UNDERSTANDING THE EFFECTS OF CHILD SEXUAL ABUSE

Child sexual abuse is a global problem that negatively affects many women and girls. Therefore, it has long been of concern to feminists, and more recently mental health activists. *Understanding the Effects of Child Sexual Abuse* draws on this revolutionary legacy to re-evaluate mainstream and feminist approaches to understanding women and child sexual abuse. The book aims to contribute to the ongoing development of a knowledge-base for those working with abused women and girls.

Understanding the Effects of Child Sexual Abuse draws on feminism and post-structuralism to critically examine current ways of understanding women, girls and child sexual abuse in psychology, psychiatry, the mass media, and by radical feminist and mental health activists. The book demonstrates the need to question the use of formulaic methods when working with abused women and girls and calls for an explicit concern with politics, principles and ethics in the related areas of theory, research and practice.

Using research on women who have been sexually abused in childhood, and who are detained in maximum-security mental-health care, Sam Warner explores and identifies key principles for practice. A social-recovery model of intervention is developed and case study examples are used to demonstrate its applicability in a range of practice areas. These include abuse psychotherapy; expert witness reports in child protection; work with domestically abused mothers of abused children; and psychotherapy with women and girls in secure care contexts.

This thorough investigation of this emotive issue provides a clear theoretical and practical framework for understanding and coping with child sexual abuse. This book will be of interest to anyone who works with children and adults who have been sexually abused. This includes clinical psychologists, therapists and other professionals that work in mental health, psychotherapy and social services, and legal settings within both community-based and secure-care contexts. It should also be essential reading for students and academics in this area.

Sam Warner is a freelance consultant and chartered clinical psychologist, and a research fellow, Department of Psychology and Speech Pathology, Manchester Metropolitan University, Manchester, UK.

WOMEN AND PSYCHOLOGY
Series Editor: Jane Ussher
School of Psychology, University of Western Sydney

This series brings together current theory and research on women and psychology. Drawing on scholarship from a number of different areas of psychology, it bridges the gap between abstract research and the reality of women's lives by integrating theory and practice, research and policy.

Each book addresses a 'cutting edge' issue of research, covering such topics as post-natal depression, eating disorders, theories and methodologies.

The series provides accessible and concise accounts of key issues in the study of women and psychology, and clearly demonstrates the centrality of psychology to debates within women's studies or feminism.

The Series Editor would be pleased to discuss proposals for new books in the series.

Other titles in this series:

THE THIN WOMAN
Helen Malson

THE MENSTRUAL CYCLE
Anne E. Walker

POST-NATAL DEPRESSION
Paula Nicolson

RE-THINKING ABORTION
Mary Boyle

WOMEN AND AGING
Linda R. Gannon

BEING MARRIED. DOING GENDER
Caroline Dryden

UNDERSTANDING DEPRESSION
Janet M. Stoppard

FEMININITY AND THE PHYSICALLY ACTIVE WOMAN
Precilla Y.L. Choi

GENDER, LANGUAGE AND DISCOURSE
Anne Weatherall

THE SCIENCE/FICTION OF SEX
Annie Potts

THE PSYCHOLOGICAL DEVELOPMENT OF GIRLS
AND WOMEN
Sheila Greene

JUST SEX?
Nicola Gavey

WOMAN'S RELATIONSHIP WITH HERSELF
Helen O'Grady

GENDER TALK
Susan A. Speer

BEAUTY AND MISOGYNY
Sheila Jeffreys

BODY WORK
Sylvia K. Blood

MANAGING THE MONSTROUS FEMININE
Jane M. Ussher

THE CAPACITY TO CARE
Wendy Hollway

SANCTIONING PREGNANCY
Harriet Gross and Helen Pattison

ACCOUNTING FOR RAPE
Irina Anderson and Kathy Doherty

THE SINGLE WOMAN
Jill Reynolds

UNDERSTANDING THE EFFECTS OF CHILD SEXUAL ABUSE

Feminist Revolutions in Theory, Research and Practice

Sam Warner

Routledge
Taylor & Francis Group

LONDON AND NEW YORK

First published 2009 by Routledge
27 Church Road, Hove, East Sussex BN3 2FA

Simultaneously published in the USA and Canada
by Routledge
270 Madison Avenue, New York, NY 10016

Routledge is an imprint of the Taylor & Francis Group, an Informa business

© 2009 Psychology Press

Typeset in Times by Garfield Morgan, Swansea, West Glamorgan
Printed and bound in Great Britain by TJ International Ltd, Padstow, Cornwall
Paperback cover design by Terry Foley

This publication has been produced with paper manufactured to strict environmental standards and with pulp derived from sustainable forests.

British Library Cataloguing in Publication Data
A catalogue record for this book is available from the British Library

Library of Congress Cataloging in Publication Data
Warner, Sam.
Understanding the Effects of Child Sexual Abuse: Feminist revolutions in theory, research, and practice / Sam Warner.
p. cm.
Includes bibliographical references and index.
ISBN 978-0-415-36027-2 (hardcover) – ISBN 978-0-415-36028-9 (pbk)
1. Child sexual abuse. 2. Adult and child – sexual abuse victims. 3. Abused women – mental health. 4. Abused women – institutional care. 5. Sexually abused children – mental health. 6. Psychotherapy. 7. Feminist theory. I. Title.
HV6570.W37 2008
362.7601–dc22
2007021592

ISBN 978-0-415-36027-2 (hbk)
ISBN 978-0-415-36028-9 (pbk)

FOR MY PARENTS THELMA AND GEOFF LIDSTER, AND MY SON MILES BRYAN MOORHOUSE.

CONTENTS

List of figures   xi
List of tables   xii
Acknowledgements   xiii

PART 1
Theory   1

1   Ethical praxis: applying a feminist post-structuralist
    perspective   3

2   Disordered and abnormal mainstream misrecognition
    of women and child sexual abuse   15

3   Dangerous desires: child sexual abuse, mental disorder
    and the mass media   34

4   Using radical politics to understand child sexual abuse:
    changing concerns in women's theory, activism and
    therapy   53

PART 2
Research   73

5   Critical research practices and ethical methodologies:
    researching women and child sexual abuse   75

6   Mad, bad or dangerous? Women's routes into 'special'
    maximum-security mental hospitals   91

7 Women surviving in secure care: making sense of the
effects of childhood sexual abuse   117

8 Special care and childhood sexual abuse: working with
women in secure mental hospitals   144

PART 3
Practice   **165**

9 Visible Therapy with women and girls: reworking the
effects of childhood sexual abuse   167

10 Critical practices in child protection: social framework
evidence and the expert witness   187

11 Mothers, children and protective practices: making
links between domestic violence and child sexual abuse   208

12 Beyond deviance and damnation: working with women
and girls in secure care contexts   227

Epilogue: Why the personal is still political: revolutions,
recoveries and utopias   247
References   253
Index   277

FIGURES

5.1   Example of scale and number of statements   86
5.2   A schematic example of a completed response grid from
      the 'routes' study   87
9.1   Triangle of Reality   175
9.2   Triangle of Communication   181
10.1 Assessment Framework   193
10.2 Assessment Diamond   194
12.1 Adaptation of Yerkes-Dodson's Law   241

TABLES

6.1	Factor array – personality disorder	95
6.2	Statements from the 'routes' Q study	115
7.1	Discourses about effects study	140
7.2	Statements from the 'discourses about effects' Q study	142
8.1	Statements from the 'representations of effects' Q study	161

ACKNOWLEDGEMENTS

I thank the many survivors who have shared some of their lives with me. I thank Ashworth Special Hospital and Rampton Special Hospital for their participation in the research described in Part 2. I thank Marcia Worrell for her valuable feedback on earlier drafts of the book, and Michael Scholes who ensured that the manuscript was in a fit state to submit. I thank Jane Ussher, Series Editor, and the anonymous reviewers whose comments have enabled me to write a better book than I had hoped. I also thank Erica Burman, Dave Harper, Diane Mansell, Roger Moorhouse, Yemisi Osolake and Jayson Rees-Hughes. Finally, I want to remember my cats Ruby and Alice, who shared much of this journey with me.

Part 1

THEORY

This book is concerned with how the effects of child sexual abuse are understood and how this affects the treatment and representation of abused women and girls. The different ways we understand child sexual abuse give rise to competing versions of reality that have markedly different effects on the lives of abused women and girls. My aim throughout this book is to detail some of these different ways of understanding in order to develop practical strategies that enable, rather than condemn, abused women and girls, and which offer hope, rather than despair. Hence, although this book covers a wide range of concerns in relation to women, girls and child sexual abuse, all these chapters are united by a sustained focus on the relationship between understanding and practice, and by the desire to develop ways of working that are both useful and ethical.

The book is organized into three sections: theory, research and practice. In this first section of the book I begin, in Chapter 1, by outlining the theoretical traditions within feminism and post-structuralism that I draw on to develop my approach in thinking through practices regarding women, girls and child sexual abuse. My aim is to make transparent my own ways of understanding. I then use this framework to critically interrogate the ways in which child sexual abuse is made sense of in mainstream mental health services (Chapter 2), by the mass media (Chapter 3) and by radical political activists in feminism and mental health (Chapter 4). The aim is to make visible the wider cultural and political arenas that contextualize practices around child sexual abuse, and women and girls across the age span, in contemporary culture. These chapters are not only about theory, in terms how child sexual abuse is understood by different sections of society. They also address how these different understandings are implicated in contrasting approaches to intervention.

As noted, my concern is to develop practices around child sexual abuse that are both useful and ethical. I begin this process in Chapter 1 by demonstrating how feminism and post-structuralism can be utilized to develop a practical moral framework for understanding and working with women, girls and child sexual abuse in a wide variety of contexts. The chapter demonstrates how a feminist desire for emancipation can be sustained, even when our political goals are multiple and continue to evolve, and how this can help guide ways of making sense of child sexual abuse in theory, research and clinical practice.

In Chapter 2, I explore the impact of diagnostic systems (*qua* psychiatry) and functional formulations (*qua* psychology) on shaping the ways in which women who have been sexually abused are understood and treated in mainstream mental health services. I demonstrate how progressive approaches to mental health that focus concern on the social foundations of individual misery are restricted by an over-reliance on notions of pathology. Particular attention is drawn to the difficulties faced by abused women who are made subject to compulsory treatment.

Chapter 3 critically examines how child sexual abuse is represented in the mass media. Common narrative structures that frame stories about victims and abusers are identified; and normative assumptions about gender that shape public debates about sex and abuse are elaborated. I argue that there is a constant desire to locate child sexual abuse outside of the nuclear family, and that this is achieved through the appropriation of medical and psychological discourse to transfer abuse to pathological outsiders. This chapter also considers the status of children, themselves, in debates about childhood sex.

Chapter 4 builds on this critique to explore changing concerns in feminism and radical mental health activism regarding women and child sexual abuse. This chapter further locates my particular ways of understanding by providing a detailed account of the theoretical and political context I locate myself within, and feel myself to be accountable to. I chart some of the different ways that women have thought through and organized around the issue of sexual violence. The argument is made for the ongoing relevance and impact of radical politics in shaping contemporary approaches to understanding and addressing child sexual abuse, and indeed in directing my work with abused women and girls, as detailed throughout this book.

1

ETHICAL PRAXIS

Applying a feminist post-structuralist perspective

Introduction

How we theorize, recognize, talk about and act in relation to child sexual abuse changes according to history, geography, culture, law and social policy. As such, in order to understand what child sexual abuse is, it is necessary to be specific about the various issues that shape where we speak from and what we speak about. In this chapter, I begin the process of making my ways of understanding explicit by identifying some of the key theoretical practices that underpin my approach to making sense of, and working with, the effects of child sexual abuse as they relate to women and girls across the age span. This book, therefore, addresses issues that affect adult women, as well as children and young people (with the focus being on girls). As with other books in this edited series, I draw on ideas from outside psychology. In part this is because psychology has a tendency to individualize complex social problems, such as child sexual abuse. Additionally, psychology is too often viewed as an impartial practice, in which perspective is viewed with suspicion. By contrast, not only do I think that perspective is always implicated in our meaning-making, but also my political beliefs are integral to what I want to achieve with psychology.

I am explicitly concerned with illuminating hidden assumptions about femininity that are implicated in constructing familiar representations of women and child sexual abuse, and which sustain normative gender hierarchies. My aim throughout this book is to challenge taken-for-granted assumptions about femininity that restrict how women's and girls' experiences of child sexual abuse are understood and how they are responded to. The politics I draw on to enable this process are feminist. I am aware that feminism covers a vast terrain and that any overarching approach (whether feminism or psychology) fails when its ability to 'speak the truth' is unquestioningly assumed. It is here that I use post-structuralism to guard against the automatic acceptance of any grand narrative or ideology by maintaining a space for critical reflexivity. And it is this intersection, between feminism and post-structuralism, which is at the heart of the work I do with, and in, psychology.

This book, therefore, provides a sustained argument for the applicability of feminism and post-structuralism within psychology. Each chapter uses the framework outlined here to think through how we work with, and represent, abused women and girls. Hence, although this book covers a wide range of issues, service contexts and clinical practices in respect of women, girls and child sexual abuse, it is united by a common theoretical approach. In this sense the book is polemical. It does not seek to cover all the disparate literature that reflects the many different methods that are used to make sense of work in this area. Rather, this book aims to demonstrate that when thinking through child sexual abuse, in terms of culture, research and clinical practice, feminism and post-structuralism can be used to provide a clear and compelling guide regarding what we do, and how we make sense of what we know. This chapter represents the first stage in building this argument. Specifically, I detail ideas from feminism and post-structuralism that inform my sense of ethics and morality, which embed my practices as an academic and clinical psychologist, and which shape the ways in which I make myself accountable for the work I do.

Feminist and post-structuralist intersections: recognizing the limits of women's knowledge base

As noted, feminism represents a wide array of political strategies and theories (some of which are discussed in Chapter 4). Whilst these may be highly contested, there are some recurring concerns. These can be described as being with the systematic subordination of the female subject and a desire to challenge gender inequalities by providing an emancipatory framework for social transformation. Hence, feminism, as theory and practice, has focused on identifying wrongs perpetrated against women and strategies for addressing these wrongs (Ramazanoglu and Holland 1999). It is little wonder, therefore, that feminism has demonstrated a sustained concern with the sexual exploitation of women (and children) within patriarchal systems and societies. In this sense, gender has been a defining construct in determining feminist politics. However, there are problems with assuming gender differences are intrinsic, stable and distinct.

If we assume gender is defined by born-with characteristics, and that there is some essential value that can be attached to masculinity and femininity, assumptions of similarity within gender categories can be over-stated. Differences between women may then be underestimated, and dominant westernized, heterosexualized versions of femininity may then be taken to represent the norm. Indeed, when either difference or similarity is assumed, gender ultimately acts as a mechanism of exclusion (Butler 1990).

4

Hence, '[t]he category *women* (as well as the more obviously contentious *Woman*)' (Stanley 1997: 274) cannot be thought of as an unproblematic term or as a stable social category. This is an important issue because when women are understood to be a disparate and shifting group, it calls into question the automatic right of any woman to speak about issues such as sexual violence on behalf of all women, as we will experience things differently. Additionally, it also challenges the assumption that women have greater access to the 'truth' about sexual violence.

Hence, if we are to claim a feminist voice, whilst not denying our differences, it is crucial to theorize, rather than simply accept gender distinctions. This is where post-structuralism begins to intersect with feminism. According to post-structuralism, reality is understood to be socially constructed through language (Foucault 1978, 1991, 1971/1992). Thus, all knowledge is understood to have epistemological equivalence in that all knowledge is socially produced and regulated. Therefore, post-structuralism, as with feminism, challenges the assumption of a natural social order. Language use is understood to be strategic, rather than transparent. Hence, the production of knowledge can never be benign. Knowledge, then, is more verb than noun: it is a practice that does things (Grosz 1995). Such approaches directly challenge the modernist assumption of an objective world, and with this the implication of any singular understanding of women and child sexual abuse, or the automatic right of any one group (of women, men, etc.) to define the truth about sexual violence. Therefore, normative values are no longer hidden (as natural), but exposed (as regulatory fictions) and, in this way, are opened up to critique (Deleuze and Guattari 1984).

Like feminism, therefore, post-structuralism is concerned with how the landscape of reality is constituted through the relationships between power and knowledge (Foucault 1991, 1971/1992). For some, including modernist/realist feminists, power is depicted as being a negative force, in that men's power over women is understood to be the thing that maintains patriarchal control. By contrast, in post-structuralist terms, power has no intrinsic value, and as such can be both 'a generative force, as well as a restrictive opportunity' (Ramazanoglu 1993: 109). Power is understood to be a practice, rather than a possession. As Deleuze and Guattari (1988: 27) argue, '[p]ower has no essence; it is simply operational. It is not an attribute but a relation.' The question of whether power is nefarious or benign, therefore, is rooted in the particular forms of knowledge it sustains, and the types of cultural relationships it affirms. In this sense, power forms a mutually constitutive triad with knowledge and subjectivity (Henriques *et al.* 1984).

From this perspective, human subjectivity is understood to be produced through culture, rather than something that exists before culture. In this sense, post-structuralism mobilizes a more complex reading of femininity that allows difference and similarity to be theorized rather than assumed. When woman as a natural category is rejected, women's essential epistemic advantage over men is also called into question (Bordo 1990). Women can no longer claim to have access to a purer form of knowledge about social and personal oppressions, such as child sexual abuse; rather, feminism, alongside other bodies of knowledge, such as psychology, is treated as part of the discursive mechanisms through which the reality of women and child sexual abuse is constructed.

This means guarding against the belief that feminism can, in any absolute fashion, determine what constitutes the right way to understand sexually abusive experiences. This is why it is crucial that feminists make their own ways of understanding explicit and the positions from which we (or I) speak visible. Hence, I call the therapeutic approach I describe in Chapter 9 Visible Therapy (Warner 2000, 2001a, 2003b) in order to highlight the need to account for both *what* is talked about and *how* talking proceeds in therapeutic relationships. 'Visibility' remains partial because all knowledge is selective and incomplete. Nevertheless, in aiming for visibility I commit myself to, as far as possible, making the interests and ideas that inform my work clear and explicit (in other words, visible). This is in contrast to abusers who deliberately hide their interests and the operations of power in order to trick and manipulate others.

Post-structuralism invites this type of critical reflection precisely because it calls into question the right of any group to determine the truth. Hence, whilst feminism guides my analyses throughout this book, post-structuralism acts as constant mediator that reminds me to question the assumptions that feminism sometimes invites me to make. This is why I argue that both feminism and post-structuralism are needed to enable the development of a morally dense approach to working with women, girls and child sexual abuse.

Moral maps for mobile subjects: feminist ethical praxis

Post-structuralist revisions of feminist theory have, over the years, invoked concern and suspicion from some feminists (see Benhabib 1995; Jackson 1992), mainly because relativism has been criticized for leading to nihilism and paralysis (Weissen 1971/1993). The concern is that deconstruction of a knowing feminist subject leads to political indifference because it undermines women's sense of collective history and knowledge. Hartsock (1990: 163–4) typifies this concern in the following lament:

> Why is it that just at the moment when so many of us who have been silenced begin to demand the right to name ourselves, to act as subjects rather than objects of history, that just then the concept of subjecthood becomes problematic? Just when we are forming our own theories about the world, uncertainty emerges about whether the world can be theorised. Just when we are talking about

the changes we want, ideas of progress and the possibility of systematically and rationally organising human society become dubious and suspect. Why is it only now that critiques are made of the will to power inherent in the effort to create theory?

Obviously, as Haraway (1991: 79) notes, '[a]n epistemology that justifies not taking a stand on the nature of things is of little use to women trying to build a shared politics.' And speaking from principled positions is necessary to any political enterprise (Kitzinger and Perkins 1993). It is possible, however, to maintain a political stance whilst retaining a post-structuralist perspective. This is because although all knowledge is seen to be *epistemologically* equivalent, in that it is socially constructed, this does not mean that all knowledge is necessarily ideologically, or *morally* equivalent (Curt 1994). Hence, whilst hierarchies of knowledge and power are no longer fixed, a feminist ethic, however mobile, can still be utilized in practice, to inform judgements about child sexual abuse, for example. Morality and ethics emerge at the junctures where feminism and post-structuralism meet.

Morality refers to the rules or norms that govern life in particular times, societies or cultures (Montero 2002). Morality is, therefore, a set of social practices that reflect dominant beliefs about what is 'good' and 'bad', for example, regarding children and sex. For Foucault (1991) morality can be further defined as the way in which individuals obey or resist regulation, for example, regarding their sexual desires, etc. The precepts we obey or resist and our beliefs about what is good and bad necessarily change. This does not mean they disappear. However, it does mean that we need to find a way of developing a flexible moral system that is, nevertheless, anchored somewhere. Hartsock's (1983) *feminist standpoint theory* provides a means through which a feminist ethic can be operationalized. According to Hartsock, structural privilege (such as male power) impedes clarity of thought because there is no impetus to theorize 'the norm' (what it means to be a man in patriarchal society). By contrast structural marginalization, such as female oppression, increases clarity of thought. This is because women not only have access to dominant understandings about how male power works for men, but also have access to 'abnormal' or subjugated perspectives about how both women and men are negatively affected by this.

As Harding (1993) argued, those at the top of social structural hierarchies are, therefore, limited in what they can understand about themselves and the worlds in which they live because of the ways they organize their actions in the world. They are organized to hide structures of domination. Making sense of these structures forces questions that undermine the naturalized order of things. By contrast, the actions of those at the bottom of these various social hierarchies provide rich starting points for everybody's thinking, research and social inquiry. Accordingly, women may have greater access to knowledge about gendered power than men, precisely because in patriarchal societies women are marginalized. This knowledge hierarchy, however, is not absolute.

Because societies are stratified, not only in terms of gender, but also in respect of issues such as race, class, geography, sexuality, ability and religion, there are multiple standpoints that can be drawn on to enrich understanding. Hence, gender marginalization cannot be *the* starting point for understanding the social world. Additionally, from a post-structuralist perspective, knowledge is not located in stable subjects (female or otherwise), but in *positions* of subjugation. Standpoints, therefore, are mobile, as well as multiple, and refer to *where* we speak from, rather than *who* we really are. Such an approach 'directly undermines the point-of-viewlessness of objectivism while refusing the relativism of interpretationism' (Harding 1990: 97). As Haraway (1991) has argued, both objectivity and relativism avoid issues of responsibility by being nowhere and everywhere respectively. Therefore, neither provides good guidelines for conducting ethical and morally located research and clinical practice. Rather, as Haraway (1991: 196) also suggests, '[t]he only way to find a larger vision is to be somewhere in particular.' To be moral, then, is to be located.

Being somewhere: some limited reflections on where I speak from

When 'who I am' is replaced with 'where I speak from', morality is a more dense and complex cultural, historical, economic and political practice. It allows a principled approach to research and therapy to be retained without universalizing or fixing what that approach is or will always be (Curt 1994). The marginalized standpoints that extend our understanding do not exist in a fixed formalized hierarchy as there are no epistemological grounds for predetermining an order of concerns. Rather, different standpoints will have different meanings and relevance in different situations, and for different people. Standpoints and concerns may converge and diverge at different times, and no one perspective can be right for all people all of the time. This is why within a diverse and disparate feminist community, women continue to have conflicting and contrasting agendas. For example, sometimes it may be more important to address economic oppression than it is to focus on sexual exploitation. At other times the two may be intimately linked. Hence, there cannot be one 'correct' feminist response. As Stanley (1997: 277) argues:

> This opens up possibilities (and closes down dubious assumptions) for feminism. No longer claiming, 'I am right, you are wrong', we necessarily move into the realm of the ethically/morally/politically *preferable*, into the realm of minded choice.

Making 'minded choices' involves tracing our understandings back and through different communities of concern to whom we feel variously accountable. As, Ramazanoglu and Holland (1999: 389) argue:

> [T]he feminist subject is socially and discursively located in relation to socially produced 'communities' that validate the right to speak as this kind of knowing subject . . . Since the knowing feminist self is a social/discursive production, understanding experience requires identifying the collectivities feminists are socially situated in, think within, and are accountable to. There must be some 'community' within which knowledge is validated, when this is not simply a male-centred, scientific community.

For example, in thinking through my practices with women and girls who have been sexually abused, I seek feedback from abuse survivors, service users and providers, feminist academics, mental health activists, etc., all from a range of socio-cultural and economic backgrounds. I also consider my work in respect of other writers who share overlapping theoretical and/or practice concerns about women, girls and child sexual abuse. I look to shared epistemic communities to validate my views, rather than seek validation through the rules of science. The value of a particular understanding of child sexual abuse, therefore, is no longer about its approximation to the truth, but rather in terms of what it means, to whom, in which situations and under what conditions. Further, because women's experiences of child sexual abuse cannot be simply and unproblematically represented, we must consider why particular experiences are raised or ignored and what institutions and institutional practices these invite and sustain (Foucault 1978).

Hence, although as the author of this book I am still responsible for the views I express, and the experiences I choose to write about, I accept that my partial perspective is, and should be, socially located and thereby open to cultural critique and revision. My responsibility to the women and girls who have been sexually abused, and who my writing directly and indirectly refers to, is not undermined by accepting that any analysis is incomplete. I do not aim to speak *for* these abused women and girls; rather my concern is to speak *about* how women and girls are constructed through stories about child sexual abuse. The primary aim of this analysis, therefore, is to examine the discourses that are drawn on to represent women, rather than tell their story or advocate their particular point of view (Weatherall *et al.* 2002). Nevertheless the ways in which I write my stories will, by default, illuminate particular versions of identity. So I am never absolved from my responsibility to my participants even when it is ways of understanding, rather than individual women, that are the focus of my analysis.

It is, therefore, crucial to address what interests motivate what we do in theory, research and practice. Hence, a recurring aim throughout this book is to illuminate who may benefit and who may be harmed by the ways we make sense of women, girls and child sexual abuse in these various contexts. Whilst judgements can be made about the broad consequences of different forms of understanding, it is crucial to remember that the value of different ideas is always subject to contextual variation. For example, both feminists and child abusers might voice an account of child sexual abuse that emphasizes that children gain from such experiences. In the former this might be to emphasize that children are survivors not victims and, hence, grow strong through adversity; for the latter such an account provides a warrant to have sex with children. Such stories cannot be studied or evaluated as disembodied discourses, but must be located specifically, and their effects explored. As indicated, in determining the value of any particular understanding of child sexual abuse I am guided by different communities of knowledge that provide a critical framework to enable me to reflect on the limited conclusions that I draw. These particular knowledge communities are not incidental, but are reflective of my politics – and my experiences.

Locating myself: making the relationship between knowledge and experience visible

The referential communities that I draw on are ones that make moral sense to me because they are explicitly concerned with challenging the structural oppression of marginalized, misunderstood, disenfranchised and abused cultural groupings of individuals. Part of my felt sense of allegiance with these particular (oppressed) communities is forged through my own socially mediated experience of power inequalities. My experiences are therefore important in the development of my ideas and how I have come to know the world as I do. However, who I am, and how my experiences constitute me, is not straightforward. And listing my membership of various social (valued and devalued) groupings does not provide a transparent shorthand for my views, nor does it provide a simple indicator of my routes to collective action.

Who I am is something to be thought through, rather than assumed, and referred to, unproblematically. As Maracek (2002) argues, how I understand my sense of self is crucial to my moral and political commitments and to my sense of ethical agency and freedom. I act from within collective cultural meanings and their mediation of my experiences of oppressive social relations, although my awareness of these is never complete (ibid.). Hence, although there may be multiple positions from which I can speak, and multiple identifications I can make, in practice my sense of self and ability to act is always culturally constrained. As Stainton-Rogers et al. (1995) point out, we face different structural invitations and barriers that restrict how we can position ourselves and that determine what we may do.

My experiences, whilst crucial to my meaning-making, cannot therefore act as the ultimate foreclosure on what I know and articulate. I cannot speak 'as a woman' because to do so obscures the multiple relations of power that are implicated in that familiar, but infinitely contested, category. I draw on feminism, but refuse any notion of transcendental femininity. As such, I locate my view from somewhere within marginalized perspectives, rather than within 'me' – my essentialized ontological state (as academic, therapist, expert witness, woman, and/or survivor etc.). This is because 'speaking from experience' is not only theoretically problematic, but often acts to mute dissent. I do not deny my experiences, but I accept they are not simple signifiers of my self or my intent.

Nevertheless, it is still important to account for how my experiences have been shaped by the communities of knowledge I refer to, and still locate myself within. This is why, in Chapter 4, I detail some radical political approaches to understanding and addressing matters of sex, violence and mental health. The description of feminist politics and radical mental health activism reflects the world in which I live and work. It also provides a means of sharing what sustains and motivates me to work in the way I do, as detailed in the following 'research' and 'practice' sections of this book. The various marginalized perspectives I draw on, throughout the book, reflect and reveal some of the tensions that I experience in embodying the academic, therapist, activist, and survivor, in contexts that are also strati-fied according to race, gender, sexuality, ability, economics and law. Indeed, my sense of identity (and the identifications I make) shifts in and through these different contexts. For example, sometimes it is strategically important to emphasize my credentials as a psychologist (when being an expert witness in court, for example) rather than my experiences of being a woman (although such experiences may inform my practices in court). What and how I know is not always visible, but making attempts to detail processes and structures of meaning-making enable more open systems of morality, as my practice of ethics can be traced and accounted for.

Ethical accountability: future actions and feminist revolutions

Adopting a situated, yet shifting, moral code forces changes in the ways that practices of social enquiry are traditionally understood. From this perspective, the subject of knowledge (the researcher/therapist) is an equal consideration in the construction of the object of knowledge (women and child sexual abuse). This is because making 'minded' choices involves, as Harding (1993) argues, exploring the unexamined and 'unconscious' beliefs that individual meaning-makers hold as members of historically-located social communities (be that feminism or psychology, for example). Harding (ibid.) suggests that this process can be thought of as 'strong reflexivity'. It invites a more dense reading of what is understood as 'methodology' as the relationships between subject and object are recognized to be unstable and complex.

From this perspective, the observer is never outside the thing being observed as both exist in a mutually constitutive social space. Any knowledge gained is produced through and with the system, the researcher or clinician, and the other participants in the research or therapy enterprise. Accordingly, the complex relationships between ontology (who we are), epistemology (how we know) and methodology (what we do) have to be examined. This refusal of universal truth puts into question psychology's traditional distinction between theory and method, as how we understand what we know already shapes the kinds of questions we may ask and the ways in which we represent our analysis. The production of knowledge is further complicated by those that read the research or clinical story and who also bring their own systems of meaning-making into this process. Hence, there can never be a final account of research or therapy as multiple readings may be given of any piece of information.

Ethical praxis is not, therefore, only an issue of how I represent myself, and my alliances, but is also about how I represent others and what effects my representational practices might have on the people I refer to. Because mainstream psychology practice is orientated towards a norm that is westernized, heterosexualized and male, being represented at all remains an ongoing challenge for many marginalized communities. This is why, according to liberation politics, such as feminism, (re)presenting marginalized groups, such as women, is an important intervention within psychology because it challenges psychology's 'male-stream' misrepresentation and misogyny (Weatherall et al. 2002).

It is not enough to be represented, however, because being present and visible does not empower if social stereotypes are validated rather than challenged (Bhavnani 1990). Hence, this book seeks to dismantle normative values that reify existing gender hierarchies. My aim is to elaborate how women and child sexual abuse is constructed through and into practices of psychology. I make no claim to represent a purer, more authentic version of womanhood or 'other' devalued cultural groupings. Rather my aim is to explore how particular versions of identity are mobilized to promote and secure existing cultural inequalities. Hence, the concern is with how we differentiate women, rather than who different women really are. 'Experience', then, must be problematized and not simply reappropriated (see Spivak 1993).

Representing self and others, therefore, requires a critical analysis not only of whose experience is raised, but the tactics of raising such experience, in particular ways, with particular words. This is crucial if the sexually-abusive experience of women is to be understood and interrogated, rather than simply reproduced. When we theorize our lives and the lives of others, issues of accountability are necessarily raised through working out whom our theories serve (Ramazanoglu and Holland 1999). We cannot avoid making judgements and knowledge-claims when we speak or write about the social world (see Stanley 1996). Hence, this is not so much a problem to be avoided; rather it is central to the project of detailing and working with subjugated perspectives. Accountability, then, does not only refer backwards to various communities of concern, but also forwards to where our ideas can prospectively impact on women's lives. Attending to issues of morality invites us to take responsibility as our actions in the world invite consideration of their future effects (Henriques *et al.* 2002), not only in terms of what could be done, but also what *should* be done. This is concordant with a feminist ethic. As Fraser (1995: 71) argues:

> [f]eminists need both deconstruction *and* reconstruction, destabilisation of meaning *and* projection of utopian hope.

Accordingly, my aim is to develop an analytic strategy that does more than simply uncover hidden, subversive and contradictory accounts (see Derrida 1978), because, as Parker and Shotter (1990) have pointed out, deconstruction does not necessarily lead to reconstruction. Critique must be more than reactive and do more than deconstruct, otherwise prevailing systems are affirmed as necessary and beyond transformation as no viable alternative can be articulated (Gross 1992). This is why I look to feminism to enable a situated appraisal of a contested social world. If we want to change things, we need both a sense of what is wrong, as well as some notion of what might be right, and some means of working out what kind of 'right' we are variously working towards. Our goals may be unstable, but without some (albeit situated and limited) utopian vision, we have nowhere to go. Hence, this is why I draw on a feminist legacy to question what counts as the truth about the relationship between sex and power, and I use this book to extend an open invitation to psychology to share in some of the revolutionary practices of feminism.

I remain mindful, however, that there is always a tension between the feminist theories I draw on to guide my representational practices of knowing and the permanent process of critique that post-structuralism promotes (see Game 1991). But it is precisely the requirement to reflect on our political theories that is crucial to ethical practice. As argued, the feminism of which I speak is not a monolithic, corporate body of knowledge, but is a dynamic, questioning and highly contested frame of reference. As will be seen, in Chapter 4, feminism has a stormy and passionate history, has got things right, as well as got things wrong, but still keeps striving for emancipation and equality.

It is in this context, in respect of this history, and with this shared passion, that this book is written. I also have a long and stormy relationship with feminist theory and activism. I have been variously inspired, challenged and sometimes dismayed by the authors I have read and the people I have worked with. These conflicting experiences have shaped my ideas and focused my work around child sexual abuse. I am acutely aware that the ways we theorize child sexual abuse have a profound impact on how we intervene. At the same time, I know practical changes in strategy and action have driven theoretical revisions in feminism. This book reflects this dynamic interrelationship between understanding and practice. The context for this dialectic is psychology. I maintain a passionate desire to revolutionize received psychological wisdom. I also accept that I keep learning and what I do is always open to revision, and its own feminist revolutions. Hence, in representing women and child sexual abuse in this book, I seek always to explore what these representational strategies conceal, constrain and construct. In the following chapter, I develop this analytic strategy further to interrogate taken-for-granted assumptions implicit within mainstream medical and psychological accounts of women, child sexual abuse and mental health.

2

DISORDERED AND ABNORMAL

Mainstream misrecognition of women and child sexual abuse

Introduction

In the previous chapter I began the process of detailing how feminism and post-structuralism can be used to provide a critical framework for thinking through matters concerning women and child sexual abuse. My aim is to draw attention to the impact that different forms of understandings have on the ways we represent and work with abused women and girls. In this chapter I begin by exploring dominant mental health approaches that act as reference points for those that work in mainstream services. These dominant approaches act as either theoretical and practice formulae to follow or, as with this book, injunctions to critically contest and challenge. Whatever our particular relationship with mainstream mental health approaches, there is seemingly some emerging common ground.

Specifically, within westernized societies, child sexual abuse is increasingly accepted as being a relatively common experience endured by children from all socio-economic and cultural backgrounds; exactly how common, however, is vigorously contested. This is because, as argued in Chapter 1, what counts as sexual abuse, who is invited to speak about it, and how childhood is constituted changes according to specific historical and cultural contexts and is mediated by shifting concepts of gender, sex, race and ability. Any statistical claims, therefore, are necessarily limited and unstable, and function primarily to raise or restrict concern about particular groups of individuals (Warner 2003a). Nevertheless, one statistically significant trend has been reproduced in most cultural and historical contexts. Categories of abuser and victim are heavily gender-saturated in that women predominate as victims and men predominate as abusers. For example, a review of the literature from around the world found that up to 30 per cent of women have been sexually abused in childhood; that women are about three times more likely than men to have been subject to child sexual abuse; and that men make up about 95 per cent of sexual offenders (British Department of Health DH 2002b).

There can never be a final account of child sexual abuse because how we define and understand it changes across time and location. Hence, how it affects people and what should be done about it also remains a significant matter for social dispute and public debate. Again, there is some consensus internationally that, although not inevitable, child sexual abuse is largely associated with negative psychological and social consequences (e.g. Briere 1992). This is demonstrated in a wide array of personal testimony (e.g. Angelou 1984; Fraser 1989) and is evidenced by reference to the high incidence of child sexual abuse within clinical populations (e.g. Harris and Landis 2001; DH 2002b). Given that women predominate as victims of sexual abuse, it may not be incidental that they also predominate as users of mental health services (Nelson and Phillips 2001). Child sexual abuse is, therefore, a prime, if sometimes unacknowledged, concern for all those who work with women in mental health care. Psychiatry and psychology, as significant organizational frameworks within mainstream services, have a profound impact on the ways in which sexually abused women are understood and treated. This chapter draws out some of the negative implications that these traditional approaches have for those women who have been sexually abused and who are in need of mental health services.

The misdiagnosis of misery: women, child sexual abuse and the medical model

Medicine has been the predominant force in determining what counts as mental health in westernized cultures throughout the twentieth and into the twenty-first century. Sonuga-Barke (1998: 117) argues that:

> Historically, psychiatry emerged as a discipline when shared systems of diagnosis based on informal rules of categorisation were developed to aid the drawing of appropriate distinctions between 'health' and 'illness' and then between different types of 'illness'.

In this context, a moral concern with social degeneracy gave way to a medical concern with categorizing 'psycho'-pathology (Foucault 1971/1992; Parker *et al.* 1995). From the perspective of medicine, misery is understood to be an internal, categorical and relatively enduring property of the self. The assumption is that there are a limited number of discrete disorders made up of interconnected symptoms that differ from each other according to aetiology, prognosis, intervention, etc. (Pilgrim and Rogers 1993). Diagnosis, then, is central to the practice of medicine because through diagnosis mental disorder is differentiated, named and fixed (Warner and Wilkins 2003).

Diagnosis is understood to be a complex activity that requires trained professionals to decipher those symptoms that are taken to be indicative of different forms of mental disorder. 'Expert opinion' acts as authorization for the veracity and appropriateness of the diagnosis reached through this process. And even though the very notion of 'opinion' invites recognition that this is an artful and interpretative practice, the denotation of 'expert' acts to reassure us that this process is more about fact than fancy. This process of regulation is sedimented through reference to diagnostic manuals, such as ICD-10 (World Health Organization 1992) and DSM-IV-R (American Psychiatric Association 1995). These actively construct mental distress in traditional medical terms that focus on issues of pathology rather than health. Misery is transformed into madness through diagnostic specification. Attributes are presented as entities (Sonuga-Barke 1998) and verbs transmute into nouns, such that 'to be disposed' becomes immobilized as 'to have dispositions' (Butler 1990). This results in a false foundationalism through which such categories assume a reality unto themselves. Diagnostic pronouncements may then be assumed to reflect real and stable categories of disorder rather than being regulatory mechanisms that structure how mental distress can be experienced, talked about and addressed.

Boyle (1990) suggests that this is an example of the 'fundamental attribution error' in which we tend to attribute others' behaviour to stable internal dispositions and underestimate contextual issues. Negative social experiences, such as child sexual abuse, superficially fracture the disease model of mental disorder by contextualizing distress. Within this framework, child sexual abuse may be understood to act as a 'trigger' that activates dormant mental illness or, more directly, is implicated in the development of personality disorders. Yet, whilst aetiological stories may be expanded, existing beliefs about diagnosis, prognosis and treatment are retained, and ultimately distress is disinvested of its social foundations. The focus of concern continues to centre on diagnostic classification. Women's reasonable responses to trauma are decontextualized as 'symptomatic' behaviour. Treatment is then orientated away from women's lives (e.g. exploration of what they do to cope) and back towards internalized disorder (e.g. pharmaceutical management of their 'disease').

For example, there are multiple ways in which women learn to cope with experiences of repetitive sexual abuse. As the abused child, they may have first responded with denial. If abuse continued, they may have utilized distraction and dissociation during these episodes to ward against the physical and emotional pain they are experienced (Warner 2000b, 2001a, 2003b). Such coping strategies may then have extended beyond the primary experiences of abuse, and prolonged dissociation may result in people hearing voices or seeing visions that capture some of their original fears and anxieties. The meaningfulness of these visions and voices is lost when so-called hallucinations are understood as symptoms of mental disease rather than historically-located coping strategies. This in turn misdirects intervention and adds to the original trauma. As Leudar (2001: 256) argues:

17

It is possible that hearing voices under the description 'a hallucination' and 'a symptom' is not so much an indication of mental illness as a cause of psychological distress.

Yet hearing voices is not even a distinguishing feature of 'mental illness' as this is a relatively mundane experience occasioned by, for example, boredom, stress, anxiety and deprivation (see Cooke *et al.* 2001). Whether it is a problem relates to the effect it has and not the hallucination itself (Leudar 2001). This cannot be determined within traditional psychiatry because any so-called hallucinatory experience is always already pathologized.

Diagnosis, therefore, discredits people's coping strategies and contributes to the 'stigmatization' people may already feel in respect of child sexual abuse. The person is not only an 'abuse victim', but is now 'schizophrenic' or has a 'borderline personality disorder', for example. Such categorization may lead to others disbelieving the person's story of abuse (Morrow and Chappell 1999): 'it's just their symptoms talking'. And 'stigma' cannot be simply removed by deferring the psychiatric identity. Although this is what, for example, the British Royal College of Psychiatrists' anti-stigma campaign implies, when they write that 'the person with schizophrenia is a person (with schizophrenia). How you say it is how you see it' (see Roberts 2000: 437). This person still has a disorder, whether the disorder is central or not. Bracketing out the disorder also separates people from their 'symptoms' and thus divorces 'symptoms' from 'causes', albeit that causes are individualized. Moreover, the notion of 'stigma', in itself, is unhelpful because it individualizes what is social discrimination. We do not talk about the 'stigma' of being female or Black, for example (Harper 2004b).

An alternative approach, by the diagnostic lobby, to the problem of how to incorporate the social foundations of individual misery into a classification system is reflected in the ubiquity of the 'post-traumatic stress disorder' label. This is increasingly used to collapse people's responses to sexual and other forms of abuse into one grand narrative about the relationship between social trauma and individual disorder (e.g. Foa and Rothbaum 1998). The social dynamic of abuse and exploitation is reduced to a purely individual, and aberrant, processing problem. Post-traumatic stress *disorder* still positions women as unreasonable, even when the social foundations of mental distress are admitted into the checklist of symptoms. Whether women are diagnosed as schizophrenic, personality disordered or suffering with post-traumatic stress, they are necessarily invited to view their responses to abuse with suspicion. By focusing on what is wrong, the medical model actively restricts women's ability to explore and appreciate their multiple experiences, as well as their feelings and beliefs about their lives.

In this way the medical model maintains a diagnostic grip on how mental distress, even that which is socially located, can be theorized and treated.

Yet for the most part, these mechanisms of control go unseen and unnoticed. As Foucault (1978) argues, regulatory systems are most effective when they hide how they operate. So deeply embedded are the assumptions that structure psychiatry, they no longer function as assumptions, but are presented as truths. Each diagnosis is a partial theory about disease that is presented as if it is a straightforward operational definition (Sonuga-Barke 1998). Each diagnostic category is presented as real, undisputed and enduring. The medical version of mental distress cannot be disputed when using these terms. We can argue about which diagnosis is most applicable, but not whether diagnosis is, in itself, a useful way of conceptualizing women's responses to child sexual abuse.

It can also be argued that women, in particular, are badly served by systems that draw on traditional assumptions around what constitutes madness. From Broverman *et al.* (1970) onwards, many studies from around the westernized world have demonstrated that women's feelings, thoughts and behaviour are consistently more likely to be defined as madness than those of men (see Chesler 1972/1989; Russell 1995; Showalter 1987; Ussher 1991; Williams 1999). It is little wonder that women's attempts to cope with experiences of child sexual abuse are too quickly defined as being symptomatic of disorder. For example, women may feel powerless to confront their abusers directly and therefore turn their fear and anger inwards. If this results in self-injury they may be judged to be personality disordered, rather than the self-injury being primarily understood as an effect of their powerlessness. As Boyle (1997: 234) suggests, psychiatric diagnosis 'involves assumptions which are not simply gender unaware but are actively hostile to women'. The medical model, then, is a powerful mechanism through which abused women's self-confidence and self-worth may be further undermined. Additionally, restricted forms of understanding also lead to restricted forms of intervention.

Pushers or providers? Psychiatrist's treatment of women and child sexual abuse

Medication is assumed to be an effective remedy for 'mental illness', so much so that it represents the main treatment in the westernized world for mental ill-health throughout most public health or 'statutory' service contexts (DH 2002b). Women who have been sexually abused represent a significant proportion of the users of psychiatric services. For example, studies suggest that over 50 per cent of American female psychiatric patients in state facilities (see Harris 2001), and as many as 70 per cent of involuntarily detained female psychiatric patients in the UK have been sexually abused in childhood (DH 2002b). Thus, it can be argued that medication can be understood to be the *de facto* mainstream treatment for sexual abuse. Here, sexual abuse remains a hidden narrative in 'mental illness'.

However, as Johnstone (2003) argues, it may be impossible to treat 'mental illness' (and by default sexual abuse) pharmaceutically because the hypothesized biological basis of any of the 'mental illnesses' has never been proven. Medication cannot, therefore, be targeted at specific disorders, and, in this sense, cannot 'treat' schizophrenia any more than it can 'treat' child sexual abuse. All that medication can do is alleviate some symptoms by cutting 'people off from their feelings, either by sedation (e.g. neuroleptics) or stimulation (e.g. SSRIs (selective serotonin re-uptake inhibitors)). In other words they make people *feel less*' (Johnstone 2003: 186).

Because medication cannot 'cure' mental distress, although it may bring relief, it is bound up in a maintenance model of intervention that militates against 'recovery' (Coleman, 1999). An over-reliance on this form of treatment is indicative of therapeutic pessimism, and justifies neglectful and restricted services. Unsurprisingly, women are more likely than men to be prescribed psychotropic (psychoactive) drugs, particularly antidepressants, anxiolytics and hypnotics (DH 2002b). This may be the result of a number of inter-linked factors, including higher levels of 'depression' and 'anxiety' in women, higher rates of help-seeking behaviour by women, and prescribers being influenced by their views on gender and mental illness (ibid.). As argued, women are more likely to be positioned within narratives of madness than men are and they continue to be variously marginalized and abused. And a history of child sexual abuse is also associated with higher rates of long-term health problems not just in Britain (DH 2002b), but around the westernized world – for example in the United States of America (USA) (see Harris and Landis 2001), Australia (see Hetherington 1991) and New Zealand (see Gavey 2003).

This association between child sexual abuse and mental health difficulties can have profound and negative consequences for women patients, particularly those who are multiply marginalized. For example, Williams (1996), in a comprehensive review of mental health services in Britain, found that not only is a history of physical and sexual abuse associated with the most severe psychiatric symptoms, but also with longer periods spent in seclusion, longer hospital admissions and higher rates of prescribed medication. Williams also found that women are the main recipients of unrequested and invasive mental health services. For example, women are two to three times more likely to receive Electroconvulsive Therapy (ECT) than men; are more likely to receive ECT without consent; and older and Black women are particularly at risk. Psychiatrists are less likely to recognize physical illnesses in women and older people. Concomitantly, mortality rates for women diagnosed as having a mental illness are higher than those for men in both hospital and community settings (ibid.). When ethnic minoritization, older age and abuse converge, women are increasingly likely to experience restricted, inadequate or enforced services. This again reflects women's treatment across most westernized contexts (e.g. in the USA, see Harris and Landis 2001; MacKinnon 1998).

Service users, unsurprisingly, when asked, do not welcome enforced treatment, question the over-reliance on medication, and regret the limited supply of talking therapies (DH 2002b). Although current policy within westernized societies is to listen to service-users' views (e.g. see DH 1999b), the fact that 'polypharmacy' and 'megadosing' are so common (Mihill 1994; Resnick 2003) suggests that service users are still being ignored. It may be that because 'evidence-based practice' is thought to be so important in determining best treatment, personal experience is still devalued (Roberts 2000). Yet, dependency on pharmaceutical solutions to mental health problems has grave consequences. For example, Mihill (1994) reported that one death a week in the UK (not including deliberate self-harm and suicide) is caused by powerful tranquillizers and other drugs given for psychiatric treatment.

Unfortunately, despite some user dissatisfaction, reliance on medication to manage social problems is likely to increase, not decrease, in westernized contexts. Pushing legal drugs is big business. Sammons and Levant (2003) note that, in the USA, drug companies spend more than US$11 billion each year on marketing and promotions, US$5 billion of which goes directly to sales representations. Mihill (1994) noted that there was an estimated one drug representative for every 18 doctors in the UK, or one for every six general practitioners (who are the main prescribers of psychiatric drugs). Resnick (2003) argues that, particularly regarding mental health problems, increasing prescribing practices are dependent on (re)creating symptoms in need of treatment. Hence, drug companies commission research that promotes drug use by stifling debate around whether old disorders, such as 'schizophrenia', exist (Parker et al. 1995). Or they present new disorders as if they always existed, and we just lacked the sophistication to recognize and treat them before ('attention deficit hyperactivity disorder' is a prime example of this).

In this way, consumers in the westernized world are increasingly invited to adopt chemical solutions for social problems. This is evidenced in the growth in use of tablets to transform mental health (e.g. Prozac), alleviate sexual dysfunction (e.g. Viagra), and focus attention (e.g. Ritalin). For example, Garfield (2002) reports that there has been a massive increase in the prescription of SSRIs (marketed as Prozac, Seroxat, etc.), although there have been serious questions about their potential negative effects. He notes that in 2000, the National Health Service (NHS) in England alone dispensed just under 12 million prescriptions of SSRIs, an increase of almost 4 million since 1997. Goodchild and Owen (2006) note that £400 million a year is spent by the NHS on psychoactive drugs. Far from becoming collectively more depressed, it can be argued that the westernized world is

becoming increasingly chemically dependent. It may be possible to cari-
cature the relationship between the pharmaceutical companies, the medics
and the patients as, respectively, that between drug barons, pushers and
users. Nevertheless, the relationships between company, doctor and patient
are complex.

There has been a dissipation of confidence in the medical profession
(Boseley 2001). It may be that the deference shown to medics has been
undermined by the increased availability of information generated through
the internet, which makes 'experts' of us all. Hence, commercial drug
pushing has had to adapt. Drugs are increasingly advertised and sold on the
internet and their increasing availability contributes to the desire for them.
Because commercial funding of research undermines credibility (Daly and
Wakefield 2002) there has been an increase in the USA of 'personal testimony' about 'disorders' to sell drugs, whereby the disease is sold rather
than the drug (Koerner 2002). 'Disease awareness' campaigns do not
require companies to list the side effects of drugs, which would be required
if advertising the drug itself. This also circumvents restrictions around the
advertisement of drugs per se, as is the case in the UK for example.

We are, therefore, encouraged to believe that our legal drug-taking is
informed by mental health need rather than being shaped by barely hidden
business policies. It is no wonder that issues of abuse are marginalized;
there is no direct chemical solution to this widespread social problem.
Pharmaceutical companies cannot make money directly from abuse, only
from its effects, and more money is made when such effects are seen to be
the problem itself. Obviously, sometimes abused (and other) women need 'a
break' from their feelings. For example, they may feel overwhelmed by
despair, or scared of and persecuted by their voices and visions. Pharma-
cology can help. Yet, the pact between traditional psychiatry and the
pharmaceutical industry does not encourage women to take an active role
in determining how they use drugs to control and manage their feelings
about abuse and other unwanted social experiences.

For example self-prescription with illegal drugs (including alcohol) is
invariably pathologized. Yet illegal drug use may serve many similar functions to legal drug use. For example, women who misuse alcohol and/or
drugs are also found to have histories of violence and abuse, poor physical
and psychological health, particularly 'anxiety' and 'depression', and have
suicidal thoughts and make suicide attempts (DH 2002b). Women may then
use illegal drugs in much the same way as prescription drugs – to mask
negative feelings associated with experiences such as abuse. Yet, good drugs
(prescribed) are predicated against bad drugs (illegal), as are respectively
users and abusers; and prescribers and pushers.

Categorization of drugs (from opium to alcohol) as good or bad is
historically unstable. Drugs also have multiple effects on different people
or the same person at different times and in different situations. Binary

reductionism, however, allows the fixing of unstable categories so that prescription drugs are viewed as being safe and therapeutic, whilst non-prescription drugs are not. This reinforces the hegemony of the medical model, privileges a paternalistic attitude to mental health care, and ultimately undermines women's own coping strategies. Pharmaceutical and technical-rich solutions are providential for commercial medical companies. It is no surprise that talking therapies have traditionally had a lesser role to play within mainstream mental health provision. However, the chemical generation is also party to a growing confessional culture that has concomitantly increased our desire to talk.

Formulating normal functioning: women, child sexual abuse, and psychology

The application of psychology to matters of mental health has a long history in westernized societies. For example, in the UK, the British Psychological Society was founded in 1901 as a sub-branch of philosophy, aligned with medicine (Newnes 1996). Clinical psychology began to grow following the Second World War, and in Britain it grew in the context of the rise of the National Health Service. The primary theoretical focus in clinical psychology within westernized societies was, and remains, behaviourism and cognitive psychology. However, competing theoretical concerns (including critical and feminist psychology) occasionally weave their way in (see, for example, Boyle 1990 in the UK; Gavey 2005 in New Zealand; Haaken 1998 and Lamb 1999 in the USA).

There are some differences in clinical psychology practice (regarding theoretical orientation, type of client, context of work, etc.) depending on the specific service being offered, how local practices have developed, and which country the clinical psychologists work in. However, there are, nevertheless, some commonalties that unite mainstream understandings and applications of clinical psychology across the westernized world. Pilgrim and Rogers (1993) argue that the statistical notion of 'normal distribution' is fundamental to mainstream understandings of psychology. According to statistics, any 'significant' deviation from the mean is necessarily abnormal. Within clinical psychology, abnormality is assumed to be fundamentally wrong, rather than simply uncommon. Practice, therefore, is directed at recuperating 'abnormal' persons back towards the mean. In traditional cognitive behavioural terms, the aim is to correct 'distorted' thinking and to change 'maladaptive' behaviour according to fixed standards of thinking and acting based on the so-called normal population.

Hence, because most people do not cut their arms, those that do are considered to have maladaptive coping strategies and to be exhibiting distorted thinking about their problems. Yet cutting one's arms may be an adaptive response to privation and abuse. Self-injury can be used to reassert control over one's body. The bloodletting can reduce tension. The physical pain can provide a distraction from troubling thoughts and feelings associated with abuse and trauma. The wounds can command attention. People may have considerable insight into their behaviour: the limitations, the dangers and the functions. Too readily assuming that any activity is wrong simply because it is abnormal restricts more helpful working practices. It invites people to be frightened of themselves, to believe they are out of control (rather than exerting whatever limited control they can).

Generic self-harm is also actually far from being abnormal. For example, drinking alcohol, smoking cigarettes, eating too much or too little, taking insufficient care with oneself are behaviours that many people engage in at some time in their lives. To some degree, the acceptance that some 'destructive' behaviours, such as generic self-harm, are statistically 'normal' obliquely underpins current trends in clinical psychology that indicate a move towards a less damning *functional analysis* regarding clients' difficulties. This is evidenced, in Britain, in the increasing reference to 'formulation' in clinical psychology practice (Crellin 1998). 'Formulation' refers to the ways in which clinical psychologists develop a functional analysis of problem behaviour: what is reinforcing in behavioural terms; what has become schematically internalized and justified in cognitive terms? In other words, how does this behaviour and/or thought work for/against the client; where did it originate; and how has it become stabilized over time?

To some degree, taking a functional analysis allows self-harm, for example, to be viewed as being adaptive for some abused people, at least some of the time. Yet a functional analysis (or formulation) is still problematic if it is structured around fixed notions about adaptation, understanding and normality (see Harper and Moss 2003). Additionally, because psychology has an individualistic focus, this can mean that psychologists, like psychiatrists, impose models of work that individualize social failures as personal disabilities. This further restricts the recognition that adaptation and understanding are situationally specific. Clinical psychology can, therefore, act in as regulatory manner as psychiatry. This conflicts with its stated aims, as the following quote about British clinical psychology exemplifies:

> The work of clinical psychologists is based on the fundamental acknowledgement that all people have the same human value and the right to be treated as unique individuals. Clinical psychologists will treat all people – both clients and colleagues – with dignity and respect and will work with them collaboratively as equal partners towards the achievement of mutually agreed goals via assessment, formulation, intervention and evaluation. Formulation [functional analysis] is the key stage as it provides a framework for

describing the problem, how it developed and how it is maintained through linking theory with practice.

(British Psychological Society, Division of Clinical
Psychology 2001b: 2)

Yet, it is difficult to treat clients as individuals when practice is circumscribed by a limited number of theoretical approaches. It is difficult to treat them with dignity and respect when we have already decided there is something 'wrong' with them. It is difficult to make them equal partners when we view their behaviour as maladaptive and their ways of thinking as distorted. It is difficult to be open to the mutability of experience when functional analysis/formulation implies that we can determine and isolate what *the* problem is. Because 'the norm' is assumed to be 'right', psychology has sometimes been guilty of not questioning the norms it relies on and, as with psychiatry, fails to account for its own role in structuring what counts as normality.

Psychology also too often relies on the idea of an objective world and psychologists' expert ability to decipher problems within it. Critique is avoided by restricting the terms of debate. It is not whether the problem exists, but how good is this test or this technique at measuring it? The search for evidence is about validating current concepts and interventions, not challenging the idea that this is a problem in need of intervention at all. Talking therapies can be as toxic for women as many psychotropic drugs are. This is the case when abused women are force-fitted into psychological narratives that still enforce dominant versions of femininity and heterosexuality. A functional analysis may have wider application than a diagnostic approach because it at least invites us to view women's actions in the context of their lives. This is because in order to explain the function of behaviours, such as self-harm, it is necessary to refer back to feelings of powerlessness, rage and despair that precede the behaviour, and the experiences of child sexual abuse, for example, that underlie such feelings. By contrast, from a mainstream medical perspective, people may be understood to self-harm simply because they are 'mentally ill' or 'personality disordered': diagnosis does not require the behaviour to have any specific function at all.

Thus tracking the functions of so-called problem behaviour has some positive value for clients who are trying to make sense of their lives and their actions. However, if clinical psychology is to be less damning of the range of human behaviour, we need to reconceptualize functional analyses as partial theories that are located and always open to change. As Harper and Moss (2003) argue, formulations about the functions of problems are made in particular social contexts, from particular perspectives, and for particular purposes. Hence, there needs to be transparency and reflexivity regarding knowledge, experience and ideas, if normative values and actions are not to be reproduced. To some degree, the need to draw on, and acknowledge, competing perspectives about mental distress and mental health, and by default women and child sexual abuse, signals current concerns within mainstream services.

Towards a social model of misery: women, child sexual abuse and mainstream services

At the beginning of the twenty-first century, there is something of a conceptual revolution happening in westernized societies regarding mainstream mental health care. There has been an apparent dissipation in confidence regarding a disease model of mental illness and a shift in focus to a more social model of mental health. This has instigated an explicit concern regarding the impact of social structural factors, such as gender, on differential patterns of mental health problems and needs. Concerns about social exclusion and inequality have meant that service-user perspectives and patient-centred care are now thought to be key when planning services. As far back as 1986, the Picker Institute was founded in Boston, USA, to investigate what patients wanted from health care and to identify how doctors and health care staff could improve the patient experience (Crompton 2006). A concern with service-user perspectives is also reflected in many current policy initiatives regarding sex, abuse and mental health from around the world. (e.g. see Parsons 2005).

In Britain, for example, the *National Service Frameworks for Mental Health* (DH 1999b) state that service users value services that can understand problems in the context of family and social settings, rather than as exclusive biomedical disorders. Emphasis is, therefore, placed on the need to build interventions around notions of hope and recovery and to develop more holistic approaches to care and assessment that 'join-up' and integrate services and service delivery. This may be a laudable aim, but current service structures militate against its implementation. In many countries, divisions exist between primary or frontline services (such as family doctors) and specialist (mental health) services, which mean there may be little opportunity for collaborative work. Moreover, access to specialist services is still determined by diagnosis.

For example, in the USA medical insurance companies will not pay for treatment unless a recognizable diagnosis has been given. The ubiquitous use of diagnosis militates against a social recovery model and also excludes those people in distress who do not readily fall into any specific diagnostic category (Nelson and Phillips 2001). Girls and women who have been sexually abused may be particularly vulnerable to being excluded from services because of their failure to fit into those diagnostic categories that would provide ready access to mental health services (see Chapter 12 for a detailed discussion of this matter). Despite these setbacks in promoting more joined-up services, there is considerable evidence of a desire to find ways to think through client need more comprehensively.

Attempts to promote integrated services are evident in those approaches that highlight commonalties between service users across different contexts of provision. For example, whilst women are a varied group, there is now a body of research that confirms the mental health needs of women differ in substantial ways to the needs of men. This knowledge has meant that increasingly gender-specific concerns are being raised in the development and planning of services. This is not always the case, particularly when other social structures of oppression are deemed to be more relevant. For example, in *Violence in indigenous communities* (Memmott *et al.* 2001), which, amongst other things, directly addressed issues of sexual violence and child abuse in Australia, most recommendations were couched in gender-neutral terms despite patterns of violence clearly differentiating men and women.

When 'women' are viewed as a distinct service-user group, the commonalties that they share can be identified and used to develop more gender-sensitive and joined-up services. For example, in a consultation document entitled *Women's mental health: Into the mainstream* (DH 2002b), it was noted that women have a significant role in the workforce and take major responsibility for childcare and homemaking. Women were also identified as experiencing low social value and status and, more commonly than men, social isolation, poverty, child and adult sexual abuse, and domestic violence. These factors are understood to interrelate and to have a significant negative impact on women's mental health and, by default, the diverse communities in which women live. Hence, by placing gender centre stage, matters of abuse, including sexual abuse, also come to the fore.

Additionally, such findings are seen to apply across service contexts. Thus, all services must be cognizant of these issues because deficits in one part of the system will have a negative impact on other aspects of provision. For example, the same document (DH 2002b: 65) notes that 'if community staff are not skilled in dealing with issues such as abuse, self-harm or in providing psychosocial interventions, hospital admissions are more likely'. Hence, making social structural oppressions the starting point for service development and planning necessarily invites consideration of a range of issues beyond the boundaries of medicine. This may also go some way towards reflecting what women themselves consider to be important. As Jacqui Smith when British Minister of State for Health (DH 2002b: 5) observed:

> We must take heed of what women are saying. They want to be listened to, their experiences validated and most of all to be kept safe while they recover from *mental illness*. They want importance placed on the underlying causes and context of their distress in

27

addition to their symptoms, support in their mothering role and their potential for recovery recognised. (emphasis added)

Unfortunately the ongoing and casual reference to 'mental illness' orientates work away from such concerns and back towards the medical model. It turns attention away from issues of abuse, just as they are finally being raised, and back towards disorder. It is little wonder then that other aspects of policy development can proceed with little or no reference to issues of abuse. For example, at the same time the aforementioned document highlighted the relationship between women's mental ill-health and their experiences of violence, sexual abuse and oppression, other policy documents were completely ignoring these matters. Specifically, the *Safety first: Five-year report on suicide and homicide by people with mental illness* (DH, 2001) and the *National suicide prevention strategy for England* (DH 2002a) do not mention sexual abuse at all. This is despite its clear relevance to mental distress and its obvious bearing upon the development of a comprehensive suicide prevention policy, particularly as it relates to women.

Recognition that abuse is a key risk factor in women's mental distress, therefore, is not enough because current models of care do not always integrate this knowledge into formulations for practice. It is unsurprising, therefore, that there is a considerable discrepancy between levels of abuse reported by women clients and the attention paid to issues of abuse by mainstream services (DH 2002b; Nelson and Phillips 2001). Child sexual abuse cannot be sensitively addressed if it continues to be separated off, and constituted as a supplementary issue, from the main concern (women's 'mental illness'). It also cannot be sensitively addressed if inevitable harm is too readily assumed and what we consider to indicate harm is not critically examined.

Symptomatologies associated with child sexual abuse invite specification of normality and police the boundaries around acceptable feminine behaviour (O'Dell 1997). The negative effects of child sexual abuse are determined, like categories of mental disorder, through reference to fixed notions of pathology, which are also gender-saturated. For example, being 'promiscuous' or 'frigid' is invariably pathologized as aberrant female behaviour (Kitzinger 1992; Warner 1996a). Neither is necessarily problematic. However, they are depicted as being so, particularly when evinced by 'sexually abused' women. Yet 'promiscuity' and 'frigidity' are not peculiar to sexually abused women. Other women may be variously passionate or cold, and may have many sexual partners or none at all. In fact, there may be few distinguishing features that differentiate abused women from non-abused women in any respect (O'Dell 2003). Reference to women's abused pasts, as with reference to psychiatric classifications of disorder, acts to discredit all of women's future sexual, and other, choices (Reavey 2003).

When child sexual abuse is understood to cause inevitable and enduring harm, women cannot be helped to recover because the damage is already done. Women's mental health problems may then become stuck because the stories that are told about abuse are too final. Diagnosing child sexual abuse can, therefore, be as unhelpful as diagnosing mental disorder. Diagnostic specification – as abused or disordered – forecloses a concern with other identifications and other relationships and can result in condemnation and therapeutic pessimism. Diagnosing child sexual abuse can serve to discredit women as everything is assumed to be determined by past abuse rather than, for example, current abuse or more generalized negative experiences of social and/or health services. Indeed, the potential for retraumatization is not just a feature of what is talked about, and how, but is also a feature of the service context.

Legislating for dangerous women: child sexual abuse and compulsory treatment

The apparent liberalization of mental health services, reflected in a patient-led, social recovery model of care, often breaks down when involuntarily detained mental health patients are considered. They may be small in number. For example, in Britain about 4 per cent of the total population of mental health service users are involuntarily detained under the current Mental Health Act (1983) (DH 2003a). However, these service users often have the greatest needs. They are likely to have severe social and mental health problems; exhibit disturbed and dangerous behaviour; be subject to greater levels of control and constraint; and represent a significant investment for public health and social care bodies (ibid.). Detained women in particular, from around the world, frequently report experiences of violence and sexual abuse (Aitken and Heenan 2004; see also Section 2 of this book and Chapter 12). Hence, because of their multiple difficulties, detained women may represent a particularly vulnerable section of the sexually abused population.

By virtue of their collective numerical insignificance, and their often complex individual social and mental health difficulties, mental health service users are the least able to argue for their rights. In addition, as detained patients they have fewer rights. Hence, they are especially vulnerable to poor service provision. Of particular concern are women in secure hospitals who, representing a minority relative to men, are at some considerable risk of sexual harassment, sexual assault and rape (by male patients and sometimes by members of staff). For example, in a survey carried out by Wassell in a British high-security mental hospital over a three year period, 1,008 incidents of verbal abuse, 64 of sexual harassment, 56 of sexual abuse and five rapes were reported (Rowden 2003). Wile (2001) also reports a similar pattern of sexual misconduct and boundary violations in inpatient settings in the USA.

Not only do women suffer actual assaults in custody, custodial systems of care also more generally reinforce and re-enact controlling relationships that can reinvoke feelings of powerlessness occasioned through earlier experiences of abuse. It is particularly important, then, that women detained in secure mental health facilities have issues of abuse taken seriously. Most countries compulsorily detain people with mental health problems when they are considered to represent a significant danger to themselves or others. They must also have a recognizable mental disorder, as defined by diagnostic manuals, such as ICD–10 (World Health Organization 1992) and DSM–IV-R (American Psychiatric Association 1995), that can be subsequently used to shore up more general legal categories of mental disorder. In Britain, for example, there are three such categories: 'mental illness', 'psychopathic personality disorder', and 'severe mental impairment/mental impairment' (Mental Health Act, 1983). Compulsory detainment is determined, therefore, by the interplay of medical and juridical concepts of pathology and culpability. Navigating women's routes into and between criminal justice and mental health systems is unsurprisingly a complicated and inconsistent process. This is not least because laws are not the same around the world nor even in states of close proximity. For example, laws change across state lines in the USA. In the UK, laws are common only for England, Wales and Northern Ireland. Laws in Scotland tend to be slightly (or greatly in the case of criminal law) different in inception time and practice (for convenience, when I discuss the law in England, Wales and North Ireland, I refer from now on to English law).

Any society must balance the safety needs of the wider community against the rights of individuals to determine how they live their particular lives. It is inevitable that conflict will exist between ensuring that abused women have access to safe and appropriate treatment and protecting others (and the women themselves) from their sometimes dangerous behaviour. This is, therefore, a highly contentious area of policy and planning. To take the UK as an example, recent years have witnessed considerable time, money and energy spent on rethinking compulsory mental health treatment (DH 1999c). The emphasis has arguably been placed on safeguarding the wider community, rather than safeguarding the rights of individual service users. Nevertheless, there has been some evidence of a more social, and less medical, reading of mental health. This is evidenced in a move from the more narrow definitions of 'diagnosis', to a broader definition of 'mental disorder' in proposed policy documents (DH 1999a). Although, as Cooke *et al.* (2001) note, this has not been balanced by specific functional criteria. Lack of specific criteria means that there is great potential for normative values to continue to structure and reinforce boundaries around health and illness. Again for those women who have been sexually abused, whose self-harming and aggressive behaviour may flout accepted limits around femininity, their vulnerability to enforced treatment may be further attenuated.

The Mental Health Act (1983) is to be extended so that this particular group of abused women may find their already limited rights eroded further. Compulsory powers are to include community-based treatment, as well as hospital detention (the latter of which is currently the case). Any extension of compulsory powers increases the ways that mental health services can enforce particular notions of normality and circumscribe the ways by which women cope with their lives (Warner and Feery 2007). Whilst these laws are peculiar to England, they do demonstrate the pernicious effects of compulsory community treatment for sexually abused women. Abused women may have good reason not to engage in services. For example, women sometimes avoid services because they feel that their experiences of child sexual abuse are marginalized. They may not want to take the prescribed medication on offer, or they may wish to stop taking that which they already know has toxic 'side' effects. They may feel they are too quickly condemned and maligned as being ill or disordered by mainstream services (see Women at the Margins 2004). Compulsory powers, therefore, sometimes further inhibit women's ability to access desired forms of treatment. This may ultimately increase, not alleviate, their mental distress.

The fear of compulsory treatment and/or detention impacts on abused women's ability to access help at points of need. It is little wonder then that women who have been sexually abused, and who also evince complex social and mental health problems, sometimes avoid services at points of crisis. Clearly, some women do behave in ways that are dangerous. However, if compulsory powers are to be used, or in the context of the UK extended, this has to be matched by the provision of a range of treatment options in safe care settings. Refusal of aversive treatments and unsafe services should not be grounds for restricting women's lives and imposing models of intervention that cause women additional harm.

Progressive mental health services: from containment to recovery

Both psychiatry and psychology have traditionally understood people in terms of deficits, dysfunction, disorders, distortions and abnormalities. Whether these forms of understanding give rise to discrete categories of disorder, or fixed formulations about the functionality of problems, they ultimately discredit the ways in which women experience and manage their, sometimes abused, lives. Because traditionally normative assumptions about pathology and abnormality are drawn on to fashion diagnosis in psychiatry and functional analysis in clinical psychology, but remain largely unexplored, how women come to recognize themselves as 'disordered' or 'abnormal' can proceed without critical challenge. Pathology and abnormality may then be internalized as a fixed, internal property of self, rather than identity being understood as a socially unstable practice.

It is precisely my dissatisfaction with normative understandings about women and mental (ill-)health that originally led me to the feminist politics, described in Chapter 4, that have continued to inform me through my working life. My desire to challenge mainstream mental health practices, particularly as they relate to child sexual abuse, has shaped the research I do (some of which is described in Section 2 of this book) and the clinical work I engage in (some of which is described in Section 3 of this book). Both feminism and radical mental health activism have helped vitalize and inspire the ways in which I work, and they provide guides for more progressive mental health practices.

Progressive mental health practices challenge the orthodoxy of fixed, pathological identity and refuse to over-determine any aspect of self-hood (whether constructed through abuse, diagnosis or functional analysis/formulation). Child sexual abuse may be a crucial issue in relation to women's mental health. However, if childhood sexual abuse is always assumed to be the defining experience, other more mundane childhood hurts may go unrecognized (Haaken 1998) and concerns about the impact of current interventions can be deferred. Hence, we cannot determine in advance the right treatment strategy for all women as knowledge and experience is always provisional. This does not mean, however, that all interventions have equal value or that all behaviour is equally acceptable. Rather, we need to make the processes of regulation explicit so that people can be enabled to make a more deliberate choice around their own conceptualizations of mental distress. We need to explore the investments both practitioners and clients have in sedimenting particular versions of reality. Some (abused) women feel a sense of relief when diagnosed as 'schizophrenic', for example, but this should not be represented as a truth, but as a possibility.

There is a pressing need to address underlying issues, and not just present symptoms. Yet, this is more principle than practice when mainstream provision continues to be structured around categories of disorder. In Section 2 of this book, I demonstrate how revolutionary changing the focus from disorder to abuse can be in developing more progressive mental health services for women. We know that women do recover from negative life experiences in the sense that they find ways to live their lives – ways that are acceptable to them. If recovery is to be a reality for women, their agency and self-determination, however provisional, has to be mobilized through narratives of hope and indeterminacy. If we restrict change through diagnostic or functional specification, we bind women to a fixed version of the past that ultimately forecloses their futures. This reinvokes a culture of victimization and passivity.

A more 'social' understanding of personal mental distress provides a means to think beyond individual symptoms because problems are no longer solely located within the pathology of the individual concerned, but are set in an ever-changing social context. And if abused women are no longer essentially pathologized, we may then provide systems of care that are committed to enabling women to recover, rather than simply containing them for evermore. Unfortunately, it is not only in mainstream mental health services that normative psychiatric and psychological approaches to working with women who have experienced child sexual abuse need to be challenged. Narratives of disorder and dysfunction seep into wider cultural debates about child sexual abuse and further shore up stereotypical versions of femininity and masculinity that compound constraints around how abused women can live their lives. Therefore, if we are concerned with changing practices within mental health systems, we must also be concerned with how child sexual abuse is understood in wider cultural debates. In the following chapter I explore some of the key ways the mass media makes sense of and represents child sexual abuse.

3

DANGEROUS DESIRES

Child sexual abuse, mental disorder and the mass media

Introduction

This chapter is about the ways in which child sexual abuse is represented in popular culture. The mass media, like psychology and psychiatry, shapes how childhood, sex and abuse are understood and experienced. Indeed, as signalled in the previous chapter, the mass media relies on mainstream mental-health understandings about child sexual abuse to inform its own ways of making sense of this issue. In this chapter I argue that mainstream depictions of victims and abusers circulate as 'master narratives'. These narratives function as benchmarks against which we measure ourselves and through which others interpret our behaviour (Harris *et al.* 2001). In this sense sexual acts and desires are never simply an individual matter of private concern, but are mediated by how sex and sexuality are deployed in culture. As Foucault (1978: 11) argued:

> The central issue . . . is not to determine whether one says yes or no to sex . . . but to account for the fact that it is spoken about, to discover who does the speaking, the positions and viewpoints from which they speak, the institutions which prompt people to speak about it and which store and distribute the things which are said.

In this chapter I elaborate common narrative structures that frame contemporary stories about child sexual abuse in westernized societies. I explore how mainstream accounts of sex and abuse rely on and reproduce familiar versions of victims and abusers that differentiate victims and abusers according to gender (Lamb 1996). I draw out the appropriation of psychiatry and psychology by the mass media who use these professional discourses to distinguish abusers from the so-called normal population and explore the often uneasy relationships between the press and the professionals who work with victims and perpetrators of abuse. Finally, I consider the disturbance caused by active consumers who do not always passively accept what they are told.

Making sex public: from confessional culture to moral panics

It would be naïve to suggest that the mass media presents a unified account of child sexual abuse or that it has an inflexible engagement with this subject. Historically, the sexual exploitation of children has flittered in and out of public consciousness (Calder 2004) and contradictions and tensions are evident in current debates about child sexual abuse. These debates reflect a diverse range of perspectives that are no longer easily located. An increasingly fragmented response from groups, such as women, has been facilitated through recent technological advances that have occasioned a rapid expansion of source material so that, 'meanings get made frequently now through crossing genres and national borders, and by cross-referencing cases, controversies and mythologies' (Atmore 1998: 9).

This chapter, then, explores common themes around sex and abuse that, it can be argued, reverberate around the globe. For westernized societies in particular, child sexual abuse has emerged as a major topic for public debate. This contrasts with previous generations, for whom child sexual abuse was largely a private matter that was seldom discussed openly. This does not mean that it went unrecognized. For example, Calder (2004) notes that at the trial of Marie Antoinette, during the French Revolution in the eighteenth century, one of the charges that was brought against her was that she had sexually abused her own son. Calder argues that this points to the fact that sexual abuse was far from being seen as 'something unimaginable, but something that just as today might be produced as a charge at a revolutionary show trial' (ibid.: 15).

However, it is perhaps only in the last few decades that child sexual abuse has been reinvented as something that requires 'remembrance and testimony' for its victims (Haug 2001: 59). A number of factors have heralded in this new age of sexual storytelling. In westernized societies, we live in an age of public confession that is reflected in our infatuation with 'reality TV' and 'docusoaps', and our ongoing obsession with talk show self-disclosure. Into this, weave feminist politics that took consciousness-raising groups as a formula for articulating and linking personal and social oppression (see Chapter 4). Feminist politics secured a hearing for traumatic accounts of child sexual abuse (Clegg 1999) and, it can be argued, provided *the* framework for how sexual abuse is currently talked about. Contemporary sexual stories reflect this legacy and conform largely to a pattern of individual 'sexual suffering, surviving and surpassing' (Plummer 1995: 49). However, although feminism may have influenced the forms that sexual stories take, ultimately the political aims of feminism have been undermined.

As will be demonstrated in Chapter 4, the point of speaking about personal experience was to build a political agenda. By contrast, current sexual stories have little to do with making the personal political. Rather, they have personal*ized* the political (Tavris 1993) through making social concerns individual matters of self-despair, self-growth and self-transformation. For example, rape is usually represented as a personal affair between the alleged rapist and alleged victim. The alleged rapist may admit to personal misunderstanding ('she didn't *say* no' or 'I thought she meant yes'), but the wider context of gender relations and gender expectations is seldom used to illuminate how such meanings are made. Yet our general expectations of men and women impact on how we make sense of sexual acts and sexual choices.

For example, an Amnesty International poll of 1,000 participants, widely reported in the UK (Amnesty International 2008), found that more than a quarter of the British public believed a woman was at least partially responsible for being raped if she was drunk or wore revealing clothes. For this section of the British public, therefore, women who are drunk or under-dressed may be viewed as *generally* consenting to sex and hence, unable to *specifically* say no to sex. Thus, alcohol and revealing clothing can be used to over-determine women's sexual choices and to misdirect attention away from other factors that may be more relevant in making judgements about forced sex.

In this way, general assumptions about women who are drunk or under-dressed, for example, are used to inform legal and other debates in specific cases of rape. Yet, personal testimony remains personalized because public debate is focused on individuals (*this* drunk and/or under-dressed woman consented to sex), rather than on general issues (*all* drunk and/or under-dressed women want sex). As a result, debate is orientated away from questioning the social and political order. The 'personal' narratives that are reported are selective; therefore, they are revealed for particular effects. Hence, a desire to confess one's experience is not, in itself, sufficient to gain a public hearing about sexual abuse as not all persons will agree what constitutes sexual abuse. In order to secure public concern, 'experience' must be transformed into 'news', whilst still remaining personal.

In order for a personal experience to be made newsworthy it has to be reconstructed as a social event. Some issues are harder to sell as news because their ubiquity breeds apathy and indifference. For example, more children in Britain, and throughout the world, are harmed through poverty than any other form of abuse. Yet newspapers are more likely to be filled with stories about sex and abuse, than stories about poverty. Poverty becomes 'news' when this general condition is transformed into a specific event (usually, but not exclusively in Britain, in respect of people in non-westernized contexts). This may be, for example, through 'natural' disasters or by marketing through association with celebrities (such as Bob Geldof's Live Aid and Live 8 music concerts in 1985 and 2005 respectively). Once made into an event, personal stories can then be retold.

'Sex' may be more obviously 'sexy' than poverty. Yet, not all stories about sex sell, particularly those about abuse. Child sexual abuse is unpleasant and distasteful. It is also still a relatively common experience that needs to be transformed into an event. Because stories of child sexual abuse pepper the world's press, a knowledgeable public may be primed to expect them, yet, at the same time, be too jaded through 'story fatigue' to keep listening (Atmore 1998; Kitzinger 2003). The familiar, therefore, must be made bizarre (Soothill and Walby 1991), yet not so bizarre that the public has no frame of reference for understanding it. In this sense, the news media can be understood to operate a formulaic approach to constituting an event as being newsworthy. As Atmore (1993: 282) argues, it must be 'both unique and repeatable, not so much as brand new as "brand news"'.

Familiarity is conferred through the use of 'framing devices'. These are 'a general scenario into which, by common consent, a particular set of events may be slotted like a picture in a frame' (Cameron 1996: 22). Plot lines that do not fit are excluded or blurred (Harris *et al.* 2001). Abusers and abused can then be 'framed' by these familiar story forms, which enable the general public to make sense of seemingly novel events. Binary categories of abnormal and normal sex are partially sustained through codifying the victim and abuser according to these familiar story forms (Atmore 1997). Yet, because these stories appear to be new, the mass media can sidestep its role in shaping what is reported (Soothill and Walby 1991). The mass media can then rehearse and reinforce existing normative values, whilst never making these values explicit.

For an event to be transformed into news, then, it must be novel, yet open to representation in familiar ways. It must also be constituted as a condition or activity that can be recognized as a significant social problem: 'bad' news sells. When these factors come together a climate of concern can be fabricated to engender a sense of 'moral panic' (Taylor-Brown 1997a, 1997b). Some issues readily lend themselves to moral indignation, such as danger to, and exploitation of, the weak and innocent (Atmore 1998). Children neatly fit into the weak, innocent role (as do animals for a large section of the British public). However, whilst inflaming moral panic may initially galvanize the public consciousness, it ensures that debate centres around the surface issue, whilst a concern with the core condition or activity is displaced. This is evident in cultural debates about 'recovered memories' (see Bass and Davis 1988) and 'false memory syndrome' (see Ofshe and Watters 1994).

According to the 'recovered memory' lobby, child sexual abuse may be suppressed in memory until triggered in adulthood by related events or through, for example, regression therapy and hypnosis. Abusers simply continue to deny that it happened. By contrast, the 'false memory' lobby argue that memories of child sexual abuse are false and have been produced by politically motivated therapists who encourage patients to tell such stories during regression therapy and hypnosis. Depending on one's perspective, then, moral panics ensue regarding concerns about abusers (who generally are male) who lie about their behaviour or therapists (who generally are female) who invoke false memories. Framing the debate in oppositional terms, as the mass media has tended to do (Kitzinger 2003), displaces the otherwise central issue of child sexual abuse. Core concerns about child sexual abuse are made peripheral to proving or disproving the existence of incompetent or politically motivated therapists, or self-serving and manipulative abusers. Obviously, there will be therapists who invoke false memories and abusers who lie about their behaviour. This is a matter of politics, rather than a matter of truth that can be decided in any final way. Therefore, because no final decision can be reached, reporting in these terms ultimately breeds social apathy.

Hence, moral panics both create concern, and at the same time militate against a critical and sustained engagement with the issue at hand. Moreover, such reporting also tends to support existing social structural hierarchies regarding male privilege and normative patterns of family life. This means that the devastating effects of being falsely accused of perpetrating abuse have been more thoroughly explored in the press than the consequences of having experiences of abuse disbelieved (Kitzinger 2003). Because the issue appears to be about individual manipulation (by nefarious abusers or incompetent therapists), gendered assumptions structure the debate, but remain veiled (as indicated, these abusers and therapists are generally assumed to be men and women respectively). By making stories about child sexual abuse (whether believed or not) personal, wider questions about normative gender relationships are displaced. Given the emphasis on recasting social inequalities as personal problems, it is little wonder that the medical model is drawn on to legitimize this individualizing approach. This is evidenced in the reverberation of the term 'paedophilia' in public discourses about children and abusive sex.

Making sense of paedophilia: the monstrous minority

There may be some public recognition that girls (and women) are most at risk of sexual and other forms of abuse within the home and from men they are familiar with. However, the 'ordinary' abuse and murder of children and women by 'ordinary' men is, on the surface at least, too mundane or common to be newsworthy. However, it is not the relatively frequency of familial abuse that is the key issue in determining public interest. Rather, and more importantly, if familial abuse were to be routinely reported it would shatter sentimental beliefs, fantasies and fictions about the inherent value, safety and sanctity of family life. In particular, recent representations of the 'new man', the father who is 'caring and sharing', would be undermined. Hence, mainstream representations of abusers tend to emphasize their difference from the norm. As Soothill and Walby (1991) have argued, sex crimes are constructed as being perpetrated by, and therefore discursively in need of, 'sex beasts' (see also Soothill 1995). Social anxiety is directed towards others, outside the westernized family.

Common misconceptions that child sexual abuse is unusual and perpetrated by a perhaps growing, but nevertheless, monstrous minority are secured in westernized societies through tales of abuse by perverse and predatory others. Recently, these have included priests (Burkeman 2002) and satanists (Levine 2002); police officers and care workers (Bright and Harris 2002); internet stalkers and sex tourists (Haug 2001). Child sexual abuse is defined in terms of exteriority, and the designation of difference is designed to build widespread panic about the world outside the domestic and familial. What all these stories do is reclaim the idea that child sexual abuse is perpetrated by an abnormal minority of men. 'New' moral panics then conform to very familiar westernized concepts of individual disorder. This perception is further secured through the casual, but repetitive, use of the term paedophile. As Kelly (1996: 45) argues:

Immediately the word *paedophile* appears we have moved away from recognition of abusers as 'ordinary men' – fathers, brothers, uncles, colleagues – and are returned to the much more comfortable view of them as 'other', a small minority who are fundamentally different from most men. The fact that they have *lives*, kinship links and jobs disappears from view in the desire to focus on difference. Attention shifts immediately from the centrality of power and control to notions of sexual deviance, obsession and 'addiction'. Paedophilia returns us to the medical and individualised explanations.

In this way, the medical model, and psychological theory, is appropriated by popular culture to construct a discursive cage around those persons who would otherwise fracture the so-called natural order. The focus of concern is the extraordinary pathology of the individual 'paedophile'. Agency is located within the 'disease' of paedophilia, and not the person who perpetrates abuse or the social structures that support it. Hence, we are encouraged to believe that abusers are out of control at the very moments they enact power (Lamb 1996). Diagnostic categorization decontextualizes exploitation and, in turn, increases cultural fears about seemingly incomprehensible predatory strangers. Anxieties about strangers can then mesh with gendered fears about the particular vulnerability of girls and women to justify restricting their movements. This has also given rise to 'Megan's Law' in the USA (and similar laws in other westernized societies, for example New Zealand). This law allows 'known paedophiles' to have their addresses and pictures made public, by publishing them on the internet, for example. Yet, girls and women are most at risk of sexual assault in the home by someone they know. And it is young men who are most at risk of physical assault on the street. This does not, however, translate into injunctions to keep young men out of public places.

Reducing the sexual exploitation of children to paedophilia has profound, and negative, consequences for how we understand the multiple issues that impact on child safety. This is also evidenced in current media reports about so-called sex tourists. As Atmore (1998) argues, when sex tourism is portrayed as paedophilia, as it has been in the Australian press amongst others, it can be disconnected from domestic abuse and attention is diverted away from the common contexts in which child sexual abuse occurs. Intervention is orientated towards individual remedies, rather than more social solutions. For example, Bainbridge and Aglionby (2005: 1), in an article entitled 'Tracking down child abusers: Police forces unite to fight world problem', note that the focus of intervention is placed on enabling more 'sex tourists/paedophiles' to be caught. This is the case even though, as they go on to say, poverty is the single most important factor in child prostitution in non-westernized contexts.

When the economic conditions that underlie child sexual abuse are deferred, individual medical and psychological solutions take precedence over addressing wider societal factors that support abusive relationships. Sex tourists need to be identified, imprisoned and/or treated. Wider discussions about the unequal distribution of wealth throughout the world can then be ignored. As Haug (2001) argues, the focus on paedophilia ultimately redirects concern from the messy world of politics back to the less complicated issue of psychological disorder. Locating child sexual abuse within the disease of paedophilia, therefore, actively restricts our abilities to develop more equitable relationships within the home and throughout the world.

Paedophilia is just one diagnostic category that is used by the mass media in westernized societies to avoid wider cultural change and, through differentiation, implicitly secure normative patterns of family life. This technique is symptomatic of a much wider practice of conflating danger with mental disorder. Direct links are made in the mass media between mental ill-health, criminality and violence. As Murray (2000: 14) argues, it is 'difficult to tell violent fact from violent fiction.' This is because coverage centres on the harm perpetrated by the 'mentally ill' to themselves or others, rather than on addressing their particular vulnerability to abuse and violence. So-called mentally disordered offenders are largely of interest to the media because of their notoriety, not primarily because of their vulnerability to abuse. Indeed, journalists continually approach workers in secure hospitals for information about socially notorious patients (personal communications 1990–2007).

Secure hospital patients, being both mad and bad, make especially 'good copy' – in the press, as well as in novels (McGrath 1996) and cartoons (Appleby 1997). Under the banner of 'public interest' the mass media appropriates the lives of such patients for entertainment, rather than to inform public debate (Linehan 1996; Runciman 1996). Sensationalist reporting, variously termed 'vulture TV' (Sutherland 2003: 5), 'trash TV', 'freak media' (Linehan 1996: 31) and 'snuff journalism' (Krajicek 1998: 2), reinforces public anxiety about madness. For example, 'schizophrenics' are believed to be more violent than other people and the closure of psychiatric hospitals is thought to have put 'the public' at increased risk of violence from the 'mentally ill' (Bunting 2004; Laurance 1995). This is not necessarily the case.

Over the last 40 years, a policy of 'care in the community' has resulted in many psychiatric hospitals and wards being closed in westernized societies and patients being resettled in the community. In Britain, during this period, the number of murders committed by people diagnosed as having a mental illness has remained consistently low and even decreased slightly. Yet the number committed by others has more than doubled from the mid-1970s to mid-1990s (see Taylor and Gunn 1999). The greatest risk factor predictive of violence, as with sexually abusive behaviour, is being male, not 'mentally ill.' Nevertheless, the common conflation of violence with madness, rather than masculinity (per se), persists. This not only deflects concern away from ordinary men (to 'madmen'), it also permits women who perpetrate sexual and violent crimes to be isolated from the 'normal population.'

Between madness and evil: displacing dangerous men and safeguarding femininity

Because women are more usually expected to be passive, weak, and/or benevolent, when they act in aggressive and abusive ways they are especially problematic for gendered society. Violent and abusive men can still be understood within the continuum of normative masculinity, albeit cordoned off at the extreme end. Such men are still men, however monstrous and mad. By contrast, women who act violently and abusively have acted outside their gender. As nature's victims it is difficult to talk about women perpetrating violence, except when their violence is a response to their own victimization (Shaw 1995). The pathologization of female perpetrators, therefore, in some ways follows a different trajectory to male perpetrators. It is precisely their failure as women, and their resulting masculinization, that is used, by the mass media, to demonstrate their individual perversity. An example of this is given by Naylor (1995: 89) referring to Beverley Allitt who, whilst working as a nurse, murdered a number of children in a British hospital:

The tabloid coverage of Beverley Allitt combined the broad-brush 'monster' image with one that emphasised her 'masculinity'. She was big, she was butch, and she beat up her boyfriend, who became

. . . 'a sex-starved target of her ugly violence'. And for good measure, she is a lesbian.

Conversely, when men commit violence and abuse they are seldom depicted as being 'ladylike', as this would appear to be a contradiction in terms. Men's internalized perversity is located through the monstrosity of the specific act rather than their failure to be men, per se. This is one reason why men are far more likely to be named as 'paedophiles' than women are (it is about an action rather than gender-confusion). This does not mean that masculinity is not differentiated at all; only that femininity cannot be easily used in this case as a signifier of depravity. Rather, male offenders are more likely to be pathologized as being inadequate (but nevertheless still) men (Atmore 1998). For example, under the headline 'Glitter's sick harem: We catch evil star with two child "brides"' (Thurlbeck 2005: 1), the *News of the World* (a British tabloid newspaper) reported a story about Gary Glitter, the 1970s pop-star, and his then alleged (he was convicted in 2006) sexual abuse of 'underage' girls in Vietnam. Thurlbeck (2005: 4), in describing one such girl, notes that, '[t]he bewildered-looking youngster was dwarfed even by Glitter's short 5ft 6ins frame.' Glitter's lack of height indicates his inadequate masculinity, and thereby signals his 'sickness' (already alluded to in the headline) and his perversity.

Using physical characteristics to codify difference and disorder is a common technique employed by the mass media; and men, like women, are increasingly having their bodies commodified (Henwood *et al.* 2002). Hence, as with Allitt and Glitter, being respectively too big and too small, is used as a shorthand for pathology (Yanovski *et al.* 1993). For women, however, the use of physical descriptions is particularly acute because women have long been constituted through their bodies rather than their minds. This is also the case for people from minority ethnic groups whose physical features are frequently used to indicate culturally inscribed negative qualities (Harrowitz 1994; Minh-ha 1987). For subjugated groups like these, identity can be deduced from the ascription of bodily features alone. For example, Hepburn (1996: 4) reports, 'A *beautiful blonde* double killer seduced a murderer in Broadmoor as part of an amazing escape plot.' (italics added)

The 'double killer', like the 'murderer' or the 'paedophile', is male until feminized through corporeal signification: 'beautiful blondes' are inevitably female. The textual body, therefore, functions as a cultural map through which social identity and deviant behaviour can be made manifest (Terry and Urla 1995). Yet the female body is an unreliable signifier of violent and sexual crime. 'Evil' women can be beautiful and ugly, exceptional and mundane (Frigon 1995). Some 'evil' women, therefore, cannot be ascribed masculine characteristics; rather, they are ascribed an idealized hyper-femininity that, through its association with crime, makes the general female condition monstrous. This is woman as temptress and seducer: the wrecker of family life against which the nuclear family stands proud, yet under siege.

Although the general female condition may be rendered monstrous by location within a discourse of hyper-femininity, individual women may in fact be excused their behaviour precisely for the same reasons. The woman who is temptress and seducer may be the wrecker of family life, yet she is still sexy. This is evidenced in reports about Debra LaFave, the American teacher, who escaped punishment for 'having sex' with her 14-year-old male pupil. Her lawyer argued that she was 'too pretty for prison' and many Americans seemingly agreed (Goldenberg 2006). This story captivated the westernized world's press precisely because her body was transformed from being an agent of abuse into an object of desire. As with male sex offenders, abuse is more readily seen, and condemned, when it is portrayed within a context of gender failure. For example, a female teacher in West Virginia was sentenced to 20 years in prison, the day after LaFave had charges dropped against her. Goldenberg (2006: 2) reports that Lyn Woods 'shared neither LaFave's good looks or youth'.

Although LaFave, as the 'hot blonde teacher', has her (abusive) monstrosity hidden, it also means she will not be forgotten. Feminine bodies that can be fetishized in this way are remembered long after other more mundane bodies (like Woods') are lost from, or indeed never register in, the collective consciousness. This is in part because they (the extraordinary bodies) exist outside the nuclear family, and hence the monsters within the family can still be ignored. LaFave, therefore, represents the opposite side of the same coin to Myra Hindley. For LaFave, being the prototypical blonde seducer inspired 'forgiveness,' for Hindley, demonization. Yet, both remain exceptional. Myra Hindley (who died in 2002) was responsible, together with Ian Bradey, for the sexual abuse, torture and murder of a number of children in Britain during the early 1960s. She remains a public obsession in the UK. Although other women have murdered and raped children, it is the repetitive use of the police photograph taken at the time of Hindley's arrest that marks her out as the exceptional face of female depravity. Glancey (2002: 5) notes that:

> Myra Hindley was fixed forever in the public eye as the peroxide-haired gorgon of that infamous police shot.
>
> Look at her defiant, evil eyes, we are meant to say. Spawn of the devil, God knows, she probably had a head of snakes, covered by a blond wig to fool us, this evil, evil woman.

This photograph is one of the icons of the twentieth century and has become, as Gerrard (2002: 14) notes, 'a nightmare inversion of Andy Warhol's Marilyn Monroe'. By contrast, Rose West's image, though more recent, is much harder to recall. Rose, together with Fred West, also abducted, tortured, sexually abused and murdered a number of young women in Britain before she was arrested and imprisoned in the 1990s. Her face may be too ordinary to remember. Additionally, Rose West reminds us that the family is the prime site of danger as it was within the home where her victims were abused and died. Hindley, by virtue of her outsider position, anchors normative heterosexual familial relations. West, as the monstrous but mundane mother, unsettles beliefs in family values and may be too frightening to be talked about and recalled. This tactic of making people who sexually abuse children into monsters and/or seducers (who are exceptional and elsewhere) is superficially reassuring. The nuclear family still *feels* safe – even if this leaves children vulnerable in abusive homes – and, as noted, ultimately misdirects money, resources and attention (Levine 2002). Vulnerability is further attenuated in the ways that victims themselves are described and the territory of victimization is understood.

Childhood victimology: gender and the special case of sex

Children are affected, both directly and indirectly, by *child* sexual abuse. Yet they are, for the most part, excluded from taking part in public debates about sex in childhood. In contemporary westernized contexts, childhood is assumed to be a 'becoming': an incomplete state of development, characterized by innocence and vulnerability. Therefore, to invite children to have opinions about sex is problematic because it prematurely signals knowledge and awareness. Children may be expected to disclose their experiences of abusive sex to therapists and investigators within the child protection arena. But to encourage children to talk about sex, except as a response to victimization, is dangerous as it recognizes them as active stakeholders in the sexual world. Accordingly, any sex that children have is pathologized, and every effort is made to stop them engaging it.

The trouble with sex is that, more than any other 'adult' activity, it seems to define the end of innocence. If childhood signifies hope and possibility, a *tabula rasa* not yet marked, sex defiles this. Yet the boundaries between childhood and adulthood are porous and children engage in many more so-called adult activities than just sex, including parenting, commerce, crime and wars (Burman 2003). Such children may be ordinarily marked off as 'other', yet many of these activities are familiar to children in westernized contexts, particularly those that live in poverty. In our rush to protect children from the 'adult world', we frequently underestimate their participation in 'adult' activities, and thereby restrict information that could enhance children's abilities to discriminate. Censorship, therefore, is not simply a response to childhood vulnerability, but is part of the mechanisms through which childhood vulnerability is maintained.

For girls, their vulnerability is further reinforced, particularly in relation to sex. Being both children and female, they are doubly positioned as being incapable of agency and self-determination. Incipient fears about the dangerousness of sex can then cluster around feminized children, who may all be thought of as being victims-in-waiting. The gendered differentiation of agency underplays the sexual choices girls make and overstates boys' complicity in sexual relationships (whether they are determined to be abusive or not). Because victimhood is constantly feminized, male victims can then be ignored or obscured. For example, the boys who were sexually abused by the aforementioned LaFave had their experiences misrecognized not simply because LaFave was a 'hot blonde', but also because boys are represented as being constantly 'up for [heterosexual] sex', and hence, cannot be abused by women.

Conversely, the particular stress on female weakness and passivity makes a virtue out of helplessness that further disables and discredits girls and women (Garner 1995). This is evidenced in contemporary debates about the aforementioned 'false memory syndrome'. Here, women's passivity is used to reposition the landscape of victimization. Women are no longer victims of sexual abusers, but victims of unscrupulous therapists. Women's essentialized victimhood is drawn on to discredit them and, thereby, justify a generalized mistrust of their memories. Men's agency (as abusers or, here, as the truthsayers) is concomitantly taken for granted and reinforced (Clegg 1999; Kitzinger 2003). By contrast, when girls and women refuse to act like victims (when they are aggressive, for example) they may also be discredited.

Unfeminine behaviour confounds vulnerability and makes guilt-by-association harder to absolve. When girls and women are tarnished by their sometimes messy lives the general public ceases to care. Ambivalence complicates stories of sexual abuse and violence, and engenders apathy. This is why the rape and murder of 'common' prostitutes and runaways is so rarely reported in the press, whilst the rape and murder of 'nice' young girls is. Dominant values about race, class, and ability structure what passes for 'nice', and sediment particular types of victims we are expected to empathize with. In general terms innocent children are easier to care about than troublesome and troubling adults. This may be why, as Burchill (1998) argues, child abuse is represented as tragedy, whilst the representation of abuse of women (and particularly marginalized women) more often seems like sport and spectacle.

For example, women who are marginalized through processes of racialization may find their abuse ignored or accommodated. Hence, although there has been long-term recognition of violence against women (Memmott *et al.* 2001) and child sexual abuse within indigenous communities in Australia (Farr 1991), such abuse has repeatedly failed to capture the public imagination. In order to galvanize the general public into caring, this 'mundane' abuse of a marginalized population had to be transformed into an exceptional tragedy by focusing concern on (very young) children. This was achieved in recent media coverage of alleged child sexual abuse in a remote Northern Territory community. The Australian Broadcasting Company's '*Lateline* program claimed children as young as five had contracted sexually transmitted diseases and that young girls were being prostituted for petrol' (Ravens 2006: 1).

Additionally, women who are marginalized through narratives of criminality and madness as being doubly deviant and doubly damned (Lloyd 1995) may also generate little public sympathy. For example, there was considerable press coverage and sustained public outrage regarding the potential (sexual) abuse of a child within Ashworth, a British high-security mental hospital (Cooper 1997). Yet the actual rape and sexual assault of women patients within that hospital over the same period (personal communications, 1994–1997) did not constitute 'news' or, indeed, even a story tacked on to the main concern. There was only one small piece in the local press, so small it had no byline, (*Liverpool Echo* 1996) that referred to one rape of a woman patient by a male patient.

If the public is to be galvanized into caring about the abuse of 'tarnished,' 'imperfect' and marginalized victims, additional guarantees (that this is still a worthy subject) are needed to secure news coverage. For example, there was some recent press interest in the widespread sexual abuse of women patients by male patients in Broadmoor, another British high-security hospital (*Guardian* 2003). However, these stories centred around the constructive dismissal of Julia Wassell, the then head of women's services at Broadmoor, who made these assaults public. Julia Wassell, as a woman with an 'excellent reputation', provided a less ambivalent focus for media concern. More usually it is when professionals are judged to be incompetent that a disinterested public can be mobilized to care about otherwise ambiguous, maligned and/or marginalized victims. For example, there was intense media interest occasioned by the public inquiry into the non-accidental death of Victoria Climbie, a child from the Ivory Coast, who whilst resident in Britain was tortured and murdered by her aunt and the aunt's boyfriend, despite considerable contact with support services (Owusu-Bempah 2003). Because Victoria was from another part of the world the sanctity of British family life could be sustained, whilst ultimately imperfect professionals could be blamed.

Guilt by association: Professional culpability and trial by media

Over the past 20 years, the mass media around the westernized world has demonstrated a sustained interest in the sexual abuse of children. As discussed above, much of this coverage is framed within well-rehearsed narratives that provide familiar, if superficially shifting, depictions of abusers and victims. Alongside a sustained public interest in victims and abusers has been, where relevant, a concomitant interest in the malpractice of professionals, identified (in the UK) in public government inquiries and debated in the press.

Public inquiries focus on the failure of the state to prevent 'preventable' harm, and aim to identify practice and procedures that can enable the development of more appropriate, proactive and responsive services. However, because the more sensational aspects of such cases are of more public interest than the minutiae of policy development, press interest is orientated to superficial short-term solutions rather than more complex long-term goals.

The 'public interest', once mobilized, can have a significant impact on the form of policy development as well as on the rate of progress. For example, restrictive, rather than progressive, mental health policies are easier to sell to the general public because of their incipient fears of madness. Goddard and Liddell (1995) refer to this as 'legislation by tabloid'. Public interest is not static, however, but is subject to cultural and historical revision. Different issues predominate at different times. In Britain, for example, the mass media has tended to report different forms of professional malpractice in respect of child abuse at different times. There was a focus on the individual non-accidental deaths of children during the late 1970s and early 1980s. In the late 1980s and early 1990s, concern turned towards the 'large-scale' sexual abuse of children (that is, where a large number of children where involved) and the perceived overzealous and intrusive state intervention that followed (Corby 2000). Children had not stopped being murdered. Indeed, murder rates are relatively stable – about 80 children are murdered every year in England and Wales (Creighton and Tissier 2006). Nevertheless, stories about child murder gave way to stories about child sexual abuse.

It may be that media coverage of child sexual abuse during the late 1980s and onwards was part of a 'backlash' against the then recent feminist successes in articulating and elaborating experiences of child sexual abuse (see Chapter 4). As Atmore (1998) notes, it was during this period that 'false memory syndrome' was invented. However, although the subject matter may change, from child murder to sexual abuse, the narrative structures used to frame the issues are reasonably consistent. Populist accounts of professional incompetence, like stories about abusers and victims, tend to support existing social structural hierarchies and undermine the need for fundamental systemic change. Again, these are both achieved through individualizing failure and avoiding issues of wider cultural accountability. Individual service providers are 'named and shamed' for providing inadequate, over-zealous, abusive or otherwise inappropriate responses; demonstrating an inability to follow procedures; and/or not recognizing clear evidence of severe abuse (see Goddard and Liddell 1995; Owusu-Bempah 2003).

Frontline workers, such as social workers and mental health nurses, who have most direct contact with clients, are usually the focus for this public and professional demonization (see, respectively, Reder *et al.* 1993; Reder and Duncan 1999; Cooper 1997; Hall and Bunyan 1997). Of the two, social workers are more frequently subject to public damnation because their usual 'victims' are innocent children. This is also evidenced in the repetitive portrayal, in American television serials about police investigations, of social workers as incompetent and/or uncaring by virtue of their limited resources, lack of time, or simply their individual stupidity, greed and self-interest; for example, *Law and order: Special victims unit* – a serial about sex crime investigations.

Mental health nurses are less subject to this public demonization. They usually fail those that have already been rejected by society, those that the public cares less about. Whether social worker or nurse, both are set up to fail. Policy decisions in child protection and mental health are usually determined in the context of crisis management, when there has been a failure in the system. This invigorates a culture of blame for both workers (whether social workers or nurses) and clients and militates against risk-taking which is essential for innovative practice (Richman and Mason 1992). Hence, both workers and clients are handicapped by a double bind, which renders them powerless to take risks, yet holds them responsible for their unwillingness to change and progress.

Psychiatry and, to a lesser extent, clinical psychology have traditionally been protected from public anger that is ordinarily directed at malfeasant social workers and, sometimes, nurses. There are fewer psychiatrists and psychologists. They spend less time with clients. Therefore they have fewer direct opportunities to harm clients and greater opportunities to share or devolve responsibility to other professionals. Perhaps, more significantly, they avoid vilification because they are often the mental health 'experts' the press refers to. However, because the medical model remains the pre-dominant reference point for such matters within the mainstream press (Cooke 1999), it is diagnosis, rather than functional analysis, that more usually structures the ways in which both mental health and social issues are understood. As I have argued, the mass media's reliance on, and reproduction of, the medical model sustains the repetitive transformation of social issues, such as child sexual abuse, into medical conditions, and reifies this particular form of knowledge and expertise. The hegemony of medicine, however, is not complete. As argued in the previous chapter, traditional notions of expertise are increasingly viewed with suspicion, and there are ever more ways in which to trade information and contest knowledge about issues such as child sexual abuse.

Recognizing the limits of mainstream manipulation: challenging the myth of passive consumption

Even as sources of knowledge expand and fragment, mainstream news reporting continues to treat its audience as if it has shared and common concerns. The assumption is that the interests of children and adults are largely unmediated by gender, sexuality, race or ability (Kitzinger 2003). Therefore, whilst the specialist press does cater to minority groups, the mainstream press avoids delineating these competing interests (except on 'women's pages', perhaps); instead, news is presented as if the processes involved in determining what is newsworthy or not are simple, straightforward and not unduly mobilized around dominant values. The only recognized divisions in the British press, for example, relate to class differences assumed to be reflected in who reads 'broadsheets' and who reads 'tabloids', and the particular party politics that each newspaper supports.

This was evidenced in contemporary British responses to reports of the abduction and murder of a young girl called Sarah Payne by 'paedophile' Ray Whiting in 2000. Working-class women were inspired by the tabloid press to march for safer communities, whilst middle-class women, supported by some of the broadsheets, worried about these vigilante tendencies (Bell 2003). The same tabloid press has more recently called for 'Sarah's law' to be established. A version of this is currently being piloted in the UK. Advocates for Sarah's law want the address of known 'paedophiles' to be published and made public, as is the case according to 'Megan's law.' Concomitantly, the broadsheets continue to express concerns about the potential for vigilantism that may result from abusers' addresses being made public, and also express worry that publicly located abusers would then go 'underground.' In fact, current plans fall short of full public access as members of the public will be able to request information about someone only when they have a personal relationship with that person, and that person has unsupervised access to their children (*The Independent* 2007: 1).

Whether broadsheet or tabloid, the role of vested interest is veiled under the aim of presenting fact, not fiction. Yet, as I have argued, common interests are created, not simply reflected, in the stories that unfold in the various sections of the press. The use of formulaic story forms does not completely suppress the shifting interests of its audiences. Indeed, the same story forms are used in different newspapers to contest and undermine competing views on the same subject. Hard news formats are used to challenge negative representations of the 'mentally ill' that circulate in other sections of the press. For example, Bunting (2004: 15), writing in the British broadsheet *The Guardian*, refers to the scandalous neglect of mentally ill people in 'the fight against prejudice' (see also Craine 1999; Skelton 1999).

In addition, although the mass media is generally complicit in perpetuating negative images of 'mentally ill' people, it has also sometimes provided the impetus for public accountability. Stephen Daggett, a patient in Ashworth, a British high-security hospital, produced a dossier about the potential abuse of a child by male patients in the same hospital. This information was only acted on when made public through the media (Cooper

1997), as were previous enquiries into all three British high-security hospitals, including Rampton during the 1970s, Ashworth (again) in the early 1990s (Pilgrim 1995), and Broadmoor more recently (*Guardian* 2003). The popular press also provides a platform that can be bought by groups seeking to challenge dominant values. For example, charitable organizations that are concerned with issues of abuse and exploitation have long taken out advertisements in the press in order to present views that they hope will shift public opinion away from blame and shame to sympathy and support (Burman 2003).

Moreover, as indicated above, information about current social issues is not confined to news reporting, but is explored on television in soap operas, sitcoms, dramas and documentaries, as well as in novels, films and, increasingly, across the internet. Whilst mainstream news and entertainment formats tend to reflect normative values, this is not always the case. For example, in the American film *The Sixth Sense* the message is that (child) psychologists, who dismiss their clients' visions and voices as being symptoms of mental disorder, rather than being meaningful and there to be explored, deserve to die. This is radical mental-health politics. However, it is the rapid expansion of relatively cheap ways to distribute information that has heralded our increasingly fragmented response to issues such as child sexual abuse.

Women have long used novels and biography to tell stories about child sexual abuse that reflect a range of hidden and subjugated perspectives (see Chapter 4). Increasingly marginalized groups, otherwise excluded from the mainstream press, have turned to the internet as a quick and effective avenue for subversive action. The one group of individuals who have had very little opportunity to produce, distribute and discuss information about child sexual abuse is children. As I have argued, it is hard enough for children to express their views about non-abusive sex. However, like other marginalized groups, children have an increasing ability to access information and to express their opinion through the growth of technology, including the internet.

Whilst access to technology, including the internet, is always restricted economically, children now have an opportunity to explore ideas in ways not previously possible. The internet provides children with a relatively 'safe', that is virtual, context in which to experiment and understand issues such as sex and abuse. It can be argued that the internet allows children to make choices around sex, something they have less freedom to do in their embodied lives, particularly in terms of the risks they sometimes face in their own homes. Yet, the positive aspects of internet use by children regarding sex are seldom reported in the mass media. The internet is problematic for westernized societies that are wedded to beliefs about childhood innocence. The fear is that *de facto* vulnerable children can be manipulated and lost within this sea of burgeoning information.

The press points to the wide availability of pornography (Hampshire 2001), with 'sex', in all its forms, reportedly being the most sought after topic on the internet (Ciclitira 2002). Stories circulate in the press about abusers stalking chat rooms, and the need for censorship is assumed rather than explored (Bright and Harris 2002; Millar 2003). Curiosity, whilst considered a virtue in respect of other aspects of childhood, is never valued when sex is at issue (Levine 2002). Yet, as I have argued, restricting information does not necessarily protect children. Practices based on a prohibition model seldom succeed, and frequently inhibit the development of responsible and considered action. Children continue to find ways to resist their positioning as passive consumers of protection. Adults sometimes need to be reminded of this.

Between manipulation and mediation

The existence of child sexual abuse is used as a primary cultural narrative for expressing fears about the deployment of sexuality. Mainstream accounts of child sexual abuse underplay its frequency and work to obscure the location of the 'ordinary' family as the primary site of abuse. This is achieved through a sustained engagement with stories about individual, non-familial abusers. Normative values about gender and family life are reinforced through dismissal of social factors in favour of individual pathology or the scapegoating of individual marginalized professionals. Dominant versions of both victims and abusers rely on, and reproduce, normative femininity and masculinity. Those people that do not act to type are contained within well-rehearsed narratives of madness and/or badness. This means that some victims are afforded recognition, whilst others are discredited. Childhood is confirmed in the public consciousness as a passive state in need of protection, children's agency is underscored, and far from being protected, their vulnerability is exacerbated. However, whilst the mass media is implicated in the manipulation of social values, this mediation is not fixed, uncontested or mono-directional.

Technological advances provide ever more ways in which opinions emerge, get shared and are contested. Although more information does not necessarily mean more informed debate, it at least increases the ways in which sex and abuse can be thought through and addressed. Whilst technology aids this process, the desire to debate, question and resist is not new. There is a long and noble tradition of countering received wisdom by those who are often most hurt by it. That we are in a position to question what counts as the truth about sex and abuse is rooted in our shared and disparate histories of oppression and resistance. In the following chapter, the ways in which feminists and radical mental-health activists have challenged normative understandings about child sexual abuse and mental health is traced through the history of second-wave and third-wave feminism. The following chapter, therefore, lies at the heart of this book as it demonstrates how the ideas and strategies outlined in this book have developed.

4

USING RADICAL POLITICS TO UNDERSTAND CHILD SEXUAL ABUSE

Changing concerns in women's theory, activism and therapy

Introduction

This chapter is about how radical politics have helped shape current understandings about, and ways of working with, women who have experienced sexual abuse in childhood. It is about how feminists and radical mental health activists have drawn on their own and others' experiences of inequality, abuse, and/or exploitation to challenge traditional forms of authority. It is a story of revolutions: about the dynamic relationships between theory and activism that continue to inspire innovations in practice to the current day. This chapter specifically reflects my own personal engagement with women's activism around sexual violence, and my own journeys in feminist and critical theory. It therefore builds on the outline given in Chapter 1, and provides a detailed account of some of the epistemic and political communities I hold myself accountable to, and which shape the principles and value base that I bring to my work.

Therefore, this chapter stands in contrast to the more mainstream approaches detailed in Chapters 2 and 3. Indeed, my engagement with the radical politics and practices that I describe here is directly linked to my dissatisfaction with traditional medical and psychological ways of understanding the effects of sexual violence, and the ways in which sex, gender and abuse have routinely been portrayed in the mass media. My particular understandings about child sexual abuse have been further shaped by my experiences within the radical political arenas in which I have lived and worked. Hence, although from a post-structuralist perspective having direct access to experience is impossible because all experience is mediated by social and historical factors, my experiences, however epistemologically problematic, are still crucial to determining the ways in which I understand the world and my actions within it. In fact, I can trace my need to make a problem out of experience to my experiences as an activist (albeit also mediated by other factors) working in women-only rape and sexual abuse survivor groups in 1980s Britain.

In order to make my journey with, and to, feminism and post-structuralism explicit, in this chapter I draw out some of the key phases of radical political thought and action regarding child sexual abuse. To this end, my account of the ebbs and flows of recent radical politics in Britain in respect of child sexual abuse is partial and strategic. I make no claims that it is definitive. The strong focus on feminism partly reflects my own particular experiences, and partly is a function of the ways sex and violence have predominated within westernized feminist activism and theory (Bindel *et al.* 1995; Haug 2001). I locate my story within the context of the Women's Liberation Movement (WLM) and the growth of second-wave, and latterly third-wave, feminism in Britain and other westernized societies. The WLM was the term used to describe women's *organized* activism and grew out of the liberation struggles of the 1960s. The British WLM newsletter was printed from 1969 to1985. The first national conference in Britain happened in 1970 and the last in 1978 – which, incidentally, was 50 years after women got the vote in the UK (see Sebestyen 1988).

The radical mental health movement is a more recent invention. I write about it here not because I want to add to the medicalization of social problems, but because I think mental health care should be part of a feminist agenda regarding the sexual abuse of women and children. This chapter is my account of how feminism and radical mental health politics thread together (see also Warner 2000a, 2004b). I also trace these developments from the 1960s to the present day, and through the various overlapping and competing theories that have predominated at different stages in this history. I explore how these theoretical shifts have translated into competing approaches, by feminists and radical mental health activists, to address the issue of women and child sexual abuse, and how this has influenced changes in the political and therapeutic agenda.

1960s–early 1970s: politics of equality
Recognizing gender hierarchies: making the personal political

Although child sexual abuse was not an explicit theme for early second-wave feminists, the changes that occurred in this era provided the context in which sex and abuse became central to a feminist agenda. Two significant factors heralded this new age in westernized societies. First, a period of relative economic stability (following the austerity of the war years) gave rise to the growth of New Left politics and related liberation struggles. Second, the 1960s were marked by the introduction of the contraceptive pill, which heralded the so-called sexual revolution. These factors set the stage for women to challenge inequalities in gender and sexual relations and to examine their roles and positions in society (see Friedan 1963). The aim was to locate women's personal difficulties within the context of wider patriarchal oppression. Women's subordination under patriarchy was understood to be modified by class, race and geography; and to be embedded in legal, economic and cultural constraints (Enns 1997).

Hence, the focus of the WLM at this time was on economic and legal parity: including that which related to sexual choices. Thus, the early demands of the WLM focused on relevant issues including decent wages, shorter working hours and shared childcare (Sebestyen 1988), as well as contraception on demand. The predominant concern, therefore, within the first phase of second-wave feminism, was to address gender inequality through emphasizing women's commonalities with men as equal subjects before the law. The tactics women used to identify what they needed for their economic, legal, and sexual emancipation also enabled women, for the first time, to create forums in which they could openly talk about what was wrong with their lives. Emancipation, whilst understood to be a collective goal, was focused on individual efforts at self-liberation. Small discussion groups were formed, these developed into consciousness-raising groups, and the slogan 'the personal is political' was born. The earliest forms of radical feminist therapy are found in these groups. Women theorized their everyday experiences of oppression and suppression, focusing on what had previously been considered to be trivial or private (Evans 1982). Links were made between women's personal feelings and experiences and the wider social triggers to which they related (Enns 1997).

Women began to discuss the different ways that they were subjugated through patriarchy. Specifically, women began to talk about their abuse by men. Women's consciousness-raising, therefore, illuminated the particular ways they were oppressed through sex and violence. Initially, women focused on inequalities in adult sexual relations and its effects, such as unwanted pregnancies, and argued for social change. For example, women campaigned for abortion on demand and, on the British mainland, abortion was partially legalized in 1967. The focus, therefore, at this point was on the ways in which women's apparent sexual choices were constrained in 'normal' adult relationships. This would pave the way for an explicit concern with rape and domestic violence, but it would be some time before the sexual abuse of *children* would be identified as a concomitant key issue.

Women used the personal insights they gained through 'consciousness-raising' groups as the dynamic foundation for political action. Building on a legacy of organized protest stretching back to the suffragettes, who had campaigned for women's right to vote earlier in the twentieth century, women came together to stage demonstrations that illuminated the social conditions that were thought to structure sexual inequalities within women's individual relationships with men. For example, women drew attention to the objectification and commodification of women's bodies by storming the stage at the 'Miss World' contest of 1971, holding banners and shouting 'We're not beautiful. We're not ugly. We're angry.' Women were increasingly vocal about the detrimental effects of patriarchal and economic oppression on women's mental health and social welfare.

Nevertheless, psychiatric abuse and detention were at this stage of limited concern within the wider WLM. Some women were writing about 'women and madness' (notably Chesler 1972/1989 in North America). However, speaking out against psychiatry in the westernized world was predominantly, at this time, a concern of professional men (e.g. Foucault 1971/1992; Laing 1960/1982; Szasz 1961; see also Parker *et al.* 1995 for overview). Such critiques seldom differentiated according to gender and were not, unlike other contemporary liberation struggles (Black, gay, women's), instigated by the oppressed themselves. Nevertheless, psychiatric survivors built on professional critique in the 1960s to develop their own political strategies for addressing oppression. For example, in 1974, a pamphlet was produced in Britain outlining the need for a mental patients' union (Irwin *et al.* 2001: 27) to call for the 'eventual abolition of mental hospitals and the repressive and manipulative institution of psychiatry' (ibid. 2001: 27). Economic and social oppression was seen as being central to understanding madness. No explicit links in this pamphlet were made to violence and sexual abuse.

Hence, the identification of the sexual and domestic oppression of women as being endemic to society and instrumental in women's ill-health had not yet emerged as a key issue for mental health activists. Equally, psychiatric oppression was not central to feminist concerns about sex and violence. At this stage, feminism and mental health activism had little point of contact. And although consciousness-raising groups may have instigated personal change for some women, they had limited impact in wider political contexts. Both the 'male-stream' and other liberation struggles, including those around mental health, failed to adequately address the particular needs of women. This set the stage for the autonomous politics that characterized the 1970s and early 1980s. In particular, it was the apparent lack of concern about widespread violence against, and sexual abuse of, women that would focus feminist concern in the proceeding era.

1970s–early 1980s: politics of autonomy
Rcognizing sexual exploitation and violence against women: the need for women-only services

During the 1970s, women, like other oppressed groups, became increasingly angry that their particular experiences of oppression were not taken seriously by the wider community. There was a gradual recognition that self-interest limited what others could be galvanized to care about. Hence, because men were thought to benefit from, rather than be oppressed by, sex and violence, women looked to each other for support and understanding. The social world was believed to be 'man-made', controlled by men in order to maintain male privilege. Because all men were deemed to benefit from the patriarchal order, all men were deemed to be guilty. And because all men were positioned as the enemy, anything associated with men and masculinity was dismissed in favour of women's values and women's ways of working. This gave rise to slogans such as 'a woman needs a man like a fish needs a bicycle'.

Therefore, a politics of autonomy developed as women increasingly recognized that liberation would not come through emphasizing similarity with men, as to do so is to be ever judged by their standards and desires. Hence, another popular slogan of the time was 'women who strive to be equal to men lack ambition'. The second phase of second-wave feminism, therefore, emphasized women's difference from men. Economics was displaced as the central concern within feminism, as the operations of patriarchy were increasingly traced through the multiple abuse women faced in their everyday lives. Women continued to break the taboo against talking about domestic violence and rape and, now, began to look backwards to identify experiences of childhood abuse and to theorize its effects (e.g. Miller 1981/1990, 1983/1990; 1983/1991). Child sexual abuse was coming out the closet and onto the feminist agenda.

Adult rape and child sexual abuse were linked as common tools of female oppression in the service of patriarchy (Brownmiller 1975). Many feminist writers and activists in this era, who placed themselves within a modernist tradition, sought to expose the 'myths' of sexual abuse (Nelson 1982/1987). According to this perspective, rape of some women and girls by some men served all men by keeping all women and girls fearful and subordinate. Rape was viewed as an abuse of power, rather than being primarily about sex, and male sexuality was understood to be about the deployment of power. This challenged mainstream understandings in psychology and psychiatry that depicted rape as being about aberrant sex perpetrated by a small number of pathological, distinct and largely unfamiliar individuals (a view that, as illustrated in Chapter 3, still circulates in the mass media today).

By contrast, feminists argued that sexual abuse is part of women's 'normal' sexual experiences and that women and girls are far more at risk from men they know than from strangers. Sexual violence of this sort was merely an extreme form of the oppression that all women and girls experience (Ward 1984). From this analysis, heterosexuality was viewed as being the central site of oppression. A result of this analysis was that some women made political choices to reject heterosexuality and to embrace sexual relationships with other women (see Faderman 1985). This was one 'personal' way in which the 'continuum of oppression' from heterosexuality to rape could be circumvented. More generally, women began to formalize their own ways of supporting each other regarding issues of abuse.

Women's unique experiences of sexual and domestic oppression under patriarchy was understood to mean that women not only needed separate services, but that women were more able than men to understand precisely what kind of separate services women needed. Hence, the principle of autonomous services 'run by women for women' was the predominant organizing principle of the day. Mainstream services and 'state-sponsored oppression' were eschewed, in favour of grass-roots activism located within the community. The idea was that women provided not simply a different, but better, perspective on the world. This is the context in which feminist standpoint theory was originally developed (see Chapter 1).

The recognition that women's mental health was disrupted not by their inherent biological inferiority, but rather by actual abuse, signalled the ways in which dominant theories of insanity would be challenged by radical mental health activists in the years to come. Not only was diagnosis condemned, but also the psychologization of social abuse was resisted. In contrast to contemporary 'trauma' talk and the burgeoning of so-called trauma clinics today, women's services in the 1970s were not organized around 'trauma', but around the actual issues that gave rise to mental distress. Sexual, psychological and physical violence were addressed through organizations such as the Women's Aid Federation and Rape Crisis Centres, both of which were established in westernized societies in the 1970s.

Valuing women's ways of working meant that such services were normally organized around collective practices rather than hierarchical structures, which were seen to be male in origin. Such grass-roots organizations were, therefore, heavily influenced by the radical feminist perspective and were active in encouraging women to make choices and to hold men responsible for oppression. Their existence demonstrated that women could control their destinies, that their bodies were their own, and that self-help was a legitimate approach to mental and social distress. The reality of women's lives was acknowledged and validated. Support was given to individual abused women, but these same women were encouraged to join in the WLM and share in the wider political agenda. Women's experiences became the new expertise, and service users often did become volunteer workers. This valorization of experience over traditional forms of expertise further acted to challenge the hegemony of the medical model and other women-blaming understandings of pathology.

Crucial to many of the women-only services established in the 1970s and early 1980s, therefore, was an explicit commitment to political struggle. The aim was to refuse to be a sticking plaster for a 'shitty' world. This meant both providing support to individual women *and* agitating for the transformation of society. This involved a commitment to educating the general public about sexual violence, for example, and to redefining the public agenda about sex and abuse. Women marched on the streets to 'reclaim the night' and took direct action against those institutions, such as porn shops, which were understood to support sexual violence against women and girls.

From this feminist perspective, rape was the practice and pornography the theory (Dworkin 1981).

Women were not uniform in supporting such understandings and actions. Indeed, some women seemed unwilling to be liberated. Radical activists viewed such women as having being been corrupted through generations of male dominance into accepting (sexually) abusive and unequal relationships, so much so that they were unaware they did it. Increasingly, for some feminist activists, a need was identified to find ways of challenging women's apparent unwitting participation in patriarchy (Radicalesbians republished 1997). The need to address women's own participation within patriarchy, and their 'acceptance' of sexually unequal relationships through internalized oppression gave rise, in some sections of feminism, to a rapprochement with previously vilified internalizing discourses such as psychoanalysis (e.g. Mitchell 1974; Rubin 1975/1997). These women, drawing on the legacy of consciousness-raising groups, argued that unless women's internalized oppression was addressed an incomplete form of liberation would result (Enns 1997).

Yet, whilst such feminists argued for a feminist appropriation of masculinist theories, more generally psychology and psychiatry were dismissed as having little to offer women (e.g. Weissen 1971/1993). Such institutions were understood to be fundamentally 'sexist' (a new word in those days) and to function as tools in the preservation of male privilege. Women attempted to counter this 'bias' by identifying it (e.g. Chesler 1972/1989) and by developing their own theories (e.g. Baker Miller 1978). Feminist therapists attempted to develop more 'women-centred' ways of working. Yet, many other feminists argued that 'therapy' could never be compatible with the aims of feminism. Radical feminists argued that therapy necessarily locates problems within individuals rather than society and, therefore, therapy was antithetical to feminist demands for social transformation because it could only ever be about personal adjustment. Hence, the emergence of a specifically feminist therapy was not universally welcomed.

Nevertheless, the 1970s were, in some ways, a golden era for feminism and for addressing 'women's issues'. It was the first time that the sexual and domestic abuse of women and girls was placed firmly on the political and therapeutic agenda. As Showalter (1987) notes, women came together for the first time in the 1970s to challenge the hegemony of psychological and medical categories of female distress and to propose alternatives, including feminist psychotherapy, women's self-help groups and political activism. Yet, differences between strategies, typified by tensions surrounding the coupling of 'feminist' with 'therapy', signalled emerging conflicts between women that still reverberate today. The mental health of abused women was clearly a central concern in this era. Yet women with long-term mental health problems, often confined in mental institutions, still remained a marginal issue for many feminists and other progressive activists.

The benefits of autonomy from men had been understood to arise from the assumption of equality and similarity between women. However, women were increasingly finding that similarities between women had been over-stated and that there was considerable need to address oppression within relationships between women. The reification of patriarchy effectively stabilized gender divisions and obscured differences not only between women, but also differences between some men and some women. More-over, feminist theories that essentialized asymmetrical gender relations were caught up in a logical trajectory that ultimately militated against liberation. If men are biologically predisposed to abuse, this partially absolves them of responsibility for abuse. They cannot change what is 'natural'. And as all women in the patriarchal order lack power, they cannot be held accountable for their own actions (Warner 1996a). Yet women were increasingly held accountable for their own investments in a structurally differentiated society. Our differences were becoming ever more evident and this would have a significant impact on how we worked around the issue of child sexual abuse. Such conditions gave rise to the politics of difference and diversity that characterized the 1980s and early 1990s.

1980s–early 1990s: politics of difference and diversity
From child sexual abuse to sexual pleasure: separatist strategies for feminist factions

Men had been an easy target for feminist anger in the 1970s and early 1980s: men were, and remain, the main perpetrators of sexual and domestic abuse, and *the* beneficiaries of patriarchy. However, in the 1980s, whilst gender was still understood to be a primary factor in structuring social relations, its pre-eminence to all other social factors was being challenged. The third phase of second-wave feminism, therefore, arose out of a concern with differences between women and in response to criticisms that feminism (and the WLM) excluded many of the women it strove to represent. Racism, ethnocentrism, classism, heterosexism and ableism seemed endemic to the WLM. Therefore, challenging the 'myth' of equality between women and addressing women's difference and diversity from each other became a new focus of concern (e.g. Hamilton and Barrett 1987). The general assumption of common experiences between women and shared goals within feminism was being increasingly scrutinized and challenged (see e.g. Davies 1981; hooks 1982; Spillers 1984).

Thus, how different women were affected by their experiences of sexual and domestic abuse could no longer be understood to be the same, nor were their needs identical. Given these differences, previously unacknowledged issues regarding multiple forms of structural oppression became part of the explicit agenda for feminist activism and therapeutic practices around sex and violence. Self-help approaches and collective work were still viewed as preferential because they encouraged power-sharing rather than hierarchical leadership. Indeed, many self-help manuals were produced during this era (e.g. Bass and Davies 1988 on child sexual abuse; Ernst and Goodison 1981 on groups). Separatist strategies, based on models developed through the 1970s, were utilized to develop more specialist services organized around ever more specific issues or groups. Gradually the strategy of autonomy from men was extended to include autonomy between groups of women. Women in therapy and self-help groups theorized their diversity through addressing the specific aspects of oppression that framed their lives. For example, therapies for Black women and for lesbians, who were abuse survivors, emerged as distinct theories and practices, developed and delivered by women who also shared those identities.

Women, as therapists and self-help facilitators, attempted to break down divisions with their clients by making explicit links between their specific, yet shared, experiences. Whilst matching Black therapists with Black clients and developing a specifically Black feminist therapy for abuse survivors, for example, went some way to addressing the needs of such women, power differences between client and therapist continued to exist. And the increasing separatist strategies failed to eradicate inequalities between women who could claim (some) shared identities. Indeed, conflating separatist strategies with essentialized identities reinstated hierarchical structures. Under the banner of 'the collective' the 'myth' of equality was maintained, but in practice 'reverse oppression' strengthened divisions. As Kelly (1991: 14) observed, identity politics exploited differences between women to establish oppression hierarchies whereby women could draw on their own experience of particular oppressions to generate guilt and silence in women deemed to be more privileged.

It was in these unsettled times that *child* sexual abuse became a significant issue for westernized feminists. Whilst sexual abuse was still understood to represent an abuse of power, the increasing specificity that characterized the politics of the day wove their way into accounts of sexual abuse. The banner term 'violence against women' was seen to obscure the particular ways that women were subjugated through sex (see Bell 1993). Women argued that physical assault just did not 'feel' the same as sexual assault. Therefore, whilst (child) sexual abuse was still conceptualized as an abuse of patriarchal power, sex was reinstated as a specific and central mechanism in the deployment of patriarchal power (Warner 1996a). This extended the analysis that all heterosexual sex is part of the continuum of rape.

Yet many women did not see themselves on a continuum that included rape when they engaged in heterosexuality; and penetrative sex by men or women was not always experienced as a violation or patriarchal subjugation. These women did not believe that their pleasure in heterosexuality and/ or penetration could all be explained away by reference to 'internalized' oppression. 'Sisters in the struggle' were increasingly doing battle with each other. Just as the assumption that heterosexuality was inevitably exploitative to women was being challenged within the feminist community, women were beginning to accept that lesbianism was not the panacea it had been held up to be. Feminists began to turn their gaze inwards to theorize women abusers and to break the silence around violence within the women's community.

As Kelly (1991) noted, however, this practice was initially resisted. 'Political' lesbians were unprepared and unwilling to recognize that the behaviour they criticized in heterosexual relationships occurred between lesbians. Such admissions seemed to undermine optimism about lesbian relationships and to contradict existing theories about the inherent problems associated with masculinity and heterosexuality. This meant that many lesbians struggled to name their experiences as abusive or violent, specifically in respect of coercive sex. Yet women, and children, are sexually abused by both lesbian and heterosexual women. Women, therefore, were forced to extend their analysis of power to include adult power over other adults and children. As the existence of women abusers within women-identified communities was increasingly recognized, women activists also reconsidered their responses to working with offenders:

> Can we afford to take the view we have with heterosexual violence, that we will not work with abusers? If we think men should work with abusive men, isn't the logical corollary that lesbians should work with abusive lesbians?
>
> (Kelly 1991: 20)

As different groups of women faced up to the particular ways in which sexual abuse impacted on their own, seemingly distinct, communities, conflicts emerged as these different groups called each other to account for marginalizing what they saw as being central issues in understanding sexual oppression. For example, white feminists were condemned for failing to demonstrate sufficient concern about Black men being framed for rape. Meanwhile Black feminists were grappling with the recognition that most sexual abuse of Black girls and women was perpetrated by Black men (see Hill Collins 1993), just as white girls and women were primarily raped by white men. Identity politics that presupposed the primacy of different forms of oppression (patriarchy or racism, for example) struggled to make sense of how they intersected with and transformed each other. Nevertheless, women were increasingly making explicit the complex interactions of different experiences of subjugation. Women would not permit their stories to be condensed or ignored.

Women, marginalized through race, class, and sexuality, wrote stories and autobiographies that elaborated the multiple forms and effects of child sexual abuse (e.g. Angelou 1984; Bass and Thornton 1983; Danica 1989;

Lewis 1997; Morrison 1981; Spring 1987; Walker 1983). Stories such as these, whilst being accorded little status in traditional academic and professional contexts, were partly responsible for provoking populist concern about child sexual abuse. In print and action, women struggled to make clear the devastating impact that child sexual abuse can have, whilst at the same time they worked hard to challenge the assumption of inevitable damage made within traditional accounts of the effects of child sexual abuse. Hence, feminist strategy of the time emphasized women's strength, agency and capacity to overcome abuse through naming the abused as survivors, and not as victims. Unfortunately, the silencing effects of identity politics, and the fragmentation of a shared sense of 'womanhood', meant that women found it increasingly difficult to talk critically with each other about child sexual abuse and its effects. As Armstrong (1991: 32) argued:

> By the time incest arose as an issue, the women's movement had already become a loose collection of the single-issued identified . . . It had already begun to splinter into a zillion often antagonistic identity groups . . . 'Survivor' became a ticket, a passport, a membership card . . . And, of course, this ghettoising of the issue served to corroborate the more general feminist population's sense that the issue was off bounds for any but card-carrying victims.

Whilst identity divisions between women may have meant that sexual abuse was increasingly difficult to talk about across these boundaries, the fragmentation of a singular feminist voice opened up a space in which women's chosen sexual practices could diversify. Because there was no longer *a* feminist perspective, the prescriptiveness of the preceding era, which took 'the personal is political' to mean that every aspect of behaviour, including sexual practices, could be mandated (Jeffreys 1990) was now challenged. For example, libertarian feminists (e.g. Califa 1980/1993 and see Vance 1984) argued against the automatic right of any group, including women, to define what was right for everyone. Sadomasochism and the explicit use of power within relationships were no longer, for some feminists, something to be avoided, but to be explored. And sex with children/cross-generational relationships was, for some, no longer an unspoken taboo, but a fantasy/practice to be articulated rather than automatically condemned (Califa 1994).

Challenges from libertarian feminists, typified in this type of sustained interest in a 'politics of pleasure', increased uncertainty and loss of confidence in feminism and its ability to understand (child and adult) sexual abuse. Already divided by simplistic identity politics, women's sisters had become strangers. It is little wonder that the organized WLM did not survive into the 1980s, even if a general concern with child sexual abuse did. However, the loss of common will was not limited to 'women's politics'. It also reflected the general slide towards individualism that typified westernized societies such as Britain at this time. In terms of therapy, there was a shift in focus during this era from radical politics to more personal solutions (e.g. Norwood 1986). Concomitantly, changes in the broad political and economic climate in westernized societies meant that there was less funding available for women's services. This meant that 'campaigning and support groups came under increasing pressure from funding agencies to lose politics and just provide support services' (Bindel *et al.* 1995: 65).

Ultimately all these factors decreased participation in feminist activism around child sexual abuse, and it was in this context that many women left grass-roots campaigning organizations for more therapeutic, individually focused services. Feminist therapy ceased to exist on the margins as an industry developed to provide personal solutions rather than revolutionary change. Therapy for women had become big business with a proliferation of approaches, texts and services. Feminism was being recuperated and the radicalism that characterized earlier times was under threat. This was reflected in how child sexual abuse was being reconstructed as a personal problem rather than as a political issue.

Psychiatry and psychology were reclaiming the ground that feminism had tried to force them to vacate. A focus on sexual desires once again replaced an analysis of the role of power in sexual violence. As Kelly and Scott (1991) noted, changing the structure of social relations was a much harder and less safe goal than breaking individual 'cycles' of abuse. Personal stories continued to be published, but now focused on personal growth rather than social transformation. 'Speaking out' was being transformed over this period from a strategy of liberation to a process of regulation. Endorsement of survivor narratives by mental health professionals served to confirm that incest was an illness in need of healing (see Armstrong 1991). As Armstrong (ibid.: 30) argued:

> We spoke of male violence and deliberate socially accepted viola-
> tion. They spoke of family dysfunction. We spoke of rage. They
> made rage a stage. We spoke of social change. They spoke of
> personal healing. We spoke of political battle. They spoke of our
> need to hug the child within . . . converting the personal-is-political
> into the political-as-personal.

Concern about oppression was being dismissed as 'political correctness'. Feminism was coming under increasing attack – and not just from the moral majority and libertarian feminists. An emphasis on women's suffer-ing had led some 'post-feminists' to criticize what they saw as 'victim feminism' (e.g. Paglia 1991; Wolf 1993). Vituperation and censure flowed from wider society and inflamed divisions that already riddled women's politics. During this period of conflict, however, not everyone was losing their sense of community. Some people were just starting to build theirs.

Radical activists in the WLM may have felt increasingly silenced, but radical mental health activists were just beginning to find their voice. As noted, the development of mainstream women's politics across the westernized world had too frequently occurred with little reference to socially disabled women with long-term mental health problems (Kitzinger and Perkins 1993).

The invisibility of 'mad' women within the wider feminist community was indicated by the absence of terms such as 'sane chauvinism' and 'mentalism' (defined as 'the negative and oppressive way in which human distress is perceived') (Plumb 1993: 175) from the more familiar list of oppressions referred to earlier. Psychiatric-system survivors, under-represented on progressive political agendas and marginalized by dominant culture, emerged in this era as a new organizing force. New organizations were established, such as 'Survivors Speak Out', a self-advocacy network that was founded in Britain in 1985 to challenge dominant models of mental health. They argued (as feminists had) that mental distress occurs 'in relation to social structures, institutions and culture' (ibid: 176), and hence change cannot be located solely inside the individual. Alliances were formed between service users and providers, and psychiatric survivors started to write about those issues that feminism had, to some degree, overlooked, such as hearing voices and self-harm (e.g. Pembroke 1994).

Service users and radical 'mad' activists were beginning to change the landscape of progressive politics. The golden era of feminism may have been long gone, but feminism had not been destroyed. It was regrouping and looking for new ways to make common cause around matters of sexual abuse and mental ill-health, for example. Ultimately, the loss of unity around the identity of womanhood provided the conditions in which some feminists turned to post-structuralism (e.g. Foucault 1978; 1991) to theorize their differences and to forge new political strategies to address matters such as child sexual abuse. Whilst these ideas had obviously been around for some time, it was in the 1990s that they were more widely detailed and developed within feminism – and radical mental health politics, which was now emerging as a significant force.

1990s–early 2000s: politics of deconstruction
Child sexual abuse and mad activism: redefining a politics of experience

The 1990s heralded a sustained attempt by some feminists to theorize experience and to question the role of identity in defining political action (e.g. Butler 1990; Haraway 1991). Hence, women turned their attention to making sense of how different theories about child sexual abuse shaped how women made sense of what had happened to them and how they came to understand themselves, as victims or survivors, for example; and, through this, how identity was an effect of, not simply a starting point for, theory and action. Hence, the notion of 'the personal' being understood as *the* route into understanding 'the political' was challenged, in as much as personal experience was understood to be a social construct, rather than a resource that was unadulterated and pure. This marked the third wave of feminism: that of deconstruction. In this phase, identity, as a shorthand for experience, was now viewed, by some feminists, with suspicion. Hence, 'hyphenated feminisms' (Bondi 1995), whereby women marked their authority to speak by listing their group memberships (e.g. *'as a* white – working class – ablebodied – survivor etc') was critiqued. Women's experiences and women's values were no longer understood to be beyond examination. The assumption that who we were and what we thought were the same thing was being challenged.

Hence, emerging out of the third phase of second-wave feminism was a related shift from a modernist understanding of absolute differences to a post-structuralist concern with how differences are socially constructed through discourse. Tactics of deconstruction were used to demonstrate how structural inequalities, in respect of sex for example, were made and maintained through language. Power was no longer understood as a possession that was essentially negative, but rather as a generative force which invoked resistance, as well as regulation (Burman *et al.* 1996). Feminists began to explore how their own representations of sex and violence were implicated in shaping how sex and abuse could be understood within contemporary cultures (Reavey and Warner 2003). Women were finding ways of speaking critically *about* (the social production of) sexually abused woman, rather than uncritically assuming they could speak *for* all abused women (or at least those who apparently shared similar identities).

As noted in Chapter 1, such tactics of deconstruction were not without their critics. Many feminists remained sceptical of approaches that appeared to deny the reality of women's shared experiences, identity and their ability to formulate collective action (e.g. Benhabib 1995; Hartsock 1990). Others argued that the role of modernism in cementing gender divisions within feminism had been overstated. For example, Jackson (1992: 31) argued that few feminists would dispute the idea that gender is culturally constructed and therefore argued that radical feminists had been caricatured as being *'essentially* essentialist'. At the same time, an emphasis on gender-as-performance (*pace* Butler 1990) seemed to trivialize and underestimate the binds of socially constructed gender. Only the privileged few can shrug off femininity and play with gender (Jackson, 1992). Finally, too much emphasis seemed to have been placed on the politics of pleasure, rather than the iniquities of abuse.

Yet some post-structuralist feminists have focused their attention on child sexual abuse (e.g. Bell 1993; Haaken 1998; Lamb 1999; Reavey and Warner 2003; Warner 2000b). Such feminists argued that child sexual abuse was not denied by acknowledging its social construction through language. Rather, understanding language use was seen as central to exposing the deployment of privilege and power within sexually abusive relationships. Charges of relativism seemed to be as overstated as charges of essentialism had been in respect of previous generations of feminists. As argued in Chapter 1, a feminist appropriation of post-structuralism still draws on feminism to provide a moral guide that challenges the naivety of relativism. Post-structuralist feminists did not abandon political activism. Rather the territory of politics changed. It was now rethought in terms of what women *want* to achieve rather than being defined by *who* women are (Yuval-Davis 1993).

Despite such assurances, however, the development of post-structuralist feminism through the 1990s was matched by a growth in liberal humanist feminism. This supported the interiorization of social problems, such as child sexual abuse, and was reflected in the increasing depoliticization of therapy for women. In the 1990s, like the decade before, consciousness-raising was being forgotten within a confessional culture where the personal remained personal and the aim of therapy was no longer inextricably linked with wider social concerns. It seemed that for some possibly more privileged women, there was a premature optimism that women's rights had been secured and abuse had been vanquished, resulting in a post-feminist concern with self-actualisation (e.g. Crossley 2000). This further contributed to the loss of common will and is despite the fact that many women across the globe still remain oppressed, abused, exploited and poor. Moreover, the professionalization of women's activism that had gained momentum during the 1980s continued. The rehabilitation of previously dismissed notions of 'expertise' marked a general move from self-help groups to feminist therapy. Additionally, the apparent failure of organizational collectives to adequately address issues of inequality meant that, for some, previously male-identified work practices, such as organizational hierarchies, were rehabilitated.

Such trends were not definitive, however. Some feminists continued to develop more critical approaches to therapy for, and research on, women (e.g. respectively Seu and Heenan 1998; ReSisters 2002 in Britain) and continued to utilize self-help models of group/personal support to address child sexual abuse (e.g. Linnell and Cora 1993 in Australia). The post-modern refusal of absolute truth reinforced the need for plurality in feminist theory, women's activism and approaches to therapy around child sexual abuse. The 1990s thus cemented the policy developed in the 1980s of forging different strategies and services for different people. Although now this was, perhaps, less prescriptive in that there was greater acceptance that women, who shared common identities, did not always want the same kind of dedicated service. For example, sexually abused women could benefit from both integrated *and* separate therapy services, within both voluntary and (some) mainstream contexts. For some feminists, however, the notion of therapy, wherever it took place, remained problematic.

Much of the therapy developed by feminists still seemed to favour privileged groups of women. Instead it was the nascent service-user movement that would address the needs of abused women with severe and enduring mental health problems. As in earlier days of the WLM, service-user activists took direct action to draw attention to the abuses they identified as being perpetrated by the mental health system. For example, the British Royal College of Psychiatrists has been picketed as a protest against compulsory treatment (Shaughnessy 2001). The growth of new technologies, such as the internet, has enabled activists to increase their effectiveness as these technologies provide a relatively cheap and accessible form of communication that facilitates local and global activism through the rapid exchange of ideas and strategies. The internet, as argued in Chapter 3, is not the destructive force it is often portrayed to be.

Service-user activists, again like feminist activists in previous years, began to organize around specific issues. These included different forms of psychiatric oppression. Some relate to gender-specific concerns such as women diagnosed with borderline personality disorder (see Women at the Margins 2004). Some addressed cross-gender concerns such as The Hearing Voices Network, which became a crucial force in resisting dominant understandings about psychosis and schizophrenia (see Romme and Escher 1993; James 2001). Direct links were made between psychosis, self-harm and the experiences often associated with these issues, such as abuse and, in particular, child sexual abuse. Child sexual abuse was becoming, for the first time, a clear issue for mental health activists, as it had previously for feminists.

Radical mental health activists (both service users and workers) came together to promulgate these ideas through staging events, providing training and publishing books (e.g. Coleman 1999; Warner 2000b). Service users challenged the orthodoxy of expertise, as previous generations of women had, by drawing on their own experiences of psychiatric abuse. Service users were becoming increasingly visible and vocal. Clients were no longer viewed as being only passive consumers of services, but recognized as consultants, trainers, evaluators and commissioners of services in their own right (Davies et al. 2001). The impact of the expanded role of service users, however, remains unclear. Small organizations, limited resources, and the growth in 'freelance' trainers means that there is often a piecemeal response to issues, and because the service-user movement is fragmented (and we've been here before), its contributions can then be marginalized (Campbell 2001).

Additionally, the recent willingness of mainstream services to listen to service users may reflect a desire to recuperate dissent, rather than revolutionize mental health practices (again a tactic that feminists are familiar with). For example, psychologists, like others in the mental health industry, are increasingly interested in service-user perspectives (see Neunes 2001;

Chapter 2). Yet few psychologists ally themselves directly with user organizations (James 2001). Also differentiating 'them from us' can ultimately sediment the divisions that already exist (see Harper *et al.* 2003) as few professionals refer to their own experiences as service users or their histories of abuse. Ultimately, whilst service users are increasingly expected to share their knowledge about mental ill-health and experiences, such as child sexual abuse, they continue to have very little control over their own treatment (see Chapter 2). In response to this, some radical mental health activists have returned to a politics of autonomy, although with a distinctively deconstructive feel.

As with 'queer' activists, 'mad' activists aim to use language to subvert social stereotypes, *and* advocate for their own autonomy and self-determination. Some activists reject the word 'user' as meaningless and bureaucratic, and embrace madness as a political term (e.g. Shaughnessy 2003). For example, 'Mad Women', established in Liverpool, England, in 1998, chose the name as 'a conscious effort to reclaim and disarm language that has been used to stigmatize and invalidate people who experience mental distress' (Mad Women 1998). Mad activists are also keen to subvert the idea that 'madness' is an inherently negative experience (Curtis *et al.* 2001). Whilst identity is still central to this radical political agenda, the instability of the use of identity in political action and the limitations of any strategy is recognized. As Morris (2001: 207) argues:

> The 'Mad Pride' virus is now loose and the term will no doubt begin to enter common currency over the next few years, leading to its eventual recuperation.

This understanding is crucial because when identities become frozen, 'speaking from experience' ends debate and restricts opportunities for change. Madness may reflect the misery associated with issues such as child sexual abuse, but it is also a context for constructive resistance. A deconstructive identity politics that seems to have influenced current radical mad activists offers the hope that this social movement may avoid some of the difficulties feminists have sometimes faced when thinking through issues of sexual violence.

Twenty-first century radicalism: where do we go from here?

Both feminists and mental health activists have made, and continue to make, significant contributions to the debate about how child sexual abuse should be responded to and understood. The fragmentation of the WLM was not simply indicative of its failure, but also indicative of the ways feminism has insinuated itself onto the mainstream agenda. Feminists directly and indirectly forced changes in institutional and legal practice regarding sexual and domestic violence and the treatment of child abuse.

Mainstream culture has absorbed some feminist ideas, and not always in a deradicalizing way. To take Britain as an example, 'Women Against Rape', which was founded in 1976, secured the legal recognition of rape within marriage in 1991 after a 15-year campaign (Hill 2002b). Child sexual abuse became part of the mainstream social care agenda in Britain during the late 1980s (see Campbell 1988). This led to the Children Act (Home Office 1989) being enacted in England and Wales in 1991 and dedicated family service units being set up by the police to deal with victims of sexual and domestic abuse.

As feminists around the world know, a legislative agenda is not without problems. As Haug (2001) has pointed out, there has sometimes been a worrying tendency for feminists and the 'moral majority' to become aligned in their desire for increased state intervention in law and order. And as mental health activists argue today, increased legislation can mean more regulation, which undermines, rather than safeguards, some people's rights. However, as legislative frameworks are part of the structures that determine how abuse can be recognized and addressed, such changes are important. There are also old battles that have not been won and which feminists and mental health activists still need to engage in. The argument that mental health and social problems arise in response to negative life experiences, such as child sexual abuse, rather than mainly in respect of born-with deficiencies, has not yet led to widespread changes in the psychiatric system. And as indicated in Chapter 3, the public's desire to reduce child sexual abuse to paedophilia and to obscure its relative banality still needs resisting. We also still need to find ways of making 'common cause' with children, who in our endeavour to protect them from talking about events they have evidently endured and survived, we exclude from political enterprise.

The various politics (equality, autonomy, difference and diversity, and deconstruction) that have shaped recent radical activism still circulate in various forms and have a role to play in helping us (whether professionals and/or activists) think through how we work around the issue of child sexual abuse. It may be that there is a necessary oscillation between the different strategies (equality, autonomy, difference and diversity, and deconstructive politics), as women still want equal treatment as well as having their differences recognized (Stanley 1997). Feminist theories and practices continue to evolve. There is debate and diversity within feminism rather than the 'orthodoxy, fundamentalism and censorious authority often attributed to it' (Ramazanoglu and Holland 1999: 382). And it is this continual engagement with, and critiquing of, feminist theories and practices that demonstrates that feminism itself remains politically relevant.

Too often, in our desire to demonstrate how innovative our current ways of working are, we too quickly dismiss that which has gone before. Without reference to our pasts we lose sense of the many changes that have been achieved and forget the lessons we have learnt – some that we can take into other forums, such as mad activism. In this sense, our collective experiences are a rich, if sometimes forgotten, resource. Hence, 'experience' may be a problem, but it is a problem worth engaging with. As Ramazanoglu and Holland (1999: 391) argue:

> Experience, and reflections on experiences of living in unequal societies, provide feminism with its foundations of rage, pain, endurance and hope for something better, without which it will wither.

Both feminists and mental health activists have demonstrated how talk about experience can be used to challenge taken-for-granted hegemonies to show how subjugated lives are edited, experience is shaped, and social interaction is constrained. Speaking rights, therefore, have a key role in defining political enterprise. Therefore, it is still politically important to foreground personal stories of sexual and psychiatric abuse, and detail personal accounts of using mental health support services as these enrich, elaborate, and provide material for discussion and contestation that theoretical work alone struggles to do (see ibid.). Our experiences give rise to the passion that sustains political activism, as well as sometimes impedes our ability to make common cause.

I was born in 1960s Britain and grew up in the golden era of 1970s feminism. I understood that sex and violence had a particular and sustained impact on how women could live their lives. Therefore, the theories and activism that women developed through these times provided the foundation for my entrée into feminist politics. To trace some of my journey so far, in 1981 I attended my first 'reclaim the night march' and joined my local 'Rape Crisis' in 1986 and 'Taboo: A community support service for women and girls who have been sexually abused in childhood' thereafter. My activism around sexual violence against women took me out of the collective (like others) and into mainstream services via my training as a clinical psychologist. By the end of the 1980s I had become tired of the divisions that separatist politics cemented. My subsequent work with women in high-security mental hospitals made me acutely aware that some women were as marginalized by some feminist organizations as they were by mainstream culture. It was in this context that I made common cause with radical mental health groups. Only some of these are women-only, and feminism is not always, for others, an explicit concern. Yet, feminists and mental health activists have many overlapping concerns, as well as sometimes common identities.

The fragmentation of political movements was not simply a tragedy, but has been, for me at least, an opportunity for cross-fertilization of ideas and strategies. I am still committed to challenging sexually abusive behaviour and to developing more egalitarian and emancipatory therapy practices and

71

mental health services. Feminism (in its many forms) remains a source of inspiration. Feminism should not, and cannot, provide all the answers. We get stuck when we start to believe we are always right. Instead, I think that feminism can be used to encourage us to ask difficult, yet relevant, questions. There cannot be one right way of working with women, but I think that we should still try to detail, situate and theorize progressive forms of action. And I make no apology for still hoping for social transformation.

Making waves: revolutions in theory, research and practice

When women rewrote their own histories they challenged the orthodoxy of received wisdom and this set the stage for revolutions in gender politics. When women articulated their personal experiences of sexual exploitation and made direct links to male privilege, they forced the issue of sexual violence onto the political agenda, and, it can be argued, this is why child sexual abuse remains such a major concern within contemporary westernized societies today. When women began to share their individual narratives of abuse, sexual exploitation was transformed from a personal experience into a political issue. Child sexual abuse was no longer isolated and uncommon, but was now viewed as a widespread social problem. This conceptual shift was a revolutionary act that continues to reverberate today, not least for many radical (women) activists in mental health (Spandler and Warner 2007).

This book is part of this radical political tradition. There are other stories about politics I could have told that reflect different aspects of 'me' or reflect different versions of history that are more directly tied to different geographical contexts. However, the account given here does largely locate my 'view from somewhere' (Haraway 1991). It is this perspective, arising out of my primary dissatisfaction with mainstream approaches to understanding child sexual abuse, and my lived experience of feminist and mental health activism, that provides the foundation for the 'research' and 'practice' sections of this book. The current chapter outlines the theoretical and political frameworks that inform my work. It demonstrates the value of utilizing personal accounts and opinions about child sexual abuse to provide the depth and detail that theoretical work alone fails to do. It therefore signals why it is important to examine our understandings about child sexual abuse through empirical enquiry and through practical application. In Part 2, I critically examine the experience of child sexual abuse by using empirical methods to research the needs of some abused women with severe and enduring mental health problems. In doing so, I also aim to focus concern on those women who have been too often overlooked within feminist politics.

Part 2

RESEARCH

In Part 1, I identified the theoretical and political frameworks that underpin my approach to understanding the sexual abuse of women and children. I used feminism and post-structuralism to demonstrate some of the short-comings associated with mainstream mental-health theories and practices, and argued for the adoption of a more radical political approach. As argued in Chapter 4, both feminists and mental health activists have demonstrated how important it is to access personal accounts of, and opinions about, childhood sexual abuse. Personal accounts of, and opinions about, childhood sexual abuse can be drawn on to enrich, inform, challenge and reshape theoretical understandings about the issue. This is why research is crucial to the development of theory and hence why the empiri-cal studies referred to in this section of the book are critical to supporting and informing the development of my working practices.

In Part 2, I focus my concern on sexually abused women in secure mental-health care. Women in such services around the world too often face misunderstanding, mistreatment, neglect and further abuse (World Health Organization WHO 2005a) and, hence, such services need major revision. Drawing on original research conducted in two British maximum-security mental hospitals, I explore how service provision may be reconfigured for such women by displacing medical diagnosis as a central organizing prin-ciple and through adopting more psychosocial recovery-orientated practices. The research presented here reflects my ongoing commitment to illuminating the specific needs of this group of marginalized and abused women. It also provides an evidence base for the development of wider practices regarding women, girls and child sexual abuse.

In Chapter 5, I demonstrate how feminism and post-structuralism can be used to develop critical approaches to research that can be adapted to investigate understandings about women and child sexual abuse within even closed systems of care and in respect of a particularly vulnerable group of women. An overview is provided of the practical processes involved in enabling professionals and patients to express a view about detained women who have experienced childhood sexual abuse. This overview includes a description of the methodologies deployed, namely a feminist post-structuralist use of interviewing and Q methodology (Stephenson, 1935a, 1935b). In the proceeding three chapters, the main points from the interviews and Q methodological studies are used to provide empirical data to support a radical, recovery-orientated mental-health agenda for abused women in secure care.

In Chapter 6, I identify key discourses (referred to as accounts) that position some sexually abused women as being 'in need' of mandatory secure mental-health care. Data from the 'routes' Q study is used to point to the ways in which detained women patients are variously understood as being 'mad', 'bad' and dangerous. In order to make the process of inter-preting accounts in Q methodology transparent, this study is reported in detail. The Q-generated accounts and interview quotes provide evidence that the medical model prevails as a dominant system for conceptualizing these women and their needs, which ultimately undervalues the role of social experiences in shaping women's experiences of madness and disorder.

In Chapter 7, the role of medicine is deliberately marginalized as concern shifts to lived experience and the specific issue of childhood sexual abuse. The empirically-generated accounts of the 'effects' of childhood sexual abuse are used to illustrate how secure mental-health services for women can be redesigned by changing the focus from 'illness' to abuse. Here, 'effects' are considered in terms of *discourses about* the impact of childhood sexual abuse and *representations of* sexually abused women patients. I explore the various ways that betrayal is depicted as affecting detained and sexually abused women patients and I consider mainstream medical and psychological means of making sense of the impact of childhood sexual abuse. I argue that mainstream approaches too often rely on normative understandings about sex and gender that can act to prescribe pathways to, and representations of, recovery. I demonstrate that it is crucial to maintain a focus on social experiences, such as childhood sexual abuse, if women are to forge different and preferred realities in which to live their lives.

In Chapter 8, I argue that psychosocial models of mental health care are better suited to enabling recovery than traditional medical ones. I again draw on empirical data (here, from the 'treatment' Q study) to elaborate the various components of a recovery-orientated secure service for women who have experienced childhood sexual abuse. Factors that empower women to take control of their lives, including safety, choice, partnership, sexual abuse therapy and remedial social skills work, are described and discussed. The research data is used to provide an evidence base that illuminates key principles for practice and which demonstrates how to make feminist post-structuralist ethics and radical politics applicable in mental-health and social-care service contexts.

5

CRITICAL RESEARCH PRACTICES AND ETHICAL METHODOLOGIES

Researching women and child sexual abuse

Introduction

Mainstream mental health services fail women, who have experienced child sexual abuse, when they conceptualize the effects of abuse, and women's coping strategies, in negative and pathological terms. In particular, the medical model has been repeatedly criticized for underscoring the impact of abuse and exploitation in shaping women's experiences of 'madness'. A corollary of this is that prescriptive pathways to recovery and health, that reflect dominant values around heteronormativity, can be reinstated as the unacknowledged goals of psychiatry and psychology. Such values are further augmented through the mass media, which perpetuates well-rehearsed and familiar narratives about abusers and victims. This means that abused women, who are further marginalized through structural oppressions such as race, culture and psychiatric status, often receive poor mental health and social care because the general public cannot be galvanized into caring about their fate. It is little wonder then that sexually abused women, with the most serious and enduring mental health problems, who end up being involuntarily detained in secure hospitals, often have the poorest service of all. Indeed, women's mistreatment in mental-health care institutions has long been documented around the world (e.g. Aitkin and Heenan 2004; Allen 1987; Chesler 1972/1989; Hemingway 1996; Horn and Warner 2000; Warner 1996b, 1996c; Wile 2001).

As demonstrated in the previous chapter, both feminists and mental health activists have attempted to challenge the hegemony of mainstream mental health practices that lead to the misunderstanding and mistreatment of sexually abused women by repeatedly drawing attention to the social foundations of madness and misery. Both feminists and mental health activists have identified child sexual abuse as a significant factor that contributes to women's experiences of marginalization, madness and misery. They have tried to resist women's pathologization by recasting women's actions as coping strategies in lives lived with few choices. Although incarcerated women with long-term mental health problems have not always been central to a feminist political agenda, mental health activists have demonstrated a sustained concern with abused women who exhibit the most severe and enduring mental health problems: namely those who are detained in secure hospitals.

The studies presented in this section of the book draw on this history of critique in order to ask questions about the role of social experiences in making sense of involuntarily detained women patients. This research specifically explores how narratives about child sexual abuse impact on the ways in which women are understood in maximum-security mental hospitals, or 'special' hospitals as they are euphemistically called in Britain. The research presented here, therefore, reflects my ongoing commitment to illuminating the specific needs of this group of marginalized and abused women. It also demonstrates the utility of feminism and post-structuralism in the provision of an ethical and practical framework for practice, including investigation. My aim is to critically examine empirically the experience of child sexual abuse, drawing on a feminist post-structuralist perspective that is also informed by a radical mental health agenda. Feminist politics have led me into research, not away from it. The ways in which I seek and analyse research data has been shaped by feminist theory, which has provided a moral map that explicitly guides my decision-making throughout this process. This chapter outlines the methodological approaches that were adopted in conducting this research. I describe a feminist post-structuralist use of interviewing and Q methodology (Stephenson 1935a, 1935b). The following chapters in this section then present the main points from the studies.

Keeping things in perspective: using reflexivity to maximize ethical research practices

From a feminist post-structuralist perspective any 'method' is a dynamic process of construction. This is implicit in the etymological roots of the word 'method'. As Coleridge (cited by Fisher 1988: 5) noted:

> The Greek word *Methodos* . . . 'is literally a *way* or *path of transit*
> . . . The term method, cannot therefore, be applied to a mere dead
> arrangement, containing in itself no principle of progression'.

There are multiple factors that shape methodological paths in research. As argued in Chapter 1, the questions we ask are never neutral, but are always selective and selecting, and therefore research is inevitably a matter of politics and ethics. For example, research on 'schizophrenia' is different from research on 'hearing voices'. Research on 'schizophrenia' presupposes schizophrenia exists as a distinct (usually biological) disorder in need of (pharmaceutical) treatment. As 'hearing voices' is not constituted as an inevitable problem in need of treatment, intervention (pharmaceutical or otherwise) remains an issue to be explored rather than assumed (Warner

2004a). Rather, a focus on 'hearing voices' invites researchers to ask what such voices mean to each individual (they may be helpful or abusive; and might reflect either or both aspects of experience), instead of pre-imposing a set understanding on them (they are always indicative of pathology). Therefore, some researchers will also not take money from large pharmaceutical companies to undertake research on 'schizophrenia' because they refuse to be conscripted into reifying 'hearing voices' as a disorder in need of medical intervention.

What we choose to study, therefore, already signals our political, monetary, professional and personal alliances. Yet, the questions we ask seldom form part of the formal process of inquiry in psychology. They are typically represented as being *the* questions (Salmon 1992). By contrast, feminism, because it has a deliberate (albeit shifting) political agenda, is centrally concerned with the ways research questions construct particular versions of reality (e.g. see Clarke and Peel 2004). Feminism, like other radical politics, invites us to ask difficult questions about the vested interests we wittingly and unwittingly challenge and support in our research practices. The research that is presented in this section of this book deliberately seeks to challenge traditional approaches to working with incarcerated and abused women with long-term mental health problems, and seeks to support a radical mental health agenda.

Both feminism and post-structuralism invite us to reflect on not only *how* we represent data, but *why* we choose to do so in the first place. Matters of epistemology, therefore, have a central role in determining both the value of the methodological approaches researchers subsequently use and apply, and why delineating perspective is a recurring theme in this book. Having some sense of the perspectives we draw on to construct research agendas invites consideration of the multiple processes implicated in formulating research questions, engaging in research relationships and interpreting research data. Therefore, it forces the researcher to take a greater responsibility for her actions through the persistent demand to reflect on their effects (Banister *et al.* 1994). Reflexivity, therefore, is an integral part of critical research practices and is central to the empirical studies that follow. Reflexivity is a way of operationalizing a situated reading of ethics because, as Reay (1996: 443) argues, 'reflexive practice should constitute a process of uncovering/recognizing the difference your differences make'. Research is inevitably a process of co-construction between participant and researcher regarding how they respond to each other and how each seeks clarification and provides emphasis. Reflexivity enables this dynamic relationship to be explored.

The process of reflection can be facilitated by keeping research diaries, having discussions with colleagues, supervisors, interest groups and friends, and by reference to other authors and research papers. The use of multiple theoretical and disciplinary standpoints, methods and sources of data, to enrich understanding and enhance rigour, is termed *triangulation* (Denzin

1978; Janesick 1998). Reflexivity is the means through which triangulation may be operationalized as a post-structuralist endeavour. From this perspective, triangulation is a fluid enterprise that enables consideration of multiple sources of information. Reflexivity enables the researcher to think through how these multiple sources of information are implicated in the active construction of the data of which they speak. Hence, within this framework, triangulation is not used as an unproblematic means of checking reliability and validity, as different perspectives will be mobilized at different times for different (political) ends.

For example, because my aim is to privilege some marginalized perspectives, it is not possible or desirable to be equally accountable to all participants or participating organizations, etc. I have a deliberate desire to challenge the hegemony of psychiatry within mental health provision and I specifically adopt a situated feminist framework for my practice. The conclusions I draw, therefore, will differentially challenge and support competing interest groups. Therefore, whether my interpretation may be considered to be plausible is a function of how matters of methodology intersect with matters of accountability. The preceding chapters serve notice of my lines of accountability that underpin the specific research practices my concerns and sense of moral accountability lead me to and through.

From concern to action: researching women and child sexual abuse in maximum-security mental hospitals

From a post-structuralist perspective there can never be a final account of research. Although any account is relative, it is still possible and providential to follow and describe a clear research process. As Curt (1994: 105) argues, any investigation should be 'capable of yielding similarly *organised* (not necessarily the same, of course) output from one instance of use to another'. It is important therefore to aim, as far as is possible, for transparency in the multiple decisions that are embedded in the theoretical, methodological and representational practices of research. The first decision that is made is to determine an issue for investigation, and to have some sense of why this topic has been chosen.

As noted, the studies presented here arose out of my concern that women who have been sexually abused are too often misunderstood and mistreated within mainstream mental health services, and in particular within secure mental health care. Secure mental health care is designed for patients who are involuntarily detained because they are deemed to be mentally disordered, and who are thought to pose a significant danger to themselves and/ or others. My aim is to contribute to a critical debate about how such women may be better served. In contemporary Britain, concerns that women are detained in systems where security is in excess of, rather than commensurate with, their needs, have led to the planned closure of women's services within two of the three British maximum-security mental hospitals. Despite this, the actual number of women in 'special' maximum-security mental health care has not been reduced and has, in fact, remained relatively stable since 1995 (Ly and Foster 2005). Additionally, changing venues does not address problems associated with traditional approaches to mental ill health that frequently undermine women's attempts to negotiate their sometimes troubled lives.

The aim of these studies was to illuminate the impact that language has on shaping sexually abused women's experiences in secure mental health care. In order to explore these issues four separate, but related, areas for investigation were identified. These were: women patients' routes into special hospitals; discourses about the effects of childhood sexual abuse on these women; how such women are represented in special hospitals; and how such women should be treated there. The next step involved identifying methods able to generate textual data that would allow me to track language use and be amenable to critical cultural analysis. To this end two main techniques were adopted: semi-structured interviewing and Q methodology. As Q methodology is likely to be less familiar than interviewing, a short description follows.

Q methodology was first developed by Stephenson (1935a, 1935b, 1992) as a technique through which different perspectives on a contested social issue can be generated by getting participants to rank-order relevant statements according to whether they agree with them or not. How much or how little people agree or disagree with each statement is used to make sense of what the overall pattern of responses means. The relative distribution of the statements, therefore, provides the template for the interpretation of the account. For example, in the 'routes' study (described in Chapter 6), there were 39 different statements, each giving a different reason for why women go to special hospitals, which could be combined in many different ways, to give many different meanings, as demonstrated below.

If someone agrees strongly with the statement '*women go to special hospitals when their requests for help have been ignored*' (statement 17 from the 'routes' study) and also agrees strongly that '*other institutions cannot cope with women's violent and aggressive behaviour*' (statement 26), we might infer from this that, in this account, women's attempts to garner support have been more physical than verbal, and have failed to have the desired effect. If the statement '*women go to special hospitals because of the harmful effects of childhood sexual abuse*' (statement 10) is associated with being ignored, in this case we might infer that other institutions had failed to enable women to talk about their experiences of child sexual abuse. Thus, as Brown (1980: 55) notes:

> There is less interest in what individual statements mean theoretically than what the [participant] does with them operationally,

and it is the Q sort which gives substance to this operation. Basic-
ally, the Q sort enables the subject to provide a model of his [sic]
point of view.

Accounts produced through Q sorting can then be read in much the same
way other texts are read through various discourse-analytic techniques.
Hence, the two methods – interviewing and Q sorting – offer opportunity
for cross-referencing and reflexive methodological triangulation (Kitzinger
and Stainton-Rogers 1985). Because there are very many different sorting
patterns that may be produced, Q has the potential to produce very many
different accounts (Kitzinger 1987), which means that Q has the power
to surprise as well as confirm. It is a speculative method, rather than
hypothetico-deductive, and hence there are no predetermined hypotheses to
prove. This was of benefit to the present studies because although they
arose out of my concern with women's mismanagement in secure mental
health care, I did not want to simply present back to my audience what I
already thought that I knew.

Whilst Q methodology was originally designed to elicit subjective viewpoints or self-referential attitudes, a more social understanding of the
technique has been formulated from a post-structuralist perspective. Here
the Q sorts (the overall pattern that the statements have been sorted into)
are understood to be 'social representations, understandings, and accounts'
(Stainton-Rogers and Stainton-Rogers 1990: 1–11). (A fully laid out Q
sort complete with statements can be found on page 95 in Chapter 6.
Alternatively, see Figure 5.2 in this chapter on page 87, which simply
demonstrates how statements might be positioned.) This conceptualization
does not try to locate processes within the individual nor does it place an *a
priori* value on particular statements (Kitzinger and Stainton-Rogers
1985). Rather, Q offers a method for validating competing versions of
reality as having epistemological equivalence (Curt 1994). Thus Q provides
a means of exploring multiplicity by ensuring that lines of enquiry are not
overly restricted by the imagination of the researcher at the onset of the
research process. Q documents variability without making the assumption
that the person doing the sorting will always give the same answer, or the
issue under investigation will always be understood in the same way. In Q,
participants are assumed to give just one interpretation or account of a
number that are available to them (O'Dell 2003). Because it is a relatively
open and non-hierarchical method of investigation, it is unsurprising,
as Febbraro (1993) argues, that Q has been taken up within feminist
and post-structuralist research (e.g. Dell and Korotana 2000; Kitzinger
1987; O'Dell 2003; Senn 1996; Stenner and Stainton-Rogers 1998;
Stowell-Smith and McKeown 1999; Wilkins and Warner 2000). It was
for all these reasons that Q methodology was utilized in the studies
presented in this book.

Opening the door on closed institutions: identifying, accessing and selecting participants

As noted, there are three special maximum-security hospitals in England: Ashworth, Rampton and Broadmoor. These hospitals are designed to hold mentally disordered patients who are thought to be the most dangerous in the country – hence the need for *maximum* or *high* security. The research described here was conducted in the first two hospitals.

Because special hospitals act as closed institutions, they are not always amenable to 'outsiders' breaching their boundaries and turning a critical gaze on their practices. However, as I had worked in a variety of capacities (as clinician, researcher, trainer and consultant) in Ashworth special hospital prior to the onset of this research, this, to some degree, facilitated acceptance and support of the current studies. Ashworth hospital funded the research, which was conducted there and in Rampton special hospital (Broadmoor, the other British special hospital, declined to take part). I thus provided my own *entrée* into this world and already had some knowledge of the links between the language and culture of participants (see Fontana and Frey 1994). In Ashworth hospital I was able to use my prior relationships with workers and patients to encourage participation. In Rampton hospital, because I was new to that institution, I needed to be much more proactive in building relationships and goodwill.

To that end I spent considerable time talking informally with patients and members of staff. Under the usual conditions that research is conducted in, participants are asked to give 'informed consent' purely in terms of the research topic and procedures. Who the researcher is is not deemed relevant according to modernist versions of scientific method. Yet, according to the approach adopted here, the researcher is centrally involved in the research process. Therefore, when people agreed to take part, it was important that they had access to expected forms of information (about the nature of the research, the processes of participation, what would happen with the research, etc), but also experience of, and knowledge about, me and my views. Particularly for women patients, who often have multiple experiences of exploitation and abuse, it was crucial that they had time to form an opinion about me. Once I had gained a working level of acceptance within both hospitals, I was then able to begin the process of identifying potential research participants.

My aim was to sample the ways in which women who have been sexually abused are spoken about and understood within secure mental hospitals. Therefore, I was interested in the range of voices that circulate in such institutions, including those of the professionals who work there, and the female – and male – patients who live there. Although I was interested in generating a wide range of perspectives, this did not translate into needing large numbers of participants for the interviews or the Q studies (Cottle *et al.*

1989). I wanted to know, in simple terms, what stories were voiced; I did not want to count how many times a particular story was told. Participants were thus targeted in terms of their ability to furnish the studies with a range of perspectives. Hence, participant selection was purposive, rather than random, and a form of theoretical 'snowball' sampling was used to facilitate this. Snowball sampling is defined as a type of non-probability sampling in which participants recruit other participants and so on (Powers 1990). Theoretical snowball sampling involves asking participants to identify other potential participants who hold views that are different to their own.

Thirty-three people participated in the interviews and 60 participants completed the four Q studies ('routes', 'effects', 'representations' and 'treatment'). Because in small communities, such as secure hospitals, some voices will be recognizable to some people, in order to protect anonymity all that is presented here is an overview of the kinds of people who participated. Participants were aged between 22 years and 57 years, and had been employed or residing in the hospitals for between four months and 24 years. About half the participants were male and half female, and about a third of participants were patients, the rest members of staff. The majority of participants described themselves as white British, and where noted, as Christian. A few identified as being Black, Asian and variously European, Jewish and atheist. As people from minoritized ethnic and religious communities represent a small percentage of both patients and workers in the special hospitals studied, this is necessarily reflected in the participants who took part. In order to safeguard their particular anonymity, in the following chapters identifying characteristics are limited to gender and role.

All male patients who participated in the studies were identified by workers as perpetrators of sexual abuse and by themselves as victims of child sexual abuse. The majority of women patients who participated described themselves as having been sexually abused in childhood. The range of workers who participated came from all ranks (from assistants to senior managers) and represented all major relevant professions. These included: psychiatrists; clinical and research psychologists; nurses; social workers; patient teachers and technical instructors; lecturers; pharmacists; and occupational therapists. None of these identified their own abuse histories. Additionally, because I was part of the situation I wished to study, by virtue of my *de facto* research role and other work roles, I not only (obviously) participated in the interviews; following Curt (1994), I also acted as one of the research participants in the Q studies (I completed the four Q sorts, too).

Engaging with participants: structuring the interviews and reflecting on research relationships

There is no one particular model for conducting interviews, rather the structure and form is related to both the information that it is designed to generate and ethical concerns regarding the likely effects of the interview process on all participants. In order to encourage an exchange of views, I needed to ensure that the interviews (and the Q studies that followed) were emotionally and physically safe for both my participants and me. I recognize that child sexual abuse is an emotionally saturated discourse that represents a significant life narrative for many patients in special hospitals, as well as for some members of staff. I did not want to be unnecessarily invasive and voyeuristic. Therefore, the nature of the interviews had much in common with the Q studies in that I was concerned with 'opinion' rather than 'experience'.

It was anticipated that participants would draw on their own lived experience to give their opinion and indeed that patients, in particular, would be primed to deliver their opinion in the form of accounts about their personal experiences (some did). The focus on opinion was deliberate because it enabled information to be produced whilst retaining some emotional distance from people's lives. I did not want to cause participants undue and immediate distress. Additionally, asking after opinion militates against the idea that all participants are able to do is act as passive repositories of 'experience' which require some 'expert-researcher' to provide the definitive interpretation. Rather, whilst the interpretative gloss offered is always ultimately mine, interviews, conceived in the manner described, emphasized the active, participatory generation of meaning-making. Thus, I made no attempt to act as a 'blank screen', but shared my general views about childhood sexual abuse.

Physical security can be an over-inflated concern within secure hospitals. However, it is still a relevant consideration when engaging in short-term research relationships with clients, who sometimes have acted violently and abusively towards others, and when emotionally difficult issues are being addressed. As Taylor (1996) observed, the researcher is not always powerful. Sometimes the vulnerability of researchers is underplayed, particularly when they are understood to be an extension of the research 'tool' (rather than a person in their own right), as in modernist versions of scientific method. Therefore, my research sessions with patients took place in private rooms that were nevertheless in close proximity to other members of staff. Research sessions were deferred if patients were felt (whether by themselves or others) to be having a 'bad day' and would be unable to cope with the task. Neither of us would benefit from a violent or abusive situation. There were only a few occasions during which I felt vulnerable. For example, a male patient became aggressive and agitated and another acted in a sexually manipulative manner, which made me feel uncomfortable.

The interviews were specifically designed to elicit discursive material on women in secure care who experienced sexual abuse in childhood. The interviews were organized around the four identified areas for investigation: 'routes', 'discourses about effects', 'representations of effects' and 'treatment'. Because my aim was to generate a range of competing viewpoints and perspectives it was important that, whilst I was interested in exploring the areas identified above, the interviews were not over-structured. To this end I deliberately kept the interview schedule skeletal in order that I did not too quickly develop a habitual style and form of questioning. Rather I tailored my interviews to the particular person and, hence, was led, to some extent, by the participant's particular concerns and interests. The 33 interviews, therefore, varied in content, focus, and detail and this was reflected in how long they lasted (between 30 minutes and an hour).

Every interview was recorded on tape and then subsequently transcribed. I recognize that transcriptions are removed from the lived conversation *in situ*. As Kvale (1996: 166) notes: '[t]o *trans*cribe means to *trans*form.' Any recording is necessarily incomplete and partial and there are always multiple ways of reading text and multiple levels at which to attend (Deleuze and Guattari 1984; Massumi 1992). It is impossible to provide the 'perfect transcript' and indeed, as Hollway (1989: 20) suggests, '[t]he quest for a perfectly accurate transcript reflects the dictum of empiricism that data provide the foundation of proof.' However, a consistent convention for transcription was adopted (adapted from Parker 1992 and Harper 1994). Because I was more interested in the *content* than the *process* of these research conversations, it was unnecessary to record detailed linguistic information. These transcriptions provided a direct source of 'quotes', as well as providing statements for the Q studies that followed.

Developing the Q sample: statement collection and selection

There are a number of clearly defined steps involved in a Q methodological study. Once an issue for investigation, such as 'routes into special hospitals', has been identified the next step is to develop a sample of views on that issue. Statements in a Q study may be derived from a range of sources, including ready-made Q samples, academic and clinical literature, 'biographical' and 'fictional' accounts within the mass media, and informal conversations with colleagues and service users, for example. Often the preferred source of statements, however, is interviews with persons who are thought to be able to reflect the diversity in the target population. Population, in this formulation, refers to a sample of statements rather than of persons. The Q studies described in this book relied primarily on the interview transcripts as their source of statements. In practical terms, statement selection proceeded as follows.

All of the interview transcripts were printed out. Four document storage boxes were used to put the printed transcripts into. Each box represented a separate study and was labelled accordingly as: 'routes', 'discourses about effects', 'representations of effects' and 'treatment'. Once the boxes were in place, each interview transcript was closely examined and any relevant quote was highlighted, cut out, and placed in the relevant box. Thus, a quote relating to 'routes' would be cut out, labelled (as to the interview that it came from) and placed in the 'routes' box. The next stage was to sort through each box and to put quotes of similar themes together. Hence, the selection process becomes more detailed and discriminating. For example, all the statements in the 'routes' box were sorted through and placed in separate piles, each pile with a different theme, such as danger to others, danger to self and so on. Next, these grouped sets of statements were typed as a list and one statement was chosen from each group of statements for inclusion in the Q sample. The aim was to adequately represent a range of viewpoints, using the minimum number of statements. Therefore all direct opposites and duplications were removed. By way of illustration, see Example 1: Danger to the public, which shows the interview statements that were drawn on to develop the item on 'danger to the public'.

Example 1: Danger to the public

Statement 30

Women who go to specials are NOT usually a danger to the public.

Derived from:

Women end up in specials because they have attacked others and therefore pose a danger to society (interview 26).
Women are a severe danger to the public (interview 6).
Only very dangerous women end up in specials (interview 5).
Women end up in specials because they have committed violent offences (interview 7).

Between 30 and 80 statements are typically used (Stainton-Rogers *et al.* 1995). The viability of the Q sample is then evaluated. This process usually involves a mixture of using a small pilot run and one's own judgement (Curt 1994). The pilot run fulfils a number of functions. First, it gives an indication of comprehensibility. Second, any omissions identified by the pilot-study participants can be rectified. Third, it provides a check of how balanced the Q sample is. In Q methodology, when people rank-order the statements (according to how much they agree with them or not), a 'forced-free' response format is used. This means that a fixed number of statements are placed in a predetermined number of columns so that the final pattern of responses approximates a normal distribution. The use of a forced-free response format makes sorting easier because it breaks the conceptual task down into smaller, and therefore more manageable, stages. It also aids in subsequent analysis. Whilst it is expected that people would sort in multiple ways, clearly if everyone agreed with *all* the statements, albeit placed in different positions, than the integrity of the Q methodological approach would be compromised. This is why, in the above example, the item on 'danger to the public' is written in negative terms (i.e. *not* usually a danger).

The practical phase: getting people Q sorting

Sixty participants were given the four separate Q studies ('routes', 'discourses about effects', 'representations of effects' and 'treatment'). For each Q study, participants were asked to read through all the statements, which were typed onto separate numbered cards, and sort them, initially, into three piles: agree, disagree and don't know/unsure/ambivalent. Marker cards, indicating the scale and number of statements that were required in each column, were laid out. For example, see Figure 5.1.

Scale	−4	−3	−2	−1	0	+1	+2	+3	+4
Number of statements	2	4	5	6	7	6	5	4	2

Figure 5.1: Example of scale and number of statements

Hence, the marker card in the -4 position would also have '2' on the card to indicate that two statements are required.

Participants were asked to sort through each pile, starting with their most extreme opinions and to work inwards. To use the example in Figure 5.1, the participant would look through their 'agree' pile and choose the two statements they most agreed with, then the next four, then the next five, and so on until all their positive statements were used up. They would then go to their 'disagree' pile and choose the two statements that they most disagreed with, then the next four, etc. When all the 'agree' and disagree' statements are used up the participant considers the statements in the more ambivalent/unsure pile. This is because the statements that an individual feels most strongly about (whether positively or negatively) will be at the heart of their account. The participant is thus *forced* to use all statements, placing an appropriate number of statements in each column, but is *free* to decide the positioning of each statement (hence the term 'forced-free' format). Once participants had completed their Q sort, the statement numbers were then recorded in the corresponding position on a response grid. For example, see Figure 5.2 for a schematic example of a completed response grid from the 'routes' Q study. The numbers in the boxes refer to the statement number.

For example, in the Q sort in Figure 5.2, the aforementioned statement 30 (Example 1: Danger to the public) is in the −1 column, which means that the statement *women who go to special hospitals are NOT usually a danger to the public* is weakly disagreed with.

Rating

−4	**−3**	**−2**	**−1**	**0**	**+1**	**+2**	**+3**	**+4**
39	3	6	24	18	38	13	10	14
31	4	9	30	15	17	37	26	16
		8	19	7	21	22	27	12
			32	2	35	25	11	
			1	36	34	29	23	
				33	28	20		
				5				

(Statement numbers — vertical axis label)

Figure 5.2 A schematic example of a completed response grid from the 'routes' study

In most cases I was present whilst participants completed the Q sorts. Because a pre-arranged appointment was made to complete the Q sorts the usual difficulties associated with low response rates for postal studies were circumvented. Being able to give verbal instructions and answer questions made the task easier to understand for participants unfamiliar with Q. I was also able to make additional notes based on the comments made by participants as they completed the Q sorts. Most participants completed the task on one occasion. Some people (mainly patients) required a number of different sittings. Time taken to complete all four Q sorts ranged from 1.3 hours to about 6 hours. The aim, as with the interviews, was to offer a flexible approach that would cater to individual needs. Time was given to talk through the issues and feelings raised by the task. Most participants reported that the task was 'hard work', but interesting. A few participants felt restrained by the forced distribution grid into which they were expected to fit their statements. These participants were encouraged to draw lines on their response grids to mark their own personal boundaries for agreement and disagreement.

Non-normative number crunching: using the computer to search for patterns in the data

When 60 different people have completed the same Q study, it is not unreasonable to expect that some of the accounts will be similar to some of the other accounts. Whilst it is possible to search for patterns (commonalities and differences) in the data by hand, it is far easier to use mathematical procedures and a computer to do this. Stephenson (1935a, 1935b) developed a mathematical process called Q factor analysis for this task. In simple terms, Q factor analysis is used to search for patterns in the data and to identify similar responses. Whilst it is appropriate to offer a brief description of Q factor analysis it is beyond the scope of this book to explore the complex mathematics involved. For those readers who are interested, Brown (1980) is a good place to start, and *Operant Subjectivity*, the journal of Q methodology, is a good source of examples.

In Q methodology it is persons (or their whole Q sorts) that are factor analysed for intercorrelations. This use of factor analysis identifies persons who share similar views. Hence, Q factor analysis provides a statistical method for identifying people who have grouped themselves together through the Q sorting process (Brown 1980). This differs markedly from traditional – known as R – methodological approaches to factor analysis. In R methodology, factor analysis is used to identify individual items that cluster together to form the same or similar constructs or traits (Senn 1996). People may then be said to possess such traits in variable amounts. Hence, traditional psychological research uses factor analysis to explore how people vary over a predetermined dimension (intelligence or personality, for example).

As O'Dell (2003: 25) notes, '[s]uch an approach assumes the "subject" of such investigation has only one level, or kind of, response and will therefore give the same or similar data time after time.' The distribution of traits is therefore assumed to be stable within a given population because people do not change, and therefore can be studied objectively. In Q, the assumption is that points of view, or patterns of responses, are inconsistent (people change over time and context). Additionally, as the whole Q sort is self-referential, no external reality is assumed. Therefore, in Q factor analysis it is the pattern of items sorted by participants, not the individual's assumed stable characteristics, that are analysed against each other (ibid.). Hence, Q factor analysis identifies clusters of people from a sample of statements and R factor analysis identifies clusters of items from a sample of people. R and Q are thus suited to different tasks.

For each of the four Q studies, the 60 completed Q sorts were factor analysed using the PCQ package developed by Stricklin (1992). The reported sortings from each response grid are correlated with those from all other grids. These correlated grids are then 'reduced by factor analysis into a limited set of bunched-together similarities' (Curt 1994: 123). A process of 'factor rotation' is used to select out hypothetical underlying patterns. Participants whose accounts are similar will end up on the same factor. Brown (1980) notes that, by and large, computer technology has led to the *pro forma* adoption of automated rotational schemes. Additionally, when Q is used as a pattern-analytic method, there is little reason for theoretical rotational schemes as no one pattern has epistemological status over another (Stainton-Rogers and Stainton-Rogers 1990). Hence, the studies reported in this book use the automated scheme contained in the PCQ package developed by Stricklin (1992).

The factors produced through Q factor analysis are composite accounts that are made up by merging 'high loading' Q sorts where the participant's *loading* on each factor indicates the association between the participant and the expressed point of view. If someone has a 'high loading' on a factor, this indicates that the pattern of statements in her Q sort will be similar to the pattern of statements in the composite account. All those Q sorts that have similar patterns will end up having 'high loadings' on the same factor, and the composite account is made up by merging these similarly patterned Q sorts together. Curt (1994) observes that Q factor analysis typically yields three to ten factors. Factors may have a number of people defining them, but also, within Q, it is perfectly acceptable to accept a single sort as significant (Brown 1980). The primary aim is to identify accounts that exist, not to make claims about their relative distribution. The merged Q sorts are then reassembled in order to facilitate interpretation. The 'statistics' used here, therefore, only represent the order in which items in the Q sort have been placed (O'Dell 2003). The sorting pattern is reconstituted by laying out the actual statements corresponding to the factor arrays of the merged Q sorts. The pattern of statements is then interrogated in order to generate a reading of the expressed account. An example of this is given in Chapter 6.

Some words of caution

Q methodology, like any research method, is constructive. Q factor analysis shapes and structures the accounts it produces and some, such as Gould (1985), have argued that the methodological steps involved are too harsh and brutal. Yet, although factor analysis obviously impacts on issues, such as the number and form of the composite accounts it identifies, the primary force within Q methodology remains the people who sorted the Q sorts in the first place. It is reductive, in that the many people, whose Q sorts form part of the studies, are not addressed individually, but rather collectively as composite accounts. However, I have no desire to make claims about individual participants. Rather, my interest lies in what accounts are in social circulation and Q methodology provides a good means for generating these.

Others (Febbraro 1993; Riger 1992) have argued that because Q uses statistical procedures to analyse propositional configurations Q can act as a rhetorical device that brings rigour and quantification to feminist and other marginalized research. Yet Q's ability to extract meaningful accounts is of much greater relevance than its rhetorical merits. And, ultimately, using Q's 'inverted factor analysis' as a sort of panacea to modernist science is self-defeating (Kitzinger 1990). It implies that any statistics are better than no statistics, whatever their purpose and/or utility. Moreover, as Gould (1985: 48) observes:

It is . . . disappointing and paradoxical to find tests of statistical significance constantly reported in the Q literature . . . as though these somehow add legitimacy to the results. We cannot have our statistical cake and eat it too.

This is why statistical summaries are not used as warrants of certitude in the following chapters. Alongside other feminist and post-structuralist researchers (e.g. Dell and Korotana 2000), all that I report in the following chapters are the factor summaries (see also James and Warner 2005; Rayner and Warner 2003). The factor summaries are simply summary descriptions of the composite accounts, which reflect the pattern of responses that were grouped together by Q factor analysis. In Chapter 6 I provide a detailed description of the first composite account ('personality disorder') in the 'routes' study in order to make the process of factor exegesis explicit. Thereafter, only brief summaries are given. My intention is not to mystify the process of factor explication. I use the tactic of dispensing with over-detailed catalogues of statement positions in order to facilitate the ease with which these studies may be read. In the following chapters, therefore, the emphasis is placed on the interpretation of the composite accounts, generated through Q factor analysis, in terms of illuminating the discursive impact, on women patients, of asking questions about child sexual abuse.

6

MAD, BAD OR DANGEROUS?

Women's routes into 'special' maximum-security mental hospitals

Introduction

According to the World Health Organization (World Health Organization/ WHO 2005a) there are more than 450 million people with mental, behavioural or neurological problems throughout the world. In the USA, for example, about one in four adults suffer from a diagnosable mental disorder in any given year (National Institute of Mental Health/ NIMH 2006a). This translates into just under 60 million people. Although mental ill-health is widespread, many of the costs are in respect of a much smaller population who exhibit severe and enduring mental distress – about 1 in 17 people in the USA (ibid.). Such people are chronic users of mental health services. They are more likely to be hospitalized, sometimes under compulsory powers, and are in need of high-intensity intervention. Hence, although they may be small in number, such people represent a significant investment in terms of services, time and expenditure, the most expensive being those detained in secure care.

Secure mental health care, therefore, may cater to a minority of the total population of people in the world with mental health problems, but those people command a disproportionate amount of resources. They also represent some of the most maligned and mistreated people throughout the world. The WHO (2005a) notes that people with mental disorders face gross violations of their human rights in many prisons, psychiatric institutions and hospitals around the world. They may be restrained with metal shackles or in caged beds, deprived of basic needs for clothing, bedding, clean water and toilet facilities, and made subject to ongoing abuse. For example, in a special feature, in the academic journal *Feminism and Psychology*, on women in prisons and secure psychiatric settings, research from around the world demonstrated that incarcerated women routinely face violence and violation (see Aitkin and Heenan 2004).

That women in secure care continue to endure violence and abuse compounds many of the issues that have been instrumental in their mental deterioration. The WHO (2000) has stated that violence against women and girls is a major health and human rights issue. For example, the WHO (ibid.) notes that research from around the world confirms that up to 50 per cent of women experience domestic violence, and up to 25 per cent experience forced sex by an intimate partner or ex-partner. Women and girls are the most frequent victims of abuse within families and are at greatest risk of forced prostitution and sex trafficking. A result of this is that violence against women ultimately presents an undue burden on health and social care systems. This would also include secure care. For some women, then, sexual abuse and other violations shape women's routes into, and experience of life within, locked institutions. If we are to develop services that are responsive to this small, but significant, group of abused women then it is crucial, as mental health activists and some feminists have argued, to directly focus attention on them.

Women's routes into secure mental health care

Although the studies reported in this section of the book address women in maximum-security mental hospitals in the UK, as indicated above, concerns about the routine mistreatment of detained patients is a global issue of some significance. Hence, these studies have relevance beyond their immediate geographical context as they speak to worldwide concerns about the routine (sexual) abuse of women and girls, and their particular mistreatment in families and in institutional care. As noted in Chapter 5, these studies are focused on women in 'special' high-security care. The reason for this is that as the most secure mental health facilities in the UK, they house some of the most marginalized abused women who, it can be argued, are most in need of concern, compassion and advocacy.

At any given time, about 630,000 people use mental health services in England and Wales (Batty 2002). Less than 27,000 of these people are formally detained in hospital each year under the Mental Health Act 1983. A very few of these are detained in secure hospitals, and only a small proportion of these are women. For example, there are about 140 women patients in maximum-security mental hospitals, who represent about 13 per cent of all patients there (Ly and Foster 2005 see also Department of Health DH 2004). These figures have stayed relatively stable over a ten year period (ibid.). Maximum-security mental health services are primarily designed for men. It is unsurprising that women may be particularly badly served in such contexts. As with other aspects of mental health care, therefore, gender is a defining construct that differentiates understanding and treatment. The first stage at which gender differentiation occurs in this context is at the point that decisions are made to justify detention.

Women are formally detained in secure mental hospitals through medico-legal processes that judge them against sets of criteria laid out in the particular country's mental health act. In Britain, involuntarily detained patients must have a 'diagnosable' and treatable mental disorder, and must represent a significant danger to themselves or others. In simple terms, judgements are made about how mad, bad and dangerous they are. As suggested in Part 1 of this book, mainstream mental health services measure and assess women against normative understandings about femininity. It can be argued, therefore, that women may be in danger of enforced hospitalization when they are deemed to be too feminine (as when women are depicted as being too passive) or not feminine enough (as when women are depicted as being too assertive). And these conceptualizations, about passivity and assertiveness, are reflected in dominant understandings about both mental illness and personality disorder, which are routinely used to justify incarceration.

As this indicates, the medical model prevails around the world as a dominant system for conceptualizing these women, and their needs. This is because diagnosis, alongside dangerousness, determines entry into secure mental health services. However, the existence of radical voices within feminism and mental health activism, for example, suggest that the hegemony of psychiatry is not monolithic. In particular, the insistence that social factors, such as abuse, trigger mental disorder and dangerous behaviour signals an increasing challenge to a biological model of women's mental incapacities (see e.g. WHO 2000). The study reported in this chapter sought to trace some of the ways that these narratives about transition from community to confinement discursively shape how women patients may be understood and treated in secure mental health care.

The study identifies some of the knowledges that are drawn on by people in special maximum-security hospitals, including both female and male patients and members of staff, to discursively delineate women's pathways there. Examination of these empirically generated accounts enables explication of the ways in which mainstream and critical voices make sense of women's routes into secure mental health care. Ultimately, the aim is to provide evidential support for the need to revise how the mental health of (sexually abused) women is understood, depicted and used as warrant for involuntary detention in secure hospitals.

Using Q methodology to provide empirical data on women's discursive routes into 'special' high-security mental hospitals

As discussed in Chapter 5, Q methodology is a technique for generating different perspectives on contested social issues (such as, why women go to secure mental hospitals), by getting participants to rank-order relevant statements according to whether they agree with them or not. In this study, there are 39 different statements, each giving a different reason for why women go to special hospitals (see Table 6.2 at the end of this chapter). How much or how little people agree or disagree with each statement is used to make sense of what the overall pattern of responses means. The relative distribution of the statements, therefore, provides the template for the interpretation of the account or perspective (see Table 6.1 for an exemplar of an account).

Although there are very many patterns that 39 statements may be sorted into, it can be anticipated that some of the accounts that are generated by participants (60 in this study) will be similar to some other accounts. Again, as indicated in Chapter 5, whilst it is possible to search for patterns (commonalties and differences) in the data by hand, it is far easier to use mathematical procedures and a computer to do this. Hence, the 60 completed Q sorts were factor analyzed using the PCQ package developed by Stricklin (1992) and seven distinct accounts of why women go to special hospitals were identified.

As anticipated, these seven accounts reflect both dominant and critical approaches to understanding why women end up in maximum-security mental hospitals. These include discourses on badness and madness, which were conceptualized within, respectively, two accounts on personality disorder and four accounts on mental illness. The final account focused on dangerousness. Additionally, a concern with matters of abuse was also evident within most accounts. In the main body of this chapter, the description of accounts is restricted to the key features that delineate them. Supplementary quotes are drawn from the interview transcripts (as explained in Chapter 5). Before I enter into this discussion however, Account one 'personality disorder' (see Table 6.1) is described in detail, and then summarized, in order to make the process of factor exegesis explicit. The interpretation of each summarized account, thereafter, follows the same steps as that demonstrated in reference to this account.

In order to interpret the composite accounts, the first step involves reassembling the Q sort from the factor array (the pattern of statement positions identified through Q factor analysis), which indicates where each statement was placed in the composite account (see Table 6.1). Interpretation is then made in terms of the pattern of responses, focusing on the statements placed in the more extreme columns. 'Extreme columns', in the context of Q-methodology, refers to the columns that have the most intense value: that is, the statements in these columns have been agreed with, or disagreed with, most strongly, relative to each other. In the 'routes' study (see Table 6.1), for example, the range is from -4 (disagree) to +4 (agree). Statements from the -4, -3, -2, +2, +3 and +4 columns are interpreted. Those statements placed in the middle columns (-1, 0, +1 and) are largely ignored *precisely* because they are not key statements in the account (they have only weakly been agreed or disagreed with, or have been placed in the neutral/don't know column).

For this account, the statements from the Q sort, and their relative positions, are referenced directly. In order to clarify this process, where

Table 6.1 Factor array – personality disorder

-4	-3	-2	-1	0	+1	+2	+3	+4
39. It is UNUSUAL for women who end up in special hospitals to have been hurt or abused as adults	3. A history of drug and/or alcohol problems is NOT common in women who end up in special hospitals	6. Women who end up in special hospitals tend to have matured early and be of higher intelligence	24. Women go to special hospitals because they are looking for safety and security and so commit an offence to end up here	18. Women end up in special hospitals because the only way they can get noticed is to get into trouble	38. Being mentally ill is NOT the main reason women end up in special hospitals	13. Women go to special hospitals because they have NOT developed appropriate coping strategies to deal with their problems	10. Women go to special hospitals because of the harmful effects of childhood sexual abuse	14. Women who go to special hospitals have had abnormal childhood experiences which have led to the development of abnormal personalities
31. Women who come from unstable family backgrounds where they have received poor or inadequate parenting are LESS likely to go to special hospitals	4. Women who come from poor and deprived backgrounds are LESS likely to end up in special hospitals	9. Women with children are LESS likely to go to special hospitals because it forces them to cope	30. Women who go to special hospitals are NOT usually a danger to the public	15. 'Personality disorder' is a bucket to dump non-feminine women in and then use as a basis for sending women to special hospitals	17. Women go to special hospitals when their requests for help have been ignored	37. Women who go to special hospitals have been labelled as 'the problem' and this identity has become stuck	26. Women go to special hospitals mainly because other institutions CANNOT cope with their violent and aggressive behaviour	16. Women go to special hospitals when other support services have failed to address issues relating to their abused pasts
	8. Women who have no support networks (friends or family etc.) on the outside are LESS likely to end up in special hospitals	19. The behaviour that gets women into special hospitals should NOT be understood as a 'cry for help'	7. Women do NOT go to special hospitals because they have problems with communication	21. Women go to special hospitals because they have done something wrong and society expects them to be punished	22. Women go to special hospitals when they have got themselves in such a state about their problems they have lost control	27. Women go to special hospitals mainly because other institutions CANNOT cope with their self-harming behaviour	12. Women go to special hospitals because of the harmful effects of childhood emotional abuse	
		32. Women go to special hospitals because the legal system is more lenient to women than men and so directs them from prison into hospitals	2. Women who fail to conform sexually (e.g. promiscuous or lesbian) are more likely to end up in special hospitals	35. Women go to special hospitals because the stereotype for women is to be gentle and do as they are told and if they don't they must be 'mad'	25. Women who go to special hospitals need to behave LESS violently and be much LESS of a danger to the public than men who go to specials	11. Women go to special hospitals because of the harmful effects of childhood physical abuse		
		1. Women go to special hospitals because they have a wish to pass on the responsibility for their lives to someone else	36. Institutionalization is NOT often a reason why women end up in special hospitals	34. Black women are more likely to be punished and sent to prison than to be seen as in need of treatment and sent to special hospitals	29. Women go to special hospitals mainly because they have caused damage to property, usually by setting fires	23. Women go to special hospitals because a stressful event has caused them to break down and act in a way which has got them into trouble		
			33. Women go to special hospitals because their lawyers advise them that it is a soft option instead of prison	28. Women who go to specials feel bad about themselves and deliberately get into trouble so they will be punished	20. Women who go to special hospitals have usually suffered a traumatic event which has triggered an underlying mental illness			
				5. Women go to special hospitals because they need long-term mental health care				

statements are referred to, they are identified by the statement number, as used in the Q study, followed by their ranked position. For example, statement 1, '*women go to special hospitals because they have a wish to pass on the responsibility for their lives to someone else*', when placed in the 'most strongly agree' column (+4) reads:

> **1. +4** *Women go to special hospitals because they have a wish to pass on the responsibility for their lives to someone else.*

The composite 'personality disorder' account was formed by merging the 37 out of 60 individual accounts that grouped themselves together through Q factor analysis. The 21 female and 16 male participants associated with this account (that is those whose Q sorts had a high correspondence to the composite account) included eight patients, twelve nurses, five psychiatrists, five clinical psychologists, five social workers, one occupational therapist and one pharmacologist. This account is now described in detail.

Account one: 'personality disorder'

According to this account, in order to explain why some women end up in high-security mental hospitals it is crucial to understand the role of childhood experiences in the development of personality disorders:

> **14. +4** *Women who go to special hospitals have had abnormal childhood experiences which have led to the development of abnormal personalities.*

From this perspective the development of women's abnormal personalities can be traced back to their multiple adverse experiences in childhood. These women have been damaged by their parents' inadequacies:

> **31. –4** *Women who come from unstable family backgrounds where they have received poor or inadequate parenting are LESS likely to go to special hospitals.*

Their experiences of unstable family relationships are indicated through their multiple experiences of abuse:

> **10. +3** *Women go to special hospitals because of the harmful effects of childhood sexual abuse.*
> **12. +3** *Women go to special hospitals because of the harmful effects of childhood emotional abuse.*
> **11. +2** *Women go to special hospitals because of the harmful effects of childhood physical abuse.*

Women's abusive and unstable childhood experiences have been attenuated by living in poverty:

> **4.** **−3** *Women who come from poor or deprived backgrounds are LESS likely to end up in special hospitals.*

The implication here is that it is the *breadth* of abuse that differentiates special-hospital women patients from women who remain in the community. The cumulative effects of women's adverse childhood experiences are thought to negatively impact on their future functioning. Multiple experiences of abuse are associated, in this account, with developmental delay. These women are immature and have lowered intellectual abilities:

> **6.** **−2** *Women who end up in special hospitals tend to have matured early and be of higher intelligence.*

The inference is that because women's histories of abuse have compromised normal development this has resulted in the establishment of abnormal personalities. This is evidenced in the difficulties they continue to experience as adults. As in childhood, women are characterized as being unable to form healthy relationships in adulthood. Specifically they continue to be abused:

> **39.** **−4** *It is unusual for women who end up in special hospitals to have been hurt and abused as adults.*

Given their abnormal personalities and relationship difficulties, it is little wonder that women who end up in special hospitals have been socially isolated which further attenuates their problems:

> **8.** **−3** *Women who have NO support networks (friends and family etc.) on the outside are LESS likely to end up in special hospitals.*

Because these women continue to be abused, and are also socially isolated, motherhood acts as an additional strain in their lives:

> **9.** **−2** *Women with children are LESS likely to go to special hospitals because it forces them to cope.*

Ultimately these women, abused throughout their lives, and seemingly powerless to change things, turn to drugs and alcohol to blot out their feelings:

3. −3 *A history of drug and/or alcohol problems is NOT common in women who end up in special hospitals.*

Indeed, it might be expected that because women's social and cognitive development has long been compromised through abuse, they have had few opportunities to develop any adaptive methods for coping with their difficulties:

13. +2 *Women go to special hospitals because they have NOT developed appropriate coping strategies to deal with their problems.*

The cumulative effects of abuse, and their reliance on maladaptive coping strategies, means that eventually something will 'tip the balance' and women's subsequent inappropriate behaviour will bring them to the attention of services:

23. +2 *Women go to special hospitals because a harmful event has caused them to break down and act in a way that has got them into trouble.*

In this account, such actions are understood to represent a 'cry for help':

19. −2 *The behaviour that gets women into special hospitals should NOT be understood as a 'cry for help'.*

These women are desperate for help to enable them to make sense of their abused pasts. Unfortunately, and significantly, successive services have failed to do this:

16. +4 *Women go to special hospitals when other support services have failed to address issues relating to their abused pasts.*

It can be inferred from this account that women want help to make sense of their lives so that they can exercise greater control in them. Their attempts to garner help are about taking responsibility, not having their sense of powerlessness increased:

1. −2 *Women go to special hospitals because they have a wish to pass on the responsibility for their lives to someone else.*

Given that these women have such extensive experiences of abuse, and that successive services have not enabled women to talk about this issue, it is unsurprising that they resort to behavioural means of coping with, and indicating, their sense of powerlessness and despair. Women may turn their hurt inwards and self-harm or become increasingly aggressive towards others: none of which other, less secure, services can deal with:

> **26. +3** *Women go to special hospitals mainly because other institutions CANNOT cope with their violent and aggressive behaviour.*
>
> **27. +2** *Women go to special hospitals mainly because other institutions CANNOT cope with their self–harming behaviour.*

In this account a history of abuse is associated with the development of maladaptive coping strategies, including aggression and self-harm which, in the absence of psychotic symptoms, are, as indicated, usually associated with the development of personality disorder. The implication is that because feeder services also understand women's behaviour to be indicative of longstanding personality problems, rather than primarily signalling the failure of services to address women's abused pasts, it is women, themselves, who are pathologized. Once labelled as 'personality disordered', women can be routinely viewed as being 'the problem' and they are therefore directed to ever more secure services:

> **37. +2** *Women who go to special hospitals have been labelled 'the problem' and this identity has become stuck.*

Because, in this account, women's difficulties are conceptualized as 'personality disorder' it is appropriate that they are sent to high-security hospitals, rather than prisons – not because of issues of leniency, but for treatment:

> **32. –2** *Women go to special hospitals because the legal system is more lenient to women than men and so directs them from prisons into hospitals.*

From description to summary

As demonstrated above, the aim is to 'tell a story' that seems to encapsulate the ways in which the different statements knit together in the composite account. As can be seen, this is a detailed and lengthy process. Whilst providing this detail acts as 'warrant' for the veracity of interpretation it is cumbersome and can detract from the main thrust of the discussion. This is why only brief summaries of accounts are given in the rest of this chapter, and in the two chapters that follow. Like Worrell (2003: 212):

> I am interested in the broad ways in which . . . discourses operate as a social and cultural resource . . . As such my analysis is not concerned with the formal organisation and sequential implicativeness of talk.

Therefore, it is appropriate within this framework to effect this reduction. The summarized accounts are here to act as signposts. Direct quotes from the interview transcripts are used to elaborate these signposted concerns. Again in order to make the process of reduction explicit, two summarized versions of the 'personality disorder' account are given in Illustrations 1.1 and 1.2 below. The shortened versions can then be checked against each other, and against the detailed description given above.

Illustration 1.1 Reduction one

Account one: 'personality disorder'

The key issue to understand in Account one is how childhood adversity undermines normal development, ultimately resulting in the establishment of abnormal personalities. Women who go to special hospitals can be differentiated from women who remain in the community by the breadth of abuse they have experienced (inadequate parenting; sexual, emotional and physical abuse; and poverty) and which has led to longstanding personality problems. This is indicated by their inability to form healthy relationships in adulthood (they continue to be abused and/or isolated), and their use of maladaptive coping strategies (such as drug and alcohol abuse). These women are desperate to make sense of their histories of abuse so that they can cope with ongoing stress in their lives (occasioned through motherhood, for example). Unfortunately, their (behavioural) cries for help have been misheard and successive services have failed to enable them to talk about their experiences of abuse. Women's subsequent behaviour (aggression and self-harm) has confirmed their disordered personalities (they are 'the problem') and justified their incarceration in high-security mental hospitals. They are directed to hospital, rather than prison, because they need 'treatment' for their disorder and not because the legal system is more lenient to women than it is men.

Illustration 1.2 Reduction two

Account one: 'personality disorder'

Women who go to special hospitals have extensive experience of childhood neglect, abuse and poverty, which has led to longstanding personality problems. This is indicated by their inability to form healthy relationships in adulthood, and their use of maladaptive coping strategies. These women are desperate to make sense of their histories of abuse so that they can cope with ongoing stress in their lives. Unfortunately, their (behavioural) cries for help have been misheard and successive services have failed to enable them to talk about their experiences of abuse. Women's subsequent aggressive and self-harming behaviour has confirmed how problematic they are, and justified their need for treatment in high-security mental hospitals.

As can be seen, each reduction retains the general meaning of the account, as constructed through my interpretation of where the statements were placed in the composite account, and how the statements might relate to each other. I make no claims that this is the definitive interpretation: different people may read the same account in different ways. My intention, in providing this rather lengthy demonstration, is to show that the major part of this interpretation is based on the composite Q sort itself rather than on my values and perspective. Having now described the process of factor exegesis, in the final part of this chapter the other accounts, produced through Q factor analysis, are presented as summaries only. These account summaries, alongside quotes from the interviews, are used to illuminate how women's routes into maximum secure hospitals are made sense of by people who live and work in such systems. These are organized into three sections, which cover personality disorder, mental illness and dangerousness.

Transforming social abuse into individual dysfunction: women and personality disorder

Around the world, all patients who are detained in secure mental hospitals must be diagnosed with a mental disorder. As argued, then, diagnosis is the boundary marker around secure care:

> I just think everybody has to have a label to come in here anyway. I don't think it's because you've been abused or nothing, cause you have to have a label to come in.
>
> (female patient)

Personality disorder is the primary diagnostic construct through which women are understood in this context (DH 2002b). Hence, 'personality disorder' represents a key factor in determining women's routes into secure hospitals. That just over 50 per cent of the participants in the current study voiced the 'personality disorder' account supports this fact. This is in contrast to all other accounts in this study where only one or two people had a high association with the other Q-generated accounts. The understanding of personality disorder described in Account one reflects an increasing acceptance that people with complex social and mental health difficulties develop them over time and in respect of adversity and abuse (DH 2003b). Hence, in Account one, personality disorder is described as being a developmental condition located in women's social history, rather than their born-with pathological or diseased mind. From this perspective it is the *extent* of abuse (rather than the personality disorder *per se*) that explains women's incarceration in secure mental health care. For example, as one female nurse argued:

> There are millions of women who are sexually abused and don't
> end up in special hospitals. So trying to make sense of it for myself,
> I think the women are damaged in their experience of parenting in
> many ways.

The personality disorder that women in secure care are most frequently diagnosed with is 'borderline personality disorder' (DH 2002b). In fact, women with a diagnosis of borderline personality disorder represent 20 per cent of *all* hospital admissions in the USA (NIMH 2006b) and it is this disorder that is most readily invoked by Account one. Stern (1939) is credited with introducing the term 'borderline' to refer to patients who fell on the border between neurotic and psychotic. This remained the primary understanding until the 1970s when the work of Gunderson *et al.* (1975) and Kernberg (1975) revitalized interest in this 'condition', which is now understood as 'developmental arrest' (this is signposted in Account one, see statement **6. −2** column, in Table 6.1). In the 1980s the American Psychiatric Association (APA 1995) officially classified the borderline patient as having a personality disorder. Symptoms include instability in mood, relationships and sense of self; intense feelings of anger, abandonment, emptiness and paranoia; and self-harming and suicidal behaviours. Such 'symptoms' are frequently associated with long-term experiences of victimization which, as noted, women in secure hospitals around the world frequently report.

Understanding personality disorder as a developmental condition is of potential benefit to women in secure, and other, mental health services. This is because women can be viewed as being socially damaged, rather than essentially mad or bad. However, recognition of the social foundations of individual narratives of unhappiness does not necessarily lead to a more social model of secure mental-health care (Warner and Wilkins 2003, 2004). If historical narratives of abuse are drawn on simply to confirm the diagnosis of (borderline) personality disorder, but the disorder is defined only in terms of 'effects' (and not in respect of abuse) then the social aspects of trauma can remain hidden. The prime concern is with personality and not abuse. It is little wonder, then, that as illustrated in Account one, many feeder systems fail to address issues associated with women's experiences of abuse as being instrumental in their routes into increasing levels of secure-hospital care (see Account one, statement **16. +4** column, Table 6.1). A focus on personality enables services to avoid those issues women need to understand, but workers fear to address. Women's capacity for self-harm is significant in this respect.

The vast majority of women patients in high-security mental hospitals self-harm (over 90 per cent in Britain: DH 2002b). Hence, although self-harm is a central feature of borderline personality disorder (and self-harm has been found to lead to 9 per cent of people so diagnosed in the USA ultimately killing themselves: NIMH 2006b), it is also present for other women in secure care. Yet, the personality disorder account in this study was the only one that highlighted this aspect of their behaviour (statement **27. +2** column, Table 6.1). And the only one, therefore, that directly linked this with experiences of childhood abuse (statement **31. −4** column and **12. +3**, **10. +3**, **11. +2**, **4. −3**, Table 6.1). It may be that discussions about childhood abuse are avoided precisely because such experiences are associated with self-harm. As noted, many women with mental health problems have multiple experiences of violence and abuse (WHO 2000). Estimates suggest that at least 70 per cent of women in high-security mental hospitals may have histories of childhood sexual abuse (DH 2002b). It is possible, then, that because abused women in secure care self-harm to such a large degree, workers sometimes respond by avoiding these issues all together. As one female social worker explained:

> I think there's an issue of the behaviour, that women who've been sexually abused present, [which] scares people more because they're often into more serious self-harm. And if they have been in systems where it's been previously disclosed and not dealt with, or no attention paid to it, their behaviour is increasingly unmanageable as far as the professionals are concerned. Then they're quickly labelled as 'special hospital material'.

When workers fail to fully comprehend their negative contributions to women's ongoing difficulties they also restrict the positive contributions they could make. Both workers and patients may then find themselves locked into ambivalent relationships that are founded on powerlessness and despair. This is particularly the case in respect of those who report long histories of abuse and who are also diagnosed with borderline personality disorder. Even traditional theorists, such as Gunn and Robertson (1976), have argued that, at worst, borderline personality disorder is a statement of therapeutic pessimism that justifies neglect. This more critical reading of 'personality disorder' is elaborated in the second account in this study (Illustration 2).

Illustration 2

Account two: 'failure to conform'

According to this account the main reason women go to special hospitals is because they have been pathologized for contravening normative codes of femininity. When women are not gentle and do not do as they are told they are understood to act outside the feminine ideal, and quickly become viewed as being 'the problem'. In this account women's main offence is their unfeminine behaviour. It is for this offence that society expects them to be punished by incarceration in a special hospital. As the feminine ideal precludes aggression, it is unremarkable that this account should stress that women patients are penalized for behaving less violently and dangerously than male patients. Indeed, these women are seldom a danger to the general public at all. These women do not go to special hospitals because they are 'mad', rather they are sent there because they are 'bad'. Specifically, and in contrast to Account one, 'personality disorder' is understood to be a bucket to dump non-feminine women in and justify detention.

From this perspective (which was associated in the current Q study with two women, a nurse and a patient), secure mental hospitals function as regulatory systems that are used to punish those women who transgress the boundaries of femininity. They are not treatment facilities that blandly respond to an unproblematized notion of 'mental illness'. These women do not need long-term mental health care, nor does their behaviour warrant such secure detention. Yet, as this account suggests, women patients may be incarcerated for displaying much less 'dangerousness' than their male counterparts. According to a consultation document commissioned by the British Department of Health (DH 2002b), women are generally placed in hospitals where the levels of security are disproportionate relative to their behaviour. Women are less likely to abscond than men are. They pose less of a risk to the public. For example, they are far less likely to have committed a violent, and in particular a sexual, offence (see also WHO 2000).

Where women cause public disorder they tend to target inanimate objects, particularly through fire-setting.

Because women only infrequently cause harm to others, they do not have to have committed a criminal offence in order to be locked up. For example, in Britain, women are more usually detained in secure hospitals under civil sections of the Mental Health Act 1983 after behaviours for which they were not charged or convicted. Consequently, they are more likely to have been transferred from other public health facilities rather than prisons. Usually this is because of their self-harming behaviour and sometimes because they have assaulted members of staff (see also Ly and Foster 2005). Therefore, it can be argued that diagnosis has a greater role in determining detention, than women's actual behaviour seems to have. As the 'failure to conform' account suggests, 'personality disorder' may be better understood as a pernicious attack than as a legitimate way of conceptualizing women's distress. As one female social worker argued:

> There isn't a single woman in here that's a stereotype. The women are different, they're very demanding, they're very aggressive, they've had substance abuse problems, they've been raped, they've been commercially sex related, they're a pain in the ass some of them, they're manipulative, they're not feminine little housewives. Now is that what personality disorder is? We might as well be calling them witches.

According to this perspective, women are harmed not only through individual experiences of abuse, but also through wider practices of gender regulation. Like the first 'personality disorder' account, women are again understood to have been denied appropriate help. However, here the implication is that this is more indicative of a punitive approach to women who transgress gender than it is a result of impartial, but imperfect, mental health practices. Thus, this account is reflective of a more radical mental health agenda, as illustrated in Chapter 4, that seeks to challenge normative mental health practices. This approach contrasts with more mainstream perspectives that may be critical of other services, but fail to illuminate their own complicity in misunderstanding and mistreating women in secure care.

Containing and controlling past and current fears: the medical redemption of disorderly women

According to mainstream mental health approaches, women end up in secure care because they, quite simply, have mental health problems (see for example WHO (2005b), on mental health legislation in Australia). This is reflected in the following four accounts generated by the Q study. In these accounts women's emotional and behavioural difficulties that lead to their incarceration in secure hospitals are more directly attributed to mental illness:

> The main difference is that the women that come here have got some form of mental illness.
>
> (female nurse)

Therefore, although the majority of women in secure care are typically cast as suffering from personality disorders, mental illness remains a significant concept in secure mental health provision. The multiple accounts of madness, produced in the Q study, reflect an evolving value base regarding the role of experience in the development of mental ill-health. Contrasting accounts of mental illness can be distinguished from each other by the degree to which they reject, or accommodate, the significance of social history in defining women's madness. Account three (voiced by a male nurse) provides an example of the most 'pure' application of the medical model (see Illustration 3).

Illustration 3

Account three: 'mental illness'

According to this account, mental illness is the main reason women end up in high-security mental hospitals. From this perspective, social factors have no role to play in determining women's routes into high-security mental hospitals. Hence, intellectual difficulties, childhood abuse and/or deprivation are irrelevant as these have no impact on biological disorder. Consistent with this formulation is the suggestion that it is harmful for other institutions to address women's abused pasts. If women's biological illness can be stabilized pharmacologically it is unnecessary and undesirable to address 'social' hurts. Thus, the boundary marker that separates women in the community from women in special hospitals is not experience, but underlying pathology.

From the perspective illustrated in Account three, because 'mental illness' is a born-with condition, women can be understood to be impervious to social influence. In this sense the presence of mental illness renders women personality-less: they are more condition than individual. Thus, any evident 'badness' is depersonalized. Embedded in this account then is an implicit distinction between the biological foundations of mental illness and the

106

social production of personality disorder. This type of understanding is demonstrated by a male psychiatrist:

> I think it is very likely that abnormal childhood experiences, of which sexual abuse is one, will affect the personality disordered people. In the mentally ill patients my view is that sexual abuse issues are likely to be much less relevant, because I do not believe that sexual abuse is likely to be the cause of major functional psychosis. The reason women come to [special hospitals] is because they've committed some very violent acts and that would be normally related to two things. Their illness would be resistant to conventional treatment, and the other factor is to do with patients who are non-compliant, in that these are patients who don't accept medication. And in those patients I think personality issues are likely to be much more relevant. That's to say that some patients don't trust their doctors, and they don't accept their advice. And that may, perhaps, be answered in terms of them having difficulties in forming trusting relationships – which again you might hypothesize is because the trust has been abused in the past.

As with Account one, in the above quote personality disorder is implicitly understood as a developmental condition shaped by negative social experiences. 'Bad' experiences determine 'bad' personality structures, as evidenced in women's inability to form trusting relationships, including with 'their doctors'. By contrast, 'mentally ill' women 'have' a born-with biological condition. Hence social influence has no impact, and any deviance women display can be absolved. Women's redemption through mental illness can be further secured by interlacing this with reference to their additional gendered inadequacies, as demonstrated in Account four (see Illustration 4).

Illustration 4

Account four: 'infantilization'

According to this account, mental illness remains dormant until triggered by an underlying factor. Therefore, social experiences are partially implicated in women's routes into special hospitals. From this perspective, women's essentialized passivity means that they are incapable of taking care of themselves, and by default this means that they are in need of long-term mental health care. Women themselves are aware of their inadequacies. They have a wish to pass on the responsibility for their lives to someone else. They are thought to deliberately commit offences in order to gain access to the safety and security that special hospitals provide. Such women represent a

---

serious danger to the general public. However, because they are 'mad' they are not held responsible for their behaviour and sent to prison. Therefore, this account rejects the idea that women are being judged and punished for acting in non-feminine ways. Indeed, women have to act more violently and dangerously than men to end up in special hospitals.

This account (as given by one male patient) further relies on normative understandings about gender in order to justify women's need for care by others who are more powerful. This account, therefore, reflects a paternalistic (and antiquated) approach in which women are not thought capable of coping alone with difficulties associated with mental illness and social harm, as the following quotes suggest:

> They've tried to get in a place like this, away from their parents, who may have been trying it on with them.
>
> (male patient)

> I think the ladies are weaker, aren't they, than men? That's why I think a lady or wife needs a husband, like a lot of women, to take care of them.
>
> (male patient)

From this perspective, and in contrast to the 'failure to conform' account, women are not depicted as needing special hospital care because they have *transgressed* their gender role. Rather, the implication is that such women need special hospital care specifically because they have acted *according to* their gender role. Mental vulnerability is exaggerated for 'mad' women: being both 'mad' and women they are doubly weak. This account, therefore, reinforces normative values that depict women as being inevitably vulnerable and in need of care by dominant males. Less paternalistically, but along a similar theme, Account five also demonstrates that secure care can be viewed as a benevolent response to women's evident inability to manage their own lives (see Illustration 5).

Illustration 5

Account five: 'out of control'

Like the 'infantilization' account, from this perspective, mental illness, *per se*, does not differentiate women in special hospitals from women in the community. Rather, it is only when subsequent events exacerbate residual mental health problems to such an extent that women lose control and subsequently get into trouble that they go to special hospitals. From this perspective, women get into trouble because when they lose control they externalize their difficulties through aggression to others and by criminal damage, usually by setting fires. Although women may act violently within institutional settings, and cause damage to property, they are not considered to represent a serious threat to the general public. And even though women cause trouble, because they are mentally ill they are not depicted as being culpable and deserving of punishment. They do not, therefore, get sent to prison. Hence, again treatment concerns are at the heart of decision-making for all women.

Both women who are 'infantilized' and women who are 'out of control' need the care of benevolent, more powerful others. Yet they differ in terms of their willingness to accept this help. As demonstrated in the 'infantilization' account, women may recognize their own limitations and seek out care and security. By contrast, according to the perspective in the 'out of control' account (given by two women patients), women do not want others to take responsibility for them. Therefore incarceration is something that is enforced rather than something that is desired. Women's frustration at being locked up may be one reason why they are sometimes depicted (as in Account five) as being aggressive within institutions, but are not dangerous to wider society. Hence, although mental illness still underlies women's routes into secure care, again there is some recognition that the social context impacts on women. This is not just in terms of triggers in society, but as with the 'personality disorder' account, also in terms of institutional neglect in feeder systems. In the final 'mental illness' account (see Illustration 6), the negative interaction between institutionalized care and mental illness is elaborated further.

Illustration 6

Account six: 'institutionalization'

According to this account, women are again thought to end up in special hospitals because mental illness has been triggered by a stressful event. Their behaviour is disturbing rather than personally or socially dangerous. Mainly (as with the 'personality disorder' account) it is understood as a 'cry for help'. The distinguishing feature in this context is that women's actions are thought be a result of their profound problems with communication. Because of the intractable nature of their mental illness, and their inability to communicate, these women have become socially isolated and in need of long-term mental health care. Ultimately, these women have become dependent on statutory support and over time have become institutionalized. Such women are understood to be unable to cope with the harsher regimes of prison and hence, even though 'the system' is not more lenient to women than men, on advice from their lawyers, they may have sought the 'softer' option of special hospitals.

According to the perspective reflected in this account (voiced by a male patient), because women are victims of mental illness, they are not viewed as being 'the problem': their illness is. This account therefore illustrates the mainstream assumption that incarceration is a treatment decision and not (as suggested in the 'failure to conform' account) a form of punishment for women's unruly behaviour. Again their illness renders them innocent:

> Her criminal behaviour is purely an expression of her mental disorder.
>
> (male psychiatrist)

Constructing women as 'victims of mental illness', as this account does, enables secure hospitals to be conceptualized as caring, rather than punitive, systems. They are caring systems that simply seek to intervene when women are incapable of looking after themselves (even though evidence suggests this is far from being the case). Sometimes women may, indeed, need asylum. Yet whilst diagnosis of mental illness absolves women in the short term, it ultimately confirms their powerlessness and dependence. Workers may view such women with greater sympathy than their personality disordered counterparts, but this also means that they have even fewer opportunities to have their life histories heard and validated. Women's 'problems with communication' therefore may be more indicative of learnt behaviour than a result of mental deficiency. As one female patient suggested:

> Because they can't communicate with whoever and it's hard for them to feel they can trust, they end up doing a crime and they end up coming here.

Being heard and believed is crucial to how women manage their experiences of abuse (Ainscough and Toon 2000). Yet, as these accounts suggest, women who end up in secure hospitals may have never had the opportunity to disclose because their various attempts to be noticed have been repeatedly ignored or misread. As one female nurse explained:

I would say that the sort of things that years ago would have been put down to attention-seeking behaviour has happened: cries for help, cries for support, cries for understanding. They've asked for help everywhere. They've been through child psychologists, school-teachers, they've moved through welfare and probation and doctors and social workers and everybody, and they've ended up here, still undisclosing.

This may be predictable when women's behaviour is used primarily to diagnose 'mental illness' or 'personality disorder' rather than to explicate the social roots of misery. Because women's distress is misperceived, symptomatic behaviour is sustained and women's steady march into increasingly secure mental health care is ensured. They may be forgiven, but they are still at fault. Professionals can then maintain faith in their ability to effect positive change in their clients and avoid responsibility for the maintenance and exacerbation of negative behaviours. The belief that secure hospitals are primarily treatment facilities can also be justified. Accordingly, in the mental illness accounts women are seen to be deserving of, and amenable to, therapeutic intervention. By contrast, according to some mainstream approaches, treatment issues should be downgraded in importance, and women's capacity for dangerousness centralized. This is reflected in Account seven.

Tracing dangerousness: saving the world and saving women from themselves

In many ways all women in secure mental health care are dangerous. As the accounts described here suggest, all women in secure care have breached the boundaries of normative behaviour. They are variously both out of control and difficult to control even when their actual danger to others is minimal. It is unsurprising, therefore, that dangerousness is a significant issue in its own right. This is reflected in Account seven (see Illustration 7).

Illustration 7

Account seven: 'dangerousness'

According to this account women may not be as dangerous as male patients, but they certainly cause problems and have been labelled as such. Their dangerousness is exacerbated through the disinhibiting effects of drugs and alcohol, and is directly linked with adverse and abusive experiences in childhood and adulthood. Dangerousness, therefore, displaces diagnosis as *the* reason for incarceration. The main function of special hospitals is to offer containment, not cure.

Indeed from this perspective women have no need of long-term mental health care. They are not institutionalized and have few communication problems. Rather they are detained, against their will, because they are dangerous. White women, who are dangerous, end up in special hospitals because the system is more lenient to them than it is to men (not because they are advised it is a soft option). Conversely, dangerous Black women are more likely to be punished and sent to prison.

As indicated, central to this understanding (voiced in this account by a male psychiatrist and a male social worker) is the importance attached to dangerousness as the boundary marker for women's routes into secure hospitals:

There were quite high percentages really who set fires and I think it is the main behaviour that warrants them to be described as an immediate danger. The other area was in personal violence. That would happen usually in some institutional setting, and occasionally someone was killed.

(male psychiatrist)

A majority of women come in for murder and arson and things like that.

(female patient)

From this perspective dangerousness is directly linked with childhood abuse:

I've learnt to say that it's the biggest, the most difficult area, it's *the* problem. It's hard to not count the history of abuse as relevant to what they've then done. So a number of women have told me that they've killed their children in order to save them from going through what they've gone through themselves.

(female clinical psychologist)

I think that's the cause of most of the index offences. They think that if it happened to them then they'd like to do it to others.

(male patient)

As these quotes suggest, although women are much less likely to commit violent offences than men, they do sometimes represent a danger to others (WHO 2000). Because violent women are antithetical to normative femininity, dangerous women must be recuperated into the natural social order.

The medical model does just this by obscuring women's culpability for the danger they pose to others through reference to their mental incapacity. This is how diagnosis functions within criminal courts. It is the disorder that is on trial not the individual. Yet 'madness' does not 'cause' murderous impulses: there are more murderers in the general population than there are murderers with mental health diagnoses (see Chapter 3). In this final account there is no attempt to absolve women's dangerousness. Like the 'failure to conform" account, secure hospitals are viewed as being primarily about containment, even punishment. 'Dangerous' women in this account are culpably bad.

As indicated in this final account, intersections between race and gender, however, make the processes of recognizing and regulating dangerousness complex and unstable. For example, in Britain, Black women have long been over-represented in the prison system, yet relatively under-represented in high-security mental health care (Horn and Warner 2000). One in every 100 Black British adults is now in prison, according to Home Office Statistics (Bright 2003). Black people are six times more likely to be sent to prison than white people and they represent almost a quarter of Britain's jail population (Osmanand and Harris 2002). Nevertheless, it is also the case that Black people are more likely to receive invasive, forced and aversive treatment for mental health problems, which also means that they may be under-represented in outpatient treatment populations, but over-represented in inpatient psychiatric care (Surgeon General 2006a). Therefore, whilst practices of racialization are implicated in the determination of women's routes into secure facilities, there is no straightforward delineation according to race – other than to say that marginalization may increase the likelihood of misunderstanding and mistreatment.

From regulation to resistance: finding ways out from women's routes in

In this chapter I have argued that one of the reasons women are badly served within secure mental health care is because their routes to treatment reflect normative values about gender and race in relation to what constitutes madness, badness and dangerousness. Using empirically generated data, I have demonstrated that women are in danger of enforced hospitalization when they are judged to be too feminine (as when women are depicted as being too passive through madness, infantilization and institutionalization) or not feminine enough (as when women are depicted as being personality disordered, out of control or dangerous). I have drawn attention to the ways narratives about mental illness and personality disorder serve to distinguish between, respectively, more forgivable and more culpable mentally disordered women patients. I have also provided evidence of an evolving mainstream mental health agenda that is increasingly orientated to recognizing the impact of negative social experiences, such as abuse, on the development of women's mental health difficulties and personality problems.

Whilst recognition of the role of experience in the development of mental health problems is positive, potential benefits are ultimately constrained by reduction within the very frameworks they seemingly challenge. Whether women are depicted as being mentally vulnerable or personality disordered, diagnosis internalizes disorder as a fixed property determined by biology and/or social history. Locating pathology in women's past obscures the institutional maintenance of symptomatic behaviour. Hence, even when life experiences, such as abuse, are implicated in the triggering of mental illness or the development of personality disorder, women's responsibility for current relationship difficulties is overdetermined. And services will necessarily struggle to focus on the social foundations of distress, whilst admittance to mental health care is still organized around traditional diagnostic conceptualizations of pathology.

A radical revision of services is needed such that medical diagnosis is no longer used as *the* key that enables access to treatment. Medicine needs to move from centre to periphery, in community as well as secure contexts. If it does not, those women already struggling with life will continue to shoulder the burden of indifference and abuse. In the following chapters, empirical data is used to demonstrate what happens when medicine is forced to the margins of concern by insisting on a sustained focus on the specific issue of childhood sexual abuse. In the following chapter this is achieved by considering how experiences of childhood sexual abuse are thought to affect women patients in secure mental health care.

Table 6.2 Statements from the 'routes' Q study

1. Women go to special hospitals because they have a wish to pass on the responsibility for their lives to someone else.
2. Women who fail to conform sexually (e.g. promiscuous or lesbian) are more likely to end up in special hospitals.
3. A history of drug and/or alcohol problems is NOT common in women who end up in specials.
4. Women who come from poor and deprived backgrounds are LESS likely to end up in special hospitals.
5. Women go to special hospitals because they need long-term mental health care.
6. Women who end up in special hospitals tend to have matured early and be of higher intelligence.
7. Women do NOT go to special hospitals because they have problems with communication.
8. Women who have no support networks (friends or family etc.) on the outside are LESS likely to end up in special hospitals.
9. Women with children are LESS likely to go to special hospitals because it forces them to cope.
10. Women go to special hospitals because of the harmful effects of childhood sexual abuse.
11. Women go to special hospitals because of the harmful effects of childhood physical abuse
12. Women go to special hospitals because of the harmful effects of childhood emotional abuse.
13. Women go to special hospitals because they have NOT developed appropriate coping strategies to deal with their problems.
14. Women who go to special hospitals have had abnormal childhood experiences which have led to the development of abnormal personalities.
15. 'Personality disorder' is a bucket to dump non-feminine women in and then use as a basis for sending women to special hospitals.
16. Women go to special hospitals when other support services have failed to address issues relating to their abused pasts.
17. Women go to special hospitals when their requests for help have been ignored.
18. Women end up in special hospitals because the only way they can get noticed is to get into trouble.
19. The behaviour that gets women into special hospitals should NOT be understood as a 'cry for help'.
20. Women who go to special hospitals have usually suffered a traumatic event which has triggered an underlying mental illness.
21. Women go to special hospitals because they have done something wrong and society expects them to be punished.
22. Women go to special hospitals when they have got themselves into such a state about their problems they have lost control.
23. Women go to special hospitals because a stressful event has caused them to break down and act in a way which has got them into trouble.
24. Women go to special hospitals because they are looking for safety and security and so commit an offence to end up here.
25. Women who go to special hospitals need to behave LESS violently and be much LESS of a danger to the public than men who go to specials.
26. Women go to special hospitals mainly because other institutions CANNOT cope with their violent and aggressive behaviour.

continues overleaf

Table 6.2 Continued

27. Women go to special hospitals mainly because other institutions CANNOT cope with their self-harming behaviour.
28. Women who go to specials feel bad about themselves and deliberately get into trouble so they will be punished.
29. Women go to special hospitals mainly because they have caused damage to property, usually by setting fires.
30. Women who go to special hospitals are NOT usually a danger to the public.
31. Women who come from unstable family backgrounds where they have received poor or inadequate parenting are LESS likely to go to specials.
32. Women go to special hospitals because the legal system is more lenient to women than men and so directs them from prisons into hospitals.
33. Women go to special hospitals because their lawyers advise them that it is a soft option instead of prison.
34. Black women are more likely to be punished and sent to prisons than to be seen as in need of treatment and sent to special hospitals.
35. Women go to special hospitals because the stereotype for women is to be gentle and do as they are told and if they don't they must be 'mad'.
36. Institutionalization is NOT often a reason why women end up in special hospitals.
37. Women who go to special hospitals have been labelled as 'the problem' and this identity has become stuck.
38. Being mentally ill is NOT the main reason women end up in special hospitals.
39. It is UNUSUAL for women who end up in special hospitals to have been hurt or abused as adults.

7

WOMEN SURVIVING IN SECURE CARE

Making sense of the effects of childhood sexual abuse

Introduction

As indicated in Chapter 6, patients in secure mental health care represent a small but significant group of people who suffer with severe and enduring mental health problems (the American National Institute of Mental Health / NIMH 2006a). There is increasing recognition that their difficulties may be exacerbated by ongoing mistreatment and abuse (World Health Organization/WHO 2005a); and that women patients in secure services across the world may be especially vulnerable to ongoing violence and sexual exploitation (Aitkin and Heenan 2004; WHO 2005a). Women patients in secure services are some of the most maligned and marginalized women in the world, whose plight is too often ignored by a general public who prefers its victims to be more unambiguously innocent (see Chapter 3). In Chapter 6, I argued that women's mistreatment in secure mental health care may also be predicated on normative misunderstandings about gender that are drawn on to justify incarceration.

I demonstrated that women's routes into secure mental health care reflect gendered understandings about personality disorder, mental illness and concepts of dangerousness, which are also racialized. In this sense the medical model prevails as the dominant force in structuring entry into secure mental health systems because women must have a diagnosis to be (mis)placed there. Problems arise because the social roots of women's misery can be hidden within medical concepts of disorder that over-determine born-with and stable deficiencies. Nevertheless, there is some evidence that a biological model of mental disorder is being challenged by an increasing acceptance that social experiences negatively impact on mental health and personality development (WHO 2000), and this was reflected in the accounts generated through the previous Q study. Further, feminists, mental health and self-help activists have challenged the idea that mental health problems are inevitably stable or deteriorating by empha-sizing that even people with severe mental disorders do sometimes recover (the American Surgeon General 2006b).

If women patients in secure mental health care are to be enabled to recover, then social models of mental health care need to be privileged over more traditional understandings of mental disorder that internalize and stabilize pathology. Hence, medicine must be replaced as the central mechanism through which these women are understood. The first step in moving medicine from centre to periphery involves refocusing concern onto the lived experiences that seem to underpin women's mental distress. As argued, childhood sexual abuse is a key experience in the lives of people with severe and enduring mental health problems, and narratives about abuse are central to contemporary challenges to the hegemony of the medical model (e.g. Harris and Landis 2001). For example, Harris (2001) reports that over 50 per cent of state-hospital psychiatric patients in the USA have experienced childhood sexual abuse. About 70 per cent of women in maximum secure care in Britain report histories of childhood sexual abuse (Department of Health 2002b, 2004). Hence, childhood sexual abuse can be considered to be a relevant factor in making sense of women with long-term mental health problems.

In order to elaborate how abuse-talk impacts on understanding these women, I deliberately focus attention on child sexual abuse. In this chapter, I draw on empirically generated accounts of the effects of childhood sexual abuse to demonstrate how such talk can be used to rethink secure mental health care. My aim is to elucidate how services for women can be reconfigured by changing the focus from 'illness' to abuse. I begin by exploring the impact of betrayal on women who have been sexually abused and then track some of the dominant forms of understanding these effects are thought to have on women patients. In terms of mainstream approaches, I consider how the medical model incorporates an understanding of childhood sexual abuse into current conceptualizations of personality disorder and mental illness. I then explore how dominant psychological theories, reflected in cognitive and behavioural approaches, make sense of the impact of childhood sexual abuse on women in secure settings. Finally, I trace how notions of recovery have evolved in relation to women in secure mental health care. I argue that mainstream applications of psychiatry and psychology too often rely on normative understandings about sex and gender and that these normative understandings can act prescriptively to reduce the ways in which women may formulate their own pathways to recovery from experiences such as childhood sexual abuse.

Making sense of the effects of childhood sexual abuse: discourses about and representations of women in secure mental health care

Two separate, but related, studies are drawn on in this chapter to illustrate how childhood sexual abuse is variously used to make sense of mentally disordered women in secure mental health care. When we make sense of the impact of social experiences, such as childhood sexual abuse, it is usual to consider what *effects* such experiences have on the people who experience them. There are a number of ways of doing this. The first Q study identifies *discourses about* the effects of childhood sexual abuse on women patients in secure mental health care. The second study identifies *representations of* women patients in secure mental health care who have experienced childhood sexual abuse. In simple terms, discourses about effects relate to what happens to people, and representations of effects relate to who people are; that is, they are respectively verb and noun.

What happens to people, and who they are, are clearly dialogically related. However, they are not identical. They may even be functionally independent, insofar as one discourse (about madness, for example) is not always predictive of one representation (of mad women, for example). As Moscovici (1985) argues discourses are not representations, even if representations are translated through discourse. Social groups will use social representations to make sense of their social world (Moscovici 1985). For example, as indicated in Chapter 3, the mass media relies on familiar representations of abusers (as, for example, paedophilic, extraordinary) to preserve the sanctity of family life. Hence, both discourses about social issues and representations of the people affected by them shape reality. Thus, both discourses about, and representations of, effects are important in illuminating how narratives about child sexual abuse can be used to make sense of mentally disordered women in secure care.

Following the principles outlined in Chapters 5 and 6, two Q sorts were constructed to address the 'effects' of childhood sexual abuse on women patients. The first study identified accounts reflecting *discourses about* the effects of child sexual abuse (see Table 7.1 at the end of this chapter). The second study identified accounts reflecting *representations of* sexually abused women patients (see Table 7.2 at the end of this chapter). Both Q sorts were completed by 60 female and male patients and staff at Ashworth and Rampton special high-security mental hospitals. Q factor analysis was used to identify key composite accounts of *discourses about* effects in the first study, and *representations of* sexually abused women in the second study; and these were interpreted according to the method outlined in Chapter 6. Some of these composite accounts are used in this chapter, together with interview quotes, to illustrate how narratives about child sexual abuse can be drawn on to make sense of mentally disordered women in secure mental health care.

Setting the context: childhood sexual abuse, secure hospitals and betrayal

Given that women in secure mental hospitals will have demonstrated some problems with living, the emphasis in secure services is on the ways women are negatively affected by childhood sexual abuse. This emphasis was reflected in both Q studies. For example, the majority of accounts in the 'discourses about effects' study depicted all childhood sexual experiences as being *inherently harmful* (see statement 18, 'discourses about effects' study, Table 7.1). Despite this, even within secure care settings, there is some limited sense that self-destruction is not total, otherwise there would be little point in treating such people. The belief is that women are still surviving, albeit sometimes tenuously. The gap between destruction and survival can be wide, and the accounts produced through both studies indicate that even within closed institutions there are many ways of conceptualizing women's responses to childhood sexual abuse. These differences notwithstanding, most understandings of the negative impact of childhood sexual abuse emphasize the centrality of betrayal.

Betrayal has long been identified as a key factor in determining the negative effects of childhood sexual abuse (e.g. Finkelhor 1988; Kendall-Tacket *et al.* 1993; Summit 1983). Betrayal is so important because it is thought to undermine victims' trust in others and inhibit their ability to form healthy intimate relationships in the future. The centrality of betrayal to making sense of the negative effects of childhood sexual abuse was supported by empirical data from the 'discourses about effects' study. Here, most accounts suggest that 'one of the most damaging aspects of child sexual abuse is betrayal, because it leaves women unable to trust anyone' (statement 26, 'discourses about effects' study, in Table 7.1). These accounts also note that the negative effects of betrayal are exacerbated 'when the abuser is someone women know and love' (see statement 28, 'discourses about effects' study, in Table 7.1), and when women have 'not been believed' (see statement 27, 'discourses about effects' study, in Table 7.1). This is why the sustained ability to trust is often assumed to be indicative of mental health and why women's inability to trust others is laced through accounts in both the 'discourses about effects' and 'representation of women' studies as being implicitly indicative of disorder. Childhood betrayal is only part of the story for sexually abused women who end up in secure care, however. As noted previously (see Aitkin and Heenan 2004; WHO 2005a), women in secure facilities around the world continue to be betrayed by the people who are responsible for their care, and in particular remain vulnerable to further sexual assault. Women's ongoing vulnerability to abuse is illustrated in Account one, which is summarized in Illustration 1 below, and discussed thereafter.

Illustration 1

Account one: discourses about effects – 're-enactment'

The central feature of this account is women's ongoing vulnerability to abuse. They continue to be subject to actual assaults by men in the hospital. Therefore, women remain frightened of anyone in a position of power and authority. They feel helpless, which is compounded by once again having no control over what happens to them. Women, therefore, do not use their experiences of childhood sexual abuse as an excuse for their behaviour. Women may try to protect themselves from their feelings by using drugs and alcohol, and they often appear to be emotionally flat. However, they can never forget because they continue to be abused.

Account one (given by a female patient and female social worker) draws attention to the multiple factors that reinforce abused women's sense of powerlessness:

> The level of security actually strips women of everything. The worst extreme is the maximum-security ward where women have virtually nothing of their own belongings. So, I mean, they're very physically stripped of themselves as well as emotionally and the whole works: the possible injecting, sitting on, physical restraint and locking away. This is the ultimate controlled institution and clearly if we're talking about people who don't have control over their bodies, their lives, you know, it's hard to see how any of that can be therapeutic.
>
> (female clinical psychologist)

For these women, their many experiences of abuse and exploitation lead to a particular mistrust of men, which is again exaggerated within secure systems where lack of control and their proximity to abusers is assured:

> Most women don't like the idea of having male nurses on the ward. It could be bad, because a lot of us have been sexually abused, and these men just violated all of us patients and made it worse. They used to strip women, they used to kick and punch [us].
>
> (female patient)

> We're mixed in with rapists and child abusers and that, and you know that and it makes you feel worse. It doesn't make you feel any better about yourself, because they look at me and I want to cringe or be sick.
>
> (female patient)

Account one reflects the fact that women around the world are routinely assaulted in secure mental-health care:

> There was a lady, the week before last, who was raped by a fella in here.
>
> (male patient)

> I was sexually abused by a male once, in the hospital. He's still a manager and I found out that it's just not me that he's done it to. So, not a safe place, you know.
>
> (female patient)

The practice of housing sexual abusers with sexual victims is instrumental in arguments for gender-specific services. However, this does not protect women from abusive practitioners (or abusive women). Betrayal through child sexual abuse is, therefore, compounded for many women in secure services by ongoing mistreatment and abuse. The different ways betrayal is thought to affect sexually abused women in secure mental hospitals is now explored.

Childhood sexual abuse and the construction of abnormal personalities

There are a number of 'personality disorder' definitions that could be applied to abused women in secure mental health services. The Diagnostic and Statistical Manual/DSM-IV-R (American Psychiatric Association (APA) 1995), for example, provides descriptions of ten personality disorders. However, not all of these categories are routinely utilized. Consequently, in this chapter, I draw attention only to those definitions that seem to have particular relevance for abused women in secure care. These include 'borderline personality disorder', 'self-defeating personality disorder', and 'anti-social/psychopathic personality disorder'.

As previously argued, 'personality disorder' is a predominant diagnostic category for understanding women in secure mental health care, particularly those who have experienced childhood sexual abuse. This is because the development of personality disorder is frequently associated with childhood abuse trauma (see Harman 2004 for data regarding the USA; Warner and Wilkins 2003 for data regarding Britain). As indicated in Chapter 6, borderline personality disorder is the most common way of representing women in maximum-security mental health care. The disorder is defined in terms of instability of mood, self-image and relationships, and is frequently associated with repeated experiences of victimization. Hence, sexually abused women in secure care are often also represented in this way (see Illustration 2).

Illustration 2

Account two: representation of women – 'borderline'

The woman described in this account is someone with an extremely poor self-image. Because she hates herself and has little self-confidence she needs a lot of acceptance, approval and attention from others. Yet, at the same time, she does not trust people and is now sexually inhibited. She is disturbed and does not have a well-developed intact personality. She has big mood swings. Often she seems full of anger, at other times sad, depressed, and lacking in energy. She is self-destructive, self-harms and frequently sets herself up to fail. As a consequence of this she has little hope about the future. Luckily, because she has a good sense of humour she is well liked.

This Q-generated account was defined by 11 women and seven men, including five nurses, four clinical psychologists, four psychiatrists, three patients, one social worker and one lecturer. The woman described in this account typifies the 'borderline' disorder. She craves attention, yet is mistrustful of others, and is characterized by 'fight and flight' responses to intimacy. Childhood sexual abuse is one foundational experience that provokes this kind of behaviour. Women's desire for intimacy leads them into relationships, just as their fear of abuse instigates their retreat. Women so defined may then be judged to have a fixed, yet unstable, identity precisely because their behaviour is contradictory. Their self-hatred mediates their sense of self:

> She doesn't like herself. Mainly the people what have been abused don't like themselves anyway, because they let it happen.
>
> (female patient)

Self-loathing invites women to internalize their rage and depression, and cope with these feelings by self-harming, as one female social worker explained:

> Lots of self-harm, still. An inability to believe that she can ever get out of the way she's been or be herself. And the more angry she becomes the more likely she is to self-harm. It's like she just reaches a point where she feels that she's getting strong and then she self-harms again, quite severely and I think that's one way of her keeping herself back.

Self harm may have multiple protective functions for these women. Self harm may not only protect women from going into an outside world that they fear, but also, this account suggests that 'borderline' women sometimes use self-harm to protect themselves from the sexual contact they also fear and wish to avoid (indicated here by sexual inhibition):

> A lot of the patients self-harmed: you know, like scratch their arms and that. A lot of them were grossly overweight and tried to make themselves look as masculine as possible, unattractive as possible. They do say to us that no man'll ever find them attractive again because they don't ever want to go through that again.
>
> (female nurse)

As the above quote suggests, self-harm might be better understood as self-preservation (Warner 2000b). Yet, women patients in secure mental health care are frequently invited to feel shame about their coping strategies: being diagnosed as disordered confirms their shame *and* holds them accountable for their shameful acts. The pathologization of women's responses to feelings of powerlessness are elaborated further in descriptions of 'self-defeating personality disorder'. Although this disorder no longer 'exists', in as much as it was proposed in DSM-III-R (APA 1987), but excluded from the most recent DSM-IV-R (APA 1995) on the grounds that the definition was misogynist (Frey 2006), it still functions as an informal reference point. Prejudice against women patients continues within secure care, and abused women can still be viewed as provoking their own downfall (see Illustration 3).

Illustration 3

Account three: representation of women – 'self-defeating'

Like the 'borderline' woman, the 'self-defeating' one has a poor self-image, is sad and depressed, with little hope for the future. She is also extremely self-destructive. In this account, however, this does not lead to self-harming behaviour, but is demonstrated through continually setting herself up to fail. She is manipulative and rebellious, but ineffectual. She becomes obsessed with things and is very sensitive and easily upset. This is because she sees things in 'black and white', has unrealistic expectations of others, and is often unclear about what she wants. Consequently she frequently oversteps boundaries with other people. Her one redeeming feature is that she also has a good sense of humour.

The description given in the above account (voiced by two women: a patient and social worker) is consistent with 'self-defeating' personality disorder as defined by the APA (1987). Such women set themselves up to fail:

> She often protests about how the system is unfair, but then sort of does something to sabotage the rules to get her out.
>
> (female social worker)

Part of these women's putative failings is their inability to manage and negotiate social relationships. A male nurse described one such woman:

> She puts herself on people. She doesn't pick up on the cues. You know that we all miss cues, but some of the cues are really obvious aren't they? This person constantly gives me the impression that she's rejected all the time and she is, because we all do it with her to a degree even if you do it nicely with her. And when I mean nicely I mean you take time to explain and it's tedious because she wants it in so 'black and white'. You know the look of hurt is no different from if it was 'oh, get away, I haven't got time for you'.

As the above quote suggests, such women can be extremely frustrating to work with. By representing women as *being* self-defeating, workers can distance themselves from their own feelings of inadequacy. That women are failing, rather than failed, can subsequently function as a self-evident truth. This disorder embodies the notion of guilty passivity, which reflects the extreme characteristics of the female role (Tavris 1993), and also calls to mind the victim of sexual abuse, hence the ongoing application of this disorder in this context. This empirically generated account, therefore, acts as a reminder that just because a 'disorder' does not have formal recognition, it can function as a social stereotype that people in secure mental health care may still draw on to make sense of abused women. As signalled in the 'routes' study, women in secure care are penalized for being *too* feminine (either too passive or too masochistic, as in this account). By contrast, women who demonstrate 'anti-social/psychopathic' tendencies rupture rehearsed understandings about gender: they are not feminine enough.

Psychopathy was originally used to refer to all forms of personality disorder and in a medico-legal sense it still does (Department of Health DH 1983). In clinical contexts, the term 'psychopathic' (Cleckley 1976; Hare 1980) has been replaced with 'antisocial' (APA 1995) and it is a history of antisocial behaviour that is the key factor in determining the antisocial personality disorder. Inevitably, it is a deeply gender-laden category. The APA (1995: 667) distinguishes between those with borderline personality disorder as being 'manipulative to gain nurturance, whereas those with antisocial personality disorder are manipulative to gain profit, power, or some other material gratification'. The former is indicative of femininity and the latter description represents the extreme characteristics of the male role and, hence, is indicative of masculinity. Therefore, women described in these terms are unusual. Yet, as also signposted in the previous chapter, such women do exist in secure mental health care (see Illustration 4).

Illustration 4

Account four: representation of women – 'antisocial/psychopathic'

The woman described in this account causes a lot of trouble. She self-harms and is extremely aggressive, violent, and manipulative; and she therefore dominates others. She is highly emotional, has considerable mood swings and is difficult and demanding. She shows little remorse for her violent and aggressive behaviour. Hence, she is understood to be immature and to have a strong, though poorly developed, personality. Because she is so immature, this woman cannot cope well with change. Although mistrustful of others, she needs a lot of attention and has unrealistic expectations of others. As a consequence she frequently oversteps boundaries with other people. Her one redeeming quality is her good sense of humour, which means that she is still quite likeable.

The 'psychopathic' representation detailed above was given by five women and two men in the Q study: three nurses, two patients, a psychiatrist and a pharmacist. It reflects some common understandings about what constitutes an antisocial personality. For example, the account draws attention to the association between violence and emotional lability:

> She sets fires, including to herself. She's completely out of control.
>
> (female nurse)

> One minute she'll be bright and happy and the next minute she'll be screaming and threatening to kill you.
>
> (male psychiatrist)

> Well, we talked earlier about behaviour and sort of unresolved rage as a child in an adult woman, and how that spills out as an 'acting out' behaviour in a way that helps them feel better. But that can be about trying to kill other people, destruction to property, destruction to themselves.
>
> (female nurse)

Although humour redeems the type of woman described in the above account, in general little sympathy is proffered to psychopathic women. This is because they are deemed to be selfish and remorseless, and the guilt-free autonomous subject is problematic for dominant discourses about femininity. It is difficult to absolve evidently selfish women. Hence, what are defined as 'social skills' in the general population become 'manipulation' in the psychopath. As one female social worker noted:

> When a woman's drawn attention to herself because she's been abused, she finds that she gets a lot of support so she doesn't want to throw the crutch away. There's actually something to preserve it for. And I think that that's difficult especially with the psychopathic women in here, because they may be seen as exploiting it to the full and really manipulating people and that sort of thing.

The psychopath, in some ways, is the most threatening of all female patients, and the one that is viewed with most suspicion. This is because she is the only one who is thought to be able to control others through her violent and manipulative behaviour. Other diagnostic constructs, therefore, may not only signal different types of behaviour, but also signpost other women's lack of efficacy and power.

Childhood sexual abuse and the construction of mental illness

Although all diagnostic categories discredit those defined within them, categories of mental illness are particularly effective at doing so (Plumb 1993). This is because 'madness' is inferred through deficient rationality *and* lack of efficacy, and hence, such persons are doubly marginalized. This is evident in discussions about psychosis. People are considered to be psychotic when they exhibit extremely abnormal behaviour ordinarily associated with completely 'losing touch' with reality (Winn 1980). As argued previously, reality is social structured according to embedded assumptions about femininity and heteronormativity. This is reflected in the following representation of a 'psychotic' woman (given by a female patient, and a male and a female social worker – see Illustration 5).

Illustration 5

Account five: representation of women – 'psychotic'

The woman described in this account is completely out of control. She has very poor social skills, although she tries to be manipulative.

> She has little trust in people and, in particular, gets on poorly with men. She has no sense of humour and is not caring or protective of others. Rather, she is aggressive and violent, and can be difficult and demanding. She is not very bright, has little insight into her problems and is far from being sensible or responsible. Indeed, she is characterized as being psychotic. This woman appears to have no feelings. She takes little interest in the world around her, has no energy or exuberance, and lacks self-determination and motivation. Unsurprisingly, she has no hope for the future.

As this account suggests, one way psychosis in women may be defined is in terms of women's inability to get on well with men. In a heteronormative world this may indeed seem abnormal and unreasonable. Psychosis may be further assumed in reference to these women's seemingly indiscriminate violence reflected in their abortive attempts to dominate and manipulate others. Ineffective behaviour (in contrast to 'psychopathic' behaviour) may appear to be more unreasonable because it is unfocused and seemingly pointless, as the following quote suggests.

> I felt the level of disturbance in the women patients in the hospital is far greater than in the male wards somehow. As soon as I was on the ward there was an immediate rush towards me in a very aggressive sort of way. It seemed far more psychotic.
>
> (female social worker)

Anger at childhood sexual abuse may underlie these women's violent disinhibition, yet their inability to effect positive change ultimately confirms their status as 'mad' women. Nevertheless, whether personality disordered or mentally ill, as these empirically generated accounts suggest, violence is an omnipresent feature of life for abused women in secure care. These women are angry about the hurt and harm they have suffered and endured. And it may be that it is this barely concealed anger and aggression that unsettles the wider community most of all. Clearly, when abused women demonstrate dangerous behaviour there is a need to provide containment. However, that secure services around the world too often fail to provide adequate care for women patients suggests that women's anger and violence is poorly understood.

If women are deemed to have serious mental health problems then it is wholly wrong to respond with punitive services, let alone abusive and/or neglectful ones. This is why it is crucial to track different forms of understanding. Violent behaviour is less frightening when it can be contextualized because we can then target our interventions more appropriately. To illustrate this point, I draw on two accounts from the 'discourses about effects' study that delineate contrasting pathways from early experiences of abuse to different forms of violent expression. In the next account (voiced by a male social worker and two male nurses), the reasons for 'violence to self and others' are explored. See Illustration 6, Account six.

Illustration 6

Account six: discourses about effects – 'violence to self and others'

According to this account, mental illness exaggerates women's inability to cope with stress occasioned through child sexual abuse and this results in violence to self and others. Because these women are depicted as being feminine, in both their behaviour and appearance, they are understood to be more likely to hurt themselves rather than other people and are seldom thought to sexually abuse others (externalized aggression and sexually abusive behaviour are more generally associated with masculinity). Women's inability to cope ultimately results in low self-esteem and low self-confidence and means that they frequently feel suicidal.

From this perspective, women's anger is directly attributed to unresolved feelings about childhood sexual abuse. Hence, women's aggression may still be unacceptable, but it is understandable. For example, a male patient described his friend:

> She gets moody. Sometimes she causes fear amongst the staff when she thinks about things like the rape and she thinks about the murder she did.

However, it is still easier to understand women's self-harm because feminine passivity and low self-esteem means violence is more readily thought to be internalized, as the next quote suggests.

> Low self-esteem or no self-esteem, a complete lack of confidence in themselves, really. Self-loathing and self-injurious behaviour, which is about self-loathing. But it's also about the exterior reflecting the interior, you know, women cutting and harming themselves as a way of finding release from their feelings.
>
> (female nurse)

Because childhood sexual abuse reinforces women's powerlessness, women's avoidance of aggression towards others is easily recognized. Self-harm is one means by which violence is displaced. Another way abused women in secure settings are thought to displace anger and despair at abuse is through directing violence towards inanimate objects. This is illustrated in the following account (see Illustration 7).

Illustration 7

Account seven: discourses about effects – 'violence to things'

This account stresses the fact that child sexual abuse has a profoundly negative impact on women's mental health. The memories of child sexual abuse leave women feeling sad, depressed and powerless. These women frequently feel out of control of their feelings. Their powerlessness means they do not direct their anger at people. Hence, they do not act or look like men; for example they do not sexually abuse others. Rather they act out their feelings on inanimate objects, for example by setting fires. Their powerlessness means that they remain frightened of people in positions of power and authority and although hurt by men, they do not avoid them.

The long-term emotional impact of abuse is again demonstrated in this account (voiced in the Q study by two female patients) by the fact that such women are unable to forget what happened to them, for example:

> I dream sometimes about it, and I often think about it when I was younger, and you know what I'd done to some of the men who were much older than me . . . I do blame myself because I put myself in that situation, and I put myself in the situation all the time, and I never done anything to stop myself. You know, I never thought of it, it was something that would hurt and that was it.
>
> (female patient)

The distinguishing feature of the perspective illustrated in this account, however, is these women's inability to 'act like a man'. This means that because they are unable to direct their rage at other people, they direct it at inanimate objects instead. And in this context, this usually involves fire-setting. As one female nurse observed:

> She had it all [written on the wall] 'fire and fire', 'fire is the only thing that will cleanse'.

It may be that fire-setting is more common in the female population than in the male population in secure hospitals because it is associated with experiences of childhood sexual abuse (DH 2002b). Fire-setting allows anger to be expressed without directly, or deliberately, harming others. By inviting a focus on childhood sexual abuse, women's so-called mad behaviour becomes easier to understand, even if – as noted – no more acceptable. Hence, child sexual abuse enables women's behaviour to be made sense of in terms of what functions it serves.

Childhood sexual abuse and the construction of cognitive damage and sexual dysfunction

When the behaviour that is taken to be indicative of mental disorder is situated in relation to lived experience, psychology has a role to play in making sense of its functions and meanings. Psychology, therefore, has the potential to transform mainstream mental health care by reorienting services towards recovery. This is because if the function of behaviour can be identified, alternative strategies may also be identified and developed, and hence women's problems with living do not have to be final. However, as argued in Chapter 2, a functional analysis is still problematic if it is structured around fixed notions about what constitutes recovery and if social failures are too quickly viewed as being personal disabilities. This is evidenced in the mainstream applications of cognitive and behavioural theory, which, separately and in combination, represent the dominant theoretical force within clinical psychology, and hence why they are discussed here.

Cognitive theory has a significant role to play in making sense of child sexual abuse. This is because cognitive theory underpins mainstream approaches to understanding the development of post-traumatic stress disorder following experiences of sexual trauma (e.g. Foa and Rothbaum 1998). Although, as indicated, abused women in secure mental health care are likely to be diagnosed with a major psychiatric disorder (such as personality problems and different forms of psychotic illnesses), many may also be viewed as exhibiting post-traumatic symptomatology. This is helpful because it situates otherwise 'mad' behaviour in relation to real experiences. According to this model, people develop post-traumatic stress disorder when they are unable to process, and come to terms with, emotionally threatening events. People are said to re-experience these traumatic events in dreams, flashbacks, and/or as recurrent and intrusive recollections (APA 1995). This perspective is illustrated in the following account (voiced by one male and two female patients). See Illustration 8.

Illustration 8

Account eight: discourses about effects – 'cognitive damage'

From this perspective, child sexual abuse has a negative impact on women's intellectual development. They are immature, emotionally regressed and confused, and have failed at school and work. Their intellectual inadequacies also mean that they cannot process their unresolved feelings about child sexual abuse. Therefore, their memories cannot be forgotten and women continue to re-experience their abuse as intrusive thoughts and images. Hence, from this perspective, psychotic symptoms are better understood as flashbacks to the abuse. These women are unable to protect themselves, such that although they want nothing to do with men, they still end up in abusive relationships with male patients. These women internalize their hurt and self-harm, but are thought to be unlikely to hurt others and they do not set fires.

The description of 'cognitive damage', in this account, is consistent with contemporary understandings of 'post-traumatic stress disorder' (APA 1995). The 'cognitive damage' account, therefore, emphasizes the need to understand psychotic symptoms, such as hallucinations, in the following terms:

> There's a number of them where they would have freak psychotic episodes in which they would hallucinate what would actually happen to them or something analogous to what had happened to them. If it wasn't as serious as that, then they might still have some sort of imagery or vivid recollection of what had happened. So they might be fearful of the dark, they might hear footsteps and things like that outside their room.
>
> (male psychiatrist)

Because the original trauma remains unresolved, people are commonly understood to avoid stimuli associated with it (APA 1995). Again, women in the studies referenced here were frequently characterized as attempting to avoid intimate relationships, particularly with men and in respect of sex. In the 'cognitive damage' account, women are depicted as being unable to avoid abusive relationships with male patients. This may reflect their cognitive confusion, but also may be indicative of embedded assumptions within secure hospitals that heterosexuality denotes health and recovery. As one female clinical psychologist explained:

> The majority of people who've hurt them were men and that leads to them wishing to be separate from men. They are very aware that

the men in here are likely to have been abusers, and yet as time goes by, because the system is one in which it is actually advantageous to mix with men, they end up in these relationships. And I just despair really of the system that puts a vulnerable group of people with a group of abusers.

Women's vulnerability, therefore, may be less a consequence of their unresolved trauma, and more a consequence of targeting by sexually predatory men within systems that condone heterosexuality. Therefore, the reason that women may continue to ruminate and have flashbacks may have more to do with current experiences of abuse than their past histories (as suggested in the above 're-enactment' account). Hence, individualizing unresolved trauma, through narratives about post-traumatic stress, may in fact contribute to women's vulnerability in secure settings by enabling ongoing abuse to be obscured. Mainstream behavioural theories that seek to make sense of the impact of childhood sexual abuse can also undermine women's ability to recover.

According to mainstream behavioural theory, 'sex' (rather than power) is *the* primary cause and effect of sexual abuse (Warner 1996a). Hence, the main focus of concern from this type of perspective is on understanding how women's sexual responses are changed by their experiences of childhood sexual abuse. Because sex is the focus of such theories, there is plenty of scope for heteronormativity to be reinstated as the benchmark against which disorder and recovery can be measured. This is illustrated in the following account (given by a male and female patient). See Illustration 9.

Illustration 9

Account nine: discourses about effects – 'sexual dysfunction'

From this perspective, child sexual abuse is again thought to give rise to feelings of depression, low self-esteem, poor self-confidence, and an inability to cope with stress, all of which frequently results in suicidal ideation. The defining feature of this account, however, is the impact child sexual abuse has on women's sexual identity and behaviour. Whilst they make good parents themselves, and are seldom thought to sexually abuse others, these women are depicted as having difficulties in forming close relationships. They are socially withdrawn, particularly in respect of men. Specifically, these women are sexually inhibited, and avoid sexual and physical contact with male others. Failing that, they become lesbians instead.

From the perspective reflected in this account, women respond to experiences of sexual abuse by withdrawing sexually from men and, sometimes, redirecting their sexual desire towards women:

> I feel uncomfortable around the ward, especially if there are lots of men on the ward. You can have a joke with other women and you don't feel like you are egging them on, or teasing them. The women just take you for what you are.
>
> (female patient)

> I'm presuming that people who have been sexually abused as children may find it more difficult to have relationships with men and so there may be a tendency to veer towards their own sex.
>
> (female nurse)

As sexual inhibition and same-sex relationships are associated with pathological emotional states (such as being suicidal), this account functionally discredits these particular sexual choices. Hence, it reflects normative assumptions that 'sexual dysfunction' is indicated by sexual inhibition with men or, worse, sexual attraction to women, as the following quotes suggest.

> Oh I don't think [lesbianism] is typical . . . the whole idea just turns me right off.
>
> (male nurse)

> I'm quite open-minded about lesbian issues in special hospitals because they can't have normal relationships.
>
> (female nurse)

This account, therefore, illustrates how heterosexuality still functions in some secure systems as an accepted marker of recovery. By making sexual inhibition with men and lesbianism a consequence of sexual abuse, heterosexuality, by default, functions as the reference point for sexual 'normality'. And, as Wilkinson and Kitzinger (1993) have pointed out, this means trajectories of heterosexual development remain, largely, untheorized and assumed. People seldom say 'sexual abuse made me heterosexual', although the link between heterosex and abuse is made in many feminist accounts (see Chapter 4). In the proceeding section, the embedded association between heterosexuality and health is teased out further.

Survival stories: from minimization to recovery

The women described in this chapter so far can be understood to represent those whose problems dictate that they are likely to stay in secure mental health care for some time to come. By contrast the women described in this section, in varying degrees, might be thought of as women who are closer to leaving, or maybe should not have been incarcerated in the first place. The emphasis here is on survival, adaptation and recovery. As one female clinical psychologist observed:

> I often find people really have the most amazing inner strength.
> You actually think these people have survived.

Notions of survival have strategic, if not total, value (Worrell 2003) in secure care. Too many women continue to be victimized and pathologized for the ways in which they try to manage their restricted lives. The recognition that women transcend and transform their experiences of abuse is important in systems where women are routinely viewed as dysfunctional and disabled. However, it is important to explore the shape survival is thought to take. As noted, this is because heterosexuality remains a powerful marker of health and recovery. This perspective is further illustrated in the following description of the 'normal' woman (given in the Q study by three women and five men: four patients, two psychologists and two nurses). See Illustration 10.

Illustration 10

Account ten: representations of women – 'normal'

The woman described in this account epitomizes idealized femininity. She has good social skills, but she is not manipulative, and she is caring and protective of others. She is sensible and responsible. She has feelings, but is definitely not out of control. She is not violent or aggressive, nor is she described as being psychotic. In fact this woman is bright and has considerable insight into her problems. She trusts people, is not difficult or demanding, and in particular is said to get on well with men. This woman is exuberant, self-motivated and determined. She takes a great interest in the world around her. As a model patient, this woman is appropriately hopeful about the future.

According to the perspective reflected in this account, normality can be inferred by how closely women approximate idealized femininity. The 'normal' woman is caring of others.

She's very understanding, 'cause I've had chats with her about certain things and she's always there for you if you need her.

(female patient)

Hence, 'normal' women do not exceed the boundaries of acceptable feminine behaviour. They have personal insight and are no longer 'out of control'. Control, in this account, is personal and does not extend to the relational, environmental or the political (Plumb 1993). In effect, women are transformed into a self-disciplining subject (Foucault 1991). The road to recovery, according to this perspective, therefore is organized around recuperation back into the matrix of femininity and heterosexuality. The woman invoked by the 'sexual dysfunction' account is evidently more ill than the 'normal' woman precisely because she refuses to reintegrate with men. Women's survival remains incomplete whilst women fail to conform to dominant versions of womanhood. Another example of this is given in the depiction of the woman who puts on a 'brave face'. See Illustration 11.

Illustration 11

Account eleven: representations of women – 'brave face'

The woman in this account is not psychotic or mentally ill in any way. In fact she is not very disturbed at all. She is not aggressive or violent and does not self-harm. However, she still hates herself. This may be linked with the fact that she is consumed with remorse for the bad things she has done to others in the past. This is particularly the case as she is described as having a great sense of loyalty towards others. She can be sensitive and easily upset. She copes with this by putting on a 'brave face'. Thus, whilst she is described as being open about her problems the implication is that she underplays their impact through, for example, her sense of humour. This woman also takes refuge in being exuberant and extrovert. She is rebellious and does not want to blend in. Specifically, she is not feminine or ladylike. However, she is unhappy in her body and has a very poor self-image. Ultimately, then, her bravado is self-defeating.

From this perspective (voiced by two male nurses in the Q study), women's apparent recovery from childhood sexual abuse may be superficial. This is an important point because many women in secure care learn to adapt to external notions of recovery that may enable them to leave hospital, but ultimately fail to address the causes and effects of their misery. Superficial recovery, as reflected in this account, can be recognized in the way that women attempt to mask their feelings about abuse, but cannot dispel their self-hatred regarding their bodies, for example. As one female patient explained:

> Nobody knows how filthy you feel when you've been raped – on the inside and the outside. No matter how many times you change a day or how many times you have a bath, you still feel dirty. You never get rid of that.

As this account implies, women may try to avoid feminine victimization by taking refuge in their masculinized bodies. Weight gain and weight loss serve protective functions in respect of sexual abuse and within restricted environments. Women's shape, therefore, can be used to signal their place on the map of recovery. As one male psychiatrist observed:

> Quite often they end up being large women even if they start off being small women. Special hospital shapes aren't they?

We know women who put on a 'brave face' are not yet recovered precisely because their dissatisfaction with their body – as in this account – is associated with being unfeminine and unladylike. Women's humour also attests to how fragile recovery can be, and how thin the mask that is worn, as demonstrated in the following quotes.

> One of the effects [is] probably to talk about it, occasionally to talk about it to death, but actually in a very joking way, in a very flippant way, almost like, you know, 'this sort of happened to me but it doesn't really matter'.
>
> (male nurse)

> Sometimes you're sitting there and you can see how sad she really looks, and she laughs and jokes about it, but she's not really happy.
>
> (female patient)

Tenuous and fraught relationships between workers and patients can be maintained through 'humour' and most of the women described in the 'representations' study were redeemed through this. Humour is often regarded as being important to mental health, even though the serious business of 'therapy' implicitly devalues 'play'. Paradoxically, then, humour, whilst located in the body and set in opposition to rationality, becomes one of *the* signifiers of normality. Goldberg (1996) argues that female humour is powerful when women self-consciously parody that which is designed to entrap them. Yet, within a context of dependency, women are more likely to be objects, rather than subjects, of humour. For example, a male nurse recalled a women patient telling him that both members of staff and other patients would 'joke' about her abuse:

> It was quite common for other people on the wards to say, 'come on, tell us about the time you did it with a pig'.

This kind of humour does not transform women. Rather, in this location, it becomes part of the technologies of self that reproduce women as self-disciplining subjects who 'laugh off' their real concerns. Notions of survival, therefore, are not always indicative of health, but also of minimization and denial, and as with the 'psychopathic' account, humour can be used to undermine women by drawing attention to the ways in which women are sometimes understood to manipulate their social environment. As one female nurse stated:

> I do have a reservation about sexual abuse that with some of the client group that we have here, it may be a very easy hook to hang things on: 'I did this because I was abused'. So I'm wary.

Women patients, then, have much to survive, not only in terms of actual abuse, but also in terms of how their experiences of abuse are sometimes dismissed, distorted and denied.

Reconfiguring recovery

In this chapter I have used empirical data to illuminate how women in secure mental health care are made sense of. Taking the specific issue of childhood sexual abuse I have tracked the different ways mainstream medical and psychological theories depict women and their problems. The accounts referenced from both 'effects' studies, regarding discourses about, and representations of, sexually abused women, demonstrate that when people are invited to consider women patients in the context of childhood sexual abuse, the impact of women's lives can no longer remain a peripheral concern. By asking people to account for women's social histories, psychiatry has to stretch an otherwise limited model to integrate an understanding of the impact of life events and their meanings. There is still a desire, evident in some medical and psychological accounts, to restrict concern to the personal, and to invoke invariant and normalizing trajectories of recovery. Nevertheless, this chapter points to the fact that if we wish to challenge traditional forms of mental health practice we need to reconfigure the whole debate. This is why language is so important as different questions force different realities to be recognized and explored. It is much harder to dismiss the impact of social experiences, such as child sexual abuse, if we begin by asking questions about the worlds in which women live, rather than making assumptions about what's gone wrong inside their heads.

Betrayal is a key mechanism through which the negative effects of child sexual abuse impact on women. And these earlier multiple betrayals are attenuated for women in secure care where personal control remains limited and where too often abuse and sexual exploitation are an ongoing reality. Whilst not all women in secure care will experience further abuse, the fear of this can be expected to have a negative impact on all those who reside there. Hence, if we are to provide secure services that meet the needs of this particular group of sexually abused women then not only must we make every effort to contextualize women's actions in terms of their lifelong experiences, but every effort has to be made to provide safe, not simply secure, care. This is no small task as the World Health Organization (2005a) has recently admitted, and as feminists and mental health activists have long argued is the case. A focus on social issues, such as child (and adult) abuse, does encourage safer and more responsive systems, however. Women's difficulties are located in reference to the world, and their accounts of abuse cannot simply be dismissed as symptoms of their disordered minds. In the following chapter, I draw out this argument further by demonstrating, through the use of empirical data, how secure mental health services might be improved by reconfiguring service development through social issues such as child sexual abuse.

Table 7.1 Statements from the 'discourses about effects' Q study

1. Women try to forget, but the memories of child sexual abuse never really go away.
2. The most obvious effect of sexual abuse on women patients is their over-compliance and inability to say no.
3. Women patients who were sexually abused as children rarely feel like killing themselves.
4. Psychotic symptoms such as hallucinations are better understood as flashbacks/intrusive thoughts and images from when women were sexually abused.
5. There is no evidence to link drug and alcohol abuse with women patient's experiences of child sexual abuse.
6. It is important to remember that women patients have survived – they have NOT been totally destroyed by their experiences of sexual abuse.
7. Women patients who have been sexually abused end up being masculine – both in the way that they look and the things that they do.
8. Childhood experiences of sexual abuse have little impact on women patients who have a mental illness.
9. Women patients who have been sexually abused are left feeling helpless – that whatever they do they cannot win.
10. Some women patients are over-dependent on male staff which seems to be connected to their abuse by men.
11. Women patients who were sexually abused in childhood are UNLIKELY to get into abusive relationships with male patients.
12. One major reason some women patients are lesbians is because of childhood experiences of sexual abuse.
13. Sadly, the negative effects of childhood sexual abuse on women patients are made worse by actual assaults by men in the hospital.
14. Because the majority of people who have hurt them are men, women patients want nothing to do with men.
15. Women patients who have been sexually abused as children are sexually inhibited (e.g. avoid any sexual/physical contact).
16. There is NO evidence to suggest that women patients who have been sexually abused find it especially difficult to get into close relationships.
17. One major effect of childhood sexual abuse is that women patients are NEVER again frightened of anyone in a position of power and authority.
18. There is nothing inherently harmful about childhood sexual experiences.
19. Women patients who have been sexually abused often end up sexually abusing others.
20. Women patients who have been sexually abused can be so disturbed by it that they become violent to others.
21. A history of childhood sexual abuse is NOT a significant factor in understanding why some women patients end up setting fires.
22. Women patients who have been sexually abused in childhood often make poor parents themselves.
23. Women patients who have been sexually abused do not know how to form good adult relationships because they have no boundaries.
24. Women patients use their experience of sexual abuse as a convenient excuse for their behaviour.
25. Experience of childhood sexual abuse leave women with low self-esteem and a complete lack of confidence.

continues

Table 7.1 Continued

26. One of the most damaging aspects of childhood sexual abuse is the betrayal of trust which leaves women unable to trust anyone.
27. Women patients are most harmed by childhood sexual abuse when people have not believed them.
28. The effect of childhood sexual abuse on women patients is much LESS when the abuser is someone they know and love.
29. The reason women patients hurt themselves has LITTLE to do with unresolved feelings associated with being sexually abused.
30. Women patients who have been sexually abused as children are LESS likely to hurt themselves than others.
31. There is NO evidence to suggest that childhood sexual abuse has any effect on women patients' intellectual development.
32. One major effect of childhood sexual abuse on women patients is they remain immature because their emotional growth was stunted.
33. There is NO clear evidence to suggest that childhood sexual abuse causes some women patients to develop fragmented or 'split' personalities.
34. There is NO evidence to suggest that childhood sexual abuse has any effect on women patients' intellectual development.
35. Childhood experiences of sexual abuse leave women patients sad, depressed and unable to engage with the world around them.
36. Women patients who have been sexually abused in childhood are RARELY emotionally mixed up and confused.
37. Women patients who have been sexually abused as children often seem flippant and not to take things seriously because they have had to minimize their hurt.
38. The damaging effects of childhood sexual abuse are made worse by issues such as racism.
39. Because women patients who have been sexually abused as children have had to protect themselves from their feelings they often appear emotionally flat like they have got no feelings.
40. One effect of childhood sexual abuse is that it leaves women patients unable to take responsibility for their lives.
41. Women patients who have been sexually abused as children try and resolve their feelings through action.
42. One particularly damaging aspect of childhood sexual abuse is that it robs women patients of their childhoods.
43. Women patients who have been sexually abused as children are RARELY out of control of their feelings.
44. One of the most damaging aspects of childhood sexual abuse is the resultant loss and isolation from their parents and children.
45. The fact that some women patients have difficulty concentrating has NOTHING to do with childhood experiences of sexual abuse.
46. Women patients who have been sexually abused as children have a very HIGH threshold for stress (can cope with a lot of stress).
47. All women patients who have been sexually abused in childhood have been damaged by these experiences.
48. Women patients who have been sexually abused as children are very good at judging other people's characters.
49. One effect of childhood sexual abuse is that women patients have often done badly at school and failed to find jobs.
50. The effects of childhood sexual abuse are made worse by being in a special hospital where women, again, have no control over what happens to them.

Table 7.2 Statements from the 'representations of effects' Q study

1. Difficult and demanding.
2. Needs a lot of attention.
3. Emotionally up and down/has mood-swings.
4. NOT very bright.
5. Seems unhappy in her body.
6. Seems young for her age.
7. Exuberant and full of energy.
8. Shy and introverted/wants to blend in.
9. Enjoys physical contact.
10. Takes a lot of care with her appearance.
11. Has NO sense of humor.
12. Seems consumed with remorse for what she has done.
13. Seems completely out of control.
14. Seems very sad and depressed.
15. Sensible and responsible.
16. Caring and protective of others.
17. Has good social skills.
18. Does NOT need acceptance and approval from others.
19. Sees things in black and white.
20. Does NOT cause trouble.
21. Gets obsessed with things.
22. Stubborn.
23. Has insight into her problems.
24. Has NO sense of loyalty.
25. Turns on people who care for her.
26. Puts on a brave face.
27. Takes NO interest in the world around her.
28. Oversteps boundaries with other people.
29. Sensitive/easily upset
30. Does NOT seem nervous.
31. NOT likeable.
32. Flirty/sexually uninhibited.
33. Prone to telling lies.
34. Sexually attracted to men.
35. Sexually attracted to women.
36. Makes other people afraid.
37. Psychotic.
38. Aggressive and violent.
39. Has a well-developed intact personality.
40. Mentally ill.
41. Has inner strength.
42. Feminine and ladylike.
43. Gets on well with men.
44. Gets on well with women.
45. Self-harms.
46. Poor self-image/seems to hate herself.
47. Strong personality/dominates others.
48. Seems to cope well with change.
49. Self-destructive/sets up self to fail.
50. Assertive/able to stand up for herself.

continues

Table 7.2 Continued

51. Seems full of anger.
52. Curious and inquisitive.
53. Open about her problems.
54. Self-confident.
55. Seems clear about what she wants.
56. Very trusting of other people.
57. Seems quite helpless.
58. Very disturbed.
59. Seems hopeful about the future.
60. Has realistic expectations of others.
61. Rebellious.
62. Moans a lot.
63. Self-motivated and determined.
64 Emotionally flat/seems to have no feelings.
65. Manipulative.

8

SPECIAL CARE AND CHILDHOOD SEXUAL ABUSE

Working with women in secure mental hospitals

Introduction

Women in secure care have complex mental health and social needs. As indicated in the previous two chapters, they tend to report long histories of abuse. They are often emotionally volatile, frequently self-harm and can sometimes be violent to others, and destructive to property. Additionally, women continue to be controlled and sometimes suffer further abuse and assault in systems that fail to provide adequate safety and protection. Secure mental health care for women, around the world, is in need of major revision (World Health Organization WHO 2005a). In order to develop more appropriate services for these women a significant commitment has to be made to detailing and addressing their specific needs and issues. It is in this context that mental health services are increasingly recognizing that abuse is a significant factor that must be accounted for in planning new secure, and other, mental health services for women (WHO 2000; British Department of Health DH 2002b).

As noted in previous chapters, childhood sexual abuse, in particular, represents a major negative life experience reported by detained women patients. Therefore, any service that seeks to address matters of abuse must incorporate an understanding of childhood sexual abuse into the matrix of care. Service providers should also be mindful of the potential for childhood abuses to be exacerbated by adult experiences of betrayal in both community and hospital. In Chapter 7, I suggested that by focusing on social factors and life experiences (such as abuse) the potential for ongoing mistreatment and misunderstanding can be reduced as this focus locates women's problems in relation to real events and not just their internal world. In this chapter, I elaborate this argument further by demonstrating, through the use of empirical data, how secure mental health services might be reconfigured and improved by adopting more social and psychological, rather than medical, approaches to intervention. My aim is to contribute to the development of an evidence base for recovery-orientated services (see the American Surgeon General 2006b).

144

Following the principles outlined in Chapters 5 and 6, a 72-item Q sort on 'treatment' for women who have experienced childhood sexual abuse was constructed (see Table 8.1 at the end of this chapter). This was completed by the same 60 participants from two British 'special' maximum-security hospitals who participated in the other three studies used as illustration in this section of the book. Q factor analysis was used to identify key composite accounts about 'treatment' and these were interpreted according to the method outlined in Chapter 6. Some of these composite accounts are now used, together with interview quotes, to explore different aspects of social and psychological approaches to the treatment of mentally disordered women in secure mental health care. The discussion of these accounts is organized around the themes of empowerment, psychological therapies and socio-communal approaches to care.

Taking control: understanding childhood sexual abuse

In the two previous chapters I demonstrated that the medical model provided the main filter in secure psychiatric care for making sense of women patients. This is partially a pragmatic issue as diagnosis determines entry into secure mental health systems. However, the medical model may have little positive to contribute to the understanding of how to treat women patients, particularly those who have also experienced childhood sexual abuse. This is because talking about child sexual abuse necessarily draws attention to social events and away from internal pathology, and hence away from medical diagnosis and the merits of medication. This was reflected in the 'treatment' study. For example, Account one specifically rejected the use of *psychiatric diagnosis as the starting point for any effective treatment plan* (statement 36, in Table 8.1). And none of the accounts drew attention to the role medication can play *in the management of some symptoms of child sexual abuse, such as depression* (statement 16, in Table 8.1).

The reduced role of the medical model in respect of child sexual abuse may also be indicative of traditional distinctions that are drawn between the treatment of 'personality disordered' and 'mentally ill' clients. According to the medical model, personality disorder is viewed as being less amenable to drug therapy than mental illness. As indicated in the previous chapters, because childhood sexual abuse is more usually associated with the development of personality disorder than mental illness, medical intervention is, by default, marginalized. Because medicine is displaced it follows that greater attention is given to psychosocial forms of intervention, which form the primary foci in this chapter.

As noted in Chapter 7, childhood sexual abuse represents a betrayal of trust for many women that is compounded by ongoing abuse and, particularly within secure care, extended and extensive feelings of powerlessness. In order to enable women to recover from experiences of childhood sexual abuse it would seem that it is crucial that women have the opportunity to develop safe relationships and are encouraged to take back control of their lives. This type of approach is reflective of a 'social empowerment' model and is illustrated in Account one from the 'treatment' study. See Illustration 1.

Illustration 1

Account one: 'social empowerment' model

According to this account, women patients who have experienced childhood sexual abuse are best helped by treating them respectfully and enabling them to regain a sense of power in their lives. Women are not helped by members of staff who make too many judgements about them or when too much emphasis is placed on controlling women. Therefore, women's views about treatment should take precedence over those of professionals. This means that although women are thought to need to talk about their experiences of sexual abuse, they should not be made to do so against their will. Treatment decisions should be based on individual need, rather than diagnostic category, and should reflect women's specific racial and cultural background. Hence, they require access to a range of treatment options, including creative therapy techniques, as it is unlikely that one method will suit all.

In order for women to feel able to address their experiences of childhood sexual abuse they need continuity and stability in their treatment and the people who care for them. It is particularly crucial that they find someone they can trust to talk to and someone who understands child sexual abuse, such as specialist counsellors or women who have themselves survived such experiences. The aim of therapy is to help women to understand their behaviour and mental processes and have the opportunity to express their feelings. Specifically, women should not be expected to forgive their abuser(s). Rather, women are thought to need help in recognizing that the abuse they suffered was not their fault. Women need support to engage in this necessarily painful process and to access the strength they have demonstrated in surviving both sexual abuse and 'the system'.

This account was voiced by 17 female and 11 male participants in the Q study: seven patients, seven nurses, six social workers, five clinical psychologists, two psychiatrists and one lecturer. This account draws attention to the need to enable abused women to regain control of their lives. According to an 'empowerment' model, as reflected in this account, women's ability to make their own choices about treatment should be recognized and encouraged. Forcing treatment is untherapeutic. As one female patient noted:

> They try and get me to talk about it and I just say, 'no, when I'm ready I'll talk about it' and that really annoys them 'cause they try and get you to talk about it. And I think that's a disadvantage because you only talk about it when you're ready to and not when the staff think you are ready to.

From a social empowerment perspective, diagnosis is understood to undermine women's ability to take control of their treatment as it underplays women's individuality. Therefore, it has little role to play in a social empowerment approach, as demonstrated in the following quote.

> [Diagnosis is] irrelevant in the work that you're doing because that's about understanding someone's distress and what that's about. And I think, sometimes, diagnosing someone can be inflexible. A woman seems to become a group symptom then, rather than a person.
>
> (female clinical psychologist)

Hence, from the social empowerment perspective, if women are to take control they must be treated as individuals, which means developing more flexible and patient-led services. In the Q-generated account of 'empowerment' particular attention is drawn to the role of creative therapeutic methods, such as writing, artwork and drama. Creative therapies have been used within high-security hospital settings (Cox 1992); with male and female offenders (Baim *et al.* 2002); with women and children who have been sexually abused (Bannister 1992; Meekums 2000); with patients diagnosed as borderline personality disordered (Hudgins 2000); and with patients who experience psychosis (Casson 2004). However, there still remains a reluctance to make use of such techniques within secure hospitals. The fear is that women are barely contained and that the system, whilst physically secure, fails to provide psychological security. Hence, techniques that are thought to increase the likelihood of behavioural disturbance are often avoided. This is why women who are demonstrably expressive are often discouraged from being so in secure care. As one male teacher of patients noted:

> I always get the feeling that, you know, their disturbed behaviour, there's quite a punitive aspect to it. You know that you don't go out on trips if they're being disturbed or don't get kind of rewards. So it's almost kind of making things worse.

In particular, as previously noted, sexually abused women patients who self-injure may engender extreme levels of fear and anxiety in those who work with them, and hence they may be specifically discouraged from articulating their feelings. As one female nurse noted:

> We've got an awful lot of very vulnerable ladies out there and we were frightened that we were going to go blindly in, wanting to do something but with no knowledge, no expertise, no backing particularly. That we were going to go in and we were going to end up with five or six patients dead on our hands.

Workers clearly need access to training about child sexual abuse in order that they have some understanding of the key concerns facing women who have suffered such abuse. In some ways, what women need is relatively easy to identify, although it may be harder to put into practice. Given that betrayal is such a significant and negative factor in women's experiences of childhood sexual abuse, it follows that women need to feel safe in their relationships in order to recover. Hence, whatever therapeutic 'technique' is adopted, as the 'empowerment' account suggests, a key issue for women who have experienced childhood sexual abuse is that they find someone they can trust to talk to. This would go some way to providing a salve for the negative effects of betrayal. Issues of stability, consistency, acceptance and understanding are instrumental in facilitating trust. For example, women need to know that they will not be blamed for the abuse they have endured.

Author: Who'd be good to talk to?

Female patient A: Somebody who'd been abused by somebody and who was a survivor and came through it. And would say how it wasn't their fault and who learned to stop themself hurting themselves, and who knew some answers.
and

Female patient B: I think they should be counselled, but by somebody who understands and who will talk to them and try to make them feel that they're not guilty and it wasn't their fault. So they could make the person feel a bit better and not blame themselves.

A crucial factor in empowering abused women, therefore, is in the amelioration of feelings of guilt. This was reflected in most other accounts generated through the Q study, which also emphasized that women need to know they are not responsible for the abuse they endured. Hence, asking about the *event(s)* of abuse is replaced with concern about the psychological *effects* of abuse (see Chapter 9). Women's survival strategies can then be recognized and tracked. This refocusing is empowering because, as van der Kolk *et al.* (1994: 726) argue:

> Many therapists seem to lose sight of the fact that these patients have demonstrated the capacity to adapt to extreme circumstances, and, instead, are tempted to infantilise patients and control every aspect of their behaviour.

Empowerment comes in many different forms which are also reflected in the ways that different forms of therapy promote different routes into the taking of control. In the following section, key psychological treatment models are elaborated in terms of their application within secure mental health care systems, and regarding how they enable women to make choices within controlled and controlling environments.

Individualizing distress: psychological models of intervention

As argued, psychosocial forms of intervention have more direct relevance for sexually abused women patients than do medical interventions, such as pharmaceutical management of their symptoms (see Chapter 2). Accordingly, psychology has a potentially significant role to play in the development of more appropriate services for abused women in secure mental health care. For example, according to a cognitive model of distress, women's visions and voices are best understood in terms of unresolved trauma, rather than as psychotic symptoms *per se* (see Chapter 7). By locating symptoms in reference to life events, a cognitive approach provides directions for how aspects of a social recovery model of therapy might be developed. See Account two (Illustration 2) for an illustration of this approach.

Illustration 2

Account two: 'cognitive' model

According to this account, women who have experienced child sexual abuse would benefit most from a cognitive model of therapy. The aim of cognitive therapy is to directly address the negative impact of trauma and to mobilize women's existing survival capacities. This is thought to be achieved by helping women to re-evaluate their understanding of abuse so that they learn not to blame themselves, but to hold their abusers accountable. This is a specialist area of work that requires specialist counsellors in sexual abuse, as well as specialist training for all workers. Personal experience of sexual abuse is not thought to provide sufficient insight. As it is a specialist approach, untrained workers, who exceed their own limits, are thought to do

---

> more harm than good. Because the expression of painful feelings can, in the short-term, exaggerate dangerous behaviour, according to this account the general public require protection from these women. Hence, from this perspective, secure mental hospitals are thought to provide an appropriate level of containment during treatment. Therefore, it is not helpful to enable women to 'play the game' in order to get out.

According to the perspective illustrated in this account (voiced in the Q study by two male psychiatrists and one female occupational therapist), women's mental disorder is directly attributed to women's inability to resolve trauma associated with abusive experiences. The reason they remain traumatized is traced back to their distorted and confused thinking about what happened to them, as the following quote suggests.

> Well, feeling bad. I always felt dirty and wary of men. But I don't know really because I was sort of like difficult at the time. I wasn't really asked to, but I thought that if I was around them that sex was what was supposed to happen. You know I weren't thinking properly. I was only about 12 or 13.
>
> (female patient)

Cognitive therapy can be used to enable women to re-evaluate and rework their entrenched 'misreading' of the past and to develop more helpful survival strategies. A female clinical psychologist gives an example of this.

> At night when she was locked in her room everything about the past came up and all the issues about abuse, and she was seeing a vision of her abuser on the wardrobe and it would really frighten her. He was about to abuse her, and then she would try to tie her neck up. So what we were doing is trying to look at that in a lot of detail and to look at what she could do herself to try and stop that process becoming frightening. It's about her developing more coping strategies.

In the short-term, the coping strategies of many women in secure care may be quite dangerous (tying ligatures for example). Therefore, as this account suggests, for some women some level of security may be beneficial. As one female nurse notes: 'I think it's about people understanding that containment could be therapeutic.' Unfortunately, as noted, locking women up does not necessarily keep them safe. Women in secure mental health care settings sometimes share space with men who have committed sexual offences, and sometimes are assaulted by them or have relationships with them. In such circumstances containment is clearly compromised and cognitive therapy may be misdirected. Telling women what they already know (sex offenders make poor life partners, for example), does not facilitate change, particularly when they are restricted to living in close proximity to them. Additionally, as indicated Chapter 7, it is important that templates for recovery do not promote a too narrow version of femininity. A more flexible approach to cognitive therapy that is closely attuned to the misuse of power (within both social and therapeutic relationships) is more likely to be achieved if, as the 'empowerment' account suggests, workers have access to specialist teaching on childhood sexual abuse, and patients access to specialist counsellors. Without access to appropriate training and support, workers are more likely to abuse the use of power within therapeutic relationships. A female clinical psychologist gives an example of this.

> It was to do with a nursing staff who was not qualified, doing sexual abuse counselling with a patient I was also seeing. Because a patient raised to me in a session that this person had touched her inappropriately I had to bring that up. This person was asked to withdraw sensitively, but just cut himself off from the sessions and that was very punishing for this patient. I think it's just this kind of desire to get right in there and talk to them about their abuse, without the right kind of experience really or supervision perhaps.

A cognitive approach, when appropriately applied, enables women to gain greater control over their lives. This occurs when women are helped to understand how their beliefs about self and others have been shaped by unresolved trauma in their lives and by encouraging women to develop alternative, less harmful, coping strategies. This does not have to mean that women stop self-harming (although this is often a goal in normative psychological therapy – see Chapter 2), but that women develop greater control of the strategies that they use to survive (see Chapter 9). The need for patients to make sense of the specific impact of child sexual abuse in therapy, however, is only one aspect of developing more empowering services within secure mental health care. Another major problem that detained patients face is that of institutionalization.

Women in secure mental hospitals are detained for between three and four times as long as their women peers in prison and longer than their male peers in secure hospitals (Aitken and Logan 2004). Hence, there is a great need to address the impact of incarceration itself. The aim is to countermand the ways in which the secure environment reinforces dependency and isolation. Therefore, this type of approach draws on behavioural theory to empower abused women who are also incarcerated. The use of behavioural theory to address the needs of sexually abused women has gathered momentum in recent years. For example, Dialectical Behaviour Therapy (particularly for those women also diagnosed with borderline personality disorder) has been positively evaluated (the American National Institute of Mental Health NIMH 2006b), although not all service users find it personally beneficial (Spandler and Warner 2007). In the following account (voiced by a female and male patient in the Q study), the more general benefits of adopting a 'behavioural' model for intervention with women patients in secure care are elaborated. See Illustration 3.

Illustration 3

Account three: 'behavioural' model

From this perspective, sexual abuse plays a peripheral role in directing treatment concerns. The emphasis is on remedial work to counteract the impact of institutionalization. Hence, women need to be understood in the context of their whole lives, including their specific racial and cultural background, as it is to this that they must be helped to return. A 'common-sense' approach is adopted. These women need practical help (such as attending educational classes and workshop activities) rather than therapy or counselling. They need friends more than therapists as they need the opportunity to develop 'normal' relationships in order integrate back into mainstream society. In particular, women need help to enable them to learn to trust men again. Thus, mixed activities and wards are useful because they provide women with real opportunities for developing normal relationships with men.

Additionally, links should be encouraged outside of the hospital, otherwise institutionalization, and the stigma and isolation associated with sexual abuse, will only be reinforced. Where sexual abuse continues to trouble patients, this should be addressed outside of women's primary relationships. Workers should not share their own experiences of sexual abuse with women patients, and patients should not be encouraged to talk to each other about these experiences. Rather, there is a need for specialist counsellors in childhood sexual abuse who can keep therapy private. Whilst sexual abuse may be relevant, because of greater concerns about incarceration, addressing women's index offence should be the main focus of therapy. This is a pragmatic concern as women will not be released unless the index offence has been addressed.

According to the perspective illustrated in this account, women's powerlessness is partially determined by the gradual erosion of their living skills through prolonged experiences of institutionalization. As one male teacher of patients noted:

> It must be a hell of an adjustment because some of them have been here a long time. Some of them don't know how to do the shopping.

Therefore, empowerment cannot be achieved purely by addressing past experiences of abuse. Indeed, women's original problems associated with abuse may be long gone, resolved even. It is now their general inability to function in the world that is compromised. Therefore, there may be a need to adopt a 'common-sense' and pragmatic approach to treatment for this particular group of abused women. This is essentially a 'behavioural' approach in that the aim is to provide real opportunities for women to redevelop their practical living skills. For example, in order to increase motivation, women need to be encouraged to believe that they will, one day, leave secure care. This can be achieved by helping women maintain contact with the outside world. As one male psychiatrist suggested:

> I'm a firm believer in getting people out of the hospital as much as possible. I think it's very depressing to be locked up in a place like this. The more they see of the real world, then the more they are reminded that there is a real world out there. We can forget that and become enmeshed in the internal world.

Accordingly, anything that prolongs detention is thought to be unhelpful. This may be one reason why, in the 'behavioural' model account, therapy for sexual abuse is thought best kept private as general knowledge within the hospital increases the pathologization of women and restricts their ordinary life expectations of privacy:

> I won't talk about the rapes. I don't think that it's right to talk to them [members of staff] about it, because they know me. And I won't talk to them about it, even more if they put it in your notes. You don't want all the staff to read about it because it's not personal then.
>
> (female patient)

According to this perspective, women need friends more than therapists because they need to relearn how to *do* ordinary relationships. Workers can help, therefore, by acting as a 'friend' might as this provides a model for what should happen in women's everyday lives.

> Well sometimes you calm them down, have a good little talk, give
> them a cup of tea and give them a cigarette and just relax a bit, to
> iron out their tensions.
>
> (male teacher of patients)

In this account, enabling women to develop 'normal' relationships is about
their ultimate reintegration into mainstream heterosexual society. Hence,
there is great emphasis placed on encouraging women's actual relationships
with men as this is a key skill that women are thought to need in order to
negotiate daily living:

> Make them feel comfortable around men again, that's one of the
> things they can do. Make them feel confident enough to talk to
> men about it. Not talk about the abuse, just generally talk to them,
> to make it easier for women when they come in. Because there's
> always gonna be men about, you can't just not have them.
>
> (female patient)

This account draws attention to the dangers of adopting a pragmatic
approach to understanding women and their needs, as also argued in
Chapter 7. This is because if insufficient attention is paid to questioning
what counts as normality then intervention will be orientated around the
uncritical acceptance that reintegration with men is the benchmark for
recovery (from sexual abuse *and* institutionalization). Hence, narratives of
'pragmatics' and 'common sense' should always be problematized, and
hidden assumptions explored. Nevertheless, remedial social intervention is
an extremely important aspect of work with women in secure care because
over time women's ability to function in the outside world decreases. This
account also reminds us that childhood sexual abuse should never be
assumed to be the only and primary issue that circumscribes women's lives.
In the following section women's social relationships are elaborated further.

Socializing distress: communal models of intervention

Hospitals are not inert contexts in which therapy takes place, but are active
communities in which patients live and professionals work. As the 'behavioural' account suggests, the institution itself has a profound role to play
in mediating women's recovery. And as suggested in previous chapters,
powerlessness and ongoing abuse negatively contribute to women's mental
health, and this negative contribution is fortified through the general
erosion of living skills and motivation. Wider practices within the hospital
community are, therefore, relevant in determining how to help women in
secure environments. A key factor that influences the quality of service that
women patients receive is how well the multidisciplinary team is

functioning. Various factors impact on the ability of teams to work together; some of these are now highlighted in the following account (voiced by one male patient). See Illustration 4.

Illustration 4

Account four: 'multidisciplinary' model

The central feature of this account is the emphasis placed on the need for a unified and consistent approach to treatment that can provide structure and routine in women's lives. From this perspective, until staff can agree on a model for understanding child sexual abuse they will only succeed in confusing the patient more. Further, until professionals stop fighting with each other women's needs will be overlooked and women's freedom to express themselves will be undermined. Cooperation and consistency are thought to be facilitated through workers sharing their knowledge about patients with each other. Keeping therapeutic discussions secret reinforces divisions between workers. Where there is professional conflict, therapy should be avoided because workers are unable to cope with any additional disturbance and women should wait until they are released before they talk about their experiences of sexual abuse. Ultimately, however, intervention is wider than the hospital and needs to occur at a societal level as well.

This account reflects the idea that in order to encourage and sustain a therapeutic environment there is need for open communication between workers who share a common vision of recovery. The need for teamwork and clear communication is written into every aspect of work around child abuse (e.g. Corby 2000; Reder and Duncan 1999; Reder *et al.* 1993; WHO 2006b). Although it may be dangerous for some patients in secure care to be open (about index offences, for example) with other patients, it is crucial that professionals communicate with each other. Over-restriction of information can lead to divisions between members of staff and instigate incoherent and inconsistent treatment regimes that are detrimental to the patients they care for. As one male psychiatrist argues:

> If there are lots of people dealing with the same patient, there is nothing worse than for the patient to perceive that there may be different approaches. If you'd decided you were going to tackle their problems in a certain way, you should actually become consistent otherwise the patients get confused. Not only do they get confused but there are those that wish to, and will, exploit those

splits and they end up splitting staff. In the long term it's not going to help that person. So, you need to be consistent, you need to be cooperative, because I believe everybody has something to contribute, not least the patient, do not ever forget that.

It is crucial, therefore, that professionals find ways of ensuring positive relationships not just with patients, but also with their colleagues. In closed institutions, inter-professional tensions have a profound effect on patient care precisely because unresolved feelings remain within the system and cannot be discharged elsewhere. If professionals cannot collaborate with each other, it is patients who ultimately suffer. In such situations it may be best to avoid starting treatment that may be sabotaged by other workers:

> There have been occasions where the conclusion has been that it's not in the patient's best interest to continue the work and those decisions have been reached on the grounds that really the professionals are not able to get it together. It's not written up like that but that's the bottom line of what it's about.
>
> (female social worker)

As this quote suggests, when teams are so fragmented it is little wonder that women in secure mental health care too often receive a poor service. Because inter-professional conflict is thought to be harder to address in large institutions, smaller secure units have been proposed as a solution to this problem. The idea is that professional fear and anxiety is easier to contain within smaller care groups and, hence, patients' individual needs and choices can be accommodated more readily. Also, it may be that smaller units allow the external rules that govern life in large institutions to be navigated better and the effects of institutionalization minimized. As one male psychiatrist explained:

> At the end of the day we concentrate on what is required of us, by the outside, by society, by the government, by whoever. They determine rules in the hospital which are designed to try and make it reasonably safe for people inside and for people outside. But at the expense of sometimes giving people as much personal autonomy [as they need] because the risks attached to it are considered to be too great really. And one way of reducing those risks might be to actually have smaller groups. If you put me in one of those wards, you know, I'd be doing the same thing within a few weeks. In society most of us don't live with twenty people all the time even if they were, you know, not psychiatrically disturbed.

156

If workers are to manage their own fears and anxieties, they must, as indicated throughout this chapter, be recognized as being in need of support. Workers need the opportunity to reflect on their own values and attitudes regarding the women they work with. This perspective is illustrated further in the 'milieu therapy' account (voiced by two female patients, one male patient, one female social worker and one male nurse). See Illustration 5.

Illustration 5

Account five: 'milieu therapy' model

The distinguishing feature of this account is the focus on the overall context in which women are understood. From this perspective, it is very important to remember that women are patients and not criminals. Thus they need care and not punishment and are more in need of therapy than 'practical' help, such as education. According to this perspective, although women's views about treatment are important, women should not be relied on to find their own solutions to their own problems. Rather, workers should provide guidance, and hence specialist training to understand the effects of child sexual abuse is required by the workers. More generally, workers need opportunity to reflect on their own values. This is crucial because, from this perspective, workers can never be objective and so need to take responsibility for the attitudes and opinions they bring to their work. Currently, there is too little emphasis placed on using 'politically correct' language and behaviour with women. Women need to be treated with respect, and an understanding of gender differences is crucial to this. This is because women have different needs from men regarding sexual abuse and, hence, require different treatment strategies. This is about everybody's values and about women's everyday experiences. Therefore, from this perspective the support and care that women receive on the wards should take precedence over specialist therapy off the wards.

This account, like the 'behavioural' and 'multidisciplinary' accounts, draws attention to wider social factors that impact on women's recovery within secure care. From a 'milieu therapy' perspective the focus is on the attitudes and values that workers bring into their work and which circumscribe daily living. This is why this account reinforces the need to view women as patients and not criminals. Therefore, from this perspective it is the wider hospital milieu that is considered to be the defining feature of intervention. The belief is that 'the social structure of the ward, group atmosphere and ward morale [are] important elements in the therapeutic endeavour of psychiatry' (Pilgrim and Rogers 1993: 125). Hence, life on the ward is considered to have as great, if not greater, impact on women's recovery than specialist therapy does.

The continual need for self-reflection is perhaps particularly crucial for ward-based staff because they, more than others, must continually negotiate the contradictions between being both jailer and carer. Self-reflection also invites, as this account suggests, a critical look at issues of gender and culture. It reflects the understanding that mentally disordered women have different needs from men (WHO 2000). As one female teacher of patients explained:

> I think women are more difficult and demand more staff, time and energy. I don't think there's enough facilities for them, I don't think they're 'specialled' enough.

In order to address women's particular racial and cultural backgrounds, as this account suggests, there is a need for workers to reflect on their own values regarding social structural hierarchies (as evidenced in the need to use 'politically correct language', for example). Unfortunately, the culture of secure hospitals does not necessarily support processes of self-reflection. As one female nurse observed:

> I think it's absolutely essential before you start working with child sexual abuse that there has to be some staff training and some awareness of some of the issues. And that requires the staff to actually look at themselves a bit. And I mean that's a bit painful. And I don't think many of them are happy to do that. It's not part of our culture. It's a bit macho in our culture: 'we don't have problems, by God, we cope.'

If workers are implicitly encouraged to avoid addressing their feelings about the work they do, tensions and rivalries are more likely to permeate the service that is offered to women patients. Workers, already feeling under pressure, may then project their responsibilities onto the patients themselves. For example, narratives of 'empowerment' may be deployed to defer responsibility for women's treatment rather than share power with the patients themselves. For example, women patients in this study frequently reported that when they were invited to *find their own solutions to their own problems* (statement 53, in Table 8.1) they experienced this as a professional strategy for abnegating care and responsibility. Sometimes women patients want professionals do the work they are employed to do. As a female social worker explained:

> I said to [a woman patient] 'you're telling me that this isn't enough, but what do you want?' And she said to me 'well, I've been in

fucking institutions all my life. I'm institutionalized. I don't know what I want. I don't know what's available. I don't know what is left. You're the expert. You're paid lots of money. Stop sending me sodding questionnaires and work it out for yourselves'.

Reconstructing the evidence base: making practice principles explicit

As this chapter demonstrates, there are multiple factors that shape policy and practices in respect of women in secure mental health care. For example, wider cultural apathy and hostility frequently inhibit the development of progressive approaches to working with detained women patients. And inter-professional rivalries can compound societal and institutional abuse and neglect which necessarily undermines women's recovery. Therefore, in thinking through good practice with detained and abused women patients, it is necessary to remain mindful of local, social, professional, institutional, political and economic forces that ultimately restrict treatment options. At the same time it is possible to develop a general knowledge base about how to work with detained and abused women that can translate across geographical and cultural contexts and have relevance beyond secure services too.

In this chapter I have drawn on empirical data to identify and illustrate some of the key factors that would need to be considered in developing holistic, recovery-orientated practices. Specifically, I have argued that detained and abused women would benefit from flexible systems of care that are targeted around individual needs and which are reflective of the social and cultural context of women's lives. Underpinning such services should be an explicit, yet critical, commitment to empowerment that promotes partnership between service users and providers and in so doing shares responsibility for change and development. What 'empowerment' means for different women, however, cannot be predetermined in any absolute way because, as indicated, women may be 'empowered' in many different ways.

For example, some abused women who are detained in secure hospitals benefit from medication whilst others do not. Some may be more institutionalized than others and hence need greater assistance with the re-establishment of general living skills. And women around the world may need different forms of help in order to manage local pressures and demands. However, although women have individual and unique experiences, they still share a common need to exercise some control in their lives. They also share a common need for non-exploitative and non-abusive relationships. Hence, 'best practice' (regarding 'empowerment', for example) may be better understood as being about values, ethics and principles rather than being about determining a specific template for intervention that would suit every woman.

159

This approach, therefore, calls for a shift from defining 'which technique is best for this problem?' to 'what underlying principles are associated with individually defined "best outcomes"'. This move, from technique to principle, means that a much wider understanding of 'what works' can be evaluated and applied (see Spandler and Warner 2007). It is this values-based understanding of 'best practice' that the research referenced in Part 2 of the book (Chapters 5–8) has sought to address. My aim was to use the empirical data to explore what kinds of values, processes and quality of relationship benefit abused women in secure mental health care. This approach is necessarily theoretically saturated because 'what works' is always socially and culturally localized. Norms (regarding gender and sexuality, for example) are there to be explored in terms of what works, for whom, in which situations, rather than assumed to be always right. This is also why it is crucial to have an explicit ethical framework that can be used to track language use as the different ways we describe problems and their solutions gives rise to very different understandings, treatment strategies and ways of being with abused women.

For example, I have suggested that if the negative effects of women's experiences of abuse are to be mediated, then concern should focus on the *effects*, rather than the *events* of abuse. Events are located in the past and hence invite little self-reflection on the part of workers. By contrast, consideration of the effects of abuse invites workers to think through how their own relationships reinforce or challenge earlier betrayals. Such an approach does not predetermine that abuse should always be spoken about. Rather it flags up key principles that are relevant, whether they relate to ward-based activity, specialist therapy or other contexts of work. For example, in a criminal investigation, where the focus is on abuse-events (e.g. whether a rape occurred or not), rather than abuse-effects (e.g. feelings about being raped), it may still be more helpful and effective to adopt the principle of a non-coercive, non-abusive approach to questioning the victim.

In this book, identifying key principles for intervention comes out of the triangulated relationship between theory, research and practice. The empirical data referenced here provides building blocks for elaborating how to translate ethics and politics into practice. Hence, it builds on the theoretical discussions of feminism and post-structuralism (as theories and practices) that began in Part 1 (Chapters 1–4), and which have guided my critique throughout. In the final section of this book I draw on these principles and values, identified first theoretically, and then elaborated in more detail empirically, to demonstrate how such ideas can be translated into practice. This is not only in terms of abused women in secure mental health services, but includes work with children as well as adults in a number of key therapy and legal practice arenas. Therefore, the final section provides 'practice-based' evidence (Spandler and Warner 2007) for the ideas that have been developed as an 'evidence base' for practice in the first two parts of the book.

Table 8.1 Statements from the 'treatment' Q study

1. Women patients should be helped to recognize the abuse they have suffered was not their fault.
2. Child and family services should be invested in – by the time women get to special hospitals it is too late.
3. The most important aspect of treatment for women who have been sexually abused is to find someone they can trust to talk to.
4. Too much emphasis is given to planning for the future on women leaving special hospitals and where they will go.
5. Spending more money on resources for women patients is not the answer to providing a better service for them.
6. Women patients will not be helped if they are encouraged to blame all their problems on sexual abuse.
7. It is vital that women can expect continuity and stability in their treatment and the people who care for them.
8. Too much emphasis is placed on staff explaining to women patients what is happening to them and why.
9. When making decisions about treatment women patients' views should come second to the views of the professionals who care for them.
10. It is important to get women to talk about their experiences of sexual abuse – whether they want to or not.
11. Creative therapy techniques, such as writing, artwork and drama, have little to offer women patients who have been sexually abused.
12. Staff should have specialist training to understand childhood sexual abuse and the effects it has on women patients.
13. Staff will NOT be able to meet the needs of women patients who have been sexually abused until support networks for staff themselves are provided.
14. The needs of sexually abused women patients should NOT be more important than protecting the public from some very dangerous women.
15. Women patients would gain little from meeting other women who have survived sexual abuse and who have stopped hurting themselves.
16. Medication has a role to play in the management of some symptoms of childhood sexual abuse, such as depression.
17. Women patients should be encouraged to talk to each other about their experiences of sexual abuse.
18. When working with women patients who have been sexually abused the abuse should be the main focus of therapy.
19. Staff need to address their own feelings about sexual abuse before they can help women patients with their feelings about being abused.
20. Managers should spend less time with patients and more time getting on with the job of administrating.
21. Therapy for child sexual abuse could be improved by learning from therapies which help people overcome other kinds of trauma, e.g. the help offered to torture victims.
22. Staff need to recognize that they can NEVER be objective and need to take responsibility for the attitudes and opinions they bring to their work with women.
23. It is every member of staff's responsibility to understand issues around child sexual abuse and NOT leave it to those 'that are interested' or 'the experts'.

continues overleaf

Table 8.1 Continued

24. One of the main issues in therapy with women patients will be around grieving for the relationships (with family and children) which they have lost as a result of being abused.
25. Sexually abused women patients will be best helped by staff who themselves have been sexually abused as children.
26. Staff who do NOT recognize their own limits and attempt to do work for which they are NOT trained will do more harm than good.
27. It is harmful for women to talk about their experiences of being sexually abused because it only makes them more disturbed.
28. Unless women patients are encouraged to look at and accept their capacity to hurt others as well as be hurt, they will NEVER recover.
29. The support and care that women receive on the wards should take second place to specialist therapy off the wards.
30. The aim of therapy should be to support women through the pain, rather than trying to take the pain away.
31. Whilst men remain in positions of power within special hospitals, women patients' needs will NEVER be met.
32. The needs of sexually abused women patients would be best served by a designated service specifically for women.
33. Staff should help women patients understand their behaviour and mental processes, and NOT make judgements about them.
34. Psycho-dynamic therapy is the best treatment for sexually abused women patients.
35. Cognitive approaches have much to offer sexually abused women patients.
36. Psychiatric diagnosis should be the starting point of any effective treatment plan.
37. Women patients would benefit from LESS structure in their lives and LESS of a routine to follow.
38. Decisions about the treatment of women patients should be negotiated between workers and NOT be made by workers acting independently.
39. It is WRONG to suggest that until professionals stop fighting with each other, women's' needs will be overlooked.
40. The primary aim of working with women patients is to provide them with skills for living.
41. A system which locks women up and takes away their ability to make choices can only ever reinforce abused women as victims and NOT survivors.
42. Work with women patients who have been sexually abused is best informed by a feminist understanding of male abuse of power.
43. Links should be encouraged outside of the hospital otherwise the stigma and isolation associated with sexual abuse will be reinforced.
44. Until staff can agree on a model for understanding childhood sexual abuse they will only succeed in confusing the patient more.
45. It is important to credit women patients with the strength they have shown in surviving both sexual abuse and 'the system'.
46. Too much emphasis is placed on using 'politically correct' language and behaviour with women patients.
47. Sexually abused women patients will only recover when they can forgive the person(s) who abused them.
48. Women patients should be treated as individuals with individual needs and problems.

continues

Table 8.1 Continued

49. There is NO need for specialist counsellors in child sexual abuse.
50. Women patients would NOT benefit from work being undertaken with their families (who are often the ones who have hurt them).
51. The most important issue when working with sexually abused women patients is to treat them with respect.
52. Special hospitals should be closed down and smaller specialist units opened to replace them.
53. Women patients should be helped to recognize and mobilize the resources within themselves to find their own solutions to their own problems.
54. Women patients who have been sexually abused need to be taught about why children are silenced and how powerless they are.
55. The most effective way to help women patients who have been sexually abused is at a societal level because it is society which is the problem.
56. The best way women patients can be helped is to help them 'play the game' so they can get out and deal with their sexual abuse on the outside.
57. Mixed activities and wards are useful for women patients because they give them the opportunity of developing normal relationships with men.
58. The racial and cultural background of women patients is NOT important in deciding the right treatment for sexually abused women.
59. An important aspect of therapy for sexually abused women patients is to learn to trust men again.
60. Psychological treatment units where psychologists have a daily input would benefit women patients.
61. Staff should adopt a 'common-sense' approach to the problems of women patients: they need friends more than therapists.
62. Women patients will only be motivated to change when a limit of time is placed on their sentences.
63. Therapy and support on demand should NOT be given because it encourages women to remain dependent.
64. Staff should share everything they know about a patient with each other – keeping therapy a secret is NOT useful.
65. Women patients need to be understood in the context of their whole lives.
66. Women patients have too much freedom to express their feelings (e.g. crying, shouting) and should learn to control them.
67. Women patients should have access to a range of treatment options as it is unlikely one method will suit all women.
68. Instead of blaming women when things go wrong, staff would be better blaming themselves for failing to understand their patients.
69. The main purpose of treatment for women patients should be to address the index offence.
70. The needs of women patients who have been sexually abused are different from the needs of sexually abused male patients and so different treatment strategies need developing.
71. It is important to remember that women are patients and NOT criminals and are in need of care and NOT punishment.
72. Sexually abused women would benefit more from practical help (e.g. attending education classes and workshop activities) than from therapy or counselling.

Part 3

PRACTICE

As a clinical psychologist, my interest in theory and research is focused through my desire to develop applicable frameworks for practice. This part of the book, therefore, applies some key principles, identified theoretically in Part 1, and developed empirically in Part 2, for working with women, girls and childhood sexual abuse. I draw on my experience of working in a variety of service contexts in order to provide examples of how to apply feminism and post-structuralism to a range of practice issues. These include sexual abuse psychotherapy with women and girls (Chapter 9); child protection systems regarding sexually abused girls (Chapter 10) and domestically abused mothers (Chapter 11); and abused women and girls in secure care contexts (Chapter 12). Thus, Part 3 provides 'practice-based' evidence for the approach developed throughout the book. My aim is to illustrate the utility of adopting a social recovery model of intervention that challenges the despair that haunts many traditional approaches to working with abused women and girls. A brief epilogue draws the book to a close.

Chapter 9 provides an introduction to Visible Therapy (Warner 2000b, 2001a, 2003b), which is a critical, social and recovery orientated therapeutic approach to working with women and girls who have experienced childhood sexual abuse. Feminist and post-structuralist theories are used to rework key psychoanalytic principles that make sense of the relationship between past experiences and current life practices. The aim is to challenge abuser-constructed reality by exploring how the tactics of abuse determine how women and girls come to understand themselves and their relationships in the world. Emphasis is placed on validating and understanding clients' attempts to cope with experiences of abuse, such as when 'hearing voices' and/or 'seeing visions' or using self-harm.

Chapter 10 develops the Visible Therapy approach further by applying it to child protection legal proceedings with sexually abused girls, specifically in respect of addressing the role of the clinical psychologist expert witness. My aim is to encourage a feminist critical-justice agenda by describing a practice framework that socially locates expert knowledge such that the multiple factors that shape understandings about child sexual abuse and

165

child welfare are made explicit. The chapter provides a brief overview of criminal and civil litigation relevant to matters of child sexual abuse as reflected in both local and international legal practices. In order to illustrate how making social frameworks visible enables greater clarity regarding expert knowledge, I then demonstrate the use of social framework evidence in the various processes of legal instruction, assessment and evidentiary reporting.

Chapter 11 explores the issue of child protection, this time in terms of the intersections between child sexual abuse and domestic violence. My aim is to address some of the key issues that domestically abused mothers of sexually abused children face in child care proceedings in order to enable more progressive and supportive practices with them and with their children. Some of the problems associated with repositioning domestic violence within the child protection arena are discussed and some of the benchmarks against which mothers are judged are deconstructed and socially located. Practices that encourage safety are described and the limits of conceptualizing abused mothers as victims are explored.

In Chapter 12, I address the particular needs of women and girls who are detained in secure care contexts. The chapter focuses on those who have experienced childhood sexual abuse and have been diagnosed with 'borderline personality disorder'. Personality problems are reconceptualized as relationship difficulties and the chapter demonstrates how this change in understanding can be helpful in sustaining social recovery-orientated therapeutic work with sexually abused women and girls in secure care systems. The relationships between sexual abuse, drug and alcohol use, homelessness, and sex work are used to contextualize this work. The impact of the service milieu, in shaping therapeutic intervention in secure settings, is addressed and therapeutic practices in respect of self-harm are elaborated. I argue for the need to maintain a radical political agenda at both local and international levels. This point is further discussed in the Epilogue where I summarize some of the main themes of the book.

I highlight what I consider to be revolutionary ways of understanding women, girls and child sexual abuse in the inter-related areas of theory, research and practice. Specifically, I argue for an approach that is based on social recovery-orientated principles. I conclude that whilst recovery cannot, nor should not, be predefined for all women and girls, in order to work towards recovery we still need to dream, to have some ideas about where we want to go: to imagine Utopia.

The case examples referred to in Part 3 are based on women and girls I have met through my clinical work. The names used are fictional, and identifying characteristics and details have been removed, altered and/or merged in order to safeguard my clients' anonymity.

9

VISIBLE THERAPY WITH WOMEN AND GIRLS

Reworking the effects of childhood sexual abuse

Introduction

In this chapter I demonstrate how feminism and post-structuralism can be used to inform and enable therapeutic work with women and girls who have experienced childhood sexual abuse. As Chapter 4 illustrates, feminists have argued that because child sexual abuse represents a worldwide social problem it is not simply a *personal* experience, but is also a *political* issue. This is important because without a coordinated political response those that are made subject to abuse remain isolated and vulnerable. A political analysis also calls into question the ways in which those that have been abused are treated by the so-called helping professions. This is not only in reference to the additional abuse and neglect women routinely face in mental health and social care services around the world (as noted in Part 2, Chapters 5–8). It is also in terms of the ways in which therapies, whether psychological or pharmaceutical, can be used to undermine women's individual and collective empowerment by ensuring women's experiences of abuse remain internalized as personal problems.

Psychotherapy, therefore, can be as oppressive as psychopharmacology and, as post-structuralism reminds us, the benefits of either one should not be assumed. Nevertheless, as a clinical psychologist it is crucial to me that the theoretical work I do has practical application, and therefore that – as signalled in Chapter 8 – general principles can be identified and used as a knowledge base for practice. Hence, in this chapter I illustrate some key principles that, I argue, can be drawn on to guide progressive forms of psychotherapy. Specifically, I demonstrate how the ethics, politics, principles and values, identified theoretically in Part 1 (Chapters 1–4), and then elaborated empirically in Part 2 (Chapters 5–8), can be applied in the form of a critical, recovery-orientated psychotherapy for women and girls who have experienced child sexual abuse. I have called this approach Visible Therapy (Warner 2000b, 2001a, 2003b), a brief overview of which now follows. Key components of Visible Therapy are then described, discussed and illustrated with case examples. These include the nature of the therapeutic relationship;

and the ways in which identity practices, abuser tactics, coping strategies, and endings and reflections are addressed in therapy.

Introduction to Visible Therapy

Visible Therapy has been developed for working with abused children and adults. It is called *Visible* Therapy in order to draw attention to the need for transparency in both *what* is talked about and *how* talking proceeds in therapeutic relationships. I know that the notion of 'visibility' is problematic because all knowledge is partial and marked by vested interests. In Visible Therapy this term is used to highlight the need to trace and be explicit about the vested interests and ideas that inform therapeutic work and which construct therapeutic realities. This is in contrast to abusers who deliberately obscure the operations of power that structure unequal and exploitative sexual relationships.

As noted in Part 1, I trace my 'vested interests' back to feminism and post-structuralism and through some of the revolutionary struggles of feminism and mental health activism as outlined in Chapter 4. Visible Therapy has also been developed in respect of empirically derived principles and practices (see Part 2); and through my knowledge and critique of mainstream mental health approaches. Visible Therapy, in this sense, is a form of what has been termed 'critical therapy', which is defined as:

> a response to modern psychology from the inside that enriches its discipline. It is a deconstructive moment in its institution that is not anarchic but affirmative, in the sense that it attempts to think it through.
>
> (Larner 2002: 16)

In this chapter, I aim to think through how psychotherapy can become more responsive to, and respectful of, women and girls who have been sexually abused. As highlighted in Chapter 8, this includes adopting a flexible, individually targeted and culturally aware therapy that promotes 'empowerment' through the active partnership between client and therapist. Hence, as psychoanalysis suggests, the therapeutic relationship is crucial not simply in terms of a context in which to reflect on current and past relationship experiences, but in terms of providing alternative, non-abusive ones (see Malan 1979/1984). Therefore, the first step in Visible Therapy is to consider some of the processes involved in enabling democracy and partnership in therapeutic relationships. Once a 'safe-enough' context for talking has been identified, the specific issues that are raised by experiences of childhood sexual abuse can then be explored. In Visible Therapy, and as both feminism and post-structuralism suggest, this involves tracking language use in order to understand and challenge its effects.

As argued in Chapter 8, this involves a shift in focus from the *events* of abuse (for example, rape etc.) to a focus on the *effects* of abuse (feelings and thoughts about, and behaviour relative to, rape etc.). As argued in Chapter 7, abuse-effects can be understood not only in terms of what the abused *do* (emotionally, cognitively, and/or behaviourally), but also in terms of *who* the abused are (that is how they are represented by themselves and others). Therefore, a second task of Visible Therapy is to explore how the abused identity and sense of self is constructed through, and affected by, experiences of childhood sexual abuse. In Visible Therapy, abuse-effects are understood to relate to the particular (psychological, social and physical) tactics of control utilized by the abuser. Hence, a third task of Visible Therapy is to identify the tactics used by the abuser to ensure compliance, in order to explore the effects of these on the abused.

Because the control-tactics used by abusers are viewed as being forged within, and relative to, the particular cultural context in which the abuse takes place, in Visible Therapy connections are made between individual acts of abuser-control and general cultural permissions and prohibitions that support abusive relationships. Finally, Visible Therapy considers how abuse-effects are maintained and shaped through subsequent and present day experiences. Specifically, Visible Therapy aims to validate women's active attempts at survival and to explore how women's coping strategies connect to both past and present worries and experiences (cf. Malan 1979/1984). The ultimate aim is to promote empowerment and recognize recovery.

Whilst it is beyond the scope of this chapter to chart the many different and competing abuse therapies that exist, there are some psychotherapies that make a significant contribution to the development of Visible Therapy. As already indicated, the Visible Therapy approach is informed by some mainstream therapeutic traditions, notably psychoanalysis (Freud 1977, 1984, 1986). This is in terms of providing a psychological framework for understanding the (constant) processes of identity formation, survival and the connections between past and present life (see also Malan 1979/1984), albeit recast through feminism and post-structuralism (see Warner 2000b, 2001a, 2003b). For example, in Visible Therapy 'defence mechanisms' become the more validating 'coping strategies' and heteronormativity is challenged rather than accepted as the benchmark for recovery. As a critical form of psychotherapy, Visible Therapy also draws on a wide range of critical therapeutic approaches – particularly feminist ones (see Chapter 4). As a post-structuralist therapy it also shares some commonality with other social constructionist approaches that focus attention on the productive effects of language, notably narrative therapy (see White 1995). And like other radical approaches to mental health, Visible Therapy specifically advocates for recovery-orientated and reflexive practices (see ibid.; the American Surgeon General 2006b; Coleman 1999). The particular ways in which mainstream and critical understandings are woven together in Visible Therapy are described below.

Enabling collaboration and promoting therapeutic democracy

As noted, the first step in practising Visible Therapy is to consider some of the processes involved in enabling democracy and partnership throughout therapeutic relationships. The aim is to promote a forthright, but collaborative, exchange of views in order to help clients to feel more confident in their ability to sort through and make sense of their own thoughts, feelings and behaviour. Collaborative relationships between client and therapist are valued because successful outcomes are more likely to occur when clients feel that they have some control over what happens to them – that is they feel empowered. Before the therapeutic relationship is established, therefore, it is important to consider how the private domain of therapy is shaped by external demands. For example, in state services, therapists often occupy diverse roles that require them to work with a range of professionals also involved in providing a service to the client. This is particularly so in child and family work and within secure care settings. When this is the case, it may not be possible to work collaboratively with everybody. It is important, therefore, to consider when collaboration with other professionals or family members becomes a collusive act that works against the primary client (MacKinnon 1998).

In order to make the practices of collaboration and decision-making visible I always seek to explore with my clients and referrers what has prompted them to come or advocate for therapy. When the client is not likely to be the main referrer, as in child and family work or secure service settings, I try to meet with the primary referrer first. It may be this person who most requires a service. Non-abusing mothers sometimes feel too guilty to ask for support for themselves and other professionals may lack confidence in their practice. In such cases I might end up working with the mother or providing consultation to other professionals. If this preparatory work is not entered into, clients can feel forced into accepting therapy on someone else's behalf. Additionally, because a confessional culture is so pervasive in westernized societies there is a too ready and common assumption that talking about child sexual abuse is a 'good thing'. Silence may secure abuse, but it also sometimes provides protection from difficult feelings and unwanted interventions from others (Warner 2001a, 2003b). Therefore I accept that talking about abuse is not useful for everybody, and that if clients are reluctant to speak there will be a good reason.

The first task of Visible Therapy, therefore, is to explore with clients what their reasons for speaking or not speaking are about. They may fear they will not be able to cope with their feelings. They may need additional support or changes in life circumstance in order to enable them to feel safe enough to talk. Clients also need information about the particular therapy on offer. Whilst any knowledge is provisional, therapists should still provide an account of how therapy might work. Clients also need information about the limits set on confidentiality by legal requirements which may override the wishes of client and therapist. Sometimes clients need to be given explicit frameworks for gaining information without disclosing too much about themselves. For example, we might talk hypothetically about 'someone who was abused'. Through these multiple processes of enquiry both client and therapist take the first steps in developing a collaborative relationship. I accept clients who may have some ambivalence about therapy, but on balance want to give it a go, and for whom there is enough safety, support and stability to begin the process.

In order to further enable collaboration, many feminist and narrative therapies have endeavoured to democratize the therapeutic relationship by deliberately valuing client wisdom over the expertise of the therapist (Denborough 2002; White 1995). However, if the only way clients get to feel big is by therapists making themselves small, therapists have missed the point (Warner 2000b). When people adopt positions that reinforce, albeit reversed, hierarchical structures, negotiation and democracy is seldom the result. Of course, clients are never only, nor should they be positioned as, passive recipients of the therapist's expertise as this reinforces victimhood (Kaye 1999). Conversely, to deny my knowledge – about sexual abuse, for example – is to act like abusers who trick and manipulate. Therefore, giving up claims to knowledge does not automatically empower the other person (Larner 1995). Rather it obscures the knowledges that always already shape how the therapist attends to what the client is deemed to be expert in.

Binary understandings about expertise restrict the opportunities for elaborating how different forms of knowledge work for and against the client. By contrast, a more reflexive understanding of expertise invites both therapist and client to share enquiry into how meanings are made within and outside of therapy (Baker 2002; Pare 2002; Proctor 2002). The client may lead the focus of enquiry, but both client and therapist are actively involved in mutual construction and deconstruction of meaning. For example, I have worked with clients whose religious beliefs have different impacts at different points in therapy. Sometimes they help make sense of the client's world, for example something is an act of God or a manifestation of evil. Sometimes the client seeks to deconstruct God's will (regarding predestination and freedom of choice) and sometimes to deconstruct their beliefs in God (it is not God or Satan's voice I hear, but my own despair). My aim is not to provide a fixed or authoritative reading of women's visions, voices, and beliefs, but to help them find meaning in them.

Because the 'really real' is unknowable, it is impossible to provide a definitive version of reality. I cannot prove or disprove whether women's visions and voices are 'really real' or 'only really real' to them. This is why I adopt a framework of *agnosticism*. It is a deliberate position of knowing that allows me to be both inside and outside the stories clients bring. Agnosticism, constructed within a post-structuralist epistemology, refuses the modernist dead end of truth and denial and does not presuppose any one story has any greater therapeutic value than another does. Clearly there are different stories that I have more familiarity with, and knowledge about, than others (I am a therapist, not a priest, for example). Being agnostic, therefore, does not mean I am able to engage with all stories with equanimity. Some I know better than others, and some forms of under-standing I prefer over others. Therefore, I would never claim a 'not know-ing' stance as advocated within some narrative approaches to therapy (see Harper 2004a; White 1995). To do so would absolve me of responsibility for the knowledge I bring to my work. Moreover, as Pare (2002: 38) argues:

> Clients seek therapeutic conversations not merely to tap into their own subjugated knowledge, but also to expand their choices through the exposure to additional ideas and practices. To merely assume that the client ultimately knows best is to close down possibilities for the persons who consult us.

Whilst I work with the stories and beliefs that clients bring, I do make deliberate suggestions that might provide a different perspective on their stories and beliefs. I accept that when clients make the decision to come for therapy they are, to varying degrees, interested in exploring new and different ideas. This is a collaborative enterprise that can only be achieved by making conflicting ideas visible not by avoiding disagreement through denial of different perspectives. In order to make my practices of knowing explicit, I adopt a position of *situated honesty* in which I share my general opinion about the issue under discussion (Warner 2001a, 2003b). When sharing my perspective I avoid telling stories about 'myself' because there is always a limit on self-disclosure, whilst few on opinion. However, when working with young children and people with learning disabilities I sometimes offer my opinion in terms of stories of self because abstraction can be difficult to understand. See Illustration 1.

Illustration 1

Karen, a five-and-half-year-old white girl, had been placed in foster care following sexual abuse by her father. The Social Services had some concerns about her mother's ability to keep Karen safe and all contact between them was supervised. Karen had lots of questions she wanted to ask her mother about why she was in care, but it seemed that she did not know how to begin. In our therapy sessions Karen

---

started playing with a plastic phone and told me she was 'speaking' to her mother. These conversations were very short until one day Karen passed the phone to me and said 'it's your Mum on the phone'. I 'spoke' to my mother about some of the worries I thought Karen had, as if they were mine (for example, so, you're not angry with me for saying stuff about home . . .). Karen then took the phone from me and this time had a longer 'conversation' with her mother. Through this play in therapy, Karen rehearsed some of things she wanted to talk with her mother about and which she eventually did.

Karen needed explicit permission to talk about her worries. If I had tried to stay 'neutral' (as the observers in family contact sessions are expected to be), Karen would have interpreted this as tacit disapproval of her desire to talk to her mother. Silence can be extremely controlling precisely because any social interaction is always already circumscribed by brought-with knowledge and expectations. Making knowledge explicit helps in deconstructing the therapist's power because once opinion is in the open it can be contested and challenged. Obviously clients will be more able to contest knowledge if it is presented as opinion, rather than fact. Hence, it is not only what is shared, but also how we negotiate our sharing. If therapists are too dogmatic in their approach they may still oppress, even when their stated aim is emancipation (Pare 2002).

Partnership processes are also supported by practical structures that further encourage both client and therapist to make their understandings visible. For example, having set therapy review dates invites both client and therapist to take shared responsibility for evaluation and reflection, as both know there is a clear context in which this discussion will happen. Additionally, if the client and/or the therapist is avoiding 'difficult' issues this provides a context in which to make them visible again. Inviting clients to consider their options directly, through explicit review, also challenges the powerlessness routinely associated with the abused identity. Hence, in this way the lived relationship between therapist and client actively mediates past and present abusive relationship experiences as victimhood is challenged through collaboration and democracy (cf. Malan 1979/1984). Victimhood is further deconstructed by exploring how abused children come to recognize themselves in their roles as recipients of abuse.

Deconstructing the abused identity and recognizing multiplicity

People come to therapy to contest who they think they are, or who others have determined them to be (as feminist and narrative therapy suggests: see Baker 2002; Turner 2002; White 1995). Talking about 'the past', 'the present'

173

or reflecting on the 'here and now' offers multiple ways of exploring meanings of self (as psychoanalysis suggests: see Freud 1986; Malan 1979/1984). When therapists and clients explore the multiple meanings of these identities-in-relationship, it also allows therapists and clients to make sense of the ways power is transacted in relationships. This invites clients and therapists to track, use and resist power. As noted, the embodied therapeutic relationship hopefully provides a lived experience of negotiated collaboration that actively invites women to recognize and reclaim their provisional sense of agency. Therapy 'works' precisely because who one is shifts according to the relationships being talked about, lived in and embodied. Exploring the social construction of subjectivity is, therefore, an integral part of the therapeutic process in Visible Therapy.

According to Althusser (1971) people learn to recognize themselves as 'subjects' through establishing an imaginary relationship with their social network and the ideological knowledges therein that hail or interpellate them. As Elliot (2002) argues, ideological knowledge functions in such a way that people fail to recognize that their felt sense of self is always located in social processes of identification which are fashioned through their everyday experiences. Dominant power interests, therefore, are reinforced by ensuring that people come to overlook (that is, ignore and 'forget') how their identities are always under construction. Child sexual abuse is a prime 'everyday' experience that secures particular naturalized forms of subjectivity that fortify the hidden operations of power such that children become trapped into relationships they do not want, but cannot leave.

Through experiences of sexual abuse, children are interpellated into the abused identity. They are socially constructed as both all-powerful (it is my fault), yet forever victims (I cannot stop this). Through repetition such beliefs become internalized and children learn to accept that this is who they really are. These relatively private processes of identification are further sedimented in reference to wider normative social understandings about femininity that construct women and girls as seductive, yet sexually passive. Visible Therapy aims to disrupt the naturalizing of the abused identity by tracing the particular ways that the client's sense of self is secured in her everyday experiences of abuse and other social relationships. Identity practices are both discursive and corporeal in that people come to recognize who they are through how they make sense of the experiences they have lived. Thus, Visible Therapy is concerned with how clients' sense of self is shaped not simply by their experiences of abuse, but also by the ways that they make sense of their experiences of abuse, and also how clients' sense of self mediates their understandings and experiences. See Figure 9.1.

Visible Therapy, therefore, addresses how the realities in which people live, and the identities into which they are interpellated, are shaped and sustained. There is a shift from using my expertise to enable clients to see

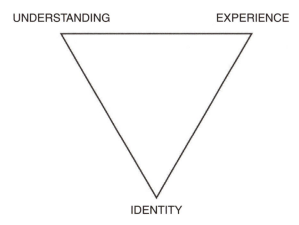

UNDERSTANDING   EXPERIENCE

IDENTITY

Figure 9.1 Triangle of Reality (Warner, 2000b)

the truth about themselves and their lives, to exploring what kinds of personhood are raised or restricted through the narratives we share in therapy. This is why it is important to work with, rather than simply dispute, disregard or attempt to disprove the identities people inhabit and talk about. See Illustration 2.

Illustration 2

Jackie, a 45-year-old white woman, told me that she was the Messiah. According to the approach adopted in Visible Therapy, identity is understood as a narrative construction and a signifier of material experience. Therefore, rather then simply try to challenge this belief my aim was to explore what 'being God' meant for Jackie in order to think through her everyday sense of powerlessness and her feelings about past abuse. Exploring what she wanted to achieve as a supreme being allowed us to talk about the things that had been, and still were, absent from her life. The more powerless Jackie felt in her everyday life, the more she invested herself with superior powers.

Jackie was trying to resist the abused identity by claiming power she did not ordinarily feel. Children also do this when they identify with comic book heroes. Because the abused identity can feel so pervasive, sometimes people believe that the only alternative to feeling all-powerless is to be all-powerful. Whilst this can lead to identification with all-powerful others, this can also result in paralysis as this transformation feels too great. It is useful, therefore, to help clients recognize the smaller acts of control they some-times exert in their lives. In this way the victim identity does not have to feel natural, inevitable and fixed, and the task of taking control in one's life so huge, daunting and far away. By making control more specific, and less global, women's felt sense of self can start to feel less stable and more constructed. As this happens women can begin to explore what it means to be a victim, or indeed a survivor, rather than accepting this is what they always will be.

They can also begin to explore other competing identities that they bring with them into therapy. Women are workers, lovers, daughters, mothers etc. and issues of age, gender, race, culture, sexuality, class, and ability interweave through all of these. Different identities may have more rele-vance at different points in therapy. We cannot, nor should not, predeter-mine which identity is most important for our clients. However, by making the social practices of identity explicit, we can explore how they might mediate individual experiences of abuse rather than assume their signifi-cance or ignore their effects. Concomitantly then, the value of 'matching' clients with therapists becomes an issue to be examined, rather than a simple straightforward act, the benefits of which can be automatically assumed.

Working out which stories of self 'work' in which situations, for which clients, is therefore an important aspect of work in Visible Therapy. This also involves reflecting on the ways in which identities are constructed through therapy. For example, do the understandings we bring reform or reinforce the abused identity? When abused women are assumed to be essentially damaged by their experiences therapists may too quickly blame their clients when the therapy does not 'work' and thereby reinforce feelings of guilt, shame and passivity (I am so damaged that I can never recover). Critical therapy approaches are, therefore, attuned to addressing how the language we use to construct who, or what, the problem is has consequences for how we work and what we focus on (Simon and Whitfield 2000). For example, diagnosis makes the client the problem by transforming what women do into who women are thought to be, and this can further reinforce women's negative sense of self. Hence, in Visible Therapy we might explore what it means for women to be diagnosed as 'schizophrenic' or 'borderline' for example, but I would not seek to apply a diagnostic category.

Because identity practices can be so deterministic, sometimes it is bene-ficial to dispense with naming rituals all together. For example, being named as a 'victim', or even a 'survivor', can overwhelm clients who are not sure what their experiences mean and how they view themselves in rela-tionship to them. This is evident when women say, 'it wasn't rape, but . . .' (see Gavey 1999). This phrase can be read both as an apologia for the abuser *and* as a rebuttal of the abused identity and all it implies. Therefore, therapists should avoid rushing to define what something is. Women may resist the identity (I'm not a rape victim), but still have feelings about the issue that they now feel unable to explore. By contrast, decentring the subject can sometimes invite greater possibilities for thought and reflection. For example, when I run groups I sometimes ask participants about their opinions rather than their experience: what they think rather than who they are. We can talk about the meanings of sexual choices, for example, without women having to claim a particular identity (such as lesbian, bisexual, or heterosexual).

The desire to enable connection between women in groups, therefore, should not be conflated with naming their shared identities. These are two separate, albeit related, practices. Hence, in Visible Therapy these separate processes are elaborated. Group participants can be encouraged to make connections with each other even when their anxieties about being 'different' mean they are reluctant to disclose information about themselves. At the beginning of groups I ask what would help participants to know about each other, but is difficult to disclose now. For girls even this can feel too exposing and so I make suggestions based on my prior knowledge of running groups for girls. Issues might include who the abuser is. I can then say, 'some of you were abused by dads, brothers etc.' In this way connection is being enabled before specific identities are claimed.

Because processes of identification that prefigure the abused identity simultaneously construct the subjectivity of the abuser, women also resist the abused identity when they reinvest the abuser's personhood. Sometimes women distance themselves from the abuser, or express their anger, through a refusal to use the abuser's given name (for example, John) or given title (for example, Dad). I always ask what to call the abuser. Names include various negative or irreverent epithets, or involve a deliberate use of pronouns, such as 'him', 'her', and 'it'. These names may change as women talk through their different feelings about the abuse. Hence, another task of Visible Therapy is to explore the different stories women can tell about their experiences of abuse. This involves tracking the abuser-tactics that were used to reinforce women's sense of victimhood.

Making the tactics of abuse visible

From a post-structuralist perspective, therapy can be understood to involve the development of alternative scripts and accounts of both past and current life in order to promote change. Miltenburg and Singer (1999) suggest that therapists can enhance strategies for change through providing or assisting in the development of 'scaffolds' around which alternative narratives can develop. In Visible Therapy, this process is encouraged by articulating the narrative structures that clients already rely on to make sense of themselves and their lives. I do not insist on 'getting a history' at the outset – as if there is a final and complete story that can be told – rather

I am interested in 'accounts' as they emerge (MacKinnon 1998). I listen carefully to these accounts and avoid early interpretation of meaning as this can foreclose the possibilities of how such narratives might unfold and where they may lead. The accounts and desires of young children are often enacted through play, drama, or drawing. See Illustration 3.

Illustration 3

Sonia, a six-year-old white girl, used drawing to indicate what she wanted from therapy. She drew a picture of a large man and a small girl. Sonia explained that the man was the person who abused her and the girl was herself. Sonia transformed this story by cutting herself out – she was now separate to her abuser. She then very carefully cut up her abuser into strips and gave each strip to me to put into the bin. We talked about how I could help her get rid of some of the sad and angry feelings she felt about him and we identified some of the things that could help her feel safe and strong, such as having a grown-up listen to her.

When clients, like Sonia, tell their stories and share their concerns they are beginning to elaborate how their beliefs about self and others are shaped and maintained. I encourage this process by asking clarifying questions and sometimes I provide a running commentary about what is happening in order to strengthen our shared understandings. I start with 'stating the obvious' regarding behavioural actions (you have just thrown the teddy on the floor; you've told me about arguing with your boss). Then I may explore more feeling interpretations (has the teddy upset you? you seem angry with the teddy; you sounded angry when you talked about your boss). I may then ask them to think of another time that they were sad and/ or angry.

The aim in talking about the present, and making links to the past, is not to produce an ultimate story of causation, but to enable exploration of the links between past and present versions of reality (Warner 2000b). The aim is not to search for 'the truth' about the past and, as noted, to adopt a position of agnosticism inhibits the desire to look for 'proof'. I work with stories that clients bring. I accept that sometimes these stories change, but that any story is told for a reason. Through this process of narrative rehearsal I maintain a willingness to 'believe' my clients. In a post-structuralist sense, belief can be understood as a willingness to listen without trying to determine what the 'really real' is. I can believe in women's sense of hurt and injustice whilst I accept that the narratives that contextualize their feelings may change over time. In this sense, belief, which, as indicated in Part 2, is so important in recovery from sexual abuse is much easier to sustain because it is always located and provisional.

The aim, then, is to explore how and why the past is remembered as it is in order to illuminate the particular tactics that were used to ensure the client's silence and acquiescence to abuse. Therefore, as signalled in Chapter 8, the focus in Visible Therapy is on the tactics that are used to control children, rather than on the details of the physical act. (Therapist's interests in this are often voyeuristic. A concern with the events of abuse is much more appropriate within criminal investigations.) The hope is that, through talking about 'tactics', women can revise, rework and reinvest their narratives about themselves. Clients can thus be enabled to reclaim their personal sense of agency by making the operations of power within abusive relationships explicit. As suggested, I do this by helping them develop more nuanced accounts of abuse that resist globalizing descriptions of self (Waller 1996). Women may then come to reinvest their stories of powerlessness with subversive resistance. When clients are specific about their attributions they can renegotiate their felt sense of helplessness: 'I was not to blame for the abuse I endured. I did find ways to survive and protect myself'. See Illustration 4.

Illustration 4

Yasmin, a 27-year-old Asian woman, believed that she was to blame for being sexually abused because she 'voluntarily' went to her abuser's bedroom every night. Yasmin's guilt was reinforced by the abuser who noted how much she 'really wanted it' because she came looking for him. We explored how, at the time, she knew that abuse was a nightly occurrence that she could not avoid. She circumvented the agony of waiting by 'getting it over with'. Her globalized feelings of guilt and responsibility hid her specific attempts at resistance from herself.

As women, like Yasmin, trace their own personal stories of regulation and resistance in the past they can extend their understandings about how they act in the present. In this way Visible Therapy encourages clients to recognize their often multiple strategies of survival and through this to explore connections between past and present life and women's ongoing constructions of self.

Creative approaches to coping under constraint

Under conditions of emotional and physical constraint children must be creative in finding ways to withstand the repetitive attacks on their sense of self. Children may cope during abuse with denial (e.g., this is not happening to me). When denial fails they may try distraction (e.g., I am not thinking about this, I am thinking about something else, I am counting numbers). Both denial and distraction are difficult to sustain and children may then resort to dissociation (e.g., I am somewhere else: I am a flower in the wallpaper, I am swimming in the sea). Many children will use a combination of these strategies, weaving back and forth. Children may cope with their subsequent feelings of powerlessness by self-harming. And, indeed self-harm (for example, self-injury or using drugs and alcohol) can provide more physical means of distraction and dissociation (see Warner 2000b, 2003b). These coping strategies (the *3Ds* – denial, distraction and dissociation – and self-harm) may generalize to other situations of abuse and deprivation, and in response to other feelings of anxiety and powerlessness. They may then become practices that women learn to rely on thereafter.

Visible Therapy is orientated towards building on these multiple strategies of survival, adaptation and creativity. Whilst, as noted, any identity – even that of survivor – ultimately constrains how individuals come to view themselves (Reavey and Warner 2001), the notion of survival does positively recognize the active ways that children manage their lives. Yet too often mainstream mental health services view such actions as being essentially pathological. This is indicated in talk about disorders or addictions. Hence, I avoid language that derogates my clients – as diseased, deficient, distorted, or dysfunctional – as this undermines their sense of agency, increases their sense of shame and denies their adaptability (Warner and Wilkins 2004). Rather my aim is to explore the connections between the ordinary thoughts and feelings that underlie women's sometimes extreme behaviour. See Figure 9.2.

According to the perspective adopted in Visible Therapy, women's actions do not have a fixed meaning. Whether any action is useful changes according to the specific context. Tracing the meaning of different forms of coping again, sometimes, involves making links between past abusive relationships and current lived experience. For example, if women have used strategies such as denial, distraction and dissociation (the *3Ds*) during episodes of abuse, and have tried not to think about their experiences afterwards, they may have few memories about what happened to them. Sometimes women need to know how memory works in order to accept that there are things that they may never recall, however hard they try. The coping strategies women use, however, can provide some connection between the past and present. Therefore, this is another reason to explore the meaning of women's coping strategies as their coping strategies may be the only bridge between past and present versions of self (Lefevre 1996). For example, the voices that people hear and the visions that they see often relate to their primary experiences of abuse, such as the abuser who torments them, or the little girl that cries out in fear or anger.

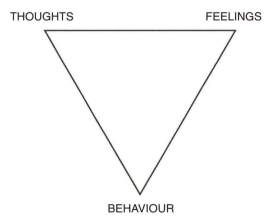

THOUGHTS   FEELINGS

BEHAVIOUR

Figure 9.2 Triangle of Communication (Warner, 2000b)

In exploring what visions and voices might mean, and in working out when and how other coping strategies work, clients can be enabled to feel a greater sense of control in their out-of-control moments. At times of heightened emotion it is difficult to think clearly and act effectively (cf. Yerkes and Dodson 1908; see also Chapter 12). Thus, having a more deliberate relationship with different forms of coping enables women to exercise greater control in their lives. Because Visible Therapy aims to increase women's sense of agency the focus is on understanding, rather than on monitoring or changing, women's actions. I accept that when women and girls have self-injured for years, for example, they have a far greater sense of what is 'safe' for them than I could know, particularly as I have no medical training. There is, therefore, no expectation in this model that women should give up their existing coping strategies such as self-harm. I assume that any action is meaningful for that person, although meaning may not always be simple and straightforward. Indeed, sometimes one action can have multiple meanings and functions for the client. See Illustration 5.

Illustration 5

Sarah is a 24-year-old African-Caribbean woman who is learning disabled. She scrubbed her skin with a wire brush and attempted to bleach herself. Sarah said she felt 'dirty' because she was abused and her skin colour felt 'wrong'. Sarah had been adopted into a white family and had grown up in a predominantly white area. Sarah had few opportunities to develop a positive sense of self. Labelling her skin scraping and bleaching behaviour as pathological, as some

---

professionals had, did not stop it happening. Indeed, it increased Sarah's lack of self-worth (she was wrong and bad all over again). Instead of focusing on Sarah's self-harm, in sessions we focused on how Sarah felt about herself. Because Sarah was quite concrete in her thinking we focused our conversations around current issues that Sarah found easier to engage with than more abstract issues from the past.

Additionally, for Sarah it seemed that it was the racism she continued to experience rather than the sexual abuse she had endured that was of immediate concern. We talked about the different ways that Sarah had been made to feel she was bad and wrong. We countered this by identifying the good things about being Sarah. I kept reminding her of these. We talked about 'being Black' and made explicit links between Sarah and Black people she knew of and liked from the mass media. Sarah did not know any Black people personally. She knew very few people at all. I identified a Black mental health community group that provided a 'befriender' for Sarah, which helped her begin to establish some positive relationships in the community. I supported her when she moved from the predominantly white district were she lived to a more ethnically diverse area. As Sarah's social relationships changed, her practices of identity were altered and her self-harming behaviour decreased.

Extending concerns within therapy to supporting activities outside of therapy contrasts with normative psychological approaches that restrict practice to psychological processes alone. Sometimes women and girls need practical help, as well as alternative narratives, to enable them to change aspects of their lives. It is important, therefore, to remain mindful that material interventions may sometimes be more useful than psychological interpretations. For example, sometimes women are referred for psychological therapy when some of their problems may be physical in nature. Sexual abuse causes physical as well as psychological trauma and physical complaints may be untreated in order to conceal abuse or because of lack of care (Nelson 2002). With this in mind, I sometimes support women and girls to have comprehensive medical check-ups. We anticipate potential outcomes in therapy and explore what impact these could have, for example if the client finds out that there is permanent damage to their reproductive system or they have a sexually transmitted infection.

Sometimes clients do not simply want their existing coping strategies validated; they want practical suggestions for how to extend their options. For example, women and girls often report difficulties with sleeping. Sexual abuse often occurs in bedrooms and falling asleep can remind people of the loss of control, and sometime dissociation, associated with experiences of abuse. This is why I do not use hypnosis as a therapeutic tool. Once asleep, people may be plagued with recurring nightmares or worrying dreams. We explore, and I make suggestions about, what would help clients feel safer going to bed at night such as having a lock on the bedroom door; having a nightlight; sleeping in a sleeping bag, etc. In respect of dreams and nightmares, we may talk about their meanings, making links to their current and past life. In order to enable clients to take some control in their nightmares, I sometimes make suggestions for how to find some sense of safety when asleep. For example, I invite clients to think about 'something or someone just before you go to sleep that will help you in your nightmares', etc.

Psychotherapy can provide an opportunity to reinvest agency by recognizing and validating women's attempts to look after themselves. I know that the method used may be directly damaging (cutting oneself) or indirectly damaging (dissociating can leave people vulnerable to harm by self or others, or people may be more likely to cause harm to others), and both forms of coping may result in constraint and diagnostic categorization. Therefore, I do worry about my clients, but accept that such actions are what women often do to preserve their life, not destroy it. If I am worried I share this with clients and explain why this is. I try to be transparent in describing my actions so that clients know why I act in the way I do. Sometimes this is about talking to other professionals if I feel clients are unable to keep themselves safe. For example, sometimes women may feel unable to resist the directives of their voices and visions to harm themselves and/or others. At such times, women need additional help. The aim is to make women aware of decisions, even when they feel most out of control, in the hope that at some point women will find ways to manage their more difficult moments themselves. In this sense it is critical to hold on to the idea that clients can 'recover' and, thus, will leave therapy one day.

The role of endings and reflexive practices in recovery

Recovery is a key issue in to the practice of Visible Therapy as it is a central discursive mechanism for resisting women's victimization and pathologization (see Chapter 2). A recovery-orientated therapy is based on the assumption that positive change is possible. It is crucial, therefore, that recovery-orientated therapists remain hopeful about their clients. Without hope there is often despair and it is when people feel hopeless rather than, or only because, they are depressed that they kill themselves. Hence, it is crucial to understand that self-harm can be a life-affirming activity and that such behaviour is often indicative of hope: if abused children had no hope of better futures they would have little need to develop coping strategies, such as self-injury, to get them there. In Visible Therapy hopefulness is sustained by recognizing that the service user will not need therapy for evermore and accepting that therapeutic relationships will end. This is why endings are a crucial consideration in Visible Therapy throughout the therapeutic relationship.

Collaborative review enables the ending process because it invites both participants to actively reflect on the immediate value of the therapeutic relationship. Structuring in specific times for review (after five and ten sessions depending on the age and needs of the client) means that relationships are less likely to drift and that endings are made 'present' throughout the relationship. After each review session, the client and the therapist may then decide to work towards ending the relationship or another planned review. This process does not ensure that everyone agrees in equal measure, but goes some way to include both client and therapist in the process of explicit decision-making.

Sometimes, the length of the relationship is determined by factors external to therapy, for example when clients move house, therapists leave the service or others stop supporting therapy. Even when this is the case I would still endeavour to enable clients to be prepared for saying goodbye. Active review enables this process as does advance consideration and post-reflection about the ways in which the therapeutic relationship changes over time and in respect of 'mini' endings occasioned by holidays or illness, for example. When endings in therapy are forced by external events I sometimes give clients transitional objects to take with them, for example a 'goodbye card'. Endings provide an opportunity for reflection and a lived experience of coping with change. Because this process is ongoing the final session does not have to include an explicit running commentary. See Illustration 6.

Illustration 6

In our final session, Joy, an 11-year-old white girl, drew a picture of a lioness in a cage and a keeper outside with a big stick. She told me that although the lion is dangerous, she is locked up. If the lion escaped, the keeper had a stick that could be used to get the lion back in the cage. During therapy Joy's anger at being abused had been a central theme. We had talked about strategies for containing it and strategies for regaining control of it. We did not need to repeat this in words. I accepted that Joy was reminding me of her strengths and enjoining me not to worry about her. Joy was still very angry, but not 'out of control'. Joy had recovered some sense of agency and validation of her feelings.

According to the understanding adopted in Visible Therapy some form of 'recovery' is a possibility for any client. This contrasts with addiction models of 'recovery' whereby clients are seen to be permanently 'in recovery', but can never recover (e.g. Narcotics Anonymous 1988). And unlike addiction models there is no template for recovery. Rather a radical social model of recovery is permissive, not prescriptive. There is no predetermined gold standard or 'cure' (see Reavey and Warner 2001). For example, for Joy her anger was affirming and she did not need to give it up. For others, it might be important to let their angry feelings dissipate. Recovery, therefore, is a multitude of things to a multitude of people. Advocating for recovery, then, should not be conflated with forcing a relentless search for solutions, as some narrative therapists suggest (Armstrong 2002; Epston 1993; White 1995). The search for unique outcomes in otherwise problem-saturated stories *requires* a problem. Yet self-harm, for example, may be both problem and solution and fixing it in either a problem story or a solution narrative undermines women's ability to understand their own multiplicity. Additionally, searching for solutions (an often masculinist endeavour) can be used to mask the avoidance of pain. Both clients and therapists can be overwhelmed by stories of abuse and avoid pain by focusing on solutions. Recovery is not always about finding answers, but is also about being able to live with, and remain hopeful in, sadness, anger, uncertainty and ambiguity.

In order that therapists are able to hear their clients' accounts of abuse, and remain hopeful in the face of such powerful emotions, they require sustained opportunity for reflection both within and outside of the immediate therapeutic relationship. Sometimes therapists assume a commonalty with their clients as women, for example, which impedes reflection. Sometimes therapists' felt sense of difference instigates a defensive reaction that undermines their ability to listen to and connect with their clients. Therapists need the opportunity to consider the multiple relationships that shape their own identities-in-action otherwise they too will act to protect their own mixed feelings about self. Being unreflective reduces our capacity to learn or, as radical feminists Daly and Caputi (1988: 230) once argued, increases our potential to act as 'the/rapist'. Supervision is a primary context for critical reflection. Indeed, there is some suggestion that there is a correlation between abuse and lack of supervision (and also seniority, and being male – see Shaw 1997).

Whilst critical approaches have been recuperated into the mainstream through the accommodation of terms such as 'reflexive practice', I use this term (*à la* narrative therapy) to signal an ongoing commitment to elaborating the relationships between theory and practice. As Cushway and Gatherer (2003) argue, this involves a deliberate deconstruction of the operations of our actions in order to improve practice. Reflexivity, as Simon and Whitfield (2000: 146) argue, is '[t]he pivotal principle through which one explores the circular and recursive relationship between theory, ideology and practice'. Through supervision we extend our accountability, increase the transparency of our knowledges, and open up our practices to scrutiny and a situated ethical evaluation. Supervision provides an opportunity to track ideas and to consider the implications of different narratives for making sense of the client's issues and concerns. We can explore how different knowledges aid in the process of reflection. For example, we can discursively investigate what a feminist reading brings to our understanding of the particular issue under discussion – and construction.

Whether in therapy, supervision, or here when writing this chapter, I constantly reflect on the ideas that shape how I work. I learn from clients, colleagues and friends and each new relationship weaves into my existing experiences and contributes to the ways in which I make sense of what I do. My ways of working continue to evolve, even as I recognize that some of my concerns are very much reflective of more general considerations that are products of this particular place and time in history. In this sense, Visible Therapy shares many of the dilemmas and issues that other forms of contemporary westernized psychotherapy face. As Elliot (2002) argues, psychoanalysis has arisen at a time characterized by fragmentation, dispersal, disconnection and multiplicity and this is reflected in concerns with splitting, otherness, ambivalence and the construction of subjectivity. Visible Therapy can also be located here. Yet, it is not a practice of despair. Feminism instigates a passionate politics that radicalizes recovery through enabling different futures to be imagined. Both clients and therapists have the capacity to change and resist the bland repetition of past generations. The stories made in therapy ripple out in many diverse and sometimes unforeseen ways that provide new narratives for clients, but also for the therapists with whom they share their lives.

From therapy to assessment

Visible Therapy follows psychological tradition in terms of trying to work out or formulate the functional relationships between how abuse survivors feel, think and behave. This has involved drawing out the connections between past and current life, and their embodiment in the therapeutic relationship. Where Visible Therapy departs from traditional psychology is in its acceptance of multiplicity and its refusal to provide a single authoritative reading of women's stories or to dictate a fixed formulae and template for recovery. This type of approach, which is both principled as well as flexible, has a wide applicability. This is not only in terms of providing a framework for thinking through abuse psychotherapy in different cultural and geographical contexts, but also in terms of guiding practice in other service settings, such as those relating to the law. Therefore, in Chapter 10, this approach is developed further by using it to inform the ways in which expert witnesses in psychology make formal assessments regarding survivors of childhood sexual abuse.

10

CRITICAL PRACTICES IN CHILD PROTECTION

Social framework evidence and the expert witness

Introduction

Sexual violence affects a great many children around the world. For example, the World Health Organization WHO (2006b) estimates that, in 2002, 150 million girls (and 73 million boys) under 18 years of age experienced forced sexual intercourse or other forms of sexual assault. If we are to help such children, and the adults they become, we must develop a range of strategies and interventions. In the previous chapter I addressed the therapeutic needs of abuse survivors and introduced Visible Therapy as a framework for enabling a culturally aware, recovery-orientated approach to abuse psychotherapy. In this chapter, I focus on abused children's legal needs and use the Visible Therapy approach to demonstrate the benefits of utilizing feminism and post-structuralism to guide the work of expert witnesses in legal proceedings that relate to sexually abused children and young people.

Expert witnesses are defined as being qualified by study or experience to help others understand the issues of the case, and their knowledge is understood to exceed that of the average lay person (Bacon *et al.* 2002; Newton 2003). Expert witnesses must limit themselves to commenting on matters that are within their range of expertise and they must have no conflict of interest with the matter under assessment (Law Society of England and Wales 2002). Whilst all psychologists could work as expert witnesses, not all of them do. This may be because they fear having their opinion scrutinized and/or they do not want to feel as if they act as 'agents of the State'. (This is the case even if experts are not appointed directly by the State. Psychologists may still feel that any engagement with legal proceedings identifies them too closely with State enterprises and concerns.) Yet, law is crucial in the fight for justice and equality, as early second-wave feminists argued (see Chapter 4). Therefore, it behoves feminist psychologists to theorize, research and critically engage with legal systems. Some already do; for example, see Gavey's (2003) research and practice regarding the expert evidence of clinical psychologists in relation to rape victims in

New Zealand. In the main, however, and unlike other aspects of psychology practice, the work of the psychology expert witness is under-theorized and under-researched.

This chapter aims to contribute to this, as yet, arguably limited knowledge base by addressing the work of the clinical psychology expert witness in child care proceedings, specifically regarding girls who have been sexually abused. I begin by outlining key laws and guidance that shape child protection practices regarding girls and sexual abuse and which provide *social frameworks* for understanding their needs. My aim is to illuminate how making social frameworks visible enables greater clarity regarding expert knowledge. I then provide examples from my work as a clinical psychology expert witness that demonstrate how explicit social frameworks can be applied through the various processes of instruction, assessment, and evidentiary reporting.

From criminalization to ambiguity in child protection

The children who are the subject of this chapter represent a minority of those who experience sexual abuse. This is because most sexual abuse remains hidden, unreported and under-recorded, and most abused children do not engage with public, state services. For example, Ashcroft *et al.* (2003), in a national study into victimization of 12- to 17-year-olds in the USA, found that 86 per cent of sexual assaults went unreported. Similarly, in a prevalence study of child maltreatment in the UK, a survey of 18- to 24-year-olds found that 31 per cent had never told anyone about their experiences of sexual abuse; and that hardly anyone had told professionals such as police, social workers, teachers or doctors (Cawson *et al.* 2000). This pattern continues into adulthood. For example, the North American National Violence Against Women survey found that only 19 per cent of adult women reported sex crimes to police (Tjaden and Thoennes 2006).

Few children and women report sex crimes because of fear and stigma. For example, WHO (2006b), in a global study of children and violence, found that this was especially the case for children in cultures where family honour is placed above the safety and well-being of children, and where reporting sexual violence can lead to ostracism, further violence or even death. Additionally, WHO (2007a) also points out that reporting rates are negatively affected by how deeply entrenched male privilege, superiority and entitlement to sex are embedded in the culture. Hence, there are multiple reasons why very few children who experience sexual violence are afforded direct protection by the state. Moreover, the service provided to the minority of children who do use state services is variable to say the least.

For example, WHO (2007a) notes, in its world report on violence and health, that in too many countries rape victims are not examined by a gynaecologist or specialist police doctor and that no standard protocols or guidelines exist. Yet, the use of standard protocols and guidelines are crucial in the improvement of the quality of treatment and psychological support of victims, as well as the evidence collected. In turn, this means that reporting rates and convictions are increased in those countries that have developed standardized protocols for investigating sexual crimes and supporting victims. This includes making use of the health sector to collect medical and legal evidence to corroborate the victim's account or to help to identify the perpetrator. For example, WHO (2007a) refers to research from Canada that demonstrates that medico-legal documentation increases conviction rates for rape irrespective of injury type (whether moderate or severe), income level, or how well the patient knew the assailant. It also helps to have a 'one-stop shop' for victims of abuse, as is the case in Malaysia's 34 public hospitals (see WHO 2007a).

In those countries where standard protocols exist, a distinction is often made regarding criminal and civil proceedings. Criminal proceedings in relation to child abuse are concerned with the prosecution of offenders. The aim of civil proceedings in relation to child abuse (the focus in this chapter) is to protect the child from the risk of significant harm. In criminal law the burden of proof is on the prosecution. In civil law the burden of proof is on the applicant (social services or the child's parents, for example). In criminal proceedings there is a high standard of proof (beyond a reasonable doubt). In civil law the standard of proof is lower (on the balance of probabilities). Tensions exist between the competing demands of prosecution (criminal law) and protection (civil law), and unfortunately these tensions frequently undermine legal attempts to safeguard children's welfare. This is because although both are important, prosecution (criminal law) needs usually determine how formal investigations proceed in child protection generally, particularly at the outset. Hence, although criminal investigations do not have the same primary goals as civil child-care (child welfare) proceedings (respectively, the prosecution of offenders versus the need to secure the best interests of the child), too often it is the need to prosecute offenders that determines early processes in *both* criminal and civil child-care investigations and assessments.

Initially, in criminal investigations (which, as argued, also shape and too often dictate child care assessments), local child-protective services, usually led by police and social workers, determine facts and make recommendations about further investigation (Merck 2006; Home Office HO 1992; HO 2002). The primary aim is to secure criminal convictions by avoiding leading questions and by gathering evidence of distinct separable offences. Yet, criminal prosecution is seldom achieved. Wattam (1997), in her review of research on reported child abuse allegations in Britain, found that 25 per cent instigated no further action at the outset. After the initial investigation 50 per cent were filtered out. The remaining 25 per cent were 'conferenced' (this is a civil law term that refers to a formal meeting of professionals which is held to determine whether the child should be placed on the child protection register and/or whether civil child-care proceedings commenced). A minority of these cases went to criminal trial, and more of the defendants were acquitted than were convicted. This pattern is also reflected in conviction rates in respect of rape. For example, Viner (2003) reports that rape convictions in Britain were 33 per cent of those charged in 1977, 7.5 per cent in 1999, and 5.8 per cent in 2002, whilst in 2002, 27 per cent more rapes were reported than in the preceding year.

Hence, although increased public awareness in westernized countries may have increased the reporting of sex crimes (Townsend 2005), this has not led to a corresponding increase in conviction rates. Prosecution evidently does not work as prosecution (too few offenders are prosecuted successfully), let alone child protection (children remain vulnerable to further abuse and their best interests are not achieved). There are multiple reasons for this. Children's experiences and accounts of sexual abuse do not conform to the narrow parameters of criminal law. Children tend to expand their accounts of sexual abuse over time rather than provide 'complete' descriptions during the course of one investigative interview. Children are not encouraged to speak by intrusive 'policing' methods that the emphasis on prosecution invites. Additionally, children (like adult women) do not make credible witnesses because they are assumed to be immature with an active fantasy life and imagination (see Wattam 1997). It is often their word against an often more 'credible' – male – other.

Therefore, securing evidence of child sexual abuse is never a straight-forward event, but is shaped by wider cultural beliefs and mores that determine what can be articulated and who is believed (Steele 2002). For example, reporting and conviction rates for sexual assault are further depressed in patriarchal cultures by lax investigation and court procedures whereby relevant information is 'lost'. Also, rape victims can be deterred from reporting through fear of being punished for filing an 'unproven' rape allegation (see WHO 2007a). There are, therefore, many reasons why criminal cases fail. This has led Wattam (1997: 97) to argue that:

> the prosecution of child abuse is neither achieved nor achievable in the majority of cases and . . . the assumption on which the criminalisation of child abuse is based should be challenged.

Yet, particularly in respect of child *sexual* abuse, criminalization is being extended, not reduced. This is evidenced in legislative change within many westernized cultures that seek to increase the ways in which the law circumscribes *any* sexual experiences children engage in. Hence, in order to understand the legislative context of child sexual *abuse*, it is also necessary to understand the wider legal dynamic of the child's ability to *consent* to sex. Children's ability to consent to sex has been questioned as greater public awareness about child sexual abuse has led to an ever-increasing concern that children are essentially vulnerable. This has, in turn, steadily increased the pathologization of children's everyday sexual behaviour in North American culture, for example (Levine 2002). This is also reflected in Britain where sex laws have undergone their most radical overhaul for at least 50 years (see Tavris 2003). The specific aim is to reduce child vulnerability to sex.

Of particular relevance is the assumption in law that the under 16s cannot consent to sex and that *any* sexual activity by the under 16s would be unlawful; see the Sexual Offences Act (HO 2003). This is in contrast to section 34 of the Crime and Disorder Act 1998 (HO 1998) which has abolished the rebuttal presumption that a child is *doli incapax*, i.e. incapable of telling the difference between serious wrong and simple naughtiness. For the purposes of the criminal law, this means that children in Britain who are under the age of criminal responsibility (10- to 13-year-olds) are subject to the same treatment as other juveniles (14- to 17-year-olds) when deciding whether or not prosecution is appropriate. Hence, the presumption that children between 10 and 14 years are incapable of criminal intent has been withdrawn (Bacon *et al.* 2002).

This paradox suggests that 'good' children have no agency around sex, whilst 'bad' children are treated as *de facto* adults. This implies that, in British law at least, rape is understood to be a crime of morality (children know right from wrong and therefore can be prosecuted for sex crimes), but not of passion. Children are deemed to be developmentally incapable of understanding their sexual feelings, and hence consent or force cannot be determined by reference to sexual desires. Children are therefore sometimes culpable and sometimes vulnerable. Hence, as Levine (2002: 59) argues, '[j]ust like the word *abuse*, the word *consent*, is subject to multiple meanings.' Such meanings, however, are socially prescribed and thus any ambiguity around the meanings of abuse and consent are not equally distributed between genders.

Boys and girls are differentiated according to received notions of gendered agency such that sex is understood to be something that men and boys do to women and girls (see MacKinnon 1989; Atmore 1998). Therefore, 'consent' is a questionable concept when boys are assumed to be more culpable in respect of sex and are much more likely to be prosecuted for unlawful (that is underage) sex than girls, who are overwhelmingly assumed to be their victims. Whilst, as indicated earlier, sexual assault is largely perpetrated by men against the feminized victim, the automatic presumption of male culpability restricts how comprehensive investigations can be. This is because assumptions about gender make the ambiguity that surrounds children and sex invisible. Nevertheless, ambiguity is at the heart of both the dicta and practices of the law. This is because protecting children – as with adults – is not straightforward. How we recognize child sexual abuse, understand consent and differentiate gender roles shapes how we investigate, prosecute offenders and/or support victims thereafter. Hence, addressing ambiguity (that is, as Visible Therapy suggests, being socially and culturally aware) is a key factor in critical child protection practices.

Explicit and implicit concerns in child protection

In order to maximize the ways in which children's safety needs can be supported through the law, both global and local issues need to be addressed. Hence, international treaties are as necessary as domestic laws and policies that reflect the specific cultural context (WHO 2007a). This is because children's rights may be better enforced through international law than domestic policies, particularly, as previously argued, in patriarchal cultures that place family honour above children's need for safety. It is in this context that recent international laws have been developed to support children's safety needs around sex. These include laws on sexual trafficking, female genital mutilation, child marriage, and rape during armed conflict (WHO 2007a). In this way, international law is used to restrict ambiguity around children's rights relative to sex. Conversely, some laws secure children's rights by incorporating an understanding of ambiguity into the Treaty or Act itself. For example, Article 12 of the United Nations Convention on the Rights of the Child states that children should be afforded the right to express their view, weighted in accordance with their age and maturity (see Lee 2003). In Article 12, therefore, a generalization about children is used as grounds for determining children's rights to participate in decision-making. However, ambivalence is manifested in, respectively, the specifics of age and maturity.

Article 12 provides an example of when the law invites those who work within it to be reflexive practitioners. And it is this general approach that can be used to inform local child-protection practices. As Seden (2001: 50) suggests, reflexivity involves refusing to define 'reality according to one set of cultural assumptions and stereotypes'. When practitioners view reality as being socially constructed it enables a reflexive process, because what counts as the truth is always seen to be open to discussion, critique and mediation. This does not represent a *laissez-faire* attitude towards the law. Rather, the aim is to encourage greater clarity regarding the ways in which the law is *practised*. By making individual values and how social and legal realities are shaped explicit, the potential for idiosyncratic practice can be reduced as the *processes* of working within a legal framework become more visible and thereby open to detailed evaluation (Warner 2003a).

For example, in Britain, current directives in child protection are arguably now based on a more flexible (that is ambiguous) understanding of

Figure 10.1 Assessment Framework (DH, 2000b)

children and their welfare. This is reflected in governmental guidance on the assessment of children in need and their families (Department of Health DH 2000b). Drawing on ideas from social constructionism (see Seden 2001), this current framework attempts to systematically tailor assessments to the particular family and environmental context in which individual children live rather than having a policy of 'one model fits all'. See Figure 10.1.

This type of model addresses an increased concern with emotional abuse and neglect. This is reflected in Figure 10.1 in the focus on parenting capacity, which implicitly relies on Attachment Theory (Bowlby 1969, 1973). Emotional abuse and neglect represent the majority of child protection referrals in most countries (DH 1995; WHO 2006b). A focus on emotional abuse and neglect instigates a shift in emphasis from incidents of actual abuse (physical or sexual) to more general concerns regarding the quality of life provided by parents to children (Corby 2000). Hence, the British approach moves away from an incident-based criminal justice model. It is more reflective of how abuse is often experienced and remembered, and provides a more open framework for addressing ambiguity.

However, because such frameworks are deliberately orientated towards issues of emotional abuse and neglect they are inevitably poor at illuminating issues concerning sexual abuse. Positive 'parenting capacity', for example, may be used to conceal sexual abuse. Conversely, sexual abuse may be extra-familial and so not immediately evident within a family-focused assessment model. Alternatively, the impact of abuse on the child's development may be recognized, but scant attention is given to why it has occurred (that is because of parenting capacity and/or social context) (see Horwath 2002). This type of model, therefore, is not equally applicable to all forms of abuse, nor are all aspects of the model necessarily applied.

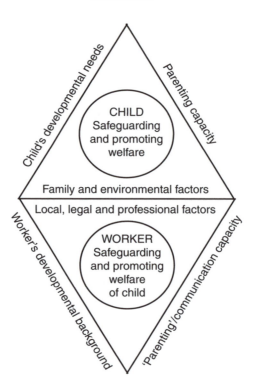

Figure 10.2 Assessment Diamond (Warner, 2003a)

Hence, a recurring problem with this, and many other, assessment models is that because the emphasis is on content (*what* needs to be assessed: child, parent, family/social context), there is insufficient concern with process issues (*how* the assessment proceeds). This is because process issues are seldom identified within these kinds of working models. Yet, how a model of intervention is applied will have a profound effect on outcomes. Hence, content models are incomplete because they obscure the impact that the style of intervention has on family outcomes. Therefore any model of intervention must address both content and process issues. So, for example, the basic triangle of concern identified in Figure 10.1 would have to become – at least – a diamond of concern comprising ecologies of both client and professional. See Figure 10.2.

Any comprehensive assessment, therefore, should address explicit factors associated with the child, as well as give due consideration to the practitioner's own personal history, style of communication, and the specific local, legal and professional context in which she works. All of these factors contribute to how children are assessed and how ambiguity can be understood and managed in assessment processes. Hence, I recognize the need to make visible the social frameworks that underpin and influence my under-standings about children and abuse. This then provides an explicit frame-work for addressing ambiguity and guiding my practice, which is now described and discussed.

Revising 'the questions' and situating my knowledge

Child clinical psychologists are typically called on, in civil law, to write reports during the final stages of child protection investigations, when the criminal justice process has been largely completed. At this point there is often conflict in the system, particularly between parents who feel persecuted and social workers who feel the burden of responsibility. Both parties may feel stuck and embattled and the child's agenda may become lost in this process. The introduction of an 'independent' expert has the potential to unsettle these habitual ways of relating that have become fixed over time. For example, in British (civil) child care proceedings, all represented parties must first agree to who they want appointed as the expert witness. The expert's name is then put forward to the court, which then approves the appointment by including the appointment in a court order (e.g. Dr Sam Warner, clinical psychologist, will file a report on Ms Smith by 4pm on 3 October 2009 and will attend court to give evidence). Because, as indicated, in civil proceedings all parties represented must agree to the expert's appointment, the use of external expertise already undermines fixed positioning because the expert is not, at the outset, perceived to have allegiance to any one party. No one party can suppress the findings of the report as it is available to all, although they can of course challenge the findings at the final hearing. Although the court remains responsible for any judgment made, some of this responsibility is redistributed. As Gavey (2003) found in her research on the judicial system in New Zealand, this extends further the opportunity for fixed and conflicted relationships to be provisionalized again.

In order to ensure that all parties are agreeable to an expert being appointed, they need some information regarding how that expert works and the relevant experiences she has. A process of negotiation usually begins between the expert witness and one of the legal representatives who is tasked with the responsibility of instructing the expert on behalf of all the parties. This person, who is called the 'lead solicitor' in the UK, outlines the case and identifies the parameters of the assessment. A formal 'letter of instruc-tion', which will have been approved by all the legal representatives, is sent by the lead solicitor to the expert. Issues identified in the letter of instruction for assessment may include: whether a care order is necessitated; the nature and effects of abuse; presence and impact of any psychological disorder or disability; consideration of contact issues and living arrangements; risk assessment regarding particular behaviours; and scale, type and timing of interventions with child, birth family and/or other caregivers, including with regard to therapy. The expert then outlines what they feel able to do and how they intend to go about doing it. Hence, this is the first key stage in which perspective and ambiguity can be made transparent, such as regarding which assessment procedures are to be used.

For example, although child psychologists traditionally make use of standardized tests, I do not use them. Hence, I need to explain why this is the case and what I do instead. I note that there are – as post-structuralism suggests – problems with judging personality and behaviour against a fixed standard that may be culturally inappropriate (Smith 2003). And although standardized tests can be used creatively, as signposts to guide more detailed analysis for example, they can also be too reductive. This is particularly so if clients are categorized too rigidly after brief assessments made on the basis of limited face-to-face contact. Therefore, I indicate why I favour more open assessments that, whilst structured around the assessment questions, are not limited to a predetermined set of procedures or psychometric tests. I note that I need sufficient time to establish a working relationship with my client(s): children (and adults) tend to expand their accounts over time; and children's needs, and their families' ability to support them, also change (Jones and Ramchandani 1999) and evolve through discussion. I typically see children individually for four to six sessions and parents for a similar number of times. I would also expect to meet with parents together (if this is still their relationship) and observe contact between children and parents, children in the foster home and also at school. I also underline that I need to see all relevant written reports and have leave to consult with all relevant professionals and any other significant family members and carers, etc.

In this way a comprehensive context for making judgements is developed by triangulating different types of information that have come from different sources. These include written texts (reports, records and test scores, if formal tests are undertaken, etc.); spoken words (taken from interviews and meetings with the child, relevant adults including other professionals); and 'enacted' information gleaned from how the child is with me and my observation of the child with others. As Smith (2003) suggests, assessments should be based only on available information and there needs to be clarity about what one knows, what one does not know, and where each source of information comes from in order that any limitations are made explicit. Therefore, I do not rely solely on third-party evidence to formulate evaluations, and I try to avoid giving an opinion on any person not directly assessed.

If this approach is acceptable I then invite the lead solicitor to send me a formal 'letter of instruction'. This is the next point at which perspective can be made visible and negotiation can take place. Questions may be extended, reduced, and/or amended. I encourage movement from categorization of people (who they are) to understanding their behaviour in context (why they act in particular ways in particular situations and what set of circumstances and processes may enable their safety and which ones would undermine it). To this end I sometimes amend instructions by adding a contextualizing paragraph. See Illustration 1.

Illustration 1

The aim of this psychological report is to address those issues laid out in the letter of instruction and which are listed below:

1. How likely is Kylie to injure herself or others in this placement.
2. What impact sexual abuse has had on her emotional development, and any treatment needs in respect of this.
3. Whether Kylie is likely to engage in inappropriate and unsafe sexual practices.
4. There are references in the paperwork provided to me of Kylie's drug-taking. Assessment of Kylie's propensity for substance dependence and abuse.

Supplementary paragraph:

In order to address these current concerns it is necessary to consider them in the context of Kylie's whole life. Therefore this report begins by addressing Kylie's primary relationship experiences and considers the effects of these on her current feelings, beliefs and behaviours. I address the development of Kylie's coping strategies, including self-harm, aggression, sexual behaviour and drug use, in the light of Kylie's relationship history and negative life events, including sexual abuse. I then offer an opinion regarding the issues laid out in the letter of instruction and provide a framework for meeting Kylie's placement, relationship and therapeutic needs.

By including the supplementary paragraph I signal that I understand children to have an agentic relationship with their world. When the expert locates children's behaviours in a social and life context, the idea that children are passive or simply disordered can be resisted. Reframing 'risky behaviours' as 'coping strategies' moves away from a medical model that would otherwise take symptomatic behaviour to be indicative of internal mental pathology. The social contextualization of behaviour emphasizes its provisionality (it is what children sometimes do, rather than is indicative of who children always are). Expert witnesses and practitioners who view children's coping strategies as social practices, rather than as symptoms of internal disorder, enable the social processes of support and intervention to be more successful. Consequently, there is increasing interest in this type of reformulation in civil proceedings (Jones and Ramchandani 1999). Hence, a social recovery model of distress, as applied in Visible Therapy, has an increasing role to play within the more prescribed arena of child protection.

Assessing the child: communicative contextual practices

I begin my assessment by reading all the information that has been collated on the child and her family, and by talking to some of the people that know her. My aim is to develop an understanding of the context of the concern. This process enables me to begin to get a sense of the implicit reasons for my appointment. For example, do social services want me to 'rubber-stamp' decisions or is there enough ambiguity and curiosity in the system to support changing relationships? No one perspective is necessarily more true than any other, but all help situate the particular child, and it can be helpful to trace the ways different accounts of the child have developed. Like MacKinnon (1998: 113), I prefer the word 'account' to 'history' because this signals that information about the past is:

> [constructed] in the present and [is] influenced by the person's present interests and [is] understood through the discourses in which the person operates. This is true of all information, whether it is received from the family, the CP [child protection] Worker, or from other professionals. In this sense, the parents' account is no more or less credible than that of the CP Worker.

I am also mindful of more general issues that affect children involved in child care proceedings. For example, because of low prosecution and conviction rates in criminal proceedings abused children often feel even more let down, disbelieved, and powerless. And although children are the primary subject of care plans they may feel they have very little control over what happens to them and that their perspective carries little credibility. Therefore, when I conduct comprehensive assessments I try to be open to what the child tells me, whilst also being clear not to promise what I cannot deliver. Abused children may have multiple experiences of being tricked and manipulated and expert witnesses should reflect on how their own practices do, or do not, replicate those of abusers. Effective abusers, like effective psychologists, are also good communicators. In order to signal my difference from abusers I endeavour to be clear and transparent regarding what I do and why I am there. Children experience a greater sense of control when rules are explicit. I begin by explaining my role as a clinical psychologist and exploring each child's understandings about such people. One 4-year-old girl told me that 'a psychologist is someone who looks at the stars' – which is sometimes true.

I talk with the child about the particular questions that are to be addressed. Through doing this, I begin the reflexive process in my head of identifying potential conflicts in the different parties' agendas. I tell the child that I will give an opinion based on the information I have access to. Hence, I make clear why it is important she is involved in this process. Obviously children can refuse to talk to me about all or any of the matters of interest to the court. As in Visible Therapy, I accept that deciding not to speak is a valid choice and I never assume that speaking is a natural activity. If children decide not to take part in the assessment process I still outline what I will do (and note the child's decision not to take part as a clear limitation in the final report).

Although the admissibility of evidence is relaxed in civil proceedings, experts are still not expected to use too many leading questions. However, how children tell stories is not helped by abstraction and sometimes they need permission to talk. Hence, I do provide some direction for children. For example, I introduce abuse explicitly by referring to what I have been told and read. I do not act as a 'blank screen'. I ask open questions, but will tell children generally what I think. For example, I sometimes voice what I think their worries and concerns are if the child appears to be too frightened to say. I also give permission by suggesting activities that enable children to begin talking about their families. For example, I might ask children to draw a picture of their family or 'all the people that are important to you'. Drawings are useful both symbolically in terms of what they represent (see Furth 1988) and also as a starting point for thinking and talking about the child's relationships. I do not make judgements in isolation, but triangulate this with other sources of information. See, for example, Illustration 2.

Illustration 2

Selena, a six-year-old African-Caribbean girl, had been removed from her parents because of sexual abuse by her father, Lee. The Social Services Department was reluctant to return Selena to her mother's care, even though Lee had left the family home. Although the Social Services accepted that Selena's mother, Sharon, was not involved in Selena's sexual abuse, they questioned her ability to protect Selena in the future. Part of this concern related to the fact that Selena did not speak about either of her parents to the social worker or foster carers, and the assumption was that this indicated a poor attachment relationship with both parents.

In our first session together I asked Selena to draw a picture of her family. In the picture Sharon and Selena were close together, and Lee was at some distance. This indicated that there may be some

---

emotional connection between Selena and her mother – and some distance from her father. Selena's closeness to her mother was further suggested by her play. During each session, Selena played with dolls and talked to them as if they were Mum and Dad. Through this play we explored her mixed feelings about Sharon and Lee. Selena was cooperative with me, but could also say no to activities that she did not want to do. This suggested that she had developed some expectation of how to have safe and reciprocal relationships, which further suggested that Sharon was not entirely inadequate as a parent; presumably this expectation was less likely to have come from her relationship with Lee.

From my conversations with others I learnt that Selena had cried and resisted vigorously when removed from Sharon, but had been silent thereafter. Selena's silence seemed to be indicative of her fear regarding the perceived actions of her social worker and foster carers, rather than her lack of attachment to her mother. Because I was not involved in the initial removal, Selena did not apparently view me as part of this frightening process and hence was more able to share her feelings about her family with me.

Because the expert witness has a privileged 'outsider' position, it enables different narratives to emerge, whose strands can then be drawn together with existing ones. Through this process I try to build and explore a plausible, rather than definitive, account of the situation that can make sense of what, sometimes, feels like contradictory information. I make my noticing things explicit, such as how people cope with the process of assessment (get upset, angry, dissociated, etc.). We can then explore the relative merits of different coping strategies in practice, in our meetings and in reference to life. Thus, like action research, post-structuralist assessments are orientated to ongoing change and mutual evaluation. This is in contrast to traditional assessment practices that view 'data gathering' as a finite, one-way and objective procedure. Hence, I recognize that any assessment is also an intervention long before I share my assessment with others.

Giving social framework evidence

As noted, in child care proceedings the introduction of an 'independent' expert disperses responsibility, and through this can enable workers, children and their families to revise their ways of being with each other. Relationships that have felt fixed may feel more open and the possibilities of positive change may be reinvigorated. In my reports I aim to enhance the possibilities of positive change by extending the context of understanding.

These types of critical post-structuralist reports are necessarily long-winded because they do not rely on reductive psychometric formulations. However, in my experience and that of others, those involved in civil procedures welcome such reports because they contextualize information (see also Jones and Ramchandani 1999). They also address, rather than avoid, ambiguity.

Difficulties associated with psychologists 'hedging their bets' and the court's need to make a definitive judgment are lessened when ambiguity is located rather than denied. I cannot make definitive predictions, but I can indicate under which circumstance, when approached in which ways, children are likely to respond and hence what they might need and how this may change according to different circumstances. I link specific knowledge about the child who is the subject of court proceedings with more general understandings about children. Like Gavey (2003) in New Zealand (see also Department of Health DH 2000b), I make an explicit commitment to detailing people's strengths. This does not mean I avoid problems, but situate them. The more specific and located these descriptions are, the more difficult it becomes to fix my descriptions as enduring characteristics of children or their carers. See Illustration 3.

Illustration 3

Keira, a 15-year-old white girl, was placed in care because of sexual abuse by members of her extended family and her parents' inability to cope with her subsequent difficult behaviour. Major concerns were expressed about her sexual activity. I was asked to address this aspect of her behaviour in my report and in that report I said:

Keira has been sexually abused by her uncles from an early age. Through this she has learnt that her body can be used by men. Her subsequent feelings of self-loathing and low self-esteem mean that she has little value for herself and her body. This has been made worse because of her felt rejection by her parents. It is unremarkable that Keira views her body as a commodity. Keira told me that the first time she 'sold her body' was when she was about 13 years old and she had run away from home. She said that she was scared and sometimes did not want to do it, but she needed the money. She said, 'I just blanked out, closed my eyes and afterwards I'd just cry and cry'. Keira told me that she preferred 'going out' with older men. They bought her things and made her feel wanted.

Keira has used sex – the one thing she has learnt she can exchange – for negotiating the world in which she lives. Keira uses sex as a means of keeping people close, bringing her status and expanding her options for negotiating the material world. Exchanging sex for money

---

and friendship has immediate benefits for Keira, but in the longer term adds to her self-loathing. If Keira is in a placement where she feels valued, respected and secure, there will be less need for Keira to exchange sex for friendship, status or material gain. Increasing Keira's self-worth through stable and secure relationships in foster care should encourage Keira to develop more healthy relationships with her peers and enable her to make more positive choices around her body. It should be noted, however, that many young women believe that their self-worth is indicated through whether they have a boyfriend or not, and that older boyfriends bring greater status. Thus, the general pressures of being an adolescent girl may still impact on her decisions around sex.

Keira's sexual behaviour was contextualized in relationship to her own life history and with regard to other girls of a similar age. As indicated in this example, when I write about the behaviour children exhibit I deliberately write about what they do (sell their bodies, use drugs and/or alcohol) rather than who they might be (prostitutes, addicts or alcoholics). This ensures that a space is opened up for articulating when they do not use a particular behaviour, or when a particular behaviour means something else (e.g., Keira uses sex for multiple reasons). In order to understand the various meanings of behaviour it helps to make the implicit knowledges that frame our understandings explicit. Reports that deliberately contextualize knowledge in this way provide a form of what has been termed social framework evidence (see Raitt and Zeedyk 2000).

This approach is derived from the idea that all knowledge is socially produced and therefore understanding is enabled by providing a framework through which to makes sense of the information presented. The aim is not to direct what conclusions should be drawn. That is a matter for the judge (and/or jury in criminal trials). Rather the aim is to enable perspective to be made explicit in expert witness reports in order that existing concepts might be reworked, by providing a different framework in which to understand them. Take the concept of post-traumatic stress disorder (PTSD), which is a popular way of conceptualizing some of the negative effects of child sexual abuse and other forms of abuse trauma. For example, Ashcroft *et al.* (2003) report that in their study of 12- to 17-year-old abuse victims in the USA about 10 per cent of girls had PTSD symptoms and that over 1 million girls had met the criteria for PTSD (as of 1995, when this data was collected). As this 'disorder' is relatively common and familiar it can be used as a social framework for acknowledging that child sexual abuse has negative effects.

Hence, when children report recurrent intrusive recollections, dreams, or sudden feelings that are connected with the abuse that they have suffered, the court can draw on the concept of PTSD to frame its understandings about the link between past abuse and current difficulties. And although, as argued throughout this book, I might think that diagnosis can be an unhelpful practice, I do not want to be drawn into equally unhelpful arguments about whether such syndromes exist or not. Therefore, I adopt a position of agnosticism (as utilized in Visible Therapy) and emphasize points of consensus, as indicated in the brief extract below, which is also taken from my report on the aforementioned Keira:

> Some people talk about effects in these terms, and we could dispute whether this indicates PTSD exists or not. What we can all agree on is that this child has recurring nightmares and intrusive thoughts about the sexual abuse, which have a negative impact on her current life.

Because PTSD is such a popular framework for understanding abuse trauma, sometimes it is necessary to emphasize that PTSD cannot account for every victim's response to sexual abuse. This is crucial because if we assume there is a particular response, those victims who do not suffer in this way can be deemed to be untrustworthy. The implication is that non-typical reactions are taken to mean that it is not true. Depicting children in formulaic victim terms, implied by PTSD formulations, can also mean that, for example, aggressive, sexually active girls may be poorly served by the courts because they seem less deserving. Girls have multiple experiences of sexual abuse and cope in many different ways and therefore there may be common patterns, but there is no typical reaction to rape (Holmstrom and Burgess 1978; Lees 1996). For example, whilst girls often avoid and fear their abusers, sometimes they still want to be with their abusers – they may have no other close relationships, etc. Therefore, the presence or absence of any particular 'symptom' has no meaning in isolation.

Moreover, whilst sexual abuse can be devastating it is seldom the only important feature of children's lives. This is why reports should reference other significant life events and relationships, as well as consider both short- and long-term effects of abuse. This is because the impact of abuse may not be felt until later in the child's life. As Wattam (1997) argues, harm may not be immediately apparent – except regarding physical abuse – or during childhood at all. There are problems then regarding how judgements are made in respect of 'significant harm' (see, for example, governmental guidance on the Children Act 1989 (DH 1991)). 'Suffering' should not be the sole factor in determining whether an offence has occurred or whether a service should be provided. Cawson (2002) suggests, therefore, that a distinction should be made between harm and endangerment. By making social frameworks explicit when we talk about 'harm' and endangerment (that is providing detailed definitions, etc.), we enter into a much richer understanding of the information under discussion.

As Raitt and Zeedyk (2000: 177) argue, the use of social framework evidence, therefore, has an additional educational function because 'it provides a broader or alternative context within which to "make sense" of the factual information presented in a specific case'. Hence, diagnosis, for example, can be challenged by exploring its utility through the provision of an alternative reading. See Illustration 4.

Illustration 4

Ella, a 16-year-old white girl, had been referred to by other experts as having an emerging 'borderline personality disorder'. My report provided an alternative conceptualization for her problems:

Ella has experienced a significant amount of neglect, abuse and exploitation throughout her life. This has resulted in fears about and avoidance of intimacy, lack of trust in others and low self-esteem. Ella has coped with this by self-harming, getting angry and being emotionally volatile. The types of feelings and behaviours that Ella exhibits are consistent, as indicated by other mental health experts, with the diagnosis of 'borderline personality disorder'. Whilst this may be the case, I think it is an unhelpful description. In the context of child and adolescent mental health we more usually talk about issues concerning 'attachment and bonding'. I think this is far more helpful.

When someone is diagnosed with a personality disorder the implication is that this is an enduring and stable condition. However, 'borderline' behaviour is largely understood to develop in response to neglectful and abusive experiences in childhood. If we consider that people's personality (how they think and how they act) is shaped by the relationships that they have – that is, the nature of the attachments they form – we invite consideration of the social environments people find themselves in. A concern with 'attachments', therefore, directs concern to the mediating effects of good relationships on those who have suffered abuse and neglect. Change her experiences and Ella may no longer appear to have a 'borderline' personality.

This shift in focus from personality disorder to attachment relationship is crucial because, it can be argued, it instigates a social-recovery model of intervention by focusing on the quality of relationships rather than individual pathology. As WHO (2006b) found in their global study of violence and children, good relationships mediate the effects of most forms of abuse. WHO found that *protective* factors include good parenting, the development of strong attachment bonds between parents and children and positive non-violent discipline. *Resilience* factors are associated with strong positive attachments to an adult family member, high levels of paternal care, warm relationships with the non-abusing carer and supportive relationships with peers not involved in substance abuse and criminal behaviour. Where children have not experienced such relationships, this is what is aimed for in foster care and group homes. It is essential, therefore, when making assessments to consider the social and relationship context.

Hence, as Ella's report demonstrates, I seek to place the individual's difficulties in a social context. My aim is to demonstrate that how an individual behaves is a function of their own experiences and expectations, *and* the ways that they are treated by others. Therefore, in my reports I address both explicit concerns and implicit influences (see the Assessment Diamond, Figure 10.2). Opportunity is given for professionals to consider how, for example, their style of intervention may shape outcomes. Hence, when I make recommendations, I describe not simply what I think needs to be done, but also how and when. For example, Martha, a 15-year-old white girl who had been sexually abused, was viewed as being uncooperative and aggressive. My report aimed to disperse responsibility for this behaviour. See Illustration 6.

Illustration 6

Previous reports have emphasized Martha's aggressive behaviour, lack of cooperation and inability to take responsibility for the harm that she has caused to others. By contrast, Martha has cooperated fully in the assessment process with me and has expressed some considerable regret about her past actions. I think that Martha feels so bad about her previous violence that it is almost unbearable for her to talk about it. Martha needs to prove to herself, as much as to others, that she can be a 'good person'. It is much easier to acknowledge one's failings when one is confident about one's abilities, and Martha is not. Martha is best able to talk about her faults when questions regarding her status as a 'good person' seem not to be centre stage. Anyone working with Martha, therefore, needs to make every effort to emphasize what she can do, in order to enable her to accept help regarding the things that she finds difficult.

In order to encourage my clients to feel that they have an active stake in the process of assessment I always discuss my opinion with them prior to attending court. They should have every opportunity to challenge what I write and also to express their feelings, particularly because sometimes I do not agree with them. It is common practice, in civil proceedings, for the different parties to take their lead from the expert's report. For example, Richman *et al.* (2002) found that in their experience British psychologists are required to defend their reports in open court in less than 5 per cent of civil cases. Because these reports carry such weight, it is right that experts should make explicit how they arrive at their opinions rather than rely on their *de facto* status as expert to limit challenges to their views. Social framework evidence invites open discussion by providing a detailed, but accessible, account of how an opinion is developed and formed. Using the idea of social framework evidence to construct my reports also has consequences for how I give oral evidence. Ordinarily, expert witnesses are advised to 'answer the question' and to 'keep it simple'. However, when knowledge is socially located there are no simple, straightforward questions or answers. Hence, when I am called on to defend my report I use this opportunity to socially frame the ideas and concerns we discuss.

Social legal practices

Acting as an expert witness necessarily means stepping outside the world of psychology because it involves working in multi-agency systems. It inevitably involves working with different, and competing, frames of reference. The information that is presented is always theoretically and culturally saturated. Yet when perspectives are hidden under the veil of objectivity the opportunity for discussion is restricted. By contrast, social framework evidence extends the ways in which any piece of evidence can be understood. Social framework evidence reports, therefore, have multiple functions. They are written to assist the court in making judgments about children's lives. They are written to offer a way of understanding that may enable children and their carers to make sense of themselves and those around them. They also provide a framework for enabling the relevant professionals (social workers, psychologists, lawyers etc) involved to consider how they enact the decisions so made. They provide a means for educating other professionals about how to understand and challenge psychological expertise and knowledge. By contrast, when social frameworks remain hidden this can support unreflective practice that promotes blame and rigidity and decreases opportunities for cooperation and positive change. Without a reflexive approach we, like our clients, sometimes fail to learn and adapt. This is why a strong process-orientated and social approach to assessment is crucial in enabling expert witnesses to support a critical justice agenda within the expanding arena of child protection.

A critical justice agenda is also served by recognizing that child sexual abuse is both a personal mental health issue and a familial, cultural, and global social problem. If criminal, as well as civil, legal systems are to support, rather than undermine, abused children, the emotional impact of abuse should not be forgotten in the pursuit of criminal justice, or indeed in civil child-care proceedings. Otherwise child protection will remain offence-event focused as it is in many countries where legislation addressing violence against children concentrates on sexual and physical assault, yet fails to take account of psychological violence (WHO 2006b). In contexts that underestimate the psychological impact of abuse, protection and penalties are focused on, whilst recovery, reintegration and redress receive much less attention. Indeed, prevention can be misperceived as being addressed simply through protection and the penalty aspects of legislation. This is why – as feminists have long argued – personal, individual experiences of abuse have to be understood as wider political issues (the personal is still political).

Hence, as indicated, international commitments to end the abuse and exploitation of children should be strengthened through the adoption of common legal frameworks that support children's rights and which can be used in tandem with domestic initiatives. Clearly, laws can be badly applied and legislative change is too often used to suppress the weak. However, child sexual abuse is also a legal issue. Therefore, if abused children are to report acts of sexual violence, and perpetrators are to be prosecuted, there is a need to create accessible and child-friendly systems where there is clear criminal, civil, administrative and professional accountability regarding proceedings and sanctions (WHO 2006b). Underpinning such changes has to be a specific and global commitment to addressing the gender dimension of sexual violence (WHO 2006b). As argued, boys and girls, men and women, are made subject to abuse and violence in different ways. Girls and women are particularly vulnerable to sexual violence by adult males within the home (WHO 2007a). Therefore, if we are to address gendered violence, commonalties between abused girls and women need exploration and illumination. In the following chapter, connections between sexually abused daughters and domestically abused mothers are explored, specifically regarding supporting mothers within child protection systems.

11

MOTHERS, CHILDREN AND PROTECTIVE PRACTICES

Making links between domestic violence and child sexual abuse

Introduction

Clinical psychologists, who work in the field of child protection, are called on to make judgements about children, and also the people who care for them. Therefore, in order that clinical psychology expert witnesses are enabled to support a critical justice agenda in child protection it is necessary to consider the rights, responsibilities and needs of adults, as well as children, within this context. A *critical* justice agenda is one which is concerned with the ongoing development of theoretically and empirically robust child protection practices that are based on progressive principles of empowerment and collaboration. Part of this process involves identifying and addressing potential commonalties between abused children and abused adults. Specifically, as the World Health Organization WHO (2006b) has pointed out, the gender dimension of sexual and physical violence must be addressed if both international and domestic laws, policies and guidance are to succeed in supporting abused children and adults. As feminists have long argued, women and girls are particularly vulnerable to abuse within the home (see Chapter 4; WHO 2007a). The family system represents a prime site in which abusers can justify, enable and conceal abuse, and both girls and women may be subject to sexual exploitation and violent domination by their relatives. Thus, it is unsurprising that sometimes the sexual abuse of children coincides with the domestic abuse of adults, or that like child sexual abuse, the domestic abuse of adults is relatively common.

For example, according to the British Department of Health DH (2000a) just over one-quarter of women and about one-sixth of men report experiences of domestic abuse. Here the term domestic *abuse* is used to cover the multiple forms of physical, social, psychological, sexual and financial control that a focus on domestic *violence* can mask (both terms – abuse and violence – are used in this chapter). In a survey published by the Australian Bureau of Statistics, 42 per cent of women reported an incidence of violence by a previous partner (Australian National Campaign against Violence and

Crime NCAVAC 1999). And the National Domestic Violence Hotline NDVH (2007) reports that 4 million American women experience a serious assault by a partner during an average 12-month period. Finally, WHO (2007b), in a multi-country study of women's health and domestic violence, found that between 15 per cent and 71 per cent of ever-partnered women had experienced physical or sexual violence or both by an intimate partner in their lifetime. The least violence was found in Japan, and the most tended to be in rural communities such as Bangladesh, Ethiopia, Peru, and the United Republic of Tanzania.

Whilst women may suffer in multiple ways, they are particularly vulnerable to the physical consequences of domestic abuse. Women are more likely than men to sustain injuries that require intervention, hospitalization and have long-term effects. In Britain, domestic violence accounts for one-quarter of all violent crime and is the most common crime perpetrated against women. Every week, two women in Britain are killed by current or former partners (see DH 2000a; Horner, 2002), and every day an average of three women are murdered by husbands and boyfriends in the USA (NDVH 2007). Horner (2002) reports that 63,000 women and children use refuges each year in Britain and that family breakdown costs the government approximately £5 billion annually. Of the adult female population in Australia, 3 per cent (or about 300,000 women) contact the domestic crisis service annually and violence against women consumes more police time than any other police business except traffic accidents. Estimates suggest that the total costs of domestic violence in South Australia alone is about Australian $100 million per year – about 14 times the amount of funds spent on direct services to victims (NCAVAC 1999).

Domestic abuse – like child sexual abuse – therefore represents a significant global social, financial, health and personal problem. And as WHO (2007b) argues, it is also a human rights issue that affects all sectors of society. Women who have experienced domestic abuse have many different needs that reflect the many different ways that they have been hurt, controlled and exploited. My aim in this chapter is to explore the intersections that occur between child sexual abuse and domestic abuse within the context of child protection. Therefore, this chapter builds on Chapter 10 (which addressed the needs of sexually abused girls in child protection systems) to explore how to work with domestically abused mothers in the same context of child protection. My aim is to elaborate some of the ways in which clinical psychologists can navigate a critical path through a sometimes confusing and conflicted system. I begin by outlining some of the dilemmas that arise when matters of domestic violence are raised regarding parents during child protection investigations and critique some of the standards against which mothers are judged. I consider the role of victimhood in shaping practices around safety and explore ways in which women's sometimes increasingly fragile sense of agency can be enabled.

Between women's rights and child protection: A conflict of interests

Women with children constitute a significant group of those affected by domestic abuse, and it is estimated that between 133 and 275 million children worldwide witness domestic violence annually (WHO 2006b). It may be unsurprising that mothers represent a significant group of abused women given that domestic violence often starts or intensifies during pregnancy (DH 2000b). For example, NDVH (2007) reports that in the USA about 30 per cent of women who experience domestic abuse do so for the first time during pregnancy. The domestic abuse of adults, therefore, frequently has a negative impact on children as well, and there is considerable overlap between the abuse of adults and children in the same home. For example, in a national survey of over 6,000 American families, 50 per cent of the men who frequently assaulted their wives were also found to have abused their children (see Carter and Schechter 1997). Additionally, Humphreys *et al.* (2001) note that, in Britain, approximately two-thirds of children in social services' care come from homes where domestic violence is also present.

Although a clear relationship exists between domestic violence and child abuse, Carter and Schechter (1997) note that in the USA recognition that domestic violence is a child abuse issue is inconsistent, and there is little productive collaboration between child protection services and domestic violence programmes. By contrast, in the child protection arena in Britain, the recognition of a correspondence between the abuse of adults and children in families has led to considerable legislative change. This change has coincided with greater concern about the general quality of life parents provide to children (see Chapter 10). The UK government now considers that safeguarding the welfare of children frequently converges with safeguarding the welfare of the abused – usually female – carer:

> Everyone working with women and children should be alert to the frequent inter-relationship between domestic violence and the abuse and neglect of children. Where there is evidence of domestic violence, the implications for any children in the household should be considered, including the possibility that the children may themselves be subject to violence and harm. Conversely where it is believed that a child is being abused, those involved with the child and family should be alert to the possibility of domestic violence within the family.
>
> (DH 1999d: 71)

Hence, although abused women may need help in their own right, within the context of child protection they are seen to be deserving of intervention because supporting victimized mothers is understood to be the most effective way of promoting the child's welfare. Some contemporary approaches to child protection, therefore, recognize that the non-abusing carer is a crucial ally in supporting abused children, including those that have experienced sexual assault. By contrast, traditionally, women whose partners have sexually abused their children have been viewed with suspicion. As the British Psychological Society (BPS) (2001a: 26) notes:

> Early literature on sexual abuse focused on how mothers contribute to a child's victimisation rather than how a mother's support and belief can play a key role in a child's ability to resolve abusive experiences.

An important aspect of statutory work in respect of child sexual abuse, therefore, is to reinforce the non-abusing carer's power, strengthen the bond between the carer and child, and restrict the power and control of the abuser (BPS 2001a: 26). Such approaches dovetail with those designed to address the impact of domestic violence, whereby the aim is to empower and enable women to regain control of their lives. This is thought to be achieved through identifying responsibility, informing women of their legal rights, assisting women and children to escape, and supporting non-abusing carers to make safe choices for themselves and their children (DH 1999d).

Superficially the increasing recognition that domestic violence shares a common domain with child abuse is to be applauded, yet the partial repositioning of domestic violence into the child welfare arena is not uniformly positive. Because domestic violence is now considered to *be* a form of child abuse (it necessarily contributes to the emotional climate in families), the state has an expanded responsibility to intervene in the lives of domestically abused women and their children. Mothers are expected to be allies in child protection, yet there are multiple reasons why many mothers involved in child care proceedings feel in conflict with professionals.

Unfortunately, many mothers of sexually abused children still feel undermined rather than supported as latent suspicion reinforces feelings of inadequacy and guilt. They may feel blamed and have a deep sense of failure, precisely at the moment that they are expected to work out how to keep their children safe and when they are also coming to terms with big questions about their own abilities and identity (see Colclough *et al.* 1999). Mothers must cope with their own feelings of distress and guilt whilst attempting to manage their children's difficult emotions (Jones and Ramchandani 1999). Because women are expected to care for and protect children they are held in greater contempt than men when things go wrong. If mothers exhibit their own insecurities and confusion, or demonstrate their own domestic vulnerabilities, they may feel further judged and undermined. Mothers may then be reluctant to ask for help because they feel blamed and/or undeserving. Alternatively if the abuser is out of the household and the mother appears to be 'safe' she may receive very little formal support at all.

When mothers are also victims of domestic violence they may feel doubly damned. As O'Hara (1995) argues, mothers worry that if they cannot protect themselves their ability to protect their children will be additionally nega- tively judged, which may increase their reluctance to talk about domestic violence. As Schechter and Edleson (1994) argue, a 'best interests of the child' perspective can mean that violent men and their adult victims are treated as equally problematic parents because the same judgement is applied to both: who can keep the child safe? Women who cannot protect themselves are not judged to be able to protect their child, and hence battered women can quickly become labelled as mothers who 'failed to protect'.

Fears of being negatively judged may be reinforced by abusers in order to maintain control in families. For example, in a study of women from minoritized ethnic communities in Britain (Batsleer et al. 2002), abusive partners were described as using children to ward against mothers accessing help from outside the family. They emphasized well-founded concerns that children from minoritized ethnic communities are over-represented in the care system, and that provision for them is inadequate and inappro- priate. If children are subsequently removed into care, the perils of speaking out confirm mothers' fears and increase their isolation. Furthermore, as Carter and Schechter (1997) note, some abusers directly undermine women's parenting abilities by injuring them, keeping them awake all night, and generally undermining their self-confidence through years of terror and trauma.

Therefore a concern with domestic violence cannot simply be 'added in' to child protection policies, otherwise this increases attention on the mother's 'failure to protect' (Humphreys et al. 2001), rather than providing a platform for support. This is because constituting domestic violence as a form of child abuse 'leads to monitoring and surveillance rather than support and help because it fails to differentiate victims from perpetrators' (Humphreys et al. 2001: 185). Mothers may then justly feel more powerless than empowered, as they exchange the master in the home for the pan- optican of state surveillance (Foucault 1991). If intervention procedures in child protection are to enable abused mothers more, and undermine them less, it is crucial therefore that the impact of different forms of abuse are differentiated within 'risk' assessments. Otherwise when assessments are made of parents' capacity to care for their children, these assessments may camouflage more than they reveal.

Assessing parenting capacity: differentiating carers and illuminating the impact of different forms of abuse

Although the court may be sympathetic to the plight of domestically abused women, in child care proceedings the primary concern with mothers is in regard to their capacity to care for their children. This focus means that professional relationships with mothers may be strained. Additionally, *child* care practitioners may have only limited understanding about the domestic abuse of *adults*. Misunderstanding is further exaggerated when gendered patterns of care are assumed, but not theorized. As noted, because women predominate as carers they may be held in greater contempt than men when they fail to protect children and, hence, their own victimization may be underestimated. For example, in Reder and Duncan's (1999) comprehensive study of fatal child abuse in Britain, there is no reference to domestic violence in the book's subject index. Yet domestic violence may be crucial. A study of 67 child fatalities in Massachusetts, USA, found that 43 per cent of mothers identified themselves as victims of domestic violence (see Schechter and Edleson 1994). And Carter (2005) reports that the American Advisory Board on child abuse and neglect suggests that domestic violence may be the single major precursor to child abuse and neglect fatalities in America.

Yet because domestic violence remains hidden, child protection is undermined. This is because, as O'Hara (1995) argues, child protection practice fails to appreciate how power dynamics are differentially actioned within families according to gender and age. Mothers clearly have a duty of care to their children, but they are not directly responsible for abuse perpetrated by others. In order to make the operations of power clear, it is important, then, to identify the different roles, relationships and responsibilities people have within families. When parents are homogenized, insufficient distinction is made between abusing and non-abusing parents, and the power relationships in family and society that sustain domestic and sexual abuse remain unexamined (O'Hara 1995). See Illustration 1.

Illustration 1

Theresa (a 29-year-old white woman) had been with her partner, Mark (a 43-year-old white man) since she was 16 years old. Throughout their relationship Mark had been violent and abusive to Theresa. They have one daughter, Donna (12 years old). Over the years Mark had controlled all aspects of Theresa's life. Theresa had become isolated from her friends and family, she did not work, and was dependent on Mark for all her emotional and financial needs. Mark interspersed physical violence with sexual assault, and continually verbally attacked Theresa. Theresa coped with this by getting drunk. Mark undermined Theresa's relationship with Donna by calling Theresa names, etc. when Donna was present. He also made Donna watch when he hit Theresa, so that Donna knew what happened to 'bad' women. If Theresa threatened to leave, Mark told Theresa she would lose Donna because of her 'alcoholism'.

Because of general concerns at school about Donna's welfare, she was referred to Social Services and subsequently sexual abuse was considered to have taken place. A criminal conviction was not obtained (sexual abuse could not be proved 'beyond a reasonable doubt'), but in the Findings of Fact in the civil child-care proceedings, the judge determined that on 'the balance of probabilities' sexual abuse had occurred, and that this was perpetrated by Mark. In his summing up, the judge acknowledged that Theresa did not know about the sexual abuse of her child, but that her evident alcoholism had caused a significant strain in the marital relationship and indicated her inadequacies as a parent. Therefore, Theresa should take some responsibility for Donna's abuse.

It may be that Theresa's use of alcohol reduced her capacity to notice things around her. However, the domination and control exerted by Mark over both Theresa and Donna (and which preceded Theresa's drinking) is far more relevant in determining Theresa's ability to protect herself and her child. No reference was made to the impact of domestic abuse by this judge in his summing up. Without a social framework within which to make sense of the impact of domestic violence, mothers like Donna may be routinely condemned for actions that are beyond their control. Challenging such judgments is made possible when social framework evidence (see Chapter 10) is used to make sense of gendered behaviour by making trajectories of responsibility explicit so that they can be tracked. This involves highlighting the impact domestic violence can have, and resisting the medicalization of social problems. As Humphreys *et al.* (2001: 185) argue:

> [the] slippage towards an emphasis on other problems such as mental ill health or alcohol misuse, [means] . . . that domestic violence becomes invisible as an interconnected or coexisting issue.

If mothers are to be supported through child care proceedings, then the capacities of each parent to exert control, as well as their individual capacities to care for their children, must be judged separately. Yet a general concern with 'parenting capacity' fails to highlight the distribution of power within families (see Figure 10.1, Chapter 10). Parenting capacity is frequently judged (*à la* Attachment Theory, Bowlby 1969, 1973) in general terms of carers' abilities to provide basic care and ensure safety through providing guidance and boundaries in the context of emotionally warm and stable relationships and a stimulating home environment. Whilst it may be self-evident that loving, stable relationships are better than destructive, unpredictable ones, whether a family unit can provide basic care does not distinguish one parent from the other, nor can we know how parenting capacity actually promotes or inhibits a child's welfare and development.

In the preceding example it may be obvious that there were serious failings in both parents' capacities to provide adequate care. However, unsituated notions of 'parenting capacity' and 'secure attachments' fail to account for how the (mis)use of parenting and relationship skills within apparently 'good' families provide the conditions for promoting and concealing child sexual abuse or domestic violence. The abusing family is viewed as being distinct from the non-abusing family; the securely attached child from the insecurely attached child; and the woman in a poor relationship from the woman who has a good relationship with her partner. These oppositions fail because they assume a template for good parenting or good relationships that is socially and temporally invariant and assumes that parents and children, or adult partners, have only one experience of relationship with each other (Warner 2001b).

As argued in Chapter 10, children may attach to a sexually abusing parent. Sexually abusive parents are also sometimes the same parents who take children to the park, play with them, buy them presents, and do a myriad of things which are not, in themselves, abusive. Women may love the partner who abuses them. Violent men can sometimes be funny, romantic, and caring too. Loving relationships are effective contexts for ensuring children and women's silence and compliance with abuse. Love acts as a counter to the fear engendered by sexual and physical aggression. Thus, the conditions that are assumed to give rise to emotional security are precisely the conditions in which abusers may exercise power to enact and conceal sexual and domestic abuse.

Furthermore, narratives of 'good parents' and 'good families' are culturally sedimented to restrict concern over white, middle-class and two-parent families, whilst mobilizing concern over Black and working-class families which fail to conform to the nuclear ideal. For example, an American study conducted by Jenny et al. (1999) found that doctors missed nearly four in ten abuse-related head-injury cases in white children or those from two-parent families, whilst missing two in ten cases in non-white children or those living with a single parent. Therefore, unacknowledged assumptions regarding race, class and family structure may be actioned through the multiple processes of assessment to raise or restrict concern regarding the lives of particular women and children.

The ability to form good relationships and to demonstrate good 'parenting capacity' does not definitively distinguish sexually abusive or domestically violent men from non-abusive men. Therefore, it is crucial that women and children are talked to if domestic and sexual abuse is to be recognized and addressed. This may seem an obvious point, but an over-reliance on Attachment Theory within systems that are orientated to consider matters of emotional abuse can fail children and women who are not 'neglected', but who are sexually and/or physically abused. The global application of seemingly benign theory contributes to the dangers that these women and children face because it hides certain forms of abuse by masking the conflicting and unstable nature of relationships and the unequal distribution of power within families. Supporting mothers involved in child care proceedings, then, involves challenging dominant structures of understanding by making alternative social frameworks visible, such that, for example, alcohol use or attachment relationships can be re-read through the lens of domestic violence. This approach invites a more specific and located reading of behaviour that is always mindful of the practices of power.

Reassessing 'poor outcomes': from categorical judgements to social contextual practices

As WHO (2006b) found in their global study of violence and children, children need strong, positive, warm, consistent and non-violent relationships with carers in order to mediate the effects of most forms of abuse. Whether parents can be helped to provide such relationships to their children is the primary concern when judgements are made about reuniting children with parents following abuse and/or neglect. A range of factors are understood to predict poor outcomes for families. Such factors largely direct attention to the shortcomings of parents, rather than the iniquities of the system. Yet, the process of assessment, and the values that assessors draw on, may be as important because, as indicated in Chapter 10, process and values have a direct impact on the end result.

Mothers may be particularly liable to negative parenting assessments, even when they have not directly abused their children. Because mothers are assumed to be selfless and beneficent, their failings may be judged more harshly than fathers' failings. Their behaviour, as primary caregivers, comes under exaggerated scrutiny, not least because mothers are more likely than fathers to attend appointments. Additionally, it is not uncommon for professionals, who are predominantly women, to avoid meetings with men they also fear (O'Hara 1995). Hence, whilst there may be generic factors that indicate 'poor outcomes' for reuniting parents with their children, mothers may be judged more harshly than men against these standards. For example, this may be the case when women are judged to be uncooperative and/or in denial. See Illustration 2.

Illustration 2

Poor outcomes: 'the abusing parent completely or significantly denies any responsibility for the child's developmental state or abuse' and 'the relationships within the family and with professionals remain at breaking point'. (DH 1999b: 59)

Safia, a 25-year-old African-Caribbean woman, refused to admit her responsibility for failing to protect her 6-year-old daughter, Chantelle, from the father (Pete, a 25-year-old white man) who sexually and physically abused her and who also domestically abused Safia. When social workers attempted to get Safia to acknowledge that she had failed to intervene when there was at least clear evidence of physical abuse, Safia said that she had not witnessed the abuse and that her partner had provided 'reasons' for any physical injury to her daughter. When pressed, Safia responded by becoming verbally and physically abusive. Safia shouted and would push people out of the way as she stormed off. Service providers felt that there was good evidence that Safia was unfit to care for her child: she denied any responsibility, and her relationship with professionals was constantly at 'breaking point'.

For Safia, the negative responses of others reinforced her shame and increased her indirect methods (swearing, pushing others) of exhibiting distress. Whilst these exhibitions of distress gave her immediate relief, ultimately these socially problematic communications and coping strategies became intrinsic to the negative perceptions of others. Women's violent conduct is tolerated less well than men's and is, therefore, more likely to be viewed as being indicative of personality rather than a situated response to an emotionally charged interaction. This may be especially the case for Black women, like Safia, because of racial stereotyping. By contrast, men may be forgiven for violent behaviour precisely because its cause is located outside of them. For example, Hinsliff (2003) reported, in the British press, that:

Joseph McGrail walked free in 1992 with a suspended sentence for kicking his wife to death, after pleading provocation on the grounds that she was an alcoholic and swore at him. The judge said the dead woman 'would try the patience of a saint'.

In Safia's case, her aggressive behaviour with professionals had become entrenched and those factors external to Safia that contributed to her actions could no longer be seen. Armed with the knowledge that strained relationships with professionals and denial of responsibility for abuse is associated with poor outcomes, existing workers were ever more pessimistic about Safia's capacity to change. Because these markers of 'poor outcomes' had been located and fixed within Safia, the professionals felt powerless to effect any positive change. In the hope that this stalemate could be resolved, all parties agreed to the appointment of an 'independent' expert. As the independent expert, I was in a privileged position in that I was outside of the established negative interaction cycle. Hence, as argued in Chapter 10, there was greater possibility for different forms of interaction to take place.

Providing a new context for assessment, in which different narratives could emerge, enabled me to introduce an alternative social framework for making sense of Safia's behaviour. It seemed that Safia's aggressive stance masked her vulnerability and service providers who continued to heap opprobrium on her increased her sense of vulnerability, which provoked more defensive anger. I invited the other professionals in her care to consider that Safia felt frightened and undermined and that if they resisted the desire to tell her that she was guilty, she would be more able to talk about her shortcomings and to accept support. When the other professionals decreased their negative interactions Safia was able to admit her sense of vulnerability and feelings of guilt, and this proved to be a positive turning point in the relationship between the professionals and Safia.

The 'expert' witness does not necessarily possess greater or better knowledge than other professionals. However, the opportunity to engage with clients anew does sometimes provide the impetus to provisionalize relationships that otherwise would remain stuck (as Gavey (2003) found in New Zealand). Moreover, drawing on social frameworks that invite greater consideration of the unequal distribution of power (such as feminist theory) and which focus attention on the social context in which individual actions unfold (such as post-structuralist theory) enables greater change within systems. This is because responsibility for change is dispersed rather than restricted to only one party, such as the mother. It is crucial, therefore, to contextualize the multiple factors that shape 'poor outcomes' in child care proceedings. This is because contextualization invites consideration of all relevant influences on outcomes (whether good or bad), and hence, contextualization increases the ways in which change can be promoted (it is no longer just about the mother, for example).

A key aspect of the work of the clinical psychologist in child protection involves challenging the use of diagnostic categorization, a step which further decontextualizes women's actions. As argued previously, making the mental health status of women the focus of concern works against them as the abuse that underpins their feelings and behaviour is hidden. The personality of the woman, or the diagnostic category so assigned, is then set at issue, rather than the experiences she has coped with and endured. For example, 'post-natal depression' internalizes women's distress at a time characterized by great social upheaval, and it may not be incidental that, as noted, domestic abuse often starts or intensifies during pregnancy. Stark and Flitcraft (1996) argue that domestic abuse is also a factor in at least 25 per cent of suicide attempts by women (see also Chantler *et al.* 2001). As Fundudis *et al.* (2003) suggest, the key to assessing parenting capacity is not found in diagnostic category or personality 'type', but is found in the background experiences and current competencies that women indicate. This is because they locate women's behaviour in a social context, which brings meaning to their actions. See Illustration 3.

Illustration 3

I was asked to assess whether Stella, a 32-year-old white woman, whose daughter Jess (11 years old) had been sexually abused by Stella's husband, Ray (a 36-year-old white man), could protect her daughter in the future. Stella was depicted as having 'personality problems'. She was described by the social worker as being 'cold and indifferent' towards her child because she showed no emotion when told that Jess might not be returned to her care.

In order to find out about Stella's parenting capacity, I needed to find out about Stella as a social being. I asked about her life experiences and how she coped with them and also reflected on how she coped with the assessment process. It seemed to me that Stella 'spaced out' when she felt emotionally threatened – for example when talking to the social worker. Stella confirmed that was how she felt. She told me that she had been like that for most of her life. She said that she had learnt to cope by 'spacing out' when she was young because 'no one cared' about the sexual abuse she had experienced. Stella continued to do this in the face of emotionally difficult experiences when she felt disregarded, undermined, uncared for and abused.

Stella's husband, Ray, was verbally, physically and sexually abusive towards her. Her primary emotional state at home was to be 'spaced out'. It followed that she was unable to pick up on the distress of her daughter. Stella demonstrated that she could be emotionally present with me (she cried, expressed anger, etc.). However, my concern remained that without support, strategies and validation, Stella's ability to care for Jess would be compromised by her capacity to shut off in the face of emotional difficulty.

Understanding Stella's apparent indifference and lack of emotional warmth as being indicative of her familiar coping style seemed more helpful than using these 'symptoms' to confirm her personality problems. As noted, when we talk about 'personality' the implicit assumption is that this is who people are, and ever will be. Yet Stella's capacity to act differently with me meant that although she routinely 'spaced out', this strategy was not all encompassing. Therefore, although Stella's ability to cut off emotionally remained concerning, recontextualizing it in more social terms enabled other professionals to have some hope that by approaching their interactions with

Stella differently there was some possibility of encouraging positive change. The frameworks we draw on to theorize child protection, therefore, have a profound impact on the multiple processes of assessment and intervention that overlap to enable, and sometimes undermine, safer family systems.

Supporting safety and security: resisting victimization and enabling agency

The primary concern within child protection systems is to minimize the risk of significant harm to children. The ways we theorize this practice shape our ability to enable safer families. Because notions of 'risk' invite a negative narrative flow, it is useful to conceptualize aims within the more positive discursive framework of 'safety'. The same issues may be addressed, but attention is directed to what can be done, rather than what mothers' failures are deemed to be. This increases the likelihood of collaborative relationships between clients and professionals and is instrumental in securing safer and, therefore, less risky futures for mothers and their children. A first step in securing safer futures is to enable women's resistance to victimization by supporting women's physical separation from their abusive partners.

The State can support women's independence through, for example, legal means (such as criminal prosecution of offenders and the use of injunctive orders, e.g. non-molestation orders and occupation orders, which can be made by both criminal and civil courts, although they are usually made by civil courts); and practical means (such as providing panic buttons in the home that are linked directly to the police). However, for many abused women physical separation from their abusers is only secured by moving their families somewhere else.

Whilst social services can help women find alternative housing, it has traditionally been the community that has provided immediate refuge for women: both informally and formally. Because men's violence increases (or may start) when women leave (DH 2000a) this is a particularly dangerous time for abused mothers and their children. For example, Frohman and Neal (2005) report that approximately 75 per cent of women who were killed by their intimate partners in the state of New York in 1997 were killed when they were in the act of leaving or when they had just left the relationship. Therefore, secrecy is understood to secure safety. However, whilst advertising one's departure may not be useful, secrecy and isolation are also the context in which abuse occurs. Yet the transitional need for secrecy has become a foundation for much formal refuge provision. The assumption is that secret refuge locations are safer than published ones. This may not be the case.

In their study of national practices in the USA, Haaken and Yragui (2003) noted that the refuges with published addresses did not report higher incidence rates of violence than confidential locations. Indeed, the location of unpublished refuges is often an 'open secret'. Open shelters (the tradition within which Erin Pizzey started the refuge movement in 1970s Britain) make male violence less hidden and place more responsibility on the community to secure safety. Neighbourhoods that have low rates of violence are ones in which there is strong collective efficacy, defined as a sense of trust, shared values and community cohesion. There is some evidence that this is the case even in poor, largely unemployed and single-parent communities that are traditionally associated with high levels of violence (see Carter 2005). Hence, safety may be better assured by having open shelters within the context of encouraging more open collectivist communities.

Open shelters also repudiate the feelings of shame that secrecy can invoke. Secret locations mean women are again isolated from family, friends and community. For women and children from minoritized ethnic communities, moving to a refuge may involve moving to areas where there are few people from the same ethnic minorities. These women and children may, then, be particularly badly served as they exchange violence within the family for racial harassment on the street or in the refuge (Pantling and Warner 2002). Refuges do not offer the same experiences of safety for all women. Haaken and Yragui (2003) also argue that secrecy invites women to feel that they and their female workers are helpless and impotent in respect of men. Indeed, accessing such services invites women and children who use them to embrace particularly disempowered formations of identity. This is because services are delivered either to vulnerable adults or children in need. Thus, mothers and children are encouraged to embrace their sense of victimhood as this provides access to psychological, social and financial support. This results in a focus on weaknesses and difficulties rather than strengths and abilities (see Haaken 2002). Mothers must then navigate between being victim enough to secure support, but not so passive that the state determines them to be incapable parents. Additionally, if women, or children, demonstrate too many weaknesses they may be excluded from the very services they need to access.

Women and children who may be the least able to negotiate independence, because they have severe mental health problems and exhibit extreme forms of behaviour, have the fewest options in terms of support. For example, if women and children use drugs, alcohol or self-injury as ways of coping with the emotional effects of sexual and domestic abuse (which a significant number do – see Collins *et al.* 1999; Spandler and Warner 2007) they may be excluded from refuges. Mothers might then be directed into the mental health system where there is very little family provision, and they may become permanently estranged from their children as they get lost within the separate spheres of psychiatric ward and children's home. Some mothers may also find themselves in prison and equally estranged from their children. For example, Frohman and Neal

(2005) quote American Bureau of Justice Statistics (1999) that found 57 per cent of female prisoners in state prisons and 40 per cent in federal prisons report physical or sexual abuse – mainly by intimate partners – prior to serving their sentence. It is crucial, therefore, that every effort is made to secure safe housing for abused women and their children because without safe housing they cannot begin to build safer relationships with themselves or each other.

Many women and children do not require ongoing intervention once they have found a safe place to live. Some mothers and children, however, do need ongoing support in order to recover from experiences of abuse. Whether support is requested or mandated there are some common factors that encourage safer lives. As argued throughout this book, abusers organize reality in such a way that their victims learn to internalize their vulnerability and thereby accept abuse as deserved and/or inevitable. Because of the ways in which services are provided, women and children may be further encouraged to view themselves as victims. Therefore, an important aspect of work with domestically abused women, as with sexually abused children, is to enable them to reclaim their sense of agency. This means that, even when mothers are made subject to compulsory state intervention, they should be encouraged to make what choices they can for their families and their acts of agency need explicit recognition. For example, when women leave violent or sexually abusive partners they are already challenging the inevitability of victimization and this should be validated.

Challenging the inevitability of victimization is crucial in enabling women to reassert themselves. As Lamb (1996: 21) argues, 'being a victim means having no responsibility for who one is, and who one has become'. It also limits who one may be in the future. If we simply say, 'it was not your fault', this offers no means through which victims may renegotiate abusive relationships in the future and underestimates the intractability of internalized guilt. Moreover, we may then fail to explore the ways abused women and children did exercise their will and find aspects of control during abusive experiences. It is crucial, therefore, to identify how and when women and children take control if mothers (and children) are to be supported through changing times and changing relationships. Leaving abusive partners, therefore, involves both material and discursive changes in women's lives as their perceptions of self (as victims, for example) also come under review.

For women, in particular, changes in relationship have a significant impact on their self-concept. As Colclough et al. (1999: 168) argue, 'women's psychological development means that, more than for men, loss of attachments are experienced as a loss of self'. These transitive moments in life can leave women feeling unsure who they are, unclear about who they have been and who they could become. Their emotional uncertainty may be attenuated by material privation occasioned by living in a refuge, loss of their own paid employment, and/or the loss of access to their partner's wage. At these times women may be acutely aware of the instability of identity and feel vulnerable in their lack of clarity. They may then retreat from the uncertainty of change and go back to the violent embrace of victimization.

Points of transition are crucial times at which the forms of support that women need should be thought through carefully. When women are made to feel blamed for the abuse they or their children endure, this public recognition can invoke feelings of shame that reinforce categories of identity shaped by abuse. These 'shameful' abuse identities can then further immobilize transitional realities. Uncertainty is better tolerated when it is marked with hope and when women can shift their sense of reality gradually. This is often a difficult task in systems that must balance the safety needs of children with encouraging women to exercise control in their lives. However, if women are to be enabled, rather than undermined, service providers have to find ways of working with, rather than simply containing, 'risk. In order to encourage positive change, I adopt a framework of *safe uncertainty* (Robinson and Whitney 1999). In this framework, safety is understood to be facilitated through specification and explication of the processes involved in interventions and by being clear and explicit about the limits of acceptable action. Because the processes are detailed, the content of intervention can then be opened up such that a space of uncertainty is provided in which people might change their behaviour and their understandings. See Illustration 4.

Illustration 4

Rosy, a 45-year-old white woman, and her husband Jack, a 47-year-old white man, did not believe that their 19-year-old son, Tom, had sexually abused their 15-year-old daughter, Helen. Tom had also been physically abusive to Rosy and Helen. Tom was the 'successful' male child who was at university and would bring honour to the family. Rosy and Jack dismissed his previous violence (it was in the past and he had grown out of it). In order to accept his culpability for sexual abuse, the bright future the parents wanted to believe in could not be sustained; additionally, their ability to view themselves as 'good parents' would also come under review. Helen's evident distress and disturbed behaviour was reframed as being indicative of her status as 'the problem child' who was still loved, but would never be as successful as Tom. They noted that Tom had never been prosecuted for sexual abuse.

Helen needed help to mobilize her parents into providing some minimal protection from Tom. My aim, in meeting with the parents, was to encourage them to keep Tom away from Helen. I made clear

---

that I believed (alongside other professionals etc.) that Helen had been sexually abused by Tom, but acknowledged that Rosy and Jack did not. I then attempted to establish the extent of our shared beliefs: that Helen was 'difficult' and 'upset'; that some of this could be to do with Tom's previous violent (if not sexual) behaviour. Because Tom's previous violence was an accepted family fact (it happened to Rosy, as well as Helen) this could not be in dispute.

I noted that although Rosy and Jack believed that Tom's violence would not be repeated, Helen was still frightened of him (and this was indicated in her difficult and upset behaviour that was also not in dispute). Therefore, whether or not Rosy and Jack believed Helen's fear to be justified because – as they said – they loved Helen too, they needed to meet some of her needs. I suggested that they could act *as if* Tom was still a threat to Helen and ensure that Tom was not allowed access to her.

My aim was to change Rosy and Jack's behaviour by deferring the need to change their understanding of reality all at once. Rosy and Jack did not agree with my interpretation (Tom had sexually abused Helen and was still a threat), yet they were encouraged to act protectively (to act as if he had sexually abused Helen and was still a threat) prior to changing their own version of events. They had previously felt unable to provide protection to Helen because this would have involved too many profound changes in their beliefs about themselves and their children.

The approach described above did not protect Helen from the emotional harm of being disbelieved. My hope was that behavioural change would instigate a gradual shift into belief in the future. Helen, at 15 years old, had made a deliberate decision not to pursue a criminal case against her brother. I could not, and did not want to, force this issue. All I could do was validate Helen's own knowledge that she was sexually abused and try to ensure her brother's access to her was restricted as much as possible. Finding ways to engage parents like Rosy and Jack is difficult, messy and imperfect. Unless we try, however, the abuser-organized system remains intact. Clearly, it is not possible to enable change within all families. Yet, without a platform of hope, condemnation becomes the leitmotif that structures child protection practices.

Promoting hope and recovery: deconstructing the tactics and effects of abuse

In order to enable mothers and children to find better futures we have to have some hope that this is possible. Without hope, services become mired in crisis management and they fail to develop practices that encourage the transformation of troubled lives. This is why challenging the assumption that abused women and children are trapped in a cycle of victimization should be a recurring concern within critical child-protection practice. Although there is some evidence that early abusive experiences can be predictive of later abusive relationships or interpersonal difficulties (Roodman and Clum 2001; Rumstein-McKlean and Hunsley 2001), this is not always the case. As even professional bodies, such as the British Psychological Society (2001a: 26), acknowledge: '[e]vidence now challenges the idea of the inevitability of abusive cycles of behaviour being continued across generations'.

An overemphasis on the impact of early experience means that the impact of lifelong learning can be underestimated. When the inevitability of future abuse is assumed, this can act as a self-fulfilling prophecy for children which cements division between them and their mothers who are invited to view their children with suspicion. Frequently, a gendered reading of sexual abuse and physical violence is drawn on to differentiate girls from boys as, respectively, ongoing victims and abusers. Such understandings, in part, underpin much current refuge policy that excludes male children over the age of 13 because of their potential to be violent. Children may then be denied access to services that could mediate the effects of domestic violence and sexual abuse as they may be deemed to be already, and permanently, damaged and the mothers themselves beyond help and redemption (Pantling and Warner 2002). Mothers' feelings of guilt at the permanent damage they have 'failed to protect' their children from can then further undermine the relationship between mothers and children.

In order to enable mothers to believe that adults and children have the capacity to renegotiate their pasts and determine different futures for themselves, it is often helpful to revisit their own stories of victimization. The aim is to draw out the multiple tactics that ensure that abuse feels inevitable, but which demonstrate how constructed this is. We might talk about how abusive men seldom act abusively at the outset but, rather, over time create the conditions in which domestic abuse will be tolerated. My aim is to make the psychological, social, and structural tactics of domestic and sexual abuse visible in order that women and children can articulate their own stories of resistance and survival. Through this process mothers and children can reclaim some shared territory, not as forever-victims, but as subjects rather than objects of family and social history.

Hence, when therapists and other workers help mothers to understand how they come to accept the reality of their lives (e.g. this is what I deserve), they also enable mothers to begin to make sense of how their child's understanding of life may have been similarly constructed. When mothers recognise that they may have been trapped by similar tactics to their children, it can help in re-establishing the relationship between mother and child. Mothers and children often need separate space in which to reflect on their individual processes of victimization in order to re-establish this common ground. Shame may be evident when issues are deemed to need secrecy. However, families are not transparent all the time, and adults and children have competing concerns and desires that they do not always share. Sometimes mothers need advice about managing (monitoring, stopping, ignoring, and distracting) their children's sexualized and aggressive behaviour when the child is too young to make these connections herself. Tracing the tactics of abuse, and the subversive strategies women and children use to survive, ensures that victimization remains under revision, rather than being an inevitable and enduring consequence of abuse.

I know that sometimes for mothers change is not always possible, or proves to be insufficient, but I try not to condemn at the outset of my working relationship with them. In such situations I accept that I am part of the mechanism by which the State ultimately acts on behalf of the child. I do write reports that lead to the separation of children from mothers, but always explain to mothers why and how I have drawn the conclusions that I have by giving specific examples and referencing particular sources of information and observations. I offer the opportunity for mothers to review my report, to challenge what I have written and to explore their feelings about my recommendations. I avoid categorical condemnation by maintaining a sense of hope, even if change is not possible this time, in this set of circumstances and relationship.

Working with abused mothers in the context of child welfare systems is fraught with competing interests and dangers. It is crucial that child care workers explore their own beliefs about motherhood if they are to resist the culture of blame that undermines more positive working relationships with women. Understanding how abuse realities are made and maintained enables this process because it draws attention to ways in which mothers are frequently set up to fail. As victims of abuse mothers may be understood to be unable to actively care for their children. Yet if their victimization is not recognized their culpability may be overstated. When attention is paid to the processes as well as the content of assessment and intervention, collaborative relationships are easier to sustain and mothers' changing lives can be supported rather than constrained. Unfortunately, for some abused women and girls their difficulties may have become too entrenched. Professionals may feel community-based support is no longer viable and that secure services are required. The final chapter of this book addresses the needs of this particular disenfranchised group of abused women and girls.

12

BEYOND DEVIANCE AND DAMNATION

Working with women and girls in secure care contexts

Introduction

In this final chapter on the application of psychology in practice I focus on women and girls who are detained in secure mental health and social care services. As signalled in Chapter 11, community-based support is not thought appropriate for all women and girls who have experienced child sexual abuse and other forms of domestic abuse. Such people frequently have multiple psychosocial difficulties and have sometimes committed criminal acts that have led to their detention. Their mental distress and social difficulties have too often been exacerbated by inadequate, inappropriate or actively abusive provision. In particular, and as argued in Part 2, secure residential services routinely fail to keep women and girls safe and frequently provide a poor context for supporting women and girls to find better lives.

For example, the World Health Organization WHO (2006b) reports that there are about 8 million children in residential care worldwide. They are usually there because of disability, family disintegration, violence, abuse and poverty. WHO notes that violence by institutional staff is widespread. 'Disciplinary' procedures include beatings with sticks and hoses. Children may be tethered to furniture and left lying in their own excrement. They may be medicated to control behaviour, and have no access to education or recreation. They may also be vulnerable to violence by other inmates – whether children or adults. Children in criminal justice systems experience similar privations and abuses. For example, WHO (2006b) reports that, at least 31 countries permit corporal punishment (including caning, flogging, stoning and amputation) of children who are convicted of crimes, and some countries still apply the death penalty to children. In 1999, 1 million children were detained in prisons, and in at least 77 countries corporal and other violent punishments are accepted as legal disciplinary measures in penal institutions. Children, again, may be beaten, caned, painfully restrained, and subjected to humiliating treatment such as being stripped naked and beaten in front of other detainees. Girls in detention facilities are at particular risk of physical and sexual abuse, mainly when supervised by male staff.

There are, therefore, too many examples of abusive and neglectful secure services throughout the world. Abused and detained women and girls are in desperate need of safer services that are more responsive to their particular needs. In this chapter I build on the evidence base developed empirically in Part 2, and thus far applied generally to matters of therapy, and assessment and support of children and mothers in child protection systems, to consider the particular problems and dilemmas associated with working in secure care settings. I focus on women and girls who have experienced child sexual abuse and who have been diagnosed with 'borderline personality disorder'. This is because, as noted in Part 2, this is an increasingly common diagnosis given to sexually abused women and girls, especially those in secure care.

For example, the American National Institute of Mental Health (NIMH) (2006b) reports that about 2 per cent of adults (that is, about 5.8–8.7 million Americans) are diagnosed with borderline personality disorder. These are mainly young women, and in the USA, they represent about 20 per cent of all psychiatric inpatient admissions. The contemporary relevance of this diagnosis is also reflected in special issues of journals focused on this issue (see for example, the *American Journal of Contemporary Psychotherapy* (2004); and, in terms of more radical mental health politics, *Asylum* (2004). Additionally, the growth of the borderline category reflects an expanding mental health and social welfare concern with personality disorder in general (see, for example, the British Department of Health DH (2003b).

My aim in this chapter is to demonstrate how services for abused and detained women and girls can be improved by reframing 'personality problems' as relationship difficulties. Relationships are crucial because as WHO (2006b) found, in their global study of violence and children, the effects of most forms of abuse can be mediated by good relationships. In this chapter I explicate the range of relationship factors that impact on therapeutic work with sexually abused women and girls in secure care systems. I begin by tracing the movement of women and girls from community to confinement. I highlight factors that impact on the day-to-day relationships clients and workers have in secure care, and which influence therapeutic endeavour. Finally, I explore some key issues in therapy, legal, and political practices.

Crossing borders: survival strategies from family to street

Experiences of child sexual abuse do not inevitably result in mental health problems and social exclusion. However, as indicated in Chapter 6, the cumulative effects of abuse, coupled with additionally unstable, unsupportive and/or neglectful backgrounds, increases isolation, and intensifies vulnerability. Girls and women, who have developed socially problematic coping strategies to offset their difficulties, may find their social and psychological vulnerability further exaggerated. Girls and women who self-harm, are aggressive, or use drugs and alcohol may be excluded from social services children's homes, domestic violence refuges and/or therapeutic care (see also Chapter 11). Additionally, these girls and women may not only be excluded by others from residential care but they may exclude themselves from such care. Because of extreme experiences of abuse and betrayal, these women and girls may struggle with the intimacy of shared living, and be unable to cope within rule-bound systems.

Some of these women and girls may find themselves in temporary accommodation or living on the streets. This excludes them from more services. For example, mental health services are often unwilling to work with children or adults who are in temporary or unstable placements. Homelessness also increases the risk of abuse as women and girls must navigate between survival and exploitation. They may use their bodies as a commodity that can be exchanged for money, food and accommodation (Cusick *et al.* 2003). Sexual abuse exaggerates the understanding that feminized bodies are an exchange item, and men capitalize on this. For example, it is common for pimps to target girls in children's homes who are already distanced from family and friends. Their isolation makes them easier to control, dominate, and groom for sexual exploitation (see Barnardos 1998). Although women and girls who work in the sex trade may represent a minority of the sexually abused population, there are still too many of them. For example, WHO (2006b) estimates that every year, around the world, about 1 million (mainly female) children under 18 enter into prostitution, child pornography and other similar activities. Many are coerced, kidnapped, sold and deceived into these activities or are victims of trafficking. Therefore, in addition to the sexual violence associated with prostitution, women and girls frequently suffer physical and psychological violence, as well as neglect.

Drugs and alcohol play a significant role in the lives of many homeless women and girls who are engaged in sex work. Problems with drugs and alcohol may have led some into homelessness and sex work. For others, drug and alcohol use may have started, or increased, as means of coping with homelessness and sex work, or have been instigated by their pimps as an additional form of control. For young women living and working on the streets, crack cocaine has an increasing interaction with sexual exploitations as Chase and Statham (2005) found in the UK for example. Some of these women and girls may also hear voices and see visions, or have 'flashbacks' to their multiple experiences of abuse. Visions, voices and flashbacks can further increase use of drugs and alcohol. There is, therefore, a well-established interrelationship between homelessness, drug and alcohol abuse, mental illness and sexual exploitation – as Anderson and Chiocchio (1997) found in the USA for example. Homeless, 'mentally ill' women and girls, who misuse drugs and/ or alcohol, and work in the sex trade, may feel unable to ask for help because when they do they are treated as psychiatric patients or criminals who are more often deprived of their liberty than afforded redress (WHO 2006b). Unsupported, such women and girls may represent an increasing danger to themselves and others as their behaviour becomes more and more disturbed. See Illustration 1.

Illustration 1

Naomi is a 14-year-old white girl who first came into care at the age of seven as a result of neglect by her drug-addicted parents. Naomi's father regularly beat up her mother, and Naomi herself was physically abused at home and also in her first foster placement. At age eight, she moved to her second placement where she was sexually abused. For the next few years Naomi lived in a variety of foster placements and children's homes. She started absconding and running away when she was 11 years old. She mistrusted adult 'officials' and responded to overtures of care with aggression. At the age of 12, she began selling herself for sex. Whenever she was picked up by the police and returned to social services care she would make her escape and go off with one of the many young men with cars, money and/or drugs who congregated outside the children's home. Whilst living on the streets she had been beaten up, raped and regularly used drugs. No one had ever been prosecuted for offences against her. By contrast, at 14 years old, Naomi was eventually detained on a secure accommodation order and locked up. Naomi had made a number of attempts to kill herself.

Early intervention may represent best practice for girls like Naomi (Hester and Westmarland 2004). Yet the services that Naomi received had been sometimes abusive, frequently neglectful, and there had been inadequate attempts made to provide a comprehensive and coordinated care strategy. The final solution was to lock her up.

Naomi was detained on a care order as she was assumed to be a 'child in need' rather than a 'criminal'. This reflected an attempt to shift policy from a punishment to a welfare model in relation to young people engaged in commercial sex. 'Child prostitutes' are now called young people 'abused' or 'exploited' through prostitution (see for example, Barnardos 1998; WHO 2006b). Yet, child protection procedures often cease to apply if young people are judged to be 'persistent' and 'voluntary' prostitutes (Chase and

Statham 2005), and trying to force fit all experiences of prostitution into a framework of sexual abuse does not provide a complete solution for women and girls who are engaged in commercial sex.

Sex work may be exploitative, but not all women and girls involved in 'survival sex' (see Parsons 2005) view themselves as enduring victims. For Naomi, commercial sex helped her manage periods of homelessness. It is invidious to make this primarily a personal issue of victimization when we fail to make practical alternatives available to young people. Naomi needed to feel a sense of control that she did not experience in social services care, and she did not have access to other alternative 'safe' housing. Children throughout the world live on the streets and there are few services for them. For example, the British Broadcasting Corporation, in a programme called 'Runaways', aired on 11 November 2004, noted that there are 100,000 teenage runaways in England and Wales and only one dedicated eight-bed unit specifically for them, whilst there are about 400 women's domestic violence refuges.

Increasingly, women and girls, like Naomi, are characterized as having 'complex' social and mental health needs, and are depicted as having 'personality disorders', which are referred to as 'emergent' in the case of young women. The inexorable rise of the personality disorder label, and for these women and girls the ubiquity with which the 'borderline' syndrome is diagnosed is concerning. Some will end up in mental health facilities or secure, social services children's homes. Others will end up in prison. For example, about 50 per cent of women in British prisons are said to suffer from a personality disorder (Home Office HO 2002). Unsurprisingly, women in the criminal justice system report similar histories to their sisters in mental health facilities. For example, the British Home Office (HO 2002) notes that 50 per cent of women prisoners report histories of abuse; 37 per cent have previously attempted suicide; and 20 per cent were accommodated by social services as children compared with 2 per cent of the general population.

It is little wonder that women, and girls like Naomi, have negligible faith that State social, legal and mental health services will act in their best interest, or that they feel marginalized and stigmatized by society as a whole. It is only relatively recently that mental health services have started to target those diagnosed with personality disorders (DH 2003b, and see Part 2). This may go some way to mandating an increased range of services for girls like Naomi before they arrive in secure care. The borderline diagnosis could function as a signpost that invites consideration of the potential impact of negative childhood experiences on such clients. Yet, diagnosis ultimately pathologizes women's and girls' attempts to survive extreme and abnormal events (Linehan 1993). Too often societal failure is wrapped up as personality deficits. I do not deny that women and girls have characteristic ways of relating, but I am mindful of how the context of care and the forms of intervention we make, or fail to make, can reinforce the expectations of abuse, neglect, and exploitation that typify their lives.

Adapting to life inside: trying to take some control

Changing life circumstances, particularly those over which we have little control, engender feelings of fear, anger and anxiety. It is little wonder that involuntary detention is frequently negatively experienced by those incarcerated. For example, Ross (2003) reviewed the literature and found that there are few British studies specifically about the effects of detention. However, results suggest that a negative emotional response is common. Detainees report feeling unworthy, vulnerable, humiliated, frightened, angry, hateful, fatalistic and out of control. Yet services frequently underestimate the impact the act of detention has on detainees' wellbeing. Ross (2003) suggests that many detainees develop 'post-traumatic stress disorder'-like symptoms *following* detention. However, symptomatic behaviour is generally understood to be part of their core condition rather than an effect of detention itself.

Whilst such issues also affect male detainees, women and girls face additional problems. Women are more likely to lose their relationships with partners and children. For example, Brooks (2001) reports that the British pressure group Women in Prisons says that 80 per cent of women 'stand by' their detained male partners, compared with 17 per cent of male partners of detained women. In England and Wales, 18,000 children have imprisoned mothers – only 5 per cent of whom remain in the family home after the mother is imprisoned (see Allison 2004). In some cases, because of long-term detention, women do not have the opportunity to become pregnant and have children; and being childless represents another stigmatized role in societies that value motherhood. Brooks (2001) also argues that men are more able to adapt to the infantilization and regimentation of life inside because they do not experience the same loss of role in respect of the domestic domain (for example, regarding cooking meals) that women do. Women also have greater difficulties accepting the limited privacy around hygiene (for example, using the toilet or having a shower).

Women and girls, therefore, experience not just a loss of power at the point of incarceration, but may also experience a profound loss of purpose, role, identity and relationships. They may also feel frightened and anxious about their immediate and long-term future. Many women and girls end up feeling hopeless at this point and arrival is a time when suicidal behaviour is a significant risk. For example, around one-quarter of inpatient suicides in England and Wales occur during the first week after admission (DH 2001). Suicide is a major issue for mental health and secure services around the world: WHO (2006a) reports that about 873,000 people around the world die by suicide every year. Therefore, given that incarceration involves collapsing a range of negative life events into a very short period of time there is a good argument for providing some form of psychological support to all detainees, regardless of their known psychological status, at point of entry. Also, because powerlessness is so detrimental to mental health, it is crucial that women and girls can exercise some control over their lives not just at the beginning, but throughout their period of detention.

Kjellin *et al.* (1997), in a study of inpatient care, found that people got better when they were treated, or perceived themselves to be treated, more respectfully. This perception was associated with the degree of autonomy and choice that they experienced. Women and girls in secure care may have limited access to information about their options and few opportunities to make their own decisions without fear of immediate reprisal or condemnation. Indeed, too often the 'choices' women and girls make are taken to be indicative of their disordered personality rather than being indicative of situational factors, for example. See Illustration 2.

Illustration 2

On my first day working in a maximum-security mental hospital I was taken to the admission ward and left there for two hours (with no keys, so I could not 'escape'). Admission wards are by nature unstable. There is a constant flow of new patients, who arrive in various states of mental distress. The nurses, with whom psychologists had a historically poor relationship in this hospital, retreated to their 'station' and shut the door. I was left 'alone' with the women. Some months later I talked with a patient, called Jo, a 23-year-old white woman, about her arrival on the same ward and we reflected on our shared experiences and different coping strategies.

Both of us were frightened and unsure of our role. We knew women in maximum security were supposed to be 'mad' and 'dangerous'. We had no lived experience to mediate this understanding at this point and no one took time to introduce us to others. We adopted personally familiar ways of coping. Neither of us looked to the staff for support – it was clearly not being proffered. Jo protected herself by responding to other patients with aggression. I invited overtures from patients. I wanted at least one ally as my 'protector' and 'informant' about others. Jo's life experiences meant she had arrived with little trust in people and her coping strategies reflected her need, and her ability, to cope alone. I have more faith in others. Of greater relevance, perhaps, acting aggressively would have been inappropriate in my role as psychologist, as well as ineffective as I am small and physically unthreatening. Our choices were as much pragmatic as moral and in themselves indicated little about our relative mental health or

---

> personality structure. I think that I would have adopted the same strategy had I been a patient; my role would have changed, but my abilities would have remained the same. If she had been supported I think that Jo would have acted with less aggression; she did when supported through other novel situations subsequently.

Jo was punished by members of staff for the aggressive 'choices' that she made. For example, following aggressive acts Jo was medicated and placed in seclusion. Yet whilst aggression may be undesired, in many ways the whole manner in which secure mental health services are financed and structured tacitly rewards this type of misbehaviour. Resources for the treatment of personality disorder tend to become available when there is a risk of violence to others. As Adshead (2001) observes, patients that 'act out' are afforded a greater degree of individual input than patients who do not. Wards with 'difficult to manage' patients have higher staff–patient ratios. Such attention may not be personally rewarding, however, when it ultimately reduces the patient's quality of life and overly restricts the choices she can make.

Women's and girls' frustration with their treatment may generate more feelings of anxiety and anger. Yet they are seldom encouraged to express their feelings. Anger, occasioned by mistreatment, cannot be tolerated and indeed female anger is often judged more harshly than male anger. As Kaul (2001) points out, the institution frequently reacts to emotional excess with punitive and controlling responses such as increased use of medication, restraint, seclusion, and 'special observations' whereby the patient's every move is scrutinized. Aggression may then be turned inwards and result in increased levels of self-harm, which again invite the same acts of control that stimulate the need for more defensive strategies. It has been argued that measures such as these are intrusive and provocative, if not simply abusive (Perkins and Repper 1996).

Excessive control not only has a detrimental effect on well-being, but it also restricts women's and girls' ability to change. Whilst requirements to ensure the safety of all detainees and the professionals that work with them – as well as society in general – necessarily impact on any therapeutic intervention, if people are to be encouraged to change there must be some limited space for negotiation. Otherwise, any putative development is ultimately theoretical. For example, we can stop people self-harming by putting them on 'special observation' and removing all implements with which they can self-injure, but this does not indicate or allow the development of alternative coping strategies. This also means that women's and girls' choices about self-harm are restricted.

Women and girls may be given superficial choices about other aspects of their lives inside, for example in respect of therapy. Yet in subtle ways they are coerced into programmes, situations, or behaviours (including using medication) that reflect the workers' concerns (Cruikshank 1993). More explicitly, treatment can be mandated when patients are judged to lack insight into their condition. However, 'insight' tends to be defined in a circular way in that 'insight' is assumed to mean that the patient agrees with her psychiatrist. Her 'failure to engage' may then be taken as indicating her disordered personality rather than being indicative of her considered opinion. Hence, my ability to ensure women and girls have a choice to see me is also compromised as personal decisions are mediated by external concerns; this obviously includes legal directives as well.

Women and girls are also given mixed messages about the choices they make about their social relationships inside secure services. We know that women, in particular, are vulnerable to sexual assault by male patients and male members of staff. Yet, as indicated in Chapters 7 and 8, mixed activities are sometimes viewed as a forum in which to measure progress: women in terms of their integration with men, and men in terms of whether they have stopped assaulting women. Because even detainees have some rights to privacy, women and girls have no formal access to information about each other that might offset their vulnerability. People misrepresent themselves in the community. However, in secure care there is an increased likelihood of meeting sexual offenders. See Illustration 3.

Illustration 3

Mary, a 42-year-old white woman, was convicted for sexual offences against her children. The other prisoners were unaware of her crimes. They only knew her children had been removed. They sympathized with her and supported her sexual relationship with a much younger woman prisoner. A prison officer, wanting to 'protect' the younger woman, disclosed Mary's offences to another prisoner. Mary was badly beaten by fellow inmates and hospitalized. Her girlfriend and others felt tricked, betrayed, and abused. There was no 'safe' system for disclosing information that would have protected Mary's girl-friend, Mary and others.

Secure systems tacitly accept that sexual relationships occur, but fail to address this issue explicitly. Even when sexual relationships are not abusive there are problems when these end. In closed institutions there is nowhere to go. There is a need to develop policy and practices that address the complexity of people's relationships inside closed institutions and that both safeguards their rights and affords protection.

Detainees' capacity to consent changes over time, but people cannot practise 'safe sex' when the system fails to recognize and take active responsibility for its role in such relationships. When the structures that shape people's relationships remain hidden, vague or misleading we undermine them further. This is why (as argued in Chapter 8) the service milieu and the wider network of social relationships within the institution must be given an equal degree of concern as factors associated with the practice of therapy itself.

Professional sabotage: the institutionalization of borderline behaviour

If the institutional milieu is to be helpful, rather than harmful, the needs of workers have to be considered alongside those of their clients. Clients in secure settings can be frightening and provoke a great deal of anxiety in the professionals that work with them. Despite their commitment to therapeutic care, practitioners sometimes respond to their own fears and anxieties by increasingly controlling the relationships they have with their clients. They may justify this approach by seeing themselves as their patients' saviours (Perkins and Repper 1996). Yet, the more decisions professionals make, the more useless, powerless and deskilled clients can feel (Barker 1992). Clients may resist and become even more difficult and demanding. And when clients do not recognize our expertise, or fail to improve, workers can also feel hurt, abused and dismissed.

This is especially the case for those frontline workers, such as nurses and support workers, who like their clients may also feel devalued and dismissed within the institutional hierarchy. They are primarily also women themselves, which may further exaggerate their sense of being invalidated. Frontline workers (all of whom may be devalued in what is a feminized role) may then develop antagonistic relationships with their clients in order to secure a sense of value in systems that conflate femininity with worthlessness (Coupe 1991). Additionally, frontline workers are often the prime targets of the client's anger and aggression and must cope with the immediate physical aftermath of self-harm – all of which is much more distressing than having contained conversations within psychotherapy.

When nurses and support staff are unable to discharge their own anger at those that are dismissive of them and those that frighten and upset them, they are more likely to displace and project their feelings into the women and girls they care for (Becker 1997). In this way the clients become identified as 'the problem' and it becomes increasingly hard to recognize that the difficult behaviour of detainees may be a normal response to ordinary frustrations, rather than being indicative of their disordered personalities. For example, many of the circumstances that precede violence are well established, such as overcrowding and the congregation of clients at certain times, such as meal times (Mawson 1990). Boredom and feeling helpless increase aggression and this is why incidents often occur at weekends and evenings when there are no off-ward/-unit activities (Mawson 1990). Living in confined spaces is not easy.

Detainees frequently report multiple experiences of inconsistent, dismissive, abusive and neglectful care. If workers are not to replicate these dynamics, they also need to feel valued and listened to. Providing safe containment for clients involves rethinking security as a relational activity (DH 2002b) and not simply one that is determined by physical restraint or pharmaceutical management. This draws attention to the need to consider everyone's relationships in secure care. This is crucial if multidisciplinary work is to be supported. Good communication is essential to this practice and requires the provision, rather than the protection, of relevant information (Kaul 2001). Yet inter-professional tensions can lead to the restriction of information. For example, psychotherapists may be disinclined to share information about their clients with frontline workers, particularly when they anticipate a negative response. Therapy may then become a marginalized activity and clinical decisions, such as moves or discharge plans, may then be taken without reference to the therapeutic work (McGauley and Humphrey 2003).

In this context, splits between workers become inevitable and symptomatic behaviour associated with the diagnosis of borderline personality disorder and experiences of abuse may then become institutionalized. This is evidenced in the aforementioned overuse of medication, which is common in many secure settings. For example, Hill (2002a) reports that in Holloway women's prison in England 33 per cent of women were taking medication for mental health problems on arrival and that 95 per cent were on mental health medication within weeks of being there. Alternatively, workers may respond to existing professional tensions by finding indirect ways to sabotage the work of others, particularly when – by virtue of their own devalued role – they feel unable to directly influence clinical decisions. For example, workers may exert power by playing 'mind games' with each other and with their clients (McDermott and King 1988). See Illustration 4.

Illustration 4

I had been seeing Joyce, a 39-year-old African-Caribbean woman, in a secure hospital for weekly therapy sessions for about two months. Just before I was due to meet her one day, I was telephoned by a nurse from the ward. She told me that Joyce had 'kicked off' in the morning. She had sworn at staff and thrown furniture around the room. Subsequently she was restrained, medicated and removed to a seclusion room. The nurse told me that she was letting me know because she assumed that I would not want to meet with Joyce

because she was 'too disturbed'. I said that I thought that the opportunity to talk about what was distressing her might be particularly
important now. The nurse said, 'Well it's up to you – but she doesn't
even know who you are'.

When I went to speak to Joyce she was sitting calmly in the
seclusion room. She said, 'Oh, it's you! I couldn't work out who was
coming to see me.' The nurse had told her that 'Mrs Warner' was
coming to see her. Joyce knew me as Sam; I have never been called
'Mrs' and she did not recognize my surname – I probably only used it
at our first meeting. When Joyce had said she did not recognize the
name and wondered whether it belonged to a distant relative, the
nurse had failed to say, 'it's Sam Warner, your psychologist'. Rather,
she indicated to Joyce that her confusion was an example of how
'mad' she was.

In order to find ways of diffusing conflict between professionals and enabling more collaborative approaches to treatment it is important that workers
have sustained opportunity to reflect on their actions. Workers, like their
clients, need safe contexts in which to express and reflect on feelings without
fear of immediate reprisal or condemnation. It is important, therefore, that
workers have access to clinical, and not simply managerial, supervision and
that regular multidisciplinary meetings are held. However, whilst formal
contexts in which to reflect on and exchange information are important, it is
informal relationships that cement common ground and contribute to the
dissipation of professional barriers. When I work within secure services I
make time for these informal relationships with colleagues from different
professions. For example, I 'hang out' on wards and in units rather than
leave immediately after meetings. Without consideration of these wider
social relationships, therapy is more likely to be undermined rather than
supported.

Tracing scars and recognizing recovery: mobilizing power and control in therapy

Talking therapies are often marginalized within systems where security
needs take precedence and pharmaceutical interventions are privileged.
Women, in mixed secure care, may be particularly badly served because as
a minority there may be very little dedicated therapy space for them. This
sometimes results in women having to access mixed-gender transport to go
to male patient facilities. When women have been sexually abused in the
past, and have well-founded fears about sexual assault in the present,
therapy may ultimately be constructively denied. A consequence of this is

that therapy often takes place in interview rooms on the wards where women live. This is also the case for girls. The boundaries between therapy and life are necessarily blurred and the therapy relationship is constantly vulnerable to disruption by noise from the ward/unit, or intrusion and disturbance by other clients and members of staff.

Additionally, although any therapeutic relationship must address issues of safety, within secure settings sometimes concerns about security overly restrict the therapeutic space. Sometimes support staff are present inside, or observing outside, the therapy room. Members of staff carry personal alarms and there are emergency buttons in private rooms. This level of surveillance may have particularly negative consequences for clients who remember the voyeurism associated with childhood experiences of sexual abuse. Therefore, both therapist and client have to develop skills at screening out noise, ignoring the presence of observers, and coping with interruptions from other clients and members of staff.

My approach to therapy and assessment is consistent with the methods already described in this part of the book. I focus on underlying issues and coping strategies and avoid diagnostic formulations. However, psychiatric drift is particularly strong in secure care, and therapeutic work with incarcerated women and girls can be hampered by a system-wide focus on what is *wrong* with the client, rather than what has *happened* to the client (Scott 2004). The avoidance of the 'why' question is also reflected in the forms of talking therapies secure services often favour. 'Here and now' methods may be focused on as means of avoiding direct discussion of past abuse. This also means that coping strategies – such as self-harm – can be conflated with 'attention-seeking' behaviour, and hence their complex relationships with both past and present life can be under-recognized.

For example, Dialectical Behaviour Therapy (DBT) (see Reynolds and Linehan 2002), which was developed specifically to address the 'suicidal' behaviour that is commonly associated with borderline personality disorder, is extremely popular in secure mental-heath services (see, for example, the American NIMH 2006b). Although DBT provides a sophisticated behavioural framework for considering the wide impact of workers' actions on patients' self-harming behaviour, it can be applied in a too simplistic and narrow manner. For some workers the focus on the dialectic relationship between worker and client is reduced to identifying when self-harm invites increased attention in order to stop reinforcing this aspect of behaviour. So, for example, if a patient has self-injured then the therapy session that week is cancelled so as not to reinforce the behaviour. It is perhaps because DBT can be used punitively to castigate clients who continue to self-injure, and defensively by workers to avoid past issues, that some service users do not find this method helpful (Spandler and Warner 2007).

By contrast, in Visible Therapy (see Chapter 10) the exploration of narratives of past abuse is a crucial aspect of the therapeutic endeavour.

The narratives help make sense of the 'here and now' and so cannot be totally ignored. Therefore, although at times the 'here and now' is all that can be talked about, this needs to be an active decision rather than an inevitable focus in therapy. Additionally, self-harm has multiple significant functions, one of which is providing an integrative experience that connects past and present life narratives (Lefevre 1996). Understanding self-harm, in *both* historical and contemporary terms, is therefore a key aspect of therapy. In secure care, women and girls often have bodies that are multiply scarred by self-injury, and these scars can provide an important focus for conversations in therapy. As women and girls talk about the thoughts and feelings that are associated with specific scars and injuries they, in effect, trace their psychological journeys across their physical bodies. Scars represent a visual signifier of internal distress and viewing, and accepting and understanding these physical marks become part of the language of therapy.

For example, for some women and girls, that they feel safe enough to show their hidden scars (such as cuts and burns on their torso) indicates their trust in the therapeutic relationship. Alternatively, sometimes women and girls show their scars early as a concrete test of acceptance. When women and girls feel accepted in the relationship they may start wearing T-shirts rather than long-sleeved tops. When women and girls want to assert that they have not self-harmed they sometimes show their healed wounds with pride and as evidence of their change. Sometimes the display of a physical wound is used as an overture to invite discussion about the reasons for this particular act of self-harm. From the particular we can trace stories, and scars, back to earlier events. Scars also provide a context in which to think about the future. This might be in terms of weaving cover stories for scars, exploring with whom women and girls might share more open accounts of their bodies, and anticipating changing times. See Illustration 5.

Illustration 5

Oona, a 15-year-old white girl, was preparing to leave the secure unit in which she had lived for the last nine months. During that time we had talked about the ways that she used self-harm to cope with her feelings about past abuse and current frustrations within the unit. Over the course of our sessions, Oona's use of self-harm had ceased as she became increasingly able to express her desires verbally. We anticipated that when she left the secure unit Oona might feel some sadness at the loss of important relationships (such as with myself). We also noted that the other people in her life might not be initially as receptive of the person she had grown into, as were the people who had shared this development with her in the unit. Oona was worried that she would start self-harming again and that she would be back to being 'out of control'. I wanted to reassure Oona that even if she started self-harming again, this did not mean the changes that she had made would be lost.

In order to help Oona contextualize her self-harm I drew a diagram based on Yerkes-Dodson's Law (Yerkes and Dodson 1908) (see Figure 12.1). Sometimes it helps to provide a visual cue that people can access alongside remembered conversations. In order to function in the world everyone needs a bit of 'stress' or adrenaline to get them going as without this we are asleep. However, if we get too stressed we stop being able to perform at all (point C, in Figure 12.1). This is because we become overwhelmed by feelings. Nevertheless, it is when we are equally connected with both our thoughts and feelings that we act at our optimal level (point B, in Figure 12.1). Because it is hard to be connected with our feelings all of the time, most of us function (in therapy and other relationships) somewhere at about point A, in Figure 12.1 – that is mainly thinking (about the issue, activity or experience at hand), but in touch with our feelings (about the same issue, activity or experience).

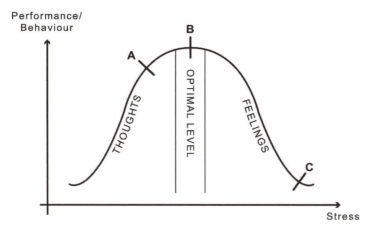

Figure 12.1 Adaptation of Yerkes-Dodson's Law (1908)

For Oona, leaving secure care represented an emotional 'crisis' that could tip her into the 'feeling' part (point C, in Figure 12.1). If this happened, her ability to 'think' would be constrained and she might then resort to self-harm as this was a very familiar coping strategy that required less conscious effort (i.e. thinking) to perform. Using this diagram helped Oona understand that even if she self-harmed this would be an indication of her temporarily overwhelming feelings, but not indicative of her personality and inability to sustain positive change. She had developed alternative coping strategies that now existed alongside the self-harm, but, at the moment, were not as familiar to her and hence needed more conscious effort to remember. When she started to feel overwhelmed by her feelings Oona used this visual cue as a reminder of this process. This diagram, which Oona carried as a picture in her head, helped Oona to make sense of her panic and avoid spiralling 'out of control'. Oona used this strategy before she left. In this way, although Oona might self-harm, this was not inevitable as she was able to take some control into her out-of-control moments.

Helping girls like Oona find ways of exerting control in their lives is a crucial task in therapy because it enables girls like Oona to believe that they have a future. The shifting of the focus from stopping self-harm to enabling greater control over self-harm (and other behaviours) recognizes that self-injury can be a life affirming activity (Spandler and Warner 2007). This understanding is extremely important when working with women and girls in secure care, particularly those diagnosed with borderline personality disorder. The emphasis on self-destruction in this diagnosis often acts as a marker of therapeutic pessimism that can ensure that both client and therapist sink into depression and lose sight of any hope that the client will one day 'get better' and leave. Believing in recovery is a radical intervention in many secure services (Warner and Wilkins 2004). And notions of recovery are easier to sustain when self-harm is understood to be a partial act of personal control, rather than being an inevitable indicator of pathology.

Recovery, in this formulation, is an idea, rather than a defined set of practices that can be measured against an inflexible standard. Thus, therapy is orientated to the particular needs of the specific client. However, because this group of women and girls tend to have had many experiences of abuse and neglect, therapy usually takes longer than therapy conducted with women and girls who can function in the community. For some women the perils of recovery feel too great. I have worked with abused women who have killed their children in a misguided attempt to keep them safe. Life inside is a punishment that they accept and they cannot bear to think and feel. So they stay dissociated and welcome being over-medicated. If such clients are to be helped to take responsibility for their lives, at some point we have to find ways to introduce the past into their present.

I accept that people are responsible for the crimes that they commit, and that diagnostic classification, in itself, is no defence; there are many people defined as being 'mentally ill' or 'personality disordered' who do not ever hurt anyone. However, if clients are to recover they also need to explore the many factors that sometimes mitigate their actions. Accepting responsibility for one's actions is a contextualizing process. In forensic settings, too often clients are expected to admit their total guilt before they can explore their own experiences of victimization. Otherwise they are seen to be making 'excuses'. Yet, if we want people to change their behaviour we need to help them to explore, connect and integrate their understandings of, and experiences as, victim and – sometimes – aggressor. This involves moving between these different identities, rather than assuming that they can be distilled and addressed separately and sequentially. If we assume that any one identity (as victim or aggressor, for example) is primary, we cannot enable clients to explore the different meanings that their roles and identities have for them in the particular social worlds that they inhabit. How women and girls feel about and understand the things that have happened to them, and that they have done, impacts on the kinds of lives they can imagine in the future.

Obviously, personal choice, or lack thereof, is mediated by complex social and economic forces, but it is also shaped by women's and girls' understandings about themselves. For example, sex work means different things to different people. Therefore, I do not assume that all women and girls who engage in sex work view themselves as victims. I accept they may have mixed feelings about commercial sex (for example, feeling variously exploited, abused, scared, trapped, in control, desired and wanted). I am also aware that without addressing the issues of pimps and homelessness, psychologizing social problems makes women and girls responsible for more than is reasonably theirs. Women and girls who have been engaged in sex work require more opportunity to exert control over their lives if they are to feel better about themselves (Chase and Statham 2005). Part of this involves exploring their own stories of self rather than forcing them to fit into predetermined narratives about the inevitable harm caused by sex work. See Illustration 6.

Illustration 6

Sarah, a 16-year-old white girl who had been sexually abused by her father, was detained on a secure accommodation order partly because she was found to be repeatedly selling herself for sex. Professionals were keen for Sarah to understand the risks she was taking as they felt that Sarah was dangerously out of control. In therapy Sarah explained that, at the time, commercial sex had helped her feel in control, not out of control. She did not have a 'pimp'. She decided when she 'worked' and she used sex to control the men who bought sex acts. This felt very different from how her father had used sex to control her. She was aware of the risks that she took and in fact it was her ability to manage these risks that seemed to further enable her sense of self-efficacy.

Rather than emphasizing her vulnerability and victimization, it was important to validate Sarah's attempts to secure control in her life. Undermining her fragile sense of self by emphasizing what is wrong with prostitution would have been unhelpful and redundant. Sarah was fully aware of the risks associated with prostitution – she experienced them – and she was more than able to articulate her mixed feelings about it; she did feel dirty and scared sometimes. When people tried to stop her, she felt controlled again, which instigated her need to exercise control in this way. Sarah needed help to make sense of the sexual abuse she had suffered, rather than educational classes on the dangers of sex work, for example. This was what we did. Sarah did not anticipate returning to prostitution in the future, but for her own reasons and not those imposed by others.

I do not advocate that prostitution is a positive life choice for girls like Sarah. However, if we simply assume that prostitution is all bad, we cannot explore the underlying reasons that underpin this behaviour, some of which may have more positive effects. That Sarah was already trying to work out her feelings about past abuse and powerlessness – albeit through commercial sex – provided a starting point for therapy. Hence, in order to enable girls and women like Sarah, it is important to listen to their narratives of life, rather than dictate pathways for them to take. The more we seek to control our clients, the more likely we are to reinforce feelings that are associated with the behaviour that we most wish to change.

The role of law and politics in securing better futures

Central to the approach described in this chapter is a commitment to an explicit concern with the operations of power in therapy, in the specific institution, and in society as a whole. Politics and the rule of law shape how both community and secure services respond to abused and exploited women and girls. Hence, increasingly, international bodies, such as the World Health Organization (WHO 2006a, 2006b, 2007a, 2007b), have identified the abuse and sexual exploitation of women and children as specific health and human rights issues that require strategic political and legal intervention at both international and local levels. For example, WHO (2006b) argues that if the number of detained children is to decrease there is a need for comprehensive child-centred juvenile justice systems that reflect international standards. Detention of children – and adults – should target only those who represent a real danger to others and investment must be made in alternatives, including community-based prevention, rehabilitation and reintegration programmes. WHO (2006b) also recommends that both *status* offences and *survival* behaviours should be decriminalized. *Status* offences are behaviours that are only a crime when committed by children, for example, absconding or truancy. *Survival* behaviours include begging, selling sex, scavenging, loitering and vagrancy; and other illegal behaviours that individuals engage in when they are victimized and forced, through trafficking or criminal exploitation, to commit illegal acts to ensure their survival.

Whilst it is important to decrease the number of women and children in detention, it is also helpful to consider how international laws can be used to secure basic standards of care when women and children are in detention. Both therapist and client are constrained by the context of care and our different roles and responsibilities. I am both advocate for my clients and also an agent of the State. The reports I write contribute to decisions about detention and release and my aim is to ensure that clients get access to the services they need. Increasingly, In Britain, the Human Rights Act 1998, which incorporates the European Convention on Human Rights into English law, is used to argue for a reasonable standard of care – as are other similar Acts and Conventions in other countries. Under mental health and social welfare legislation, and criminal law, it is the client who is on trial. It is the client who must demonstrate that she is no longer a risk to herself and/or the community. By contrast, the Human Rights Act can be used to put the service on trial. It places the emphasis on service providers to justify and demonstrate the efficacy and morality of their practices. For example, when a woman was raped by a male patient in a secure unit, a petition under the Human Rights Act was brought on her behalf to oblige her local health authority to provide alternative women-only secure accommodation. I wrote an expert witness report to attest to the detrimental impact that living in mixed accommodation had had, and would continue to have, on her mental health. The court invited the health authority to demonstrate the benefits of mixed-gender secure care for this woman. They could not, and a women-only service was provided.

Whichever court my reports are written for, they are conceived as a type of 'advance directive' (Amering *et al*. 1999) in terms of detailing what works and what does not work for the client and what would help her in the future. I view my reports as a bridging device that contributes to the enablement of more helpful transitions between services, such as from secure care to the community. Sometimes I continue to work with young women after their return to the community. Because there is usually a duty of care to children, the State is obliged to provide a range of services that facilitates transitions between care contexts. Adult women do not have the same mandated provision. They may come out of secure care having lost their homes, their children and with little hope of securing paid work, and with only limited access to social and mental health support.

Without there being comprehensive strategies in place for supporting and anticipating women's and girls' return to community living, women and girls may struggle with life outside, return quickly, or never leave at all. I have known women and girls who have deliberately self-harmed or hurt others in order to stay inside. They know that they have few caring relationships outside and/or will be victimized by pimps and others when they return to the community. I know one woman who broke back into an open prison in order to be with her friends because she missed them. Unfortunately, insufficient attention is given to the communities to which women and girls return. At the same time, for some women and girls, secure care is just another context in which they experience abuse and neglect. If we are to develop services that meet the needs of this group of women and girls then providing safe accommodation, whether community-based or secure, has to be a priority. There is little point talking about therapy if their most basic needs are not being met.

Recommendations such as these could have wide-ranging and positive consequences for the many women and girls who live and survive on the margins of society. The dialogic relationship between mechanisms of oppression and survival, such as sex, are fully recognized in strategies that seek to decriminalize such behaviours and seek to understand their utility. Rethought in this way, women and girls' behaviour may then be used to access services rather than being used to label and condemn them. This clearly involves great changes in our social welfare systems in relation to the integration of social, economic, educational and mental health policies, at both local and international levels. The language we use to describe our concerns and actions is crucial to this enterprise because it signals our intentions. 'Personality disorder' is the current flag of convenience. However, as a pathological identity it is a flawed banner that ultimately signals defeat. If we are to provide refuge and asylum for these abused and marginalized women and girls we must find different ways of describing the problems that they face. This is why I have emphasized politics, relationships, and recovery over criminality, personality disorder and despair. When the needs of abused and marginalized women and girls are understood in political and relational terms and service providers maintain faith in recovery, we may then build services that let women and girls in – a long time *before* we seek to lock them up. And we might also help transform social worlds that sustain abuse, distress and trauma into communities that are rich with equality, hope and recovery.

EPILOGUE

WHY THE PERSONAL IS STILL POLITICAL

Revolutions, recoveries and utopias

In this book I have demonstrated the dynamic relationship between theory, research and practice. My aim has been to show how these three general areas of action and inquiry enrich and inspire each other. I have attempted to do this by detailing their mutually constitutive contribution to the development of a knowledge base about women and girls, child sexual abuse, mental health and social care. I have illuminated the intersections between feminism and post-structuralism that underpin my approach and which I have used to guide a radical political agenda in theory, research and practice. I have suggested that when formulating strategies of intervention it is more useful to think in terms of ethics, principles and values than a specific test or technique. I have also elaborated some of the ways in which my ethics, principles and values have developed and the communities of knowledge I trace my ideas back to and through. I have provided detailed illustrations of how my ideas can be brought into the mainstream practice of psychology in a wide variety of service settings with abused women and girls.

This book represents my attempt to formulate and make sense of the many ways we could intervene in matters concerning child sexual abuse. Hence, this book is not simply a commentary on what currently exists, but it is also about what could be. I bring purpose and passion to my work, and hope that the theories we use, and the research we do, can help to positively revolutionize our practices with abused women and girls. In the final pages of this book I briefly reflect on what some of these revolutions might be. In particular, I argue for the value of social recovery-orientated practices and the need to hold onto some dreams of Utopia.

Revolutions

Sexual abuse is a worldwide problem that affects many millions of women and girls and which, I have argued, requires comprehensive social, psychological, economic and legislative change at local and global levels. There is, in effect, a need for revolutions in many areas of practice, provision and politics. In this book I have focused on some of the changes that impact on, and can be affected by, psychology. I have placed this book within the context of revolutionary feminism and mental health politics and have used this approach to reconsider how we theorize, research and work with sexually abused women and girls. Following feminist tradition, I have argued that inequalities in gender underpin most sexually exploitative and abusive relationships, with men predominating as abusers, and women and girls as victims. In this book I have been particularly concerned with those women and girls who seem to be most disenfranchised of their human rights. These are the women and girls who live on the margins of societies around the world and who, too often, find themselves locked up on psychiatric wards or in prison cells where they are subject to further acts of sexual abuse and violence. This focus might be thought of as revolutionary because women and girls with complex mental health and social needs have not always been high on either mainstream or feminist agendas. Hence, this is why this book is also informed by other communities of knowledge, such as radical mental health politics, in which severe and enduring mental health difficulties are an explicit and recurring concern.

My aim has been to revolutionize psychology in order that psychology can then be used to revolutionize the lives of women and girls who have experienced childhood sexual abuse. This book therefore demonstrates that, as some earlier psychoanalytic feminists suggested, there can be a productive rapprochement between radical feminist and mental health politics, and psychology. This rapprochement is itself revolutionary given that many radical activists mistrust – for many good reasons – mainstream services. Yet, I think that it is crucial not to dismiss any area of intervention outright. Even the most constraining environments sometimes can be radicalized and if we do not engage with them we leave the most vulnerable women and girls undefended. This is why I work with women and girls in secure, as well as community, settings and act as an expert witness, as well as being a psychotherapist. This book has allowed me to share some of these experiences. This is important because if we are to build alliances, as providers and users of services, we need to make our concerns and actions open and accessible to each other.

Personal accounts of child sexual abuse (by both service users and/or providers) provide debates with depth and detail, without which, as argued, theoretical work would be impoverished and mainstream understandings of abuse survivors' lives would be superficial. It is because experience is so important in the development of theory, and therefore practice, that the personal must still be thought of as being political. It is also why actively engaging with, rather than simply theorizing about, experience is a recurring concern throughout this book. Hence, research and practice form two crucial sections of the book because they demonstrate how, and why, theory works.

This book is committed to developing an evidence-base that supports the use of feminist post-structuralist ethics and radical mental health politics when working with sexually abused women and girls in mental health and social care service contexts. Because any body of knowledge is limited, I have used post-structuralism to ensure that the theories and practices I rely on, and extend, remain open to reflection, revision and further revolution. Revolutions in gender politics and practices around the world cannot be identical. Sex and sexual abuse are deployed differently in different cultures. Hence, whilst child sexual abuse, and how we understand and work around it, is a global concern, I do not presume that all understandings and actions can be universalized. However, I do think that there are common questions that could be considered across geographical and cultural contexts. This is why I am less concerned with identifying particular tests or techniques (different ones will be appropriate in different contexts, with different people), but more concerned with identifying ethics, principles and values that may be associated with good outcomes for abuse survivors. In particular, I have advocated for services to be orientated towards recovery, which is still a revolutionary idea for many of those who work in mental health and social care.

Recoveries

Alongside many abuse and psychiatric survivors, I have – in this book – called for recovery to be recognized as a legitimate organizing principle in mental health and social care. This is because I am interested in identifying ways of transforming survival into recovery. Too many women and girls live in worlds where survival is a daily struggle. There are everyday acts of survival in the home, on the streets, in cells and on psychiatric wards. There are the threats to life that are endured and the little by little destruction that is resisted. And there are the acts of survival that are stretched by additional experiences of racism, homophobia and religious persecution. We should never underestimate the fact that survival means survival for many abused women and girls and that recovery can barely be imagined.

The recovery approach adopted in this book is very different from the 'in recovery' approach detailed in 12-step programmes, such as Alcoholics Anonymous and Narcotics Anonymous. Being *in* recovery binds people to their problems and presumes that life must be lived as an ongoing crisis when, as I argue, the aim is to do more than survive each day. In order to achieve a life beyond immediate survival, I detailed a recovery-orientated psychotherapy, termed Visible Therapy, which valorizes a social model of change. A focus on the social foundations of distress invites consideration of the multiple factors that impact on how women and girls think and feel and on what they do. Therefore, it contextualizes what would otherwise be thought of as symptomatic states or behaviours. Hence, stories of abuse are not dismissed as being symptomatic of madness (as in mental illness) or manipulation (as in personality disorder). And coping strategies are not automatically condemned as being pathological (as in hearing voices and seeing visions) or essentially destructive (as in self-injury or alcohol and drug use). Thus, I have argued that revolutions in mainstream mental-health practice will be limited whilst ever they are structured around fixed notions of disease and disorder.

In Visible Therapy therefore, diagnosis is avoided and no behaviour is assumed to have an intrinsic value. Rather, the aim is to make sense of experiences, in both past and present life, that underpin mental and social difficulties. The aim is to explicate how abusive relationships cement particular versions of reality that are reinforced by subsequent experiences of abuse, neglect and constraint. Once the psychological, social and cultural structures of abuse have been identified they can then be challenged and resisted in order for new realities (that is new ways of understanding) to emerge. I have argued that this therapeutic principle can apply around the world as the need to identify abuse-structures that entrap women and girls is a necessary step to liberation, even if those structures shift according to geographical context and some are more stable and resistant to change than others.

Hence, in this book I have argued that there cannot be a fixed template for recovery. There are different battles to be fought, and different recoveries to be made, and what works for one woman may not necessarily work for another. For example, in Visible Therapy self-harm is understood as a viable coping strategy that, when used in this way, has life affirming qualities. Therefore, ceasing self-harm should not be an automatic goal for everyone in therapy, although it may still be for some. Rather, the focus is on making sense of self-harm (and other so-called symptomatic states and behaviour, such as hearing voices and seeing visions) in order to make sense of women's and girls' lives. I have also applied this type of functional analysis to legal proceedings. I have used the concept of social framework evidence to ensure expertise and perspective is made visible and thereby open to discussion and challenge.

I demonstrated that in order to support a critical justice agenda, links should be made across intersecting areas of abuse, such as the sexual abuse of children in families and the domestic abuse of mothers. Although there are obvious difficulties in working with abused mothers in the context of child welfare, I again argued that understanding how abuse realities are made and maintained is enabling because it helps focus where support is most needed. Hence, whether abused mothers can recover their ability to care for their child is, as indicated, about how they and we renegotiate relationships, rather than whether the mother is personality disordered or mentally ill. Therefore, I have argued that we need to re-evaluate the benchmarks against which we measure mothers' behaviour. If we do not challenge the stereotypes that mothers and abused women and girls are measured against, women and children who are further marginalized through structural oppressions, such as race, culture and psychiatric status, may be condemned to inferior, condemnatory and/or abusive treatment ever more.

Thus, I have argued that an understanding of recovery should be at the heart of service strategy in a wide range of service contexts. It should also inform wider cultural debates about child sexual abuse as ultimately it is the wider culture that acts to permit and/or inhibit abuse. Without changes in community values we may never build systems of care that enable women and girls to recover because we cannot imagine, and will not permit, anything more than containment. The first step in ensuring that recovery is a shared reality for women and girls around the world is, therefore, to insist that women and girls have their rights to self-determination accepted and supported in the different societies in which they live. Hence, international commitments to end sexual abuse and exploitation should lead to the adoption of common legal frameworks that support women's and children's rights around the world. Without this, abuse and exploitation may continue unchecked, and women's and girls' resistance – and recovery – may be dismissed as madness and/or punished as criminality. Therefore, although definitions of recovery may be individualized, there are still some principles regarding self-determination that should be globalized. Hence, if we want to turn complaint into statement of intent – that is move from what is wrong to what might put it right – we need some visions of Utopia. If we do not dream, how do we find the will and the way to survive, and the ability to turn survival into recovery?

Utopias

Throughout this book I have been open and transparent about my desires for personal, local and global transformations. The feminist mantra that *the personal is political* is still relevant because child sexual abuse must be thought of as both personal and political if we are to develop comprehensive strategies for intervention that can transform lives at both individual and international levels. Child sexual abuse is experienced personally; therefore individual abuse survivors need support (not necessarily therapy) to make their own journeys towards their own sense of freedom and recovery. It is also a worldwide social problem that requires a coordinated political response, without which those that are made subject to abuse remain isolated and vulnerable. A personal-political problem requires an ethical framework that can address the specific, as well as consider larger, connecting issues. It must be able to guide and inspire, as well as allow critique and reflection.

This is why a passionate and compassionate feminist political response is still needed when thinking through our practices with abused women and

251

girls. There are still revolutions that are yet to happen and – as post-structuralist theory teaches us – that we may not yet have imagined. Recovery is a possibility if we imagine it and if we find ways of working that can support it. This, as noted, requires local and global commitments to revolutionize social, psychological, economic and legal policies in respect of gender, sex and power. We need to take some shared responsibility throughout the world for the world, whilst also recognizing that we will also have local needs and individual differences that require particular and specific attention. In order to work towards these goals, we need some vision of what we want to be different. We need some vision of Utopia. We might then imagine different Utopias whose characterizations may shift and change. Women's and girls' needs around the world will always be variable and contested. Yet we can still sometimes make common cause and we do find ways to transform survival into recovery. And our desires for better futures sometimes interweave to provide paths towards worlds we might hope to live in some day.

REFERENCES

Adshead, G. (2001). Murmurs of discontent: Treatment and treatability of personality disorder, *Advances in Psychiatric Treatment*, 7: 407–16.

Ainscough, C. and Toon, K. (2000). *Breaking Free Work Book: Practical Help for Survivors of Child Sexual Abuse*, London: Sheldon Press.

Aitken, G. and Heenan, C. (2004). Editors' introduction: Women in prison and secure psychiatric settings – Whose needs, whose dangerousness?, *Feminism and Psychology*, 14(2): 215–19.

Aitken, G. and Logan, C. (2004). Dangerous women? A UK response, *Feminism and Psychology*, 14(2): 262–9.

Allen, H. (1987). *Justice Unbalanced: Gender, Psychiatry and Judicial Decisions*, Milton Keynes: Open University Press.

Allison, E. (2004, May 13). Cherie Booth: Keep women out of jail, *Guardian*, p. 9.

Althusser, L. (1971). *Lenin and Philosophy and Other Essays*, London: New Left Books.

American Journal of Contemporary Psychotherapy. (2004). 34 (3): 183–290.

American Psychiatric Association (1987). *Diagnostic and Statistical Manual of Mental Disorders (DSM-III-R)*, 3rd edn revised, Washington DC: American Psychiatric Association.

American Psychiatric Association (1995). *Diagnostic and Statistical Manual of Mental Disorders (DSM-IV-R)*, 4th edn revised, Washington DC: American Psychiatric Association.

Amering, M., Denk, E., Griengl, H., Sibitz, I. and Stastny, P. (1999). Psychiatric wills of mental health professionals: A survey of opinions regarding advance directives in psychiatry, *Social Psychiatry: Psychiatric Epidemiology*, 34: 30–34.

Amnesty International (2008). If she's drunk and wearing a short skirt, it's her own fault if she gets raped isn't it? www.amnesty.org.uk/content.asp?CategoryID= 11051 (accessed 25 January 2008).

Anderson, C.M. and Chiocchio, K.B. (1997). Homeless, addictions and mental illness', in M. Harris and C.L. Landis (eds) *Sexual Abuse in the Lives of Women Diagnosed with Serious Mental Illness*, London: Brunner-Routledge, pp. 21–37.

Angelou, M. (1984). *I Know Why the Caged Bird Sings*, London: Virago Press.

Appleby, S. (1997, May 24). 'Learning to talk', *Guardian Weekend Magazine*, p. 12.

Armstrong, H B. (2002). Narrative therapy, *Critical Psychology: The International Journal of Critical Psychology*, 7: 165–9.

Armstrong, L. (1991). Surviving the incest industry, *Trouble and Strife: The Radical Feminist Magazine*, 21: 29–32.

Ashcroft, J., Daniels, D.J. and Hart, S.V. (2003). *Youth Victimization: Prevalence and Implications*. Washington DC: US Department of Justice, Office of Justice Programs. www.ncjrs.gov/pdffiles1/nij/194972.pdf (accessed 13 February 2007).

Asylum: The Magazine for Democratic Psychiatry. (2004). Bullshit psychiatric diagnosis: Special Edition on women and borderline personality disorder by Women at the Margins, 14: 3.

Atmore, C. (1993). Branded: Lesbian representation and a New Zealand cultural controversy', in D. Bennett (ed.) *Cultural Studies: Pluralism and Theory*, Melbourne: University of Melbourne, pp. 281–92.

Atmore, C. (1997). Brand news: Using Foucault to theorise rape, the media and feminist strategies, in C. O'Farrell (ed.) *Foucault: The Legacy*, Brisbane: Queensland University of Technology.

Atmore, C. (1998). Towards 2000: Child sexual abuse and the media, in A. Howe (ed.) *Sexed Crime in the News*, Melbourne: Federation Press, pp. 1–18.

Bacon, H., Bulkeley, R., Casswell, G., Hipkin, L., Lucey, D. and Todd, L. (2002). *Managing Litigation Arising in Clinical Work with Children and Families: Some Practice Guidelines for Clinical Child Psychologists*, Leicester: British Psychological Society.

Baim, C., Brookes, S. and Mountford, A. (eds) (2002). *The Geese Theatre Handbook: Drama with Offenders and People at Risk*, Winchester: Waterside Press.

Bainbridge, B. and Aglionby, J. (2005, November 26). 'Tracking down child abusers: Police forces unite to fight world problem', *Guardian*. www.guardian.co.uk/child/story/0,,1651301,00.html (accessed 1 November 2006).

Baker, C. (2002). *Female Survivors of Sexual Abuse*. London: Routledge.

Baker Miller, J. (1978). *Towards a New Psychology of Women*, Harmondsworth: Pelican Books.

Banister, P., Burman, E., Parker, I. and Tindall, C. (1994). *Qualitative Methods in Psychology*, Milton Keynes: Open University Press.

Bannister, A. (ed.) (1992). *From Hearing to Healing: Working with the Aftermath of Child Sexual Abuse*, Harlow, Essex: Longman.

Barker, P. (1992) Psychiatric nursing, in T. Butterworth and J. Faugier (eds) *Clinical Supervision and Mentorship in Nursing*, London: Chapman & Hall, pp. 49–64.

Barnardo's (1998). *Stolen Childhood: Barnardo's Work with Children Abused Through Prostitution*, Barkingside: Barnardo's.

Bass, E. and Davies, L. (1988). *The Courage to Heal: A Guide for Women Survivors of Child Sexual Abuse*, London: Cedar.

Bass, E. and Thornton, L. (eds) (1983). *I Never Told Anyone: Writings by Women Survivors of Child Sexual Abuse*, London: Harper and Row.

Batsleer, J., Burman, E., Chantler, K., McIntosh, H.S., Pantling, K., Smailes, S. and Warner, S. (2002). *Domestic Violence and Minoritisation: Supporting Women to Independence*, Manchester: Manchester Metropolitan University.

Batty, D. (2002, September 13). 'Come back when you're really sick', *Guardian*, p. 17.

Becker, D. (1997). *Through The Looking Glass: Women and Borderline Personality Disorder*, Oxford: Westview Press.

Bell, V. (1993). *Interrogating Incest: Feminism, Foucault and the Law*, London: Routledge.

Bell, V. (2003). The vigilant(e) parent and the paedophile: The *News of the World* campaign 2000 and the contemporary governmentality of child sexual abuse', in P. Reavey and S. Warner (eds) (2003) *New Feminist Stories About Women and Child Sexual Abuse: Sexual Scripts and Dangerous Dialogues*, London: Taylor & Francis, pp. 108–28.

Benhabib, S (1995). Feminism and postmodernism, in S. Benhabib. J. Butler. D. Cornell and N. Fraser, *Feminist Contentions: A Philosophical Exchange*, London: Routledge, pp. 17–34.

Bhavnani, K.K. (1990). What's power got to do with it? Empowerment and social research, in I. Parker and J. Shotter (eds) *Deconstructing Social Psychology*, London: Routledge, pp. 141–52.

Bindel, J., Cook, K. and Kelly, L. (1995). Trials and tribulations – Justice for women: A campaign for the 1990s', in G. Griffin (ed.) *Feminist Activism in the 1990s*, London: Taylor & Francis, pp. 65–76.

Bondi, L. (1995). Locating identity politics, in M. Keith and J. Pile (eds) *Place and the Politics of Identity*, London: Routledge, pp. 95–118.

Bordo, S. (1990). Feminism, postmodernism, and gender-scepticism, in J.L. Nicholson (ed.) *Feminism/Postmodernism*, London: Routledge, pp. 133–56.

Boseley, S. (2001, September 10). 'Drug firms accused of distorting research', *Guardian*, p. 2.

Bowlby, J. (1969). *Attachment and Loss. Volume 1: Attachment*, New York: Basic Books.

Bowlby, J. (1973). *Attachment and Loss. Volume 2: Separation*, New York: Basic Books.

Boyle, M. (1990). *Schizophrenia: A Scientific Delusion?*, London: Routledge.

Boyle, M. (1997). III. Clinical psychology: Theory – making gender visible in clinical psychology, *Feminism and Psychology*, 7(2): 231–8.

Briere, J.N. (1992). *Child Abuse Trauma: Theory and the Lasting Effects*, London: Sage Publications.

Bright, M. (2003, March 30). 'One in 100 black adults now in jail', *The Observer*. www.browse.guardian.co.uk/search?search=prisons+black&N=4294964356+3097+4294963572&site=Society (accessed 3 March 2006).

Bright, M. and Harris, P. (2002, October 20). 'Child porn swoop targets 90 police', *The Observer*, p. 1.

British Broadcasting Corporation (2004). *Runaways*. Screened on 11 November.

British Psychological Society (2001a). *Child Abuse: Clinical Factors in the Assessment and Management of Concern*, Leicester: British Psychological Society.

British Psychological Society (2001b). *Division of Clinical Psychology: The Core Purpose and Philosophy of the Profession*, Leicester: British Psychological Society.

Brooks, L. (2001, January 30). 'Is a woman's place in prison?', *Guardian*. www.society.guardian.co.uk/crimeandpunishment/story/0,,431172,00.html (accessed 3 March 2006).

Broverman, I., Broverman, D.M., Clarkson, I.E., Rosenkrantz, P.S. and Vogel, S.R. (1970). Sex role stereotypes and clinical judgements of mental health, *Journal of Consulting and Clinical Psychology*, 6(5): 355–64.

Brown, S.R. (1980). *Political Subjectivity: Application of Q Methodology in Political Science*, New Haven, CT: Yale University Press.

Brownmiller, S. (1975). *Against our Will: Men, Women and Rape*, London: Secker and Warburg.

Bunting, M. (2004, July 5). 'Comment and analysis: The last taboo', *Guardian*, p. 15.

Burchill, J. (1998, May 2). 'The age of reason: Telly most horrid', *Guardian Weekend Magazine*, p. 5.

Burkeman, O. (2002, September 7). 'Jesuits pay $7.5m to two men abused for 30 years', *Guardian*, p. 15.

Burman, E. (2003). Childhood, sexual abuse and contemporary political subjectivities, in P. Reavey and S. Warner (eds) (2003) *New Feminist Stories About Women and Child Sexual Abuse: Sexual Scripts and Dangerous Dialogues*, London: Taylor & Francis, pp. 34–51.

Burman, E., Aitken, G., Alldred, P., Allwood, R., Billingham, T., Goldberg, B., Gordo Lopez, A.J., Heenan, C., Marks, D. and Warner S. (1996) *Psychology, Discourse, Practice: From Regulation to Resistance*, London: Taylor & Francis.

Butler, J. (1990). *Gender Trouble: Feminism and the Subversion of Identity*, London: Routledge.

Calder, J. (2004). Histories of abuse, *Psychotherapy Section Newsletter*, British Psychological Society, 37: 11–26.

Califa, P. (1980/1993). *Sapphistry: The Book of Lesbian Sexuality*, USA: Naiad Press.

Califa, P. (1994). *Public Sex: The Culture of Radical Sex*. Pittsburgh: Cleis Press.

Cameron, D. (1996). Wanted: The female serial killer, *Trouble & Strife: The Radical Feminist Magazine*, 33: 21–8.

Campbell, B. (1988). *Unofficial Secrets: Child Sexual Abuse – The Cleveland Case*, London: Virago Press.

Campbell, P. (2001). Surviving social inclusion, *Clinical Psychology Forum*, 150: 6–13.

Carter, J. (2005). *Domestic violence, child abuse, and youth violence: Strategies for prevention and early intervention*, Minnesota Center Against Violence and Abuse. www.mincava.umn.edu/link/documents/fvpf2/fvpf2.shtml (accessed 3 March 2007).

Carter, J. and Schechter, S. (1997). *Child Abuse and Domestic Violence: Creating Community Partnerships for Safe Families*. www.mincava.umn.edu/link/documents/fvpf1/fvpf1.shtml (accessed 4 March 2007).

Casson, J. (2004). *Drama, Psychotherapy and Psychosis: Dramatherapy and Psychodrama with People Who Hear Voices*, Hove: Brunner-Routledge.

Cawson, P. (2002). Child maltreatment: An unhappy situation, *Primary Healthcare*, 12(4): 32–3.

Cawson, P., Wattam, C., Brooker, S. and Kelly, G. (2000). *Child Maltreatment in the United Kingdom: A Study of Prevalence of Child Abuse and Neglect*, London: NSPCC.

Chantler, K., Burman, B., Batsleer, J. and Bashir, C. (2001). *Attempted Suicide and Self-harm (South Asian Women): Project Report*, Manchester: Manchester Metropolitan University.

Chase, E. and Statham, J. (2005). Commercial sexual exploitation of children and young people in the UK: A review, *Child Abuse Review*, 14: 4–25.

Chesler, P. (1972/1989). *Women and Madness*, London: Harvest/ HJB Book.

Ciclitira, K. (2002). Researching pornography and sexual bodies, *The Psychologist*, 15(4): 191–4.

Clark, V. and Peel, E. (2004). Special Feature: The social construction of lesbianism: A reappraisal, *Feminism and Psychology*, 14(4): 485–90.

Cleckley, H. (1976, 6th edition). *The mask of sanity*, St Lewis, MO: Mosby.

Clegg, J. (1999). Feminist recoveries in *My Father's House*, *Feminist Review*, 61: 67–82.

Colclough, L., Parton, N. and Anslow, M. (1999). Family support, in N. Parton and C. Wattam (eds) *Child Sexual Abuse: Responding to the Experiences of Children*, London: John Wiley & Sons, pp. 159–80.

Coleman, R. (1999). *Recovery: An Alien Concept*, Gloucester: Handsell Publishing.

Collins, J.J., Spencer, D.L., Snodgrass, J.A. and Wheeless, S.C. (1999). *Linkage of Domestic Violence and Substance Abuse Services: Final Report*. National Criminal Justice Reference Service. www.ncjrs.gov/App/Publications/abstract.aspx?ID= 194123 (accessed 4 March 2007).

Cooke, A. (1999). Clinical psychology, mental illness and the media, *Clinical Psychology Forum*, 128: 7–10.

Cooke, A., Harper, D. and Kinderman, P. (2001). DCP update. Reform of the Mental Health Act: Implications for clinical psychologists, *Clinical Psychology*, 1: 48–52.

Cooper, G. (1997, February 10). 'Ashworth staff sold drugs to patients', *Independent*, p. 15.

Corby, B. (2000). *Child Abuse: Towards a Knowledge Base*, Buckingham: Open University Press.

Cottle, C.E., Searles, P., Berger, R.J. and Pierce, B.A. (1989). Conflicting ideologies and the politics of pornography, *Gender and Society*, 3(3): 303–33.

Coupe, J. (1991). Why women need their own service, in B. Elass (ed.) *The International Handbook of Addiction Behaviour*, London: Routledge, pp. 168–74.

Cox, M. (ed.) (1992). *Shakespeare Comes to Broadmoor: The Actors are Come Hither: The Performance of Tragedy in a Secure Psychiatric Hospital*, London: Jessica Kingsley Publishers.

Craine, S. (1999). Local press campaign halts ECT suite, *Clinical Psychology Forum*, 128: 30–31.

Creighton, S.J. and Tissier, G. (2006). Child killings in England and Wales. www.nspcc.org.uk/Inform/OnlineResources/InformationBriefings/ChildKillingsIn EnglandAndWales_asp_ifega26015.html (accessed 6 November 2006).

Crellin, C. (1998). Origins and social contexts of the term formulation in psychology case-reports, *Clinical Psychology Forum*, 112: 18–28.

Crompton, S. (2006, October 28).'Father of modern patient care: Interview', *The Times, Body and Soul Section*, pp. 6–7.

Crossley, M. L. (2000). Deconstructing autobiographical accounts of childhood sexual abuse: Some critical reflections, *Feminism and Psychology*, 10(1): 73–90.

Cruikshank, B. (1993). Revolutions within self government and self esteem, *Economy and Society*, 22: 327–43.

Curt, B.C. (1994). *Textuality and Tectonics: Troubling Social and Psychological Science*, Buckingham: Open University Press.

Curtis, T., Dellar, R., Leslie, E. and Watson, B. (2001). Introduction, in T. Curtis,

R. Dellar, E. Leslie, and B. Watson (eds) *Mad Pride: A Celebration of Mad Culture*, Gloucester: Handsell Publishing, pp. 7–8.

Cushway, D. and Gatherer, A. (2003). Reflecting on reflection, *Clinical Psychology*, 27: 6–10.

Cusick, L., Martin, A. and May, T. (2003). *Home Office Research Study 268: Vulnerability and Involvement in Drug Use and Sex Work*, London: www. homeoffice.gov.uk.

Daly, M. and Caputi, J. (1988). *Webster's First New Intergalactic Wickedary of the English Language*, London: Attic Press.

Daly, R. and Wakefield, J. (2002, July 11). 'Cash and questions', *Guardian*, p. 12.

Danica, E. (1989). *Don't: A Woman's Word*, London: Women's Press.

Davies, A.Y. (1981). *Women, Race, and Class*, New York: Vintage Books.

Davies, F., Holden, L. and Sutton, R. (2001). User involvement and psychosocial rehabilitation, *Clinical Psychology Forum*, 150: 34–42.

Deleuze, G. and Guattari, F. (1984). *Anti-Oedipus: Capitalism and Schizophrenia*, London: Athlone Press.

Deleuze, G. and Guattari, F. (1988). *A Thousand Plateaus*, London: Athlone Press.

Dell, P. and Korotona, O. (2000). Accounting for domestic violence: A Q methodological study, *Violence Against Women*, 6(3): 286–310.

Denborough, D. (2002). *Queer Counselling and Narrative Practice*. Adelaide: Dulwich Centre Publications.

Denzin, N.K. (1978, 2nd edn). *The Research Act: A Theoretical Introduction to Sociological Methods*, New York: McGraw-Hill.

Department of Health (1983). *The Mental Health Act*, London: HMSO.

Department of Health (1991). *The Children Act (1989): Guidance and Regulations*, (Volumes 1–10) London: HMSO.

Department of Health (1995). *Child Protection: Messages from Research*, London: The Stationery Office.

Department of Health (1999a). *Managing People with Severe Personality Disorder: Proposals for Policy Development*, London: The Stationery Office.

Department of Health (1999b). *The National Service Framework for Mental Health*, London: The Stationery Office.

Department of Health. (1999c). *Reform of the Mental Health Act 1983: Proposals for consultation*. London: The Stationery Office.

Department of Health (1999d). *Working Together to Safeguard Children: A Guide to Inter-agency working to Safeguard and Promote the Welfare of Children*, London: The Stationery Office.

Department of Health (2000a). *Domestic Violence: A Resource Manual for Health Care Professionals*, London: The Stationery Office.

Department of Health (2000b). *Framework for the Assessment of Children in Need and Their Families*, London: The Stationery Office.

Department of Health (2001). *Safety First: Five-year Report of the National Confidential Inquiry into Suicide and Homicide by People with Mental Illness*, London: The Stationery Office.

Department of Health (2002a). *National Suicide Prevention Strategy for England*, London: The Stationery Office.

Department of Health (2002b). *Women's Mental Health: Into the Mainstream*, London: The Stationery Office.

Department of Health (2003a). *Inpatients Formally Detained in Hospitals Under the Mental Health Act 1983 and Other Legislation*, London: The Stationery Office.

Department of Health (2003b). *Personality Disorder: No Longer a Diagnosis of Exclusion – NIMHE Policy Guidance*, London: www.homeoffice.gov.uk.

Department of Health (2004). 'Statistics on admissions under the Mental Health Act 1983'. Available at http://www.dh.gov.uk/assetRoot/04/10/87/88/04108788.xls (accessed 9 March 2006).

Derrida, J. (1978). *Writing and Difference*, London: Routledge and Kegan Paul.

Dworkin, A. (1981). *Pornography: Men Possessing Women*, London: Women's Press.

Elliot, A. (2002, 2nd edn). *Psychoanalytic Theory: An Introduction*, Basingstoke: Palgrave.

Enns, C.Z. (1997) *Feminist Theories and Feminist Psychotherapies: Origins, Themes, and Variations*, New York: Haworth Press.

Epston, D. (1993). Internalizing discourses versus externalizing discourses, in S. Gilligan and R. Price *Therapeutic Conversations*, New York: Norton, pp. 161–80.

Ernst, S. and Goodison, L. (1981). *In our own Hands: A Book of Self-help Therapy*, London: Women's Press.

Evans, M. (ed.) (1982). *The Woman Question: Readings on the Subordination of Women*, Oxford: Fontana Paperbacks.

Faderman, L (1985). *Surpassing the Love of Men: Romantic Friendship and Love Between Women from the Renaissance to the Present*, London: Women's Press.

Farr, V. (1991). The nature and frequency of incest: An analysis of the records of the West Australia sexual assault referral centre, 1986–1988, in P. Hetherington, (ed.) *Incest and the community: Australian Perspectives*. Perth: University of Western Australia, pp. 148–56.

Febbraro, A.R. (1993, April). On the epistemology, metatheory, and ideology of Q methodology: An historical and critical analysis', paper presented at International Society for Theoretical Psychology, 5th conference, France.

Finkelhor, D. (1988). The trauma of child sexual abuse: Two models, in G.E. Wyatt and G.J. Powell (eds) *Lasting Effects of Child Sexual Abuse*, London: Sage Publications, pp. 61–82.

Fisher, S. (1988). *Revelatory Positivism? Barth's Earliest Theology and the Merburg School*, Oxford: Oxford University Press.

Foa, E.B. and Rothbaum, B.O. (1998). *Treating the Trauma of Rape: Cognitive-Behavioral Therapy for PTSD*, New York: Guilford Press.

Fontana, A. and Frey, J.H. (1994). Interviewing: The art of science, in N.K. Denzin and Y.S. Lincoln (eds) *Handbook of Qualitative Research*, London: Sage Publications, pp. 361–76.

Foucault, M. (1971/1992). *Madness and Civilization: A History of Insanity in the Age of Reason*, London: Routledge.

Foucault, M. (1978). *The History of Sexuality, Volume One: An Introduction*, Harmondsworth: Penguin Books.

Foucault, M. (1991). *Discipline and Punish: The Birth of the Prison*, London: Penguin Books.

Fraser, N. (1995). 'False antithesis', in S. Benhabib, J. Butler, D. Cornell and N. Fraser, *Feminist Contentions: A Philosophical Exchange*, London: Routledge, pp. 59–74.

Fraser, S. (1989). *My Father's House: A Memoir of Incest and of Healing*, London: Virago Press.

Freud, S. (1977). *7. On sexuality*, London: Penguin Books.

Freud, S. (1984). *11. On metapsychology the theory of psychoanalysis*, London: Penguin Books.

Freud, S. (1986). *4. The interpretation of dreams*, London: Penguin Books.

Friedan, B. (1963). *The Feminine Mystique*, New York: Norton.

Frigon, S. (1995). A genealogy of women's madness, in R.E. Dobash, R.P. Dobash and L. Noaks (eds) *Gender and Crime*, Cardiff: University of Wales Press, pp. 20–48.

Frohman, S. and Neal, C. (2005). *The Probation Response to Supervision of Women who are Abused*, Minnesota Center Against Violence and Abuse. www.mincava.umn.edu/documents/commissioned/probationanddv/probationanddv.html (accessed 4 March 2007).

Fundudis, T., Kaplan, C. and Dickinson, H. (2003). A comparison study of characteristics of parents of abused and non-abused children, *Educational and Child Psychology*, 20(1): 90–108.

Furth, G. (1988). *The Secret World of Drawings: Healing through Art*. Boston: Sigo Press.

Game, A. (1991). *Undoing the Social: Towards a Deconstructive Sociology*, Milton Keynes: Open University Press.

Garfield, S. (2002, April 28). 'The chemistry of happiness', *Observer Magazine*, pp. 16–25.

Garner, H. (1995). *The First Stone: Some Questions About Sex and Power*, Sydney: Pan Macmillan Australia.

Gavey, N. (1999). I wasn't raped, but ...: Revising definitional problems in sexual victimization, in S. Lamb (ed.) *New Versions of Victims: Feminists Struggle with the Concept*, New York and London: New York University Press, pp. 57–81.

Gavey, N. (2003). Writing the effects of child sexual abuse: Interrogating the possibilities and pitfalls of using clinical psychology expertise for a critical justive agenda, in P. Reavey and S. Warner (eds) (2003) *New Feminist Stories About Women and Child Sexual Abuse: Sexual Scripts and Dangerous Dialogues*, London: Taylor & Francis pp. 187–209.

Gavey, N. (2005). *Just Sex? The Cultural Scaffolding of Rape*, London: Psychology Press.

Gerrard, N. (2002, November 17). 'The end of innocence', *Observer*, p. 14.

Glancey, J. (2002, November 16). 'Image that for 36 years fixed a killer in the public mind', *Guardian*, p. 5.

Goddard, C. and Liddell, M. (1995). Child abuse fatalities and the media: Lessons from a case study, *Child Abuse Review*, 4: 356–64.

Goldberg, B. (1996). Come to the carnival: Women's humour as transgression and resistance, in E. Burman, G. Aitken, P. Alldred, R. Allwood, T. Billingham, B. Goldberg, A.J. Gordo Lopez, C. Heenan, D. Marks and S. Warner, *Psychology, Discourse, Practice: From Regulation to Resistance*, London: Taylor & Francis, pp. 152–69.

Goldenberg, S. (2006, March 24). 'Too pretty for prison'. *Guardian*. www.guardian.co.uk/g2/story/0,,1738423,00.html (accessed 31 October 2006).

Goodchild, S. and Owen, J. (2006, October 29). 'Revealed: The postcode lottery for mental health patients', *Independent on Sunday*, p. 30.

Gould, P. (1985). A new Q too?, *Operant Subjectivity*, 8(2): 42–53.

Gross. E. (1992). What is feminist theory?, in H. Crowley and S. Himmelweit (eds) *Knowing Women: Feminism and Knowledge*, London: Polity Press, pp. 355–69.

Grosz. E. (1995). *Space, Time, and Perversion*, London: Routledge.

Guardian (2003, March 8). 'Broadmoor's cover-up: Another brave whistleblower suffers', *Guardian*. Leader. www.society.guardian.co.uk/Print/0,3858,4620929,00. html (accessed 4 April 2003).

Gunderson, J.G., Carpenter, W. and Strauss, J.S. (1975). Borderline and schizophrenic patients: A comparative study, *American Journal of Psychiatry*, 132: 1257–64.

Gunn, J. and Robertson, G. (1976). Psychopathic personality: A conceptual problem, *Psychological Medicine*, 6: 631–4.

Haaken, J. (1998). *Pillar of Salt: Gender, Memory, and the Perils of Looking Back*. London: Free Association Books.

Haaken, J. (2002). Stories of survival: Class, race, and domestic violence, in N. Holmstrom (ed.) *The Socialist Feminist Project: A Contemporary Reader in Theory and Practice*, New York: Monthly Review Press, pp. 102–20.

Haaken, J. and Yragui, N. (2003). Going underground: Conflicting perspectives on domestic violence shelter practices, *Feminism and Psychology*, 13(1): 49–71.

Hall, C. and Bunyan, N. (1997, February 8). 'Child abuse inquiry at hospital', *Daily Telegraph*, p. 1.

Hamilton, R. and Barrett, M. (eds) (1987). *Questions for Feminism: The Politics of Diversity*. Norfolk: Verso.

Hampshire, M. (2001, February 5–11). Web of abuse, *The Big Issue in the North*, pp. 10–11.

Haraway, D. (1991). *Simians, Cyborgs, and Women: The Reinvention of Nature*, New York: Routledge.

Harding, S. (1990). Feminism, science and the anti-Enlightenment critiques, in L. Nicholson (ed.) *Feminism/Postmodernism*, London: Routledge, pp. 83–106.

Harding, S. (1993). Rethinking standpoint epistemology: What is strong objectivity?, in L. Alcoll and E. Potter (eds.) *Feminist Epistemologies*, London: Routledge, pp. 49–82.

Hare, R. D. (1980). A research scale for the assessment of psychopathy in criminal populations, *Personality and Individual Differences*, 1: 111–17.

Harman, M.J. (2004). Children at-risk of borderline personality disorder, *Journal of Contemporary Psychotherapy*. 34(3): 279–90.

Harper, D. J. (1994). The professional construction of paranoia and the discursive use of diagnostic criteria, *British Journal of Medical Psychology*, 67: 131–43.

Harper, D.J. (2004a). Introducing social constructionist and critical psychology into clinical psychology training, in D.A. Paré and G. Larner (eds) *Collaborative Practice in Psychology and Therapy*, Binghampton, NY: Haworth Press, pp. 157–70.

Harper, D.J. (2004b). Personal communication, 4th February.

Harper, D.J. and Moss, D. (2003). A different kind of chemistry: Reformulating formulation, *Clinical Psychology*, 25: 6–10.

Harper, D.J., Goodbody, L. and Steen, L (2003). Involving users of services in clinical psychology training, *Clinical Psychology*, 21: 14–19.

Harris, A., Carney, S. and Fine, M. (2001). Counter work: Introduction to under the covers: Theorising the politics of counter stories, *International Journal of Critical Psychology*, 4: 6–18.

Harris, M. (2001). Modifications in service delivery for women diagnosed with severe mental illness who are also the survivors of sexual abuse trauma. In M. Harris and C.L. Landis, (eds). *Sexual Abuse in the Lives of Women Diagnosed with Serious Mental Illness*, Hove: Brunner-Routledge. Pp. 3–20.

Harris, M. and Landis, C.L. (eds) (2001). *Sexual Abuse in the Lives of Women Diagnosed with Serious Mental Illness*, Hove: Brunner-Routledge.

Harrowitz, N. (1994). *Anti-Semitism, Misogyny and the Logic of Cultural Difference*, London: University of Nebraska Press.

Hartsock, N. (1983). The feminist standpoint: Developing the ground for a specifically feminist historical materialism, in S. Harding and M.B. Hintikka (eds) *Discovering Reality: Feminist Perspectives on Epistemology, Metaphysics, Methodology, and Philosophy of Science*, Boston: Reidel Publishing, pp. 283–310.

Hartsock, N. (1990). Foucault on power: A theory for women?, in L. Nicholson (ed.) *Feminism/Postmodernism*, London: Routledge, pp. 157–75.

Haug, F. (2001). Sexual deregulation or the child abuser as hero in neoliberalism, *Feminist Theory*, 2(1): 55–78.

Hemingway, C. (ed.) (1996). *Special Women? The Experience of Women in the Special Hospital System*, Hampshire: Avebury.

Henriques, J., Hollway, W., Urwin, C., Venn, C. and Walkerdine, V. (1984). *Changing the Subject: Psychology, Social Regulation and Subjectivity*, London: Methuen.

Henriques, J., Hollway, W., Urwin, C., Venn. C. and Walkerdine, V. (2002). Afterward, *Feminism and Psychology*, 12(4): 462–8.

Henwood, K., Gill, R. and Mclean, C. (2002). The changing man, *The Psychologist*, 15(4): 182–6.

Hepburn, I. (1996, January 2). 'Broadmoor girl killer seduces murderer in sex for freedom escape plot', *The Sun*, p. 5.

Hester, M. and Westmarland, N. (2004). *Home Office Research Study 279: Tackling Street Prostitution: Towards an Holistic Approach*, London: www.homeoffice.gov.uk.

Hetherington, P. (ed.) (1991). *Incest and the Community: Australian Perspectives*. Perth: University of Western Australia.

Hill Collins, P. (1993). The sexual politics of Black womanhood, in P. Bart and E. Moran (eds) *Violence Against Women*, London: Sage, pp. 85–103.

Hill, A. (2002a, December 1). 'No one leaves this place with her sanity intact', *Observer*, p. 10.

Hill, A. (2002b, November 24). 'Rape crisis centres face closure threat, *Observer*, p. 14.

Hinsliff, G. (2003, February 6). 'Crime of passion is no defence', *Observer*, , pp. 1–2.

Hollway, W. (1989). *Subjectivity and Method in Psychology: Gender, Meaning and Science*, London: Sage Publications.

Holmstrom, L. and Burgess, A. (1978). *The Victim of Rape: Institutional Reactions*, London: Wiley.

Home Office in conjunction with the Department of Health (1992). *Memorandum of Good Practice on Video Recorded Interviews with Child Witnesses for Criminal Proceedings*, London: The Stationery Office.

Home Office (1989). *Children Act 1989*, London: The Stationery Office.

Home Office (1998). *Crime and Disorder Act 1998, section 34*. London: Home Office Communication Directorate.

Home Office (2002). *Statistics on women and the criminal justice system*. London: Home Office Communication Directorate.

Home Office (2003). *Sexual Offences Act 2003*. London: Home Office Communication Directorate.

hooks, b. (1982). *Ain't I a woman: Black women and feminism*. London: Pluto Press.

Horn, R. and Warner, S. (eds) (2000). *Positive Directions for Women in Secure Environments: Issues in Criminological and Legal Psychology*. Leicester: British Psychological Society.

Horner, A. (2002, November 7). Challenging myths and stereotypes around domestic violence, paper presented at Challenging myths and stereotypes around domestic violence Conference, North Lincolnshire Women's Aid, Scunthorpe, UK.

Horwath, J. (2002). Maintaining a focus on the child? First impressions of the *Framework for the Assessment of Children in Need and their Families* in cases of child neglect, *Child Abuse Review*, 11(4): 195–213.

Hudgins, M.K. (2000). The therapeutic spiral model: Treating PTSD in action, in P.F. Kellermann and M.K. Hudgins (eds) *Psychodrama with Trauma Survivors: Acting out your Pain*, London: Jessica Kingsley Publishers, pp. 229–54.

Humphreys, C., Mullender, A., Lowe, P., Hague, G., Abrahams, H. and Hester, M. (2001). Domestic violence and child abuse: Developing sensitive policies and guidance, *Child Abuse Review*, 10: 183–97.

Irwin, E., Mitchell, L., Durkin, L. and Douieb, B. (2001). The need for a mental patients union: Some proposals, in T. Curtis, R. Dellar, E. Leslie, and B. Watson, (eds) *Mad Pride: A Celebration of Mad Culture*, Gloucester: Handsell Publishing, pp. 23–8.

Jackson, S. (1992). The amazing deconstructing woman. *Trouble and Strife: The Radical Feminist Magazine*, 25, 25–31.

James, A. (2001). *Raising our Voices: An Account of the Hearing Voices Movement*. Gloucester: Handsell Publishing.

James, M. and Warner, S. (2005). Coping with their lives: Women, learning disabilities, self-harm and the secure unit: A Q methodological study, *British Journal of Learning Disabilities*, 33: 120–27.

Janesick, V.J. (1998). The dance of qualitative research design: metaphor, methodolatry and meaning, in N.K. Denzin and Y.S. Lincoln (eds). *Strategies of Qualitative Enquiry*, London: Sage Publications, pp. 35–55.

Jeffreys, S. (1990). *Anticlimax: A Feminist Perspective on the Sexual Revolution*. London: Women's Press.

Jenny, C., Hymell, K.P., Ritzen, A., Reinhert, S.E. and Hay, T.C. (1999). Analysis of missed cases of abusive head trauma, *Journal of the American Medical Association*, 281(7): 621–6.

Johnstone, L. (2003). Prescription rights peer commentary: Back to basics. *The Psychologist*, 16(4): 186–7.

Jones, D.P.H. and Ramchandani, P. (1999). *Child Sexual Abuse: Informing Practice from Research*, Oxford: Radcliffe Medical Press.

Journal of Contemporary Psychotherapy (2004, Fall). Special issue on borderline personality disorder. *Journal of Contemporary Psychotherapy*.

Kaul, A. (2001). Confidentiality in dual responsibility settings, in C. Cordess (ed.) *Confidentiality and Mental Health*, London: Jessica Kingsley Publishers, pp. 95–108.

Kaye, J. (1999). Toward a non-regulative praxis, in I. Parker (ed.) *Deconstructing Psychotherapy*, London: Sage Publications, pp. 19–38.

Kelly, E. (1991). Unspeakable acts: Women who abuse, *Trouble and Strife: The Radical Feminist Magazine*, 21: 13–20.

Kelly, E. and Scott, S. (1991). Demons, devils and denial, *Trouble and Strife: The Radical Feminist Magazine*, 22: 33–5.

Kelly, L. (1996). Weasel words: Paedophiles and the cycle of abuse. *Trouble and Strife: The Radical Feminist Magazine*, 33: 44–9.

Kendall-Tackett, K.A., Meyer Williams, L. and Finkelhor, D. (1993). Impact of sexual abuse on children: A review and synthesis of recent empirical studies, *Psychological Bulletin*, 113: 164–80.

Kernberg, O. (1975). *Borderline Conditions and Pathological Narcissism*. New York: Harper Collins.

Kitzinger, C. (1987). *The Social Construction of Lesbianism*. London: Sage Publications.

Kitzinger, C. (1990). The rhetoric of pseudo-science, in I. Parker and J. Shotter (eds) *Deconstructing Social Psychology*, London: Routledge, pp. 61–75.

Kitzinger, C. and Perkins, R. (1993). *Changing our Minds: Lesbian Feminism and Psychology*, London: Onlywomen Press.

Kitzinger, C. and Stainton-Rogers, R. (1985). A Q-methodological study of lesbian identities, *European Journal of Social Psychology*, 15: 167–87.

Kitzinger, J. (1992). Sexual violence and compulsory heterosexuality, *Feminism and Psychology*, 2(3): 399–418.

Kitzinger, J. (2003). Creating discourses of false memory: Media coverage and production dynamics, in P. Reavey and S. Warner (eds.) *New Feminist Stories about Women and Child Sexual Abuse: Sexual Scripts and Dangerous Dialogues*, London: Taylor & Francis, pp. 94–107.

Kjellin, L., Andersson, K., Candeford, I-L., Palmsteirna, T. and Wallsten, T. (1997). Ethical benefits and costs of coercion in short term inpatient psychiatric care, *Psychiatric Services*, 48(2): 567–70.

Koerner, B. (2002, July 30). 'First you market the disease ... then you push the pills to treat it', *Guardian*, pp. 8–9.

Krajicek, D. (1998, May 11). 'The bad, the ugly and the worse', *Guardian, Media Section*, pp. 2–5.

Kvale, S. (1996). *InterViews*. London: Sage Publications.

Laing, R.D. (1960/1982). *The Divided Self*, Harmondsworth: Penguin Books.

Lamb, S. (1996). *The Trouble with Blame: Victims, Perpetrators, and Responsibility*, London: Harvard University Press.

Lamb, S. (ed.) (1999). *New Versions of Victims: Feminists Struggle with the Concept*, London: New York University Press.

Larner, G. (1995). The real as illusion: Deconstructing power in family therapy, *Journal of Family Therapy*, 17(2): 191–217.

Larner, G. (2002). Towards a critical therapy. *Critical Psychology: The International Journal of Critical Psychology*, 7: 9–29.

Laurance, J. (1995, April 18). 'Majority see mentally ill as axe-wielding maniacs', *The Times*.

Law Society of England and Wales (2002). Appendix 14 Family Division: Best Practice Guide for instructing a single joint expert. www.lawsociety.org.uk/ document/downloads/dynamy/flapper (accessed 23 January 2008).

Lee, N. (2003). Child protection and the distribution of ambiguity, *Educational and Child Psychology*, 20(1): 43–52.

Lees, S. (1996). *Ruling Passions: Sexual Violence, Reputation and the Law*, Buckingham: Open University Press.

LeFevre, S. (1996). *Killing Me Softly: Self Harm Survival not Suicide*, Gloucester: Handsell Publishing.

Leudar, I. (2001). Is hearing voices a sign of mental illness? *The Psychologist*, 14(5): 256–9.

Levine, J. (2002). *Harmful to Minors: The Perils of Protecting Children from Sex*, London: University of Minnesota Press.

Lewis, H. (1997). *House Rules*. London: Secker and Warburg.

Linehan, M.M. (1993). *Cognitive-behavioural Treatment of Borderline Personality Disorder*. New York: Guilford Press.

Linehan, T. (1996). Media madness, *Nursing Times*, 3(92): 30–31.

Linnell, S. and Cora, D. (1993). *Discoveries: A Group Resource for Women who have been Sexually Abused in Childhood*, Haberfield: Dympna House.

Liverpool Echo. (1996, April 24). 'Attack claim at hospital', *Liverpool Echo*, p. 11.

Lloyd, A. (1995). *Doubly Deviant, Doubly Damned: Society's Treatment of Violent Women*. London: Penguin Books.

Ly, L. and Foster, S. (2005). Statistics of mentally disordered offenders 2004: England and Wales. *Home Office Statistical Bulletin*, www.ho.gov.uk.

McDermott, K. and King, R.D. (1988). Mind games: Where the action is in prisons, *British Journal of Criminology*, 28(3): 357–77.

McGauley, G. and Humphrey, M. (2003). Contribution of forensic psychotherapy to the care of forensic patients, *Advances in Psychiatric Treatment*, 9: 117–24.

McGrath, P. (1996). *Asylum*, London: Viking.

MacKinnon, K. (1989). *Towards a Feminist Theory of the State*. Harvard: Harvard University Press.

MacKinnon, L.K. (1998). *Trust and Betrayal in the Treatment of Child Sexual Abuse*. London: Guilford Press.

Mad Women. (1998). *Statement of philosophy*. www.madwomen@btinternet.com (accessed 4 June 1999).

Malan, D.H. (1979/1984). *Individual Psychotherapy and the Science of Psychodynamics*. Cambridge: Cambridge University Press.

Maracek, J. (2002). Editor's introduction: The subject in question, *Feminism and Psychology*, 12(4): 423–6.

Massumi, B. (1992). *A User's Guide to Capitalism and Schizophrenia: Deviations from Deleuze and Guattari*. London: MIT Press.

Mawson, D. (1990). Violence in hospital, in R. Blueglass and P. Bowden (eds)

Principles and Practice of Forensic Psychiatry, London: Churchill Livingstone, pp. 641–8.

Meekums, B. (2000). *Creative Group Therapy for Women Survivors of Child Sexual Abuse: Speaking the Unspeakable*, London: Jessica Kingsley Publishers.

Memmott, P., Stacey, R., Chambers, C. and Keys, C. (2001). *Violence in Indigenous Communities: Full Report*, Canberra: Commonwealth Attorney-General's Department.

Mental Health Act (1983) *see* Department of Health (1983).

Merck (2006). "Introduction: Child neglect and abuse: Merck manual home edition". www.merck.com/mmhe/print/sec23/ch288/ch288a.html (accessed 13 February 2007).

Mihill, C. (1994, August 27). 'Tranquillisers kill one a week', *Guardian*, p. 4.

Millar, S. (2003, January 6). 'Chat room danger prompts new safety code', *Guardian*, p. 1.

Miller, A. (1981/1990). *Thou Shalt not be Aware: Society's Betrayal of the Child.* London: Pluto Press.

Miller, A. (1983/1990). *For Your Own Good: The Roots of Violence in Child-rearing.* London: Virago Press.

Miller, A. (1983/1991). *The Drama of being a Child and the Search for the True Self.* London: Virago Press.

Miltenburg, R. and Singer, E. (1999). Culturally mediated learning and the development of self-regulation by survivors of child abuse: A Vygotskian approach to the support of survivors of child abuse, *Human Development*, 42: 1–17.

Minh-ha, T.T. (1987). Difference: A special third world women issue, *Feminist Review*, 25: 5–22.

Mitchell, J. (1974). *Psychoanalysis and Feminism: A Radical Reassessment of Freudian Psychoanalysis.* London: Penguin Books.

Montero, M. (2002). Ethics and politics in psychology: Twilight dimensions. *Critical Psychology: The International Journal of Critical Psychology*, 6: 81–98.

Morris, S. (2001). Heaven is a mad place on earth, in T. Curtis, R. Dellar, E. Leslie and B. Watson (eds) *Mad Pride: A Celebration of Mad Culture*, Gloucester: Handsell Publishing, pp. 207–8.

Morrison, T. (1981). *The Bluest Eye.* London: Triad Grafton Books.

Morrow, M. and Chappell, M. (1999). *Hearing Women's Voices: Mental Health Care for Women.* Vancouver: British Columbia Centre of Excellence for Women's Health.

Moscovici, S. (1985). Comment on Potter and Litton, *British Journal of Social Psychology*, 24: 91–2.

Murray, I. (2000). Glass houses: An exploration of violence and abuse. *Asylum*, 12(3): 14–15.

Narcotics Anonymous. (1988, 5th edition). *Narcotics Anonymous*, Chatsworth, CA: Narcotics Anonymous World Services.

National Campaign Against Violence And Crime/NCAVAC. (1999). *Ending Domestic Violence? Programs for Perpetrators*, Canberra: Attorney-General's Department.

National Domestic Violence Helpline/NDVH. (2007). *Abuse in America.* www.ndvh.org/educate/abuse_in_america.html (accessed 4 March 2007).

National Institute of Mental Health/NIMH. (2006a). *The Numbers Count: Mental*

Disorders in America. www.nimh.nih.gov/publicat/numbers.cfm (accessed 15 November 2006).

National Institute of Mental Health/NIMH. (2006b). *Science Update: Targeted Therapy Halves Suicide Attempts in Borderline Personality Disorder.* www.nimh. nih.gov/press/targeteddbt.cfm (accessed 15 November 2006).

Naylor, B. (1995). Women's crime and media coverage: Making explanations, in R.E. Dobash, R.P. Dobash and L. Noaks (eds) *Gender and Crime,* Cardiff: University of Wales Press, pp. 77–95.

Nelson, S. (1982/1987). *Incest: Fact and Myth.* Edinburgh: Stramullion.

Nelson, S. (2002). Physical symptoms in sexually abused women: Somatization or undetected injury? *Child Abuse Review,* 11: 51–64.

Nelson, S. and Phillips, S. (2001). *Final Report. Beyond Trauma: Mental Health Care Needs of Women who Survived Childhood Sexual Abuse.* Edinburgh: Edinburgh Association for Mental Health.

Neunes, C. (ed.). (2001). *Clinical Psychology Forum: Involving Service Users,* 150.

Newnes, C. (1996). The development of clinical psychology and its values, *Clinical Psychology Forum,* 95: 29–34.

Newton, R. (2003). The role of the expert witness, *UK Casebook: Medical Protection Society,* 20: 14–17.

Norwood, R. (1986). *Women who Love too much: When you keep Wishing and Hoping he'll Change.* London: Arrow Books.

O'Dell, L. (1997). Child sexual abuse and the academic construction of symptom-ologies, *Feminism and Psychology,* 7: 334–7.

O'Dell, L. (2003). Distinctly different? Descriptions of the sexually abused and non-abused child, *Educational and Child Psychology,* 20(1): 22–33.

Ofshe, R. and Watters, E. (1994). *Making Monsters: False Memories, Psycho-therapy, and Sexual Hysteria,* Berkeley, CA: University of California Press.

O'Hara, M. (1995). Child deaths in contexts of domestic violence, *Childright,* 115: 15–18.

Osmanand, S. and Harris, P. (2002, December 29). 'Black people six times more likely to be jailed than whites', *Observer.* www.guardian.co.uk (accessed 4 April 2003).

Owusu-Bempah, K. (2003). Political correctness: In the interest of the child? *Educational and Child Psychology,* 20(1): 53–63.

Paglia, C. (1991). *Sexual Personae: Art and Decadence from Nefertiti to Emily Dickinson.* New York: Vintage.

Pantling, K. and Warner, S. (2002). Minoritisation and motherhood: Women, children and domestic violence, in J. Batsleer, E. Burman, K. Chantler, H.S. McIntosh, K. Pantling, S. Smailes and S. Warner *Domestic Violence and Minoritisation: Supporting Women to Independence,* Manchester: Manchester Metropolitan University, p. 121–33.

Pare, D. (2002). Discursive wisdom: Reflections on ethics and therapeutic knowledge, *Critical Psychology: The International Journal of Critical Psychology,* 7: 30–52.

Parker, I. (1992). *Discourse Dynamics: Critical Analysis for Social and Individual Psychology,* London: Routledge.

Parker, I. and Shotter, J. (1990). *Deconstructing Social Psychology,* London: Routledge.

Parker, I., Georgaca, E., Harper, D., McLaughlin, T. and Stowell-Smith, M. (1995). *Deconstructing Psychopathology*, London: Sage Publications.

Parsons, J.T. (ed.) (2005). *Contemporary Research on Sex Work*. New York: Haworth Press.

Pembroke, L. (1994). *Self-harm: Perspectives from Personal Experience*. London: National Self-Harm Network.

Perkins, R.E. and Repper, J.M. (1996). *Working Alongside People who have Long–term Mental Health Problems*. London: Chapman and Hall.

Pilgrim, D. (1987). Psychotherapy in British special hospitals: A case of failure to thrive, *Free Associations*, 11: 59–72.

Pilgrim, D. (1995). Psychologists and the special hospitals: The case for closure not collusion, *Clinical Psychology Forum*, 81: 9–11.

Pilgrim, D. and Rogers, A. (1993). *A Sociology of Mental Health and Illness*. Buckingham: Open University Press.

Plumb, A. (1993). The challenge of self-advocacy, *Feminism and Psychology*, 3(2): 169–87.

Plummer, K. (1995). *Telling Sexual Stories: Power, Change and Social Worlds*, London: Routledge.

Powers, A. P. (1990). *A Dictionary of Nursing Theory*, London: Sage Publications.

Proctor, G. (2002). *The Dynamics of Power in Counselling and Psychotherapy*, Ross-on-Wye: PCCS Books.

Radicalesbians. (republished 1997). The woman identified woman, in L. Nicholson (ed.). *The Second Wave: A Reader in Feminist Theory*, London: Routledge, pp. 153–7.

Raitt, F.E. and Zeedyk, S. (2000). *The Implicit Relation of Psychology and Law: Women and Syndrome Evidence*, London: Routledge.

Ramazanoglu, C. (ed.) (1993). *Up against Foucault: Explorations of some Tensions between Foucault and Feminism*, London: Routledge.

Ramazanoglu, C. and Holland, J. (1999). Tripping over experience: Some problems in feminist epistemology, *Discourse: Studies in the Cultural Politics of Education*, 20(3): 381–92.

Ravens, T. (2006, October 28). 'Minister ambushed over pedophile claims'. www.theaustralian.news.com.au/story/0,20867,20659319-29277,00.html (accessed 31 October 2006).

Rayner, G. and Warner, S. (2003). Self-harming behaviour: From lay perceptions to clinical practice, *Counselling Psychology Quarterly*, 16(4): 305–29.

Reavey, P. (2003). When past meets present to produce a sexual other: Examining professional and everyday narratives of child sexual abuse and sexuality, in P. Reavey and S. Warner (eds) (2003). *New Feminist Stories about Women and Child Sexual Abuse: Sexual Scripts and Dangerous Dialogues*, London: Taylor & Francis, pp. 148–66.

Reavey, P. and Warner, S. (2001). Curing women: Child sexual abuse, therapy and the construction of femininity, *International Journal of Critical Psychology, Special Issue: Sex and Sexuality*, 3: 49–69.

Reavey, P. and Warner, S. (eds). (2003). *New Feminist Stories about Women and Child Sexual Abuse: Sexual Scripts and Dangerous Dialogues*, London: Taylor & Francis.

Reay, D. (1996). Dealing with difficult differences: Reflexivity and social class in feminist research, *Feminism and Psychology*, 6(3): 443–56.

Reder, P. and Duncan, S. (1999). *Lost Innocents: A Follow-up Study of Fatal Child Abuse*, London: Routledge.

Reder, P., Duncan, S. and Gray, M. (1993). *Beyond Blame: Child Abuse Tragedies Revisited*, London: Routledge.

ReSisters (2002) *Women Speak Out: Women's Experiences of Using Mental Health Services and Proposals for Change*, Leeds: ReSisters.

Resnick, R. (2003). To prescribe or not to prescribe: Is that the question? *The Psychologist*, 16(4): 184–6.

Reynolds, S.K. and Linehan, M.M. (2002). Dialectical behaviour therapy, in M. Hersen and W. Sledge (eds) *Encyclopaedia of Psychotherapy* (Volume 1), Oxford: Elsevier, pp. 621–8.

Richman, J. and Mason, T. (1992). Quo vadis the special hospitals?, in G. Williams (ed.) *Private Risks and Public Behaviours*, Hampshire: Avebury, pp. 150–68.

Richman, J., Berry, M. and Hooper, J. (2002, November 11). The role of British psychologists acting as expert witnesses: Myths and realities. Paper presented at the New Laws for Forensic Psychology Conference, Manchester: Manchester Metropolitan University.

Riger, S. (1992). Epistemological debates, feminist voices: Science, social values, and the study of women, *American Psychologist*, 47(6): 730–40.

Roberts, G.A. (2000). Narrative and severe mental illness: What place do stories have in an evidenced-based world? *Advances in Psychiatric Treatment*, 6: 432–41.

Robinson, G. and Whitney, L. (1999). Working systematically following abuse: Exploring safe uncertainty, *Child Abuse Review*, 8: 264–74.

Romme, M. and Escher, S. (1993). *Accepting Voices*. London: MIND.

Roodman, A.A. and Clum, G.A. (2001). Revictimization rates and method variance: A meta-analysis, *Clinical Psychology Review*, 21(2): 183–204.

Ross, K. (2003). The psychology of being sectioned, *Clinical Psychologist*, 23: 9–13.

Rowden, R. (2003, March 12). 'Culture of abuse' *Guardian*. www.society.guardian. co.uk/print/0,3858,4623083,00.html (accessed 4 April 2003).

Rubin, G. (1975/1997). The traffic in women: Notes on the political economy of sex, in L. Nicholson (ed.) *The Second Wave: A Reader in Feminist Theory*, London: Routledge, pp. 27–62.

Rumstein-McKlean, O. and Hunsley, J. (2001). Interpersonal and family functioning of female survivors of childhood sexual abuse, *Clinical Psychology Review*, 21(5): 471–90.

Runciman, R. (1996, January 17) 'Tell the truth about Broadmoor', *The Times*.

Russell, D. (1995). *Women, Madness and Medicine*. Cambridge: Polity Press.

Salmon, P. (1992). Researching in a different voice: An invitation from the research editor, *Changes*, 10(2): 165–70.

Salmon, P. (2003). How do we recognise good research? *The Psychologist*, 16(1): 24–7.

Sammons, M.T. and Levant, R.F. (2003). Yes, but there is another question, *The Psychologist*. 16(4): 187–8.

Schechter, S. and Edleson, J.L. (1994). *In the Best Interest of Women and Children: A Call for Collaboration between Child Welfare and Domestic Violence*

Constituencies, Minnesota Center against Violence and Abuse. www.mincava. umn.edu/documents/wingsp/wingsp.html (accessed 13 February 2007).

Scott, S. (2004). VII. Opening a can of worms? Counselling for survivors in UK women's prisons, *Feminism and Psychology*, 14(2): 256–61.

Sebestyen, A. (1988). *From Women's Liberation to Feminism*. Dorset: Prism Press.

Seden, J. (2001). Assessment of children in need and their families: A literature review, in Department of Health *Studies Informing the Framework for the Assessment of Children in Need and their Families*, London: The Stationery Office, pp. 1–80.

Senn, C. (1996). Q-methodology as feminist methodology: Women's views and experiences of pornography, in S. Wilkinson (ed.) *Feminist Social Psychologies: International Perspectives*, Buckingham: Open University Press, pp. 201–18.

Seu, I.B. and Heenan, M.C. (1998). *Feminism and Psychotherapy: Reflections on Contemporary Theories and Practices*. London: Sage Publications.

Shaughnessy, P. (2001). Into the deep end, in T. Curtis, R. Dellar, E. Leslie, and B. Watson, (eds.) *Mad Pride: A Celebration of Mad Culture*, Gloucester: Handsell Publishing, pp. 15–22.

Shaughnessy, P. (2003). Stigma from personal experience, *Asylum: The Magazine for Democratic Psychiatry*, 13(4): 6–9.

Shaw, E. (1997). Reducing sexual abuse in therapy, *Clinical Psychology Forum*, 110: 47.

Shaw, M. (1995). Conceptualizing violence by women, in R.E. Dobash, R.P. Dobash and L. Noaks (eds) *Gender and Crime*, Cardiff: University of Wales Press, pp. 115–31

Showalter, E. (1987). *The Female Malady: Women, Madness and English Culture: 1830–198*, London: Virago Press.

Simon, G. and Whitfield, G. (2000). Social constructionist and systemic therapy, in D. Davies and C. Neal (eds) *Pink Therapy II: Therapeutic Perspectives on Working with Lesbian, Gay and Bisexual Clients*, Buckingham: Open University Press, pp. 144–62.

Skelton, L. (1999). United Kingdom Advocacy Network AGM stormed by BBC shock troops, *Clinical Psychology Forum*, 128: 32.

Smith, D. (2003). 10 ways practitioners can avoid frequent ethical pitfalls, *Monitor on Psychology*. American Psychological Society. www.apa.org/monitor/jan03/10ways/html (accessed 13 February 2007).

Sonuga-Barke, E.J.S. (1998). Categorical models of childhood disorder: A conceptual and empirical analysis, *Journal of Child Psychology and Psychiatry*, 39(1): 115–33.

Soothill, K. (1995). Sex crime news from abroad, in R.E. Dobash, R.P. Dobash and L. Noaks (eds) *Gender and Crime*, Cardiff: University of Wales Press, pp. 96–114.

Soothill, K. and Walby, S. (1991). *Sex Crime in the News*, London: Routledge.

Spandler, H. and Warner, S. (2007). *Beyond Fear and Control: Working with Young People and Self-harm*, Ross-on-Wye: PCCS Books.

Spillers, H.J. (1984). Interstices: A small drama of words. In C.S. Vance (ed.) *Pleasure and Danger: Exploring Female Sexuality*, London: Routledge, pp. 73–100.

Spivak, G.C. (1993). Can the subaltern speak?, in P. Williams and L. Chrisman (eds). *Colonial Discourse and Post-colonial Theory*, London: Harvester Wheatsheaf, pp. 66–111.

Spring, J. (1987). *Cry Hard and Swim*, London: Virago Press.

Stainton-Rogers, R. and Stainton-Rogers, W. (1990). What the Brits got out of Q: and why their work may not line up with the American way of getting into it! *Electronic Journal of Communication*, 1(1): 1–11.

Stainton-Rogers, R., Stenner, P., Gleeson, K. and Stainton-Rogers, W. (1995). *Social Psychology: A Critical Agenda*, Cambridge: Polity Press.

Stanley, L. (1996). 1. The mother of invention: Necessity, writing and representation, *Feminism and Psychology*, 6(1): 45–51.

Stanley, L. (1997). Recovering *women* in history from feminist deconstructionism, in S. Kemp and J. Squires (eds) *Feminisms*, Oxford: Oxford University Press, pp. 274–370.

Stark, E. and Flitcraft, A. (1996). *A Woman at Risk: Domestic Violence and Women's Health*. London: Sage Publications.

Steele, R.S. (2002). The history of memory of childhood sexual abuse: True or false? *International Journal of Critical Psychology*, 5: 92–112.

Stenner, P. and Stainton-Rogers, R. (1998). Jealousy as a manifold of divergent understandings: A Q methodological investigation, *European Journal of Social Psychology*, 28: 71–94.

Stephenson, W. (1935a). Correlating persons instead of tests, *Character and Personality*, 4: 17–24.

Stephenson, W. (1935b). Techniques of factor analysis, *Nature*, 136: 297.

Stephenson, W. (1992). Self in everyday life, *Operant Subjectivity*, 15(2): 29–55.

Stern, A. (1939). Psychoanalytic investigation of and therapy in the borderline group of neurosis, *Psychoanalytic Q*, 7: 467–89.

Stowell-Smith, M. and McKeown, M. (1999). Locating mental health in black and white men: A Q methodological study, *Journal of Health Psychology*, 4(2): 209–22.

Stricklin, M. (1992). *P. c. q. version 2.0: Factor analysis programs for Q-technique*. Nebraska, USA: M. Stricklin.

Summit, R.C. (1983). The child sexual abuse accommodation syndrome, *Child Abuse and Neglect*, 7: 177–93.

Surgeon General (2006a). *Mental Health: A Report of the Surgeon General: Overview of Cultural Diversity and Mental Health Services*. www.surgeongeneral. gov/library/mentalhealth/chapter2/sec8.html (accessed 15 November 2006).

Surgeon General (2006b). *Mental Health: A Report of the Surgeon General: Overview of Recovery*. www.surgeongeneral.gov/library/mentalhealth/chapter2/sec10. html (accessed 15 November 2006).

Sutherland, J. (2003, March 10). 'Live car chases make primetime TV in LA – and the bloodier the better. But Gulf war two won't be shown like that', *Guardian, Media Section*, p. 5.

Szasz, T. (1961). *The Myth of Mental Illness*, New York: Harper and Row.

Tavris, A. (2003, January 30). 'Grooming outlaw in abuse crackdown', *Guardian*, p. 6.

Tavris, C. (1993). The mismeasure of woman, *Feminism and Psychology*, 3(2): 149–68.

Taylor, K. (1996). Keeping mum: The paradoxes of gendered power relations in interviewing, in E. Burman, P. Alldred, C. Bewley, B. Goldberg, C. Heenan, D. Marks, J. Marshall, K. Taylor, R. Ullah and S. Warner, *Challenging Women: Psychology's Exclusions, Feminist Possibilities*, Buckingham: Open University Press, pp. 106–22

Taylor, P.J. and Gunn, J. (1999). Homicides by people with a mental illness: Myth and reality. *British Journal of Psychiatry*, 174: 9–14.

Taylor-Brown, J. (1997a). Obfuscating child sexual abuse. I: The identification of social problems, *Child Abuse Review*, 6: 4–10.

Taylor-Brown, J. (1997b). Obfuscating child sexual abuse. II: Listening to survivors, *Child Abuse Review*, 6: 118–27.

Terry, J. and Urla, J. (1995). *Deviant Bodies: Critical Perspectives on Science and Difference in Popular Culture*. Bloomington, IN: Indiana University Press

Thurlbeck, N. (2005, November 13). 'Glitter's sick harem: We catch evil star with two child brides', *News of the World*, pp. 1, 4–5.

Tjaden, P. and Thoennes, N. (2006). *Extent, Nature, and Consequences of Rape Victimization: Findings from the National Violence against Women Survey*. Washington: National Institute of Justice. www.ncjrs.gov/pdffiles1/nij/210346.pdf (accessed 13 February 2007).

Townsend, M. (2005, October 23). 'Too many rapists go free, says Solicitor General', *Observer*. www.guardian.co.uk/crime/article/0,,1598901,00.html (accessed 3 March 2006).

Turner, M. (2002). Have we seen the last chapter in narrative therapy? *Critical Psychology: The International Journal of Critical Psychology*, 7: 53–73.

Ussher, J. (1991). *Women's Madness: Misogyny or Mental Illness?* London: Harvester Wheatsheaf.

van der Kolk, B.A., Hostetler, A., Herron, N. and Fisler, R.E. (1994). Trauma and the development of borderline personality disorder, *Borderline Personality Disorder*, 17(4): 715–30.

Vance, C.S. (ed.). (1984). *Pleasure and Danger: Exploring Female Sexuality*. London: Routledge.

Viner, K. (2003, August 2). 'We live in a boom time for rape – and for rapists', *Guardian*. www.guardian.co.uk/print/0,,4725182-103677,00.html (accessed 23 January 2008).

Walker, A. (1983). *The Color Purple*. London: Women's Press.

Waller, G. (1996). Sexual abuse and the eating disorders: Understanding the psychological mediators, *Clinical Psychology Forum*, 92: 27–32.

Ward, E. (1984). *Father–Daughter Rape*, London: Women's Press.

Warner, S. (1996a). Constructing femininity: Models of child sexual abuse and the production of woman, in E. Burman, P. Alldred, C. Bewley, B. Goldberg, C. Heenan, D. Marks, J. Marshall, K. Taylor, R. Ullah and S. Warner, *Challenging Women: Psychology's Exclusions, Feminist Possibilities*, Buckingham: Open University Press, pp. 36–53.

Warner, S. (1996b). Special women, special places: Women and high security mental hospitals, in E. Burman, G. Aitken, P. Alldred, R. Allwood, T. Billingham, B. Goldberg, A.J. Gordo Lopez, C. Heenan, D. Marks and S. Warner, *Psychology, Discourse, Practice: From Regulation to Resistance*, London: Taylor & Francis, pp. 90–113.

Warner, S. (1996c). Visibly special? Women, child sexual abuse and special hospitals, in C. Hemingway (ed.). *Special Women? The Experience of Women in the Special Hospital System*, Hampshire: Avebury, pp. 59–70.

Warner, S. (2000a). "Feminist theory, the Women's Liberation Movement and therapy for women: Changing our concerns". *Changes: An International Journal of Psychology and Psychotherapy*. 18,4: 232–243.

Warner, S. (2000b). *Understanding child sexual abuse: Making the tactics visible.* Gloucester: Handsell Publishing.

Warner, S. (2001a). Disrupting identity through Visible Therapy: A feminist post-structuralist approach to working with women who have experienced child sexual abuse, *Feminist Review*, 68: 115–39.

Warner, S. (2001b). Disrupting narratives of blame: Domestic violence, child sexual abuse and the regulation of experience and identity, *Psychology of Women Section Review*, 4(1): 3–17.

Warner, S. (2003a). Critical reflections on communicating with children: Making the tactics of training and intervention explicit, *Educational and Child Psychology*, 20(1): 109–23.

Warner, S. (2003b). Disrupting identity through Visible Therapy: A feminist post-structuralist approach to working with women who have experienced child sexual abuse. In P. Reavey and S. Warner (eds) *New Feminist Stories about Women and Child Sexual Abuse: Sexual Scripts and Dangerous Dialogues*, London: Taylor & Francis, pp. 226–47

Warner, S. (2004a). Contingent morality and psychotherapy research: Developing applicable frameworks for ethical processes of enquiry. *Journal of Critical Psychology, Counselling and Psychotherapy*, 4(2): 106–14.

Warner, S. (2004b). "Radical politics from the Women's Liberation Movement to Mad Pride". *Asylum: The magazine for democratic psychiatry*. 14(2) : 30–34.

Warner, S. and Feery, D. (2007). Self-harm and the law: What choices do we really have? In H. Spandler and S. Warner (eds) *Beyond Fear and Control: Working with Young People and Self-harm*, Ross-on-Wye: PCCS Books.

Warner, S. and Wilkins, T. (2003). Diagnosing distress and reproducing disorder: Women, child sexual abuse and borderline personality disorder, in P. Reavey and S. Warner (eds) *New Feminist Stories about Women and Child Sexual Abuse: Sexual Scripts and Dangerous Dialogues*, London: Taylor & Francis, pp. 167–86.

Warner, S. and Wilkins, T. (2004). Between subjugation and survival: Women, borderline personality disorder and high security mental hospitals, *Journal of Contemporary Psychotherapy*, 34(3): 265–78.

Wattam, C. (1997). Is the criminalisation of child harm and injury in the interests of the child?, *Children and Society*, 11: 97–107.

Weatherall, A., Gavey. N. and Potts. A. (2002). II. So whose words are they anyway? *Feminism and Psychology*, 12(4): 532–39.

Weissen, N. (1971/1993). Psychology constructs the female, Or, the fantasy life of the male psychologist (with some attention to the fantasies of his friends, the male biologist and the male anthropologist), *Feminism and Psychology*, 3(2): 195–210.

White, M. (1995). *Re-authoring Lives: Interviews and Essays*. Adelaide: Dulwich Centre Publications.

Wile, J. (2001). Inpatient treatment of psychiatric women with trauma, in M. Harris and C.L. Landis (eds) *Sexual Abuse in the Lives of Women Diagnosed with Serious Mental Illness.* Hove: Brunner-Routledge, pp. 109–38.

Wilkins, T. and Warner, S. (2000). Understanding the therapeutic relationship: Women diagnosed as borderline personality disordered, *British Journal of Forensic Practice*, 2(3): 30–37.

Wilkinson, S. and Kitzinger, C. (1993). *Heterosexuality: A Feminism and Psychology Reader*, London: Sage Publications.

Williams, J. (1996). Social inequalities and mental health: Developing services and developing knowledge, *Journal of Community and Applied Social Psychology (Special Issue)*, 6(5): 311–16.

Williams, J. (1999). Social inequalities and mental health, in C. Newnes, G. Holmes and C. Dunn (eds) *This is Madness: A Critical Look at Psychiatry and the Future of Mental Health Services*, Ross-on-Wye: PCCS Books, pp. 29–50.

Winn, D. (1980). *The Whole Mind: An A–Z of Theories, Therapies and Facts.* Suffolk: Fontana.

Wolf, N. (1993). *Fire with Fire: The New Female Power and how it will Change the 21st Century.* London: Chatto and Windus.

Women at the Margins. (2004). *Asylum: Special edition on women and borderline personality disorder – Bullshit Psychiatric Diagnosis*, 14, 3.

World Health Organization/WHO. (1992). *The ICD-10 Classification of Mental and Behavioural Disorders.* Geneva: WHO.

World Health Organization/WHO. (2000). *Violence against Women.* www.who.int/mediacentre/factsheets/fs239/en (accessed 11 November 2006).

World Health Organization/WHO. (2005a). *Glaring Inequalities for People with Mental Disorders.* www.who.int/media*_Hlt160976218ce*_Hlt160976218ntre/news/notes/2005/np14/en (accessed 15 November 2006).

World Health Organisation/WHO. (2005b). *Mental Health Atlas*, Geneva: WHO.

World Health Organization/WHO. (2006a). *Denied Citizens: Mental Health and Human Rights.* www.who.int/mental_health/en (accessed 15 November 2006).

World Health Organization/WHO. (2006b). *United Nations General Assembly, Sixty-First Session: Promotion and Protection of the Rights of Children. Item 62 (a)*, Geneva: WHO.

World Health Organization/WHO. (2007a). Chapter 6: Sexual violence, *World Report on Violence and Health.* www.who.int/violence_injury_prevention/violence/global_campaign (accessed 13 February 2007) pp. 149–82.

World Health Organization/WHO. (2007b). *Summary Report: WHO Multi-country Study on Women's Health and Domestic Violence against Women: Initial results on Prevalence, Health Outcomes and Women's Responses.* www.who.int/gender/violence/who_multicountry_study/summary (accessed 4 March 2007)

Worrell, M. (2003). Working at being survivors: Identity, gender and participation in self-help groups, in P. Reavey and S. Warner (eds). *New Feminist Stories about Women and Child Sexual Abuse: Sexual Scripts and Dangerous Dialogues*, London: Taylor & Francis, pp. 210–55.

Yanovski, S.Z., Nelson, J.E., Dubbert, B.K. and Spitzer, R.L. (1993). Association of binge eating disorder and psychiatric comorbidity in obese subjects, *American Journal of Psychiatry*, 150(10): 1472–9.

Yerkes, R.M., and Dodson, J.D. (1908). The relation of strength of stimulus to rapidity of habit formation, *Journal of Comparative Neurology and Psychology*, 18: 459–82.

Yuval-Davis, N. (1993). Beyond difference: Women and coalition politics, in M. Kennedy, C. Luelska and V. Walshe (eds). *Making Connections: Women's Studies, Women's Movements and Women's Lives*. London: Taylor & Francis. pp. 3–10.

INDEX

12-step programme 249; *see also* Alcoholics Anonymous
ableism 60
abortion 55
abuse, effects of 75, 98, 148, 160, 169, 195, 224, 228; see also betrayal; child sexual abuse, effects of
abuse survivors 9, 53, 63, 120, 186, 225, 248; lesbian survivors of abuse 61
abused women and girls 1, 4, 5, 6, 9–10, 11, 14, 15, 22, 26, 28, 30, 33, 36, 45, 55, 56, 58, 62, 65, 71, 73, 78, 91–2, 97, 101, 103–4, 114, 120–1, 125, 159, 161, 171, 208–9, 213–14, 221–9, 247–8, 250, 252
abuser tactics 168, 177; *see also* abusers, tactics used by
abusers 10, 15, 19, 38–40, 45, 49, 62, 121–2, 132–3, 141, 146, 149, 150; narratives regarding 2, 34, 37, 46–7, 51, 75, 119–20; tactics used by 16, 165, 168, 169, 171, 177–9, 198, 212, 222, 226
accountability 12–13
activism 53, 68; feminist 13, 54, 60, 64, 72, 92, 117, 139; grass-roots 58, 64; mad 65, 71; mental health 1, 11, 32, 51, 56, 68–9, 71, 72, 73, 75–6, 92, 93, 117, 139, 168, 248; political 1, 2, 11, 59, 67, 71; queer 69; self-help 117; service-user 68; women's 53, 54, 67
addiction models 184–5; *see also* 12-step programme; Alcoholics Anonymous; Narcotics Anonymous

agency 32, 39, 45, 63, 174, 179–81, 183, 184, 191; of children 51, 191, 197; enabling 209, 220–4; ethical 10; and gender 45, 191
aggressive behaviour 31, 99, 100, 104, 105, 109, 115, 126, 128, 197, 205, 234, 237
agnosticism 172, 178
alcohol 22, 24, 98, 111, 115, 121, 166, 180, 213, 221, 229; and attitudes to rape 36
Alcoholics Anonymous 249; *see also* addiction models
antisocial behaviour 125
antisocial personality disorder *see* personality disorder
anti-stigma campaign 18
anxiety 22
Ashworth Hospital 46, 49, 50, 81, 119; *see also* special hospital; Broadmoor Hospital; Rampton Hospital
Attachment Theory 193, 215; attachments 204, 215; attachment relationships 199, 204, 216; *see also* relationships
attention deficit hyperactivity disorder 21

badness 51, 94, 106, 113
behavioural model 152–4, 157
behaviourism 23
betrayal 74, 118–20, 122, 138, 144–5, 148, 229
body image 42
borderline personality disorder *see* personality disorder
brave face 136–7, 142

British Royal College of Psychiatry 68

Broadmoor Hospital 46, 50, 81; *see also* special hospital; Ashworth Hospital; Rampton Hospital

Butler, Judith 4, 17, 65, 66

care in the community 41

care orders 195, 230

censorship 44, 51

child assessment 198–200

child prostitution 40, 46; *see also* commercial sex; sex work

child protection 166, 188–95, 198, 207, 208–13, 218, 220, 224–5, 228

child sexual abuse 1–2, 3, 5, 6, 7, 9–10, 11, 14, 15, 25–6, 27, 28, 31, 32–3, 36–7, 43–4, 57, 61, 63, 67–70, 72, 73, 82, 83, 96, 106, 118, 138–40, 144, 146, 152, 154, 162, 165, 169, 172–4, 182, 193, 197, 199–202, 227, 230, 247, 248, 250, 251; anger at 128–9; and the construction of cognitive damage 131–3; and the construction of mental illness 127–31; and the construction of sexual dysfunction 133–4; conviction rates 189, 198; as cultural narrative 51, 76; and dangerousness 112; debates on 35, 63, 64, 191–2; and domestic abuse/violence 165, 166, 209–19; effects of 3, 16, 20, 29, 63, 79, 100, 114, 118–23, 129, 131–4, 139, 140, 148, 157, 160, 169, 195, 202, 216, 228, *see also* betrayal; in ethnic/indigenous/minoritized communities 45–6, 212; events of 160, 169; and feminism 54, 60, 64; and gender 15, 41, 225; in institutions 227–8; as legal issue 207; and litigation 165–6; and mental illness 20, 107, 118; narratives of 119; and personality disorders 17, *see also* personality disorder; and paedophilia 70; as a political issue 167; and popular culture 34–52; prevalence of 15, 39, 188; recovery from 136–7, 169, 178, 184–5, *see also* recovery; responses to 19, 50, 120; symptomatology of 28; theories of 65; training about 148, 149, 157, 161; by women 62, 235

child sexual abuse (*statistics*) 15–16, 19, 188, 202; in clinical population 16; and post traumatic stress disorder 202; prosecutions 189–90; in rural populations 209

child welfare 166, 189, 211, 226, 250

childhood emotional abuse 95, 96, 100, 115, 193, 207, 215

childhood physical abuse 95, 96, 100, 115

children (*statistics*), with imprisoned mothers 232; in care 227; in prisons 227; and prostitution 229; witnessing domestic violence 210

Children Act (1989) 70, 203

classism 60

closed institutions 81, 120, 156, 235; *see also* custodial systems of care; secure care; secure services; special hospitals

cognitive damage 131–2

cognitive model 149–52

cognitive theory 131

commercial sex 105, 230–1, 243–4; *see also* child prostitution; prostitution; sex work

consciousness-raising 35, 55, 56, 59, 67

consent to sex 190–1

contraception 55

contraceptive pill 54

coping strategy 17–19, 75, 115, 124, 150, 151, 168, 169, 180–1, 183, 197, 200, 239; denial as 180, 216; dissociation as 180; distraction as 180; maladaptive 23, 98, 150; *see also* alcohol; drug abuse; hearing voices; seeing visions; self-harm; violence

corporal punishment 227

counsellors 146–52, 163

culpability 30, 113, 191, 223, 226

cultural analysis 79

culture 5, 34, 176; mainstream 70, 71; popular 34–52

custodial systems of care 29–30, 75–6, 78–84, 91, 101–6, 109–11; 166; 232; women surviving in 117–43; working with girls/women in 144–63, 227–46; *see also* closed institutions; secure care; secure services; special hospitals

dangerousness 101, 104, 111–13, 117
death penalty 227
deconstruction 6, 13, 65–6, 69–70, 166, 168, 171, 173, 185, 224
denial 17, 138, 172, 180, 216–17
depression 20, 22, 123, 183; post-natal 218
detention 31, 93, 105, 153, 227, 244; and abuse 29, 58; effects of 232–3; justification of 92, 104
developmental arrest 102
deviant behaviour 42
diagnosis 16–17, 26, 29, 30, 48, 58, 73, 93, 101–2, 105, 113, 114, 122, 147, 218, 250
Dialectical Behaviour Therapy 152, 239
discourse analysis 80, 100
dissociation 17, 180, 182–3, 200, 242
distraction 17, 24, 180, 226
domestic abuse 40, 59, 60, 70, 208–13, 221, 250; see also violence, domestic; rape
domestic abuse/violence (statistics) 92, 208–10: and child fatalities 213; and children in care 210; children witnessing 210; cost of 209; links to child abuse 210; by partner 92, 208–9; and pregnancy 210; and prisoners 222; refuges 209, 220–1, 231; and suicide 218, 231; see also rape (statistics)
dreams 130, 131, 183, 202
drug abuse 22, 95, 97, 98, 100, 111, 115, 121, 140, 166, 180, 197, 202, 221, 229–30, 250, 229

electroconvulsive therapy 20
empiricism 84
empower/ment 12, 74, 145–9, 151, 153, 158–9, 167–71, 208, 211–12, see also social empowerment model
endangerment 203
endings 168, 183–4
epistemology 5, 7, 8, 9, 12, 53, 77, 80, 88, 172
essentialism 66–7
ethics 4, 7, 11–12, 74, 76–7, 159–60, 167, 247, 249; see also principles
ethnocentrism 60
evil 171
expert witnesses 11, 165, 186, 187, 195, 197, 200, 206, 208, 217–18

factor rotation 88
false memory syndrome 37–8, 45, 47
families: beliefs about 38–40, 43; nuclear 2, 43–4, 215
female genital mutilation 192
femininity 11, 25, 42, 126, 142, 151; assumptions about 3, 5, 28, 31, 33, 125, 127; idealized 135; normative 51, 93, 104, 112, 115, 136; stereotypical 33
feminism 1–2, 3–6, 9, 11–14, 32, 51, 54, 56, 58, 59, 64–5, 69, 71–2, 73, 75–7, 90, 93, 160, 165, 167, 168, 169, 186, 187, 207, 218, 248; diversity within 70; gender divisions in 66; history of 13, 35, 54–69; liberal humanist 67; libertarian 63, 64; and post-structuralism 5, 7, 15, 66–7, 74, 247; second-wave 52, 54, 55, 57, 66, 187; third-wave 54, 66; victim 64: see also politics
feminist standpoint theory 7, 57
fire-setting 95, 105, 109, 112, 116, 126, 130–2, 140
flashbacks 131–3, 140, 229
formulation 24
Foucault, Michel 5, 7, 9, 16, 19, 34, 56, 65, 136, 212
foundationalism 17
framing devices 37
frigidity 28
functional analysis 24, 25, 31, 131
fundamental attribution error 17

gender 4–5, 26, 49, 176, 252; definition of 4; in the Media 53; normative understandings of 38, 117, 118, 160; and race 113; socially constructed 66
gender differences 4, 5
gender inequality 4, 55, 248
gender relations 36
God 171
guilt 61, 148, 176, 211, 218, 225; by association 45–8
guilty passivity 125

hallucinations 17–18, 131–2, 140; see hearing voices, seeing visions
Haraway, Donna 7, 8, 65, 72
hearing voices 17–18, 22, 50, 65, 68, 76–7, 149, 165, 171, 180–1, 183, 229, 250: of God/Satan 171

Hearing Voices Network, The 68
heteronormativity 75, 127–8, 133, 169
heterosexism 60
heterosexuality 25, 57, 61–2, 132, 134–6
homelessness 166, 229–30, 243
homophobia 249; *see also* oppression
human rights 91–2, 209, 244–5, 248
Human Rights Act (1998), The 245
humour: female 137; sense of 123, 124, 126, 128, 136, 137, 142
hyper-femininity 42
hyphenated feminisms 66
hypnosis 37, 183

identity 9, 11–12, 42, 71, 95, 174–7; abused 173–7, 223; and self 169, 174, 185, 211; as survivor 61, 63, 65–6, 176, 180; as victim 65, 176, 221; formation 169; in Visible Therapy 175: pathological 32, 246; personality disorder as 123; practices 168, 174–6, 182; problem as 99; psychiatric 18; sexual 133; social 42; social construction of 174–6; *see also* politics, identity
in recovery 185, 249; *see also* 12-step programme, addiction models, Alcoholics Anonymous, Narcotics Anonymous
incest 63, 64
individualism 63
infantilization 107–8, 113, 149, 232
institutionalization 109–11, 113, 151–4, 159; of borderline behaviour 236–8; *see also* personality disorder
intelligence 88, 95, 97, 115
internet 22, 39, 50–1, 68
interviews 74, 76, 79–85, 94, 100, 101, 109, 145, 190, 196, 239; structuring 82–4; transcription of 84
inverted factor analysis 89

language 5, 66–7, 138, 169; use of 7, 67, 79, 160, 168, 246
legal proceedings 166, 187–92, 195, 198, 205–7, 220, 245; civil *vs* criminal 189–90
lesbianism 62, 115, 134, 140
liberation politics 12, 54, 56

Mad Women 69
Mad Pride 69
madness 19, 41, 113, 127, 131, 250; fears of 47; and murder 113; narratives of 17, 20, 46, 51; and women 56, 65, 69, 74, 75, 107–8, 119, 251
male-stream 56
marginalization 10–12, 45, 50, 71, 75, 113, 117; gender 8, 20, 23, 45; multiple 20, 127; structural 7, 251
masculinity 4, 33, 41–2, 57, 62, 126, 129, 140; normative 41, 51; stereotypical 33
masculinism 59
masculinization 41–2
mass media 1, 2, 33, 34–52, 75, 182
master narratives 34
meaning-making 3, 11–12
media, the *see* mass media
medical model 16–19, 23, 28, 74, 75, 93, 117–18, 145, 214
medical profession 22
medication 31; shortcomings of 20–1
medication/drugs (*statistics*), deaths due to 21; marketing 21–2; in prison/ secure populations 237; prescription 21–2
megadosing 21
Megan's law 39, 49; *see also* Sarah's law
mental disorder 17, 29, 30, 91, 131, 195; biological model of 117–18; and danger 40; prevalence of 91, 92; recovery from 117; social models of 118
mental health 1, 11, 15, 23, 26, 32, 48, 65, 72, 76, 117, 169, 247; gender differences in 27; politics of 50, 65; and trust 120; women's 56, 58, 118, 221
Mental Health Act (1983), 29–31, 92, 105; statistics on admissions 118
mental health nurses 47–8
mental health services 1, 2, 15, 16, 26, 29, 33, 64, 68, 74, 75, 78–9, 91, 102, 167, 180, 231; collaboration in 170
mental illness 17–20, 27–8, 30, 40–1, 101, 104, 106–10, 114, 117, 129, 140, 230, 242, 250; images of 49; models of 26, 246

mental illness (*statistics*) 91–2; patients involuntarily detained 29, 79, 92; patients sexually abused 19
mentalism 65
methodology 11–12
milieu therapy model 157–9, 236
minded choices 8–9, 11
modernism 66, 81, 83, 89, 172
moral majority 70
moral panic 37, 39
morality 4, 7, 8, 11
multidisciplinary model 155–7
murder 38, 41, 43–4, 45, 242
murder (*statistics*) 47; child fatalities 213; at end of relationship 220; by partner 209

Narcotics Anonymous 185, 249; *see also* addiction models; Alcoholics Anonymous; in recovery
narrative structures 2, 34, 47, 177; scaffolds 177
narratives of abuse 72, 103
National Health Service 21, 23
National Institute of Mental Health (NIMH) 91, 102, 117, 152, 228, 239
new man 38
nightmares 183, 203
normal distribution 23

objectivity 8, 25
ontology 11, 12
oppression 28, 51, 55, 56, 58, 61, 62, 64–5, 246; continuum of 57; domestic 56, 57; economic 8, 56; female 7, 57; hierarchies of 61; internalized 59, 61; mechanisms of 229; patriarchal 55–6; personal 6; psychiatric 56, 68; reverse 61; sexual 62; social 6, 35, 56; state-sponsored 58; structural 10, 27, 60, 75, 251; between women 60; *see also* racism
organizational hierarchies 67

paedophilia 38–40, 42, 70; as disease 39
parenting 193, 204, 214–15, 218
paternalism 23
patriarchy 4, 7–8, 55–6, 57, 60, 62, 192; women's participation in 59
perpetrators of abuse 34, 82, 189, 207, 212; gender of 41, 60

personality 88, 103, 106, 107, 109, 114, 117, 126, 142, 196, 204, 217, 218, 234, 241; antisocial 126; problems of 99–101, 131, 166, 219, 228, 231
personality disorder 17–19, 25, 30, 90, 93, 95–107, 109, 122, 145, 204, 228, 231, 234, 242, 246, 250; anti-social/psychopathic 122, 125–6; borderline 18, 68, 102, 103, 104, 122–5, 147, 152, 166, 176, 204, 228, 231, 237, 239, 242; definition of 122; definition of, medico-legal 125; psychopathic 30, 122; self-defeating 122, 124–5; and women 101–5, 113, 114, 115, 117
personality disorder (*statistics*) 228; hospital admissions with 102; in prison population 231–2
pharmaceutical industry 21–3
pimps 229, 243, 246
political correctness 64, 157, 162
politics 7, 32, 35, 38, 244, 246; of autonomy 56–60, 70; of deconstruction 65–8, 70; of difference and diversity 60–5, 70; of equality 70; feminist 71–2, 76–7, 186, 252; identity 61–3, 69; New Left 54; of pleasure 63, 66; radical 1, 2, 3, 50, 53–72, 74, 77, 228, 247, 248; women's 63
polypharmacy 21
population (research) 84
pornography 51, 58, 59; child 229
postmodernism 67
post-structuralism 1, 3–8, 13, 53–4, 73, 76–8, 80, 90, 160, 167, 168, 169, 172, 178, 187, 200–1, 218; and feminism 5, 7, 15, 74, 247
post-traumatic stress disorder 18, 131, 202–3, 232
poverty 36, 40, 44, 97, 115
power 5, 7, 64, 66, 174, 244, 252; male 7, 162; misuse of 151, 162, 179, 216; patriarchal 61; and sex 13, 61, 63, 67
power inequalities 10, 63, 213–14, 218
power-sharing 61
powerlessness 19, 25, 30, 48, 97–99, 103, 110, 120, 124, 130, 145, 152, 154, 163, 173, 175, 179, 180, 198, 212, 232, 236, 244

principles 7–8, 32, 53, 58, 73–6, 159–60, 165–8, 208, 247–51; *see also* ethics
prisons 91, 112
prisons/prisoners (*statistics*), abused in childhood 19; black people in 113; children in 227; with history of abuse 103, 222; medication in 237; mothers in 232; and post traumatic stress disorder 232
promiscuity 28, 115
prostitution 45, 230–1, 244; *see also* child prostitution; commercial sex; sex work
psychiatric abuse 56, 71
psychiatric drift 239
psychiatric patients 19
psychiatric survivors 56, 65, 249; *see also* survivors
psychiatry 2, 16, 25, 31, 34, 48, 56, 57, 59, 64, 75, 78, 138
psychoanalysis 59, 168, 169, 174, 186
psychologists 11, 24, 25, 48, 50, 68–9, 163; child 50, 111, 195; clinical 4, 23–4, 71, 82, 96, 123, 165, 167, 195, 198, 208, 209, 218; as expert witnesses 165, 187–8, 195, 206, 208; feminist 187; research 82
psychology 2, 3–4, 6, 11, 12, 16, 23, 25, 31, 34, 57, 59, 64, 75, 131, 187–8, 227, 248; behavioural 118, 133, 151–3; clinical 23, 24, 31, 48, 149, 167, 168, 186, 187; cognitive 23, 118, 131; feminist 23; and statistics 15, 23–4
psychopathic personality disorder *see* personality disorder
psychopathy 125, 127
psychopharmacology 167
psychosis 68, 127–8, 147
psychosocial model 27, 73–4, 145, 149
psychotherapy 67, 71, 158, 163, 167, 168, 183, 186, 234, 236, 239; behavioural 151; cognitive 149; creative 161; critical 168, 169, 185; feminist 55, 59, 61, 64, 67–8, 169, 171, 173; narrative 169, 171, 172, 173, 185; recovery-orientated 167, 173, 187, 249; *see also* recovery; sexual abuse 74, 165; *see also* Visible Therapy
psychotropic drugs 20, 25

Q factor analysis 87–90, 101
Q methodology 74, 79–90, 93–4, 101–2, 104, 117, 119, 123, 126, 145, 146, 150, 161–3; and statistics 88–90

R methodology 88
race 8, 11, 15, 45, 49, 61, 62, 176, 215, 251; and gender 113; and imprisonment 112–13, 116
racial stereotyping 217
racialization 45, 113, 117
racism 60, 62, 141, 182, 221, 249
Rampton Hospital 50, 81, 119; *see also* special hospital; Ashworth Hospital; Broadmoor Hospital
rape 29, 36, 55, 57, 59, 92, 137, 169, 176–7, 187–9, 230, 245; during armed conflict 192; attitudes to 36, 45, 46, 57, 62; continuum of 61; guidelines on 189; within marriage 70, 188; reaction to 203; taboos surrounding 57, 188
rape (*statistics*) 29, 92, 209; conviction rates 190; crime reporting 188; *see also* domestic abuse/violence (*statistics*)
Rape Crisis Centres 58, 71
rape survivor groups 53
reality, construction of 5–6, 17, 32, 28, 66, 77, 80, 88, 119, 165, 171, 178, 192, 222–5, 250–1
recovered memories 37
recovery 20, 26, 28, 31–2, 74–5, 118, 131–8, 151, 154–5, 157–9, 166, 169, 179, 183–6, 207, 224, 238, 242, 246, 249–52; *see also* psychotherapy, recovery-orientated; social recovery model; Visible Therapy
recovery-orientated practices 73–4, 131, 159, 165, 169, 247
reflection 6, 8, 10, 13, 71, 77, 157, 173–4, 198; on research relationships 82; *see also* reflexivity; self-reflection
reflexivity 3, 11, 25, 77–8, 80, 185, 192, 206; reflexive practices 77, 169, 171, 183–6, 206; reflexive practitioners 192; reflexive process 199; *see also* reflection; self-reflection
regression therapy 37

regulatory systems 19
relationships 40, 49, 55, 63, 77, 97,
    100–3, 107, 114, 120, 122–3,
    132, 137, 140, 152–4, 156, 159,
    160, 162, 163, 165, 168, 174,
    182, 185–6, 195–200, 222, 228,
    232, 239–41, 246, 250; abusive
    40, 67, 132–3, 140, 169, 173,
    179, 180, 203–5, 213–18, 220,
    222, 225, 248, 250; agentic 197;
    attachment 199, 204, 216;
    controlling 30; cross-generational
    63; cultural 5; difficulties in 166,
    228; family 162, 215, 228, 240;
    heterosexual 62; lesbian 57, 62,
    134; research 77, 82–4; safe 148,
    202, 222; in secure care 151, 228,
    235–8; sexual 45, 235–6; social
    125, 151, 153–4, 174, 182,
    235–9; unequal 59, 168, 215,
    248; unstable 96; between women
    60; see also Attachment Theory;
    therapeutic relationship
relativism 6, 8, 67
religious persecution 249
residential care 227, 229
resilience factors 205
retraumatization 29

sadomasochism 63
safe sex 236
safe uncertainty framework 223
sane chauvinism 65
Sarah's law 49; see also Megan's law
schizophrenia 18, 32, 41, 68, 76–7,
    176; treatment of 20, 76; see also
    hearing voices; seeing visions
secure care 74, 83, 91–2, 101–13,
    105–6, 108–9, 111, 117–39,
    144–5, 147, 150, 152–5, 157,
    166, 170, 227–46; see also closed
    institutions; custodial systems of
    care; secure services; special
    hospitals
secure care (statistics) 19, 29, 79, 92;
    abuse within 29, 91, 227–8;
    admissions 102, 118; patients with
    history of abuse 103; self-harm in
    103; suicide in 232
secure mental heath care see closed
    institutions; custodial systems of care;
    secure services; special hospitals;

Ashworth Hospital; Broadmoor
    Hospital; Rampton Hospital
secure services 99, 117, 119, 122,
    128, 139, 159, 226, 228, 232,
    235, 238–9, 242, 244; see also
    closed institutions; custodial
    systems of care; secure care; secure
    services; special hospitals
seeing visions 17–18, 22, 50, 149–50,
    165, 171, 180–1, 183, 229, 250
self-actualization 67
self-defeating personality disorder see
    personality disorder
self-determination 32, 45, 128, 251
self-harm 30–1, 65, 68, 99, 100, 116,
    123–4, 129, 132, 141, 144, 151, 165,
    166, 185, 229, 235, 239–42, 246,
    250; as coping strategy 180–3,
    239–40, 250; generic 24–5, 102,
    105
self-hatred 123, 136, 137, 142
self-help 58–61, 67, 117
self-injury 23–4, 148, 180, 181, 183,
    197, 221, 240
self-reflection 158, 160, 168; see also
    reflection; reflexivity
separatism 61, 71
service users 21, 26–7, 29–30, 58, 65,
    68–9, 84, 152, 159, 183, 239, 248
sex beasts 39, 44
sex tourists 39, 40
sex trafficking 92, 192
sex work 92, 166, 201–2, 229–31,
    243–5; see also child prostitution;
    commercial sex
sexism 59
sexual abuse see child sexual abuse;
    domestic abuse: violence, domestic
sexual assault 29
sexual dysfunction 133–4
sexual exploitation 4, 8, 35, 46, 56, 72,
    117, 139, 208, 229–30, 244, 248,
    251
sexual harassment 29
sexual inhibition 124, 134; lack of
    142
sexual revolution 54
sexual storytelling 35
sexual violence 2, 5, 27, 53, 64, 69, 72,
    187, 188, 207; education on 58
sexuality 8, 11, 34, 49, 51, 160, 176,
    177; male 57

shelters *see* women's refuges
situated honesty 172
sleeping, difficulties with 182–3
social class 63, 176, 215
social constructionist approaches 169, 193
social empowerment model 146–9
social framework evidence 166, 200–6, 214, 250
social frameworks 166, 188, 195, 202–3, 218
social hierarchies 7
social identity 42
social recovery model 26, 29, 149, 165, 166, 198, 204; *see also* recovery
social workers 111, 112, 123; demonisation of 47–8
solicitors 195
special hospitals 76, 79, 96–101, 111, 115–16, 141; *see also* custodial systems of care; Ashworth Hospital; Broadmoor Hospital; Rampton Hospital
statistics *see* child sexual abuse (*statistics*); children (*statistics*); domestic abuse/violence (*statistics*); medication/drugs (*statistics*); Mental Health Act (1983); mental illness (*statistics*); murder (*statistics*); personality disorder (*statistics*); prisons/prisoners (*statistics*); rape (*statistics*); secure care (*statistics*); suicide (*statistics*)
stigmatization 18
structural hierarchies 38
structures of domination 7, 60
subjecthood 6
subjectivity 5; social construction of 174, 186
suffragettes 55
suicidal behaviours 102, 183, 231, 232
suicidal feelings 129, 218
suicide (*statistics*), and domestic abuse 218, 231; and self-harm 103; worldwide deaths 232
suicide prevention 28
supervision 185–6
survival sex 231
survival strategies 148–50, 228–32, 245; *see also* coping strategies
survivor narratives 64, 135–8

survivors: of abuse 9, 53, 63, 120, 148, 186, 225, 248; lesbian 61; groups 53, 65; as identity 63, 65–6, 176, 180; psychiatric 56, 65, 249

talking therapies 21, 23, 25, 238, 239
therapeutic relationship 6, 45, 151, 167–8, 173, 184–5, 226, 239; democracy in 170–1; ending of 184; partnership in 168, 170, 173
therapy *see* psychotherapy
tranquillizers 21
transitional objects 184
trauma 17, 24, 58, 115, 122, 131, 149–51, 161, 203, 212, 246
trauma clinics 58
triangulation 77–8, 80, 196

Utopia, dreams and visions of 13, 166, 247, 251–2

verbal abuse 29
victim(s) 6, 15–6, 18, 34–7, 41, 44–8, 51, 63–5, 70, 75, 82, 92, 117, 122, 125, 160–2, 166, 174, 176–7, 189, 191–2, 202–3, 210, 212, 221–2, 225, 231, 243, 248; forever-victims 225; male 45; mothers as 166, 212–13, 226; of domestic violence 212–13, of mental illness 110; of trafficking 229; rape 177, 187–8, 190
victim feminism 64
victimhood 171, 173, 177, 29, 221; feminization of 45
victimization 22, 41, 44–5, 102, 122, 137, 183, 188, 211, 213, 220, 222–3, 225–6, 231, 243–4
victimology 44–6
vigilantism 49
violence 22, 28, 40–1, 45, 54, 60, 66, 71, 112, 115, 126, 188, 221, 223–4, 228, 246; domestic 55, 57, 92, 165, 166, 208–14; gendered 207; towards inanimate objects (*see also* fire-setting) 105, 130; towards self *see* coping strategies, self-harm; in institutions 91, 117, 128, 140, 144, 151, 227, 236; male 64, 151, 220–1; psychological 207; within women's community 62; *see also* sexual violence

visibility 6
Visible Therapy 167–86, 187, 198, 199,
    239, 249–50
visions *see* seeing visions
voices *see* hearing voices

woman, as category 5, 11
Women's Liberation Movement 54–5,
    58, 65, 68, 69

women's refuges 209, 220–1, 225, 229,
    231
World Health Organization 91–3,
    103–5, 112, 117, 120, 144, 155, 158,
    187–90, 192, 204, 207–10, 216,
    227–30, 232, 244

Yerkes-Dodson 181
Yerkes-Dodson's Law 241